I got a fan letter the other day that said, "Congratulations on passing the 30-volume mark! Thirty is an excellent number! It's not too many or too few. But now you've entered dangerous waters."

I thought to myself, I need to work harder.
Oh, by the way, a second *Bleach* movie is coming out!

–Tite Kubo, 2007

BLEACH is author Tite Kubo's second title. Kubo made his debut with *ZOMBIEPOWDER.*, a four-volume series for *WEEKLY SHONEN JUMP*. To date, *BLEACH* has been translated into numerous languages and has also inspired an animated TV series that began airing in the U.S. in 2006. Beginning its serialization in 2001, *BLEACH* is still a mainstay in the pages of *WEEKLY SHONEN JUMP*. In 2005, *BLEACH* was awarded the prestigious Shogakukan Manga Award in the *shonen* (boys) category.

BLEACH
Vol. 31: DON'T KILL MY VOLUPTURE
SHONEN JUMP Manga Edition
This volume contains material that was originally published in English
in SHONEN JUMP #87–89. Artwork in the magazine may have been
altered slightly from what is presented in this volume.

STORY AND ART BY
TITE KUBO

English Adaptation/Lance Caselman
Translation/Joe Yamazaki
Touch-Up Art & Lettering/Mark McMurray
Design/Sean Lee
Editors/Pancha Diaz and Yuki Takagaki

VP, Production/Alvin Lu
VP, Sales & Product Marketing/Gonzalo Ferreyra
VP, Creative/Linda Espinosa
Publisher/Hyoe Narita

Published by VIZ Media, LLC
P.O. Box 77010
San Francisco, CA 94107

10 9 8 7 6 5 4 3 2 1
First printing, June 2010

PARENTAL ADVISORY
BLEACH is rated T for Teen and is recommended
for ages 13 and up. This volume contains
fantasy violence.
ratings.viz.com

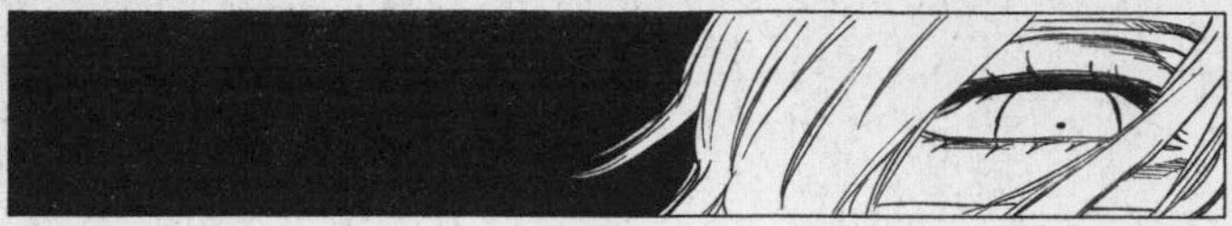

Tell me you hate me more than anything in the world.

BLEACH 31

DON'T KILL MY VOLUPTURE

Shonen Jump Manga

STARS AND

Orihime Inoue

Ulquiorra

Ichigo Kurosaki

plot

When high school student Ichigo Kurosaki meets Soul Reaper Rukia Kuchiki his life is changed forever. Soon Ichigo is a soul-cleansing Soul Reaper too, and he finds himself having adventures, as well as problems, that he never would have imagined. Now Ichigo and his friends must stop renegade Soul Reaper Aizen and his army of Arrancars from destroying the Soul Society and wiping out Karakura as well.

When the Arrancars abduct Orihime, Ichigo and his friends travel to Hueco Mundo to rescue her. After a series of harrowing battles, they finally reach Aizen's stronghold, Las Noches. Now as they penetrate ever deeper into the enemy's lair, they encounter a host of powerful foes bent on their destruction. And Rukia faces the specter of an old friend who she was forced to kill, and a chance for forgiveness—but at a terrible price.

BLEACH ALL

ザエルアポロ

Szayelaporro

阿散井恋次

Renji Abarai

Uryû Ishida

石田雨竜

STORIES

BLEACH 31

DON'T KILL MY VOLUPTURE

Contents

270. WARning

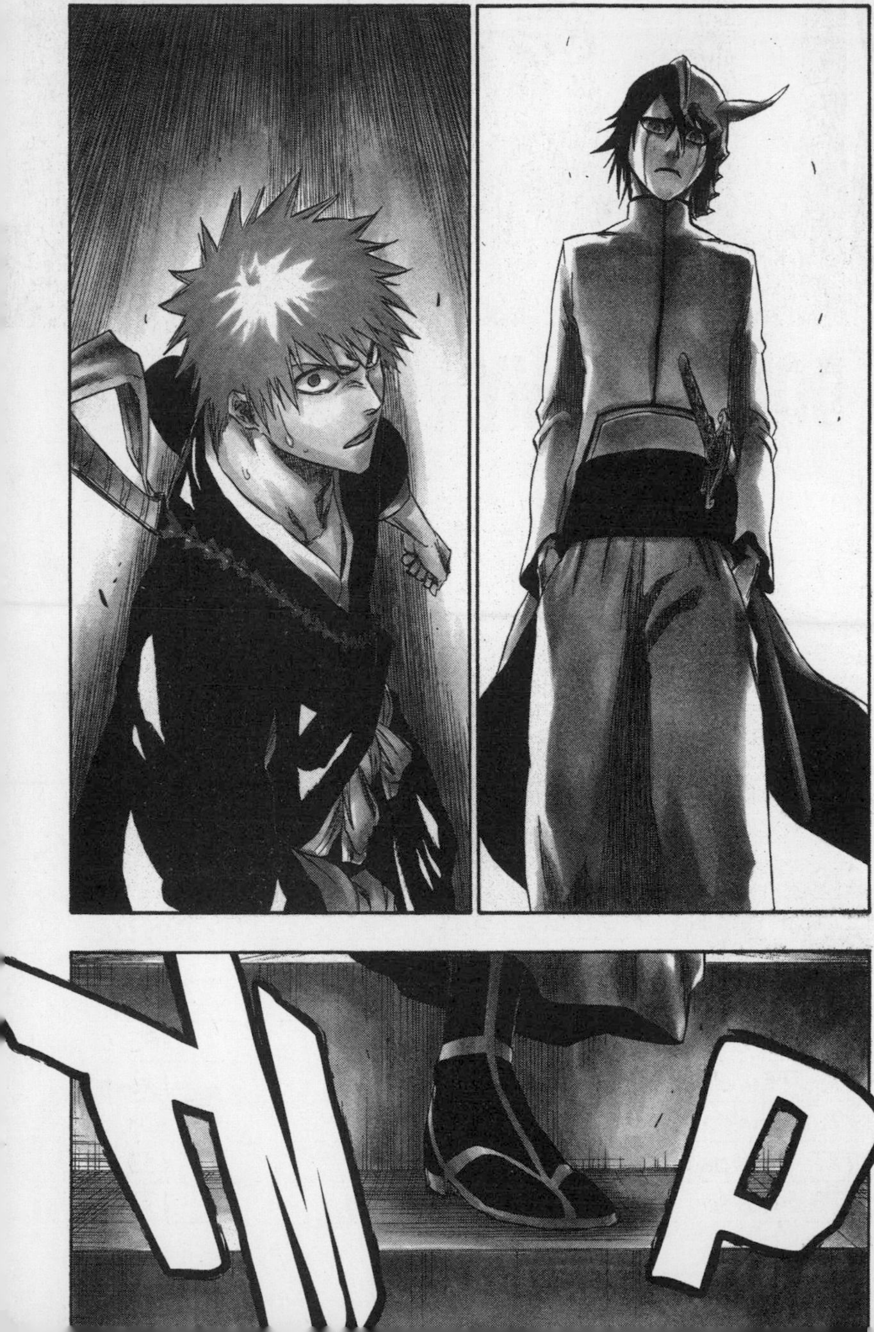
TMP

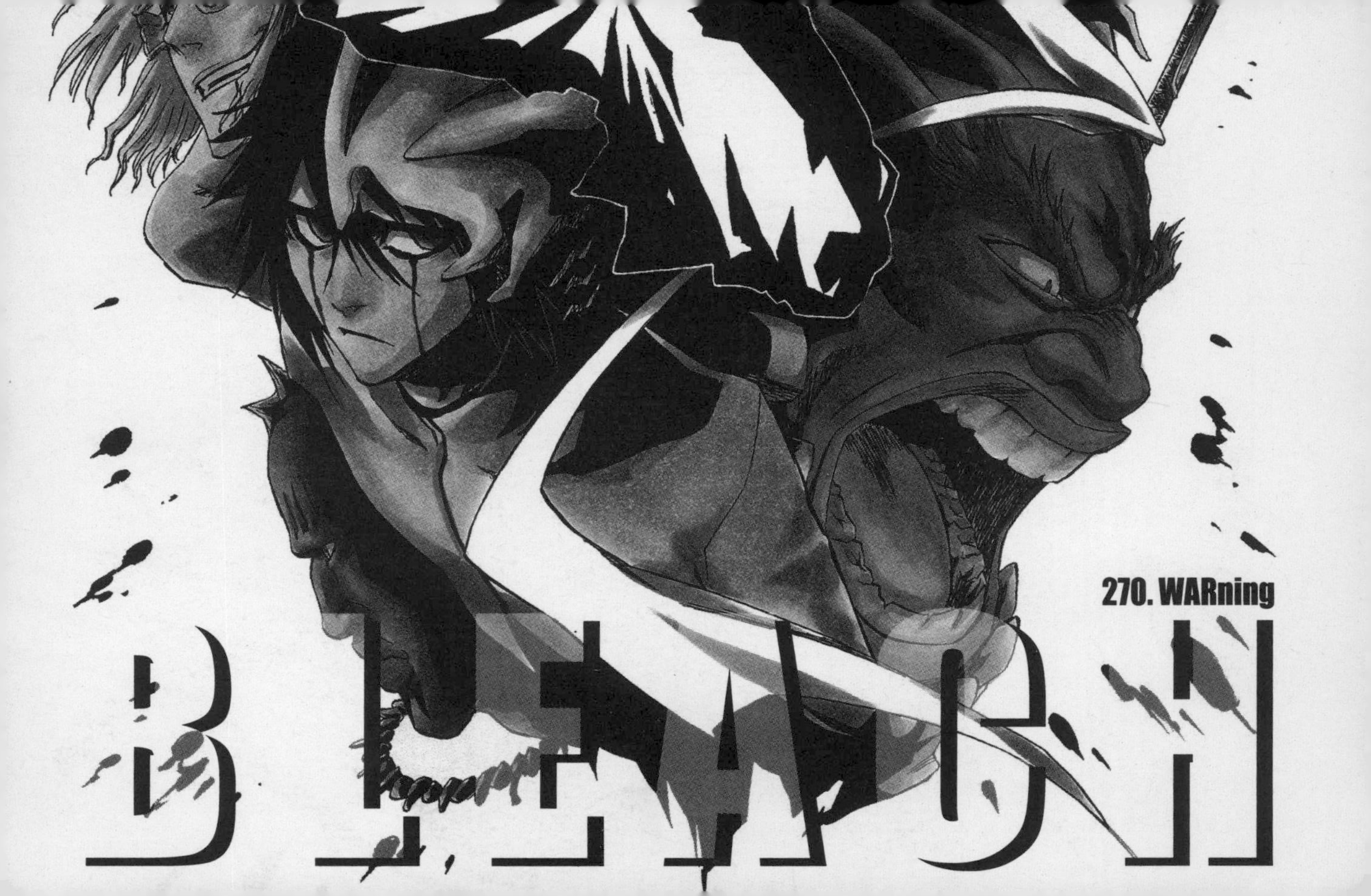
270. WARning
BLEACH

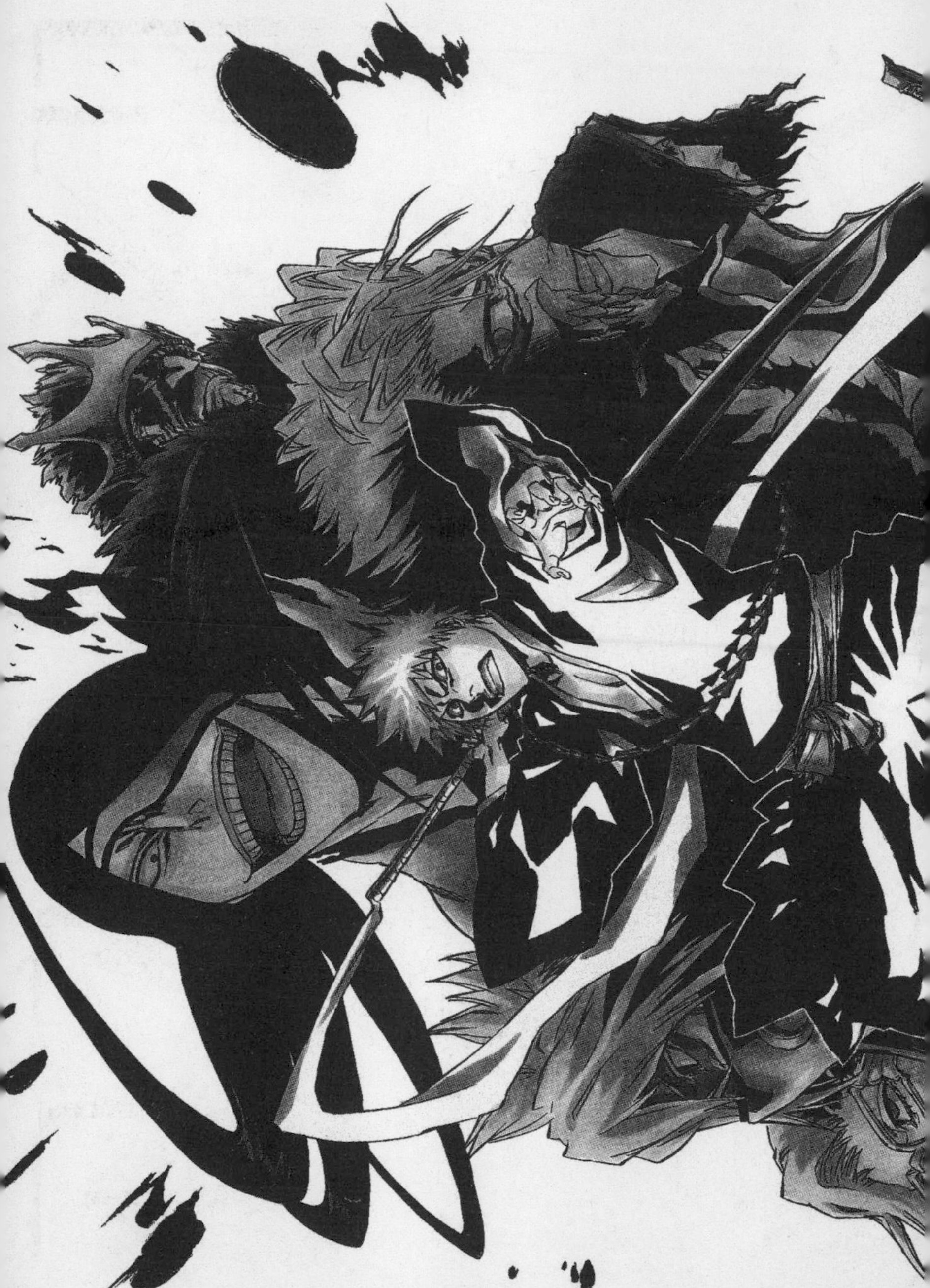

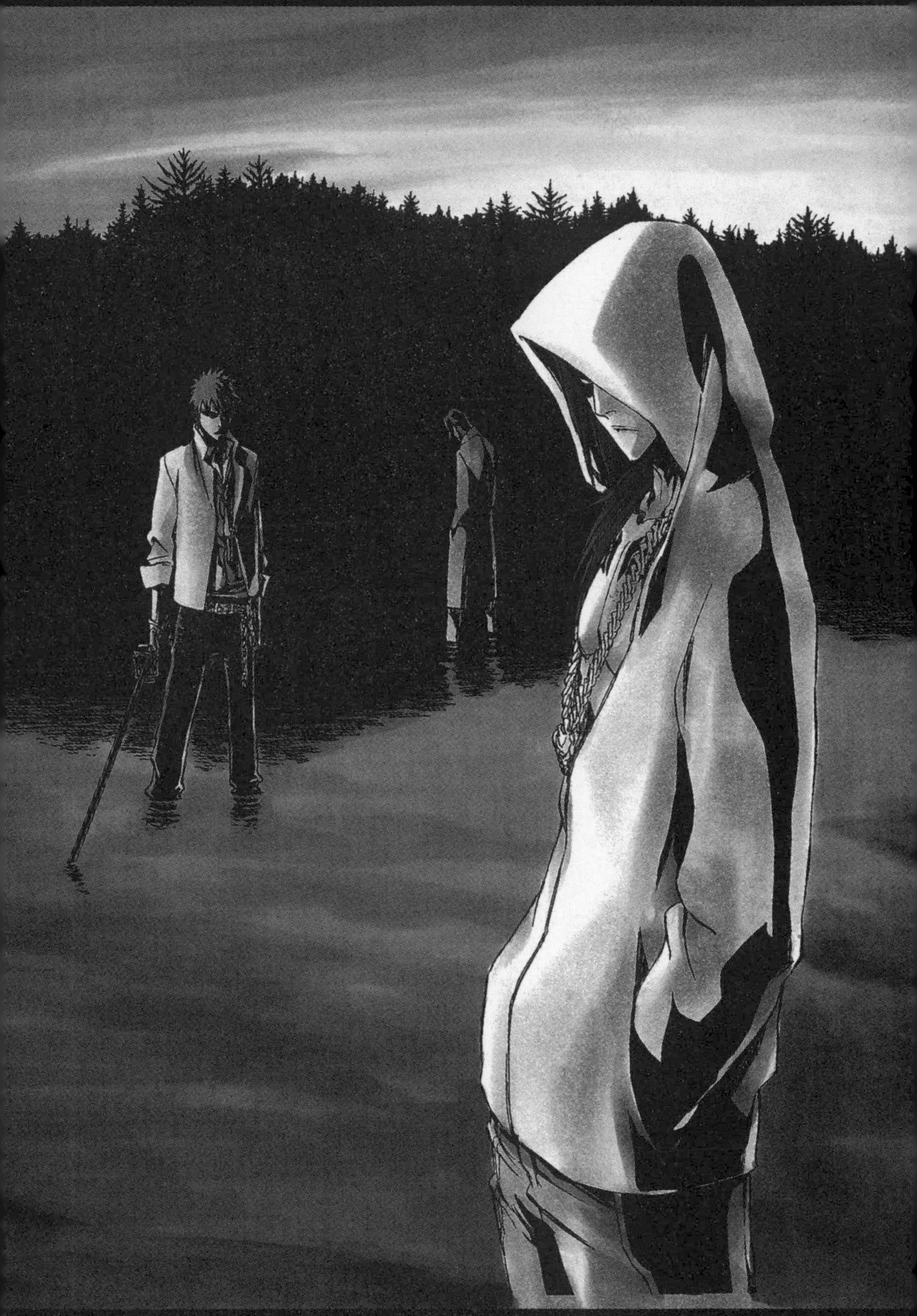

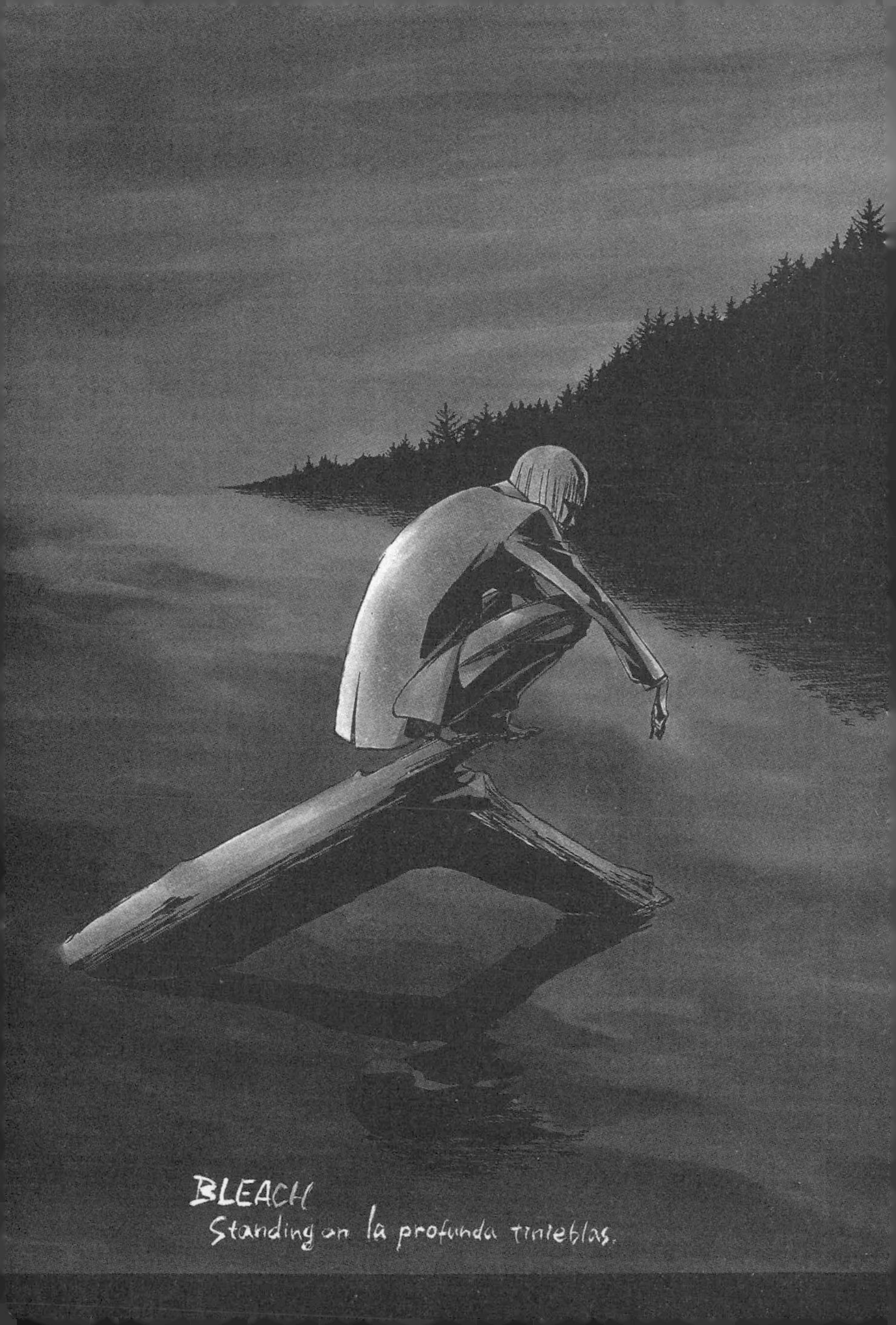
BLEACH
Standing on la profunda tinieblas.

BLEACH

ブリーチ

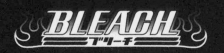

READ THIS WAY

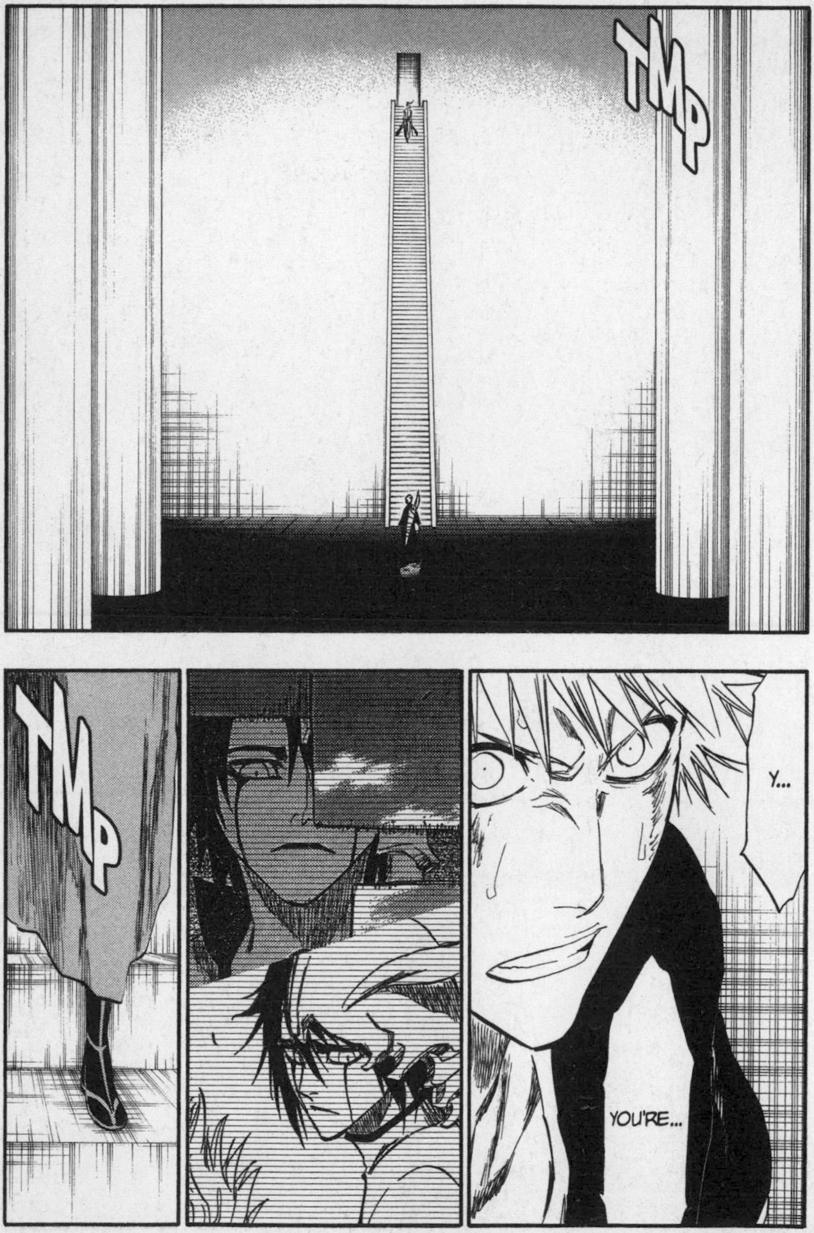
TMP
Y...
YOU'RE...
TMP

I DON'T RECALL INTRODUCING MYSELF TO YOU.

YOU REMEMBER MY NAME.

ULQUIORRA!

ANYWAY...

RUKIA KUCHIKI IS DEAD.

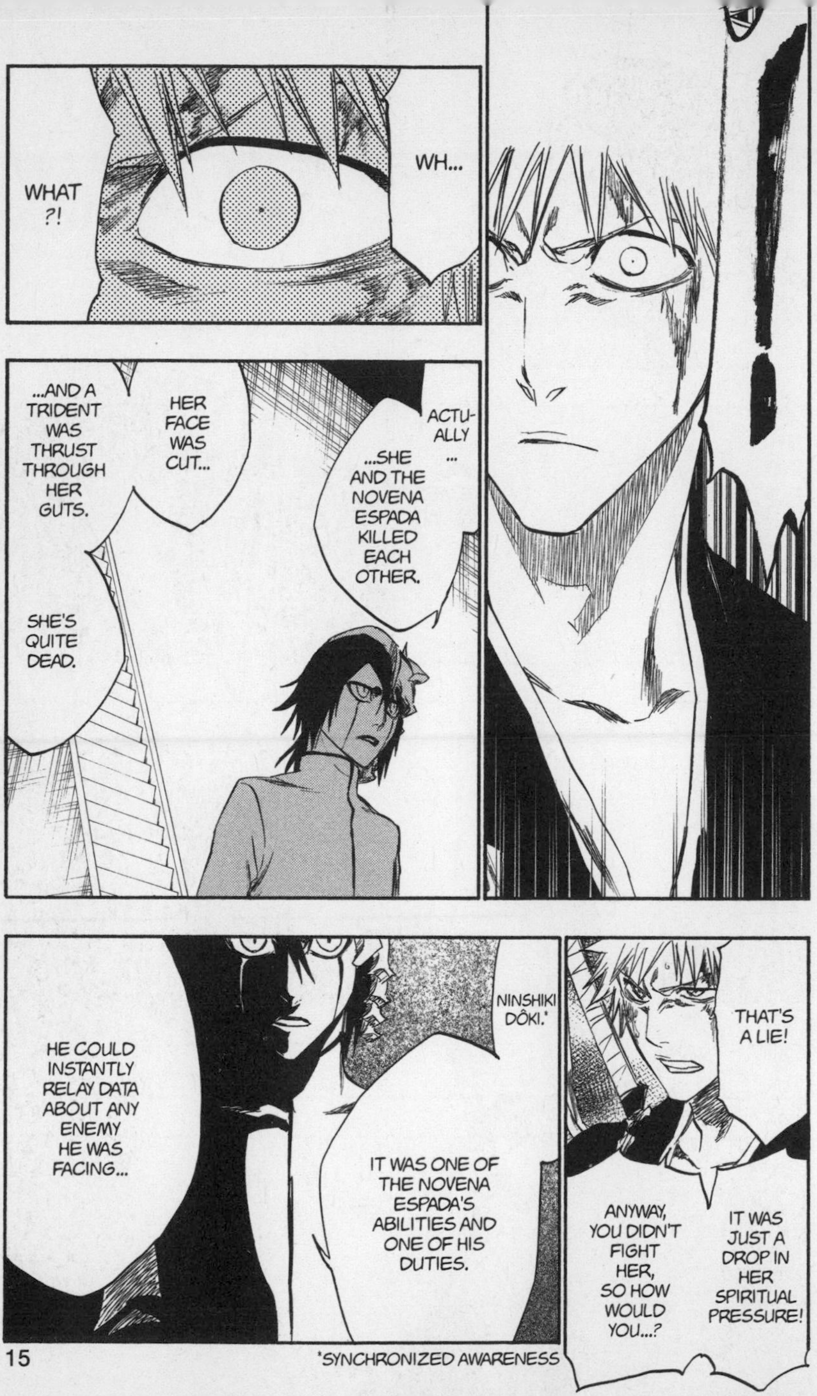
!
WH...
WHAT?!
ACTUALLY...
...SHE AND THE NOVENA ESPADA KILLED EACH OTHER.
HER FACE WAS CUT...
...AND A TRIDENT WAS THRUST THROUGH HER GUTS.
SHE'S QUITE DEAD.
THAT'S A LIE!
IT WAS JUST A DROP IN HER SPIRITUAL PRESSURE!
ANYWAY, YOU DIDN'T FIGHT HER, SO HOW WOULD YOU...?
NINSHIKI DÔKI.*
IT WAS ONE OF THE NOVENA ESPADA'S ABILITIES AND ONE OF HIS DUTIES.
HE COULD INSTANTLY RELAY DATA ABOUT ANY ENEMY HE WAS FACING...

*SYNCHRONIZED AWARENESS

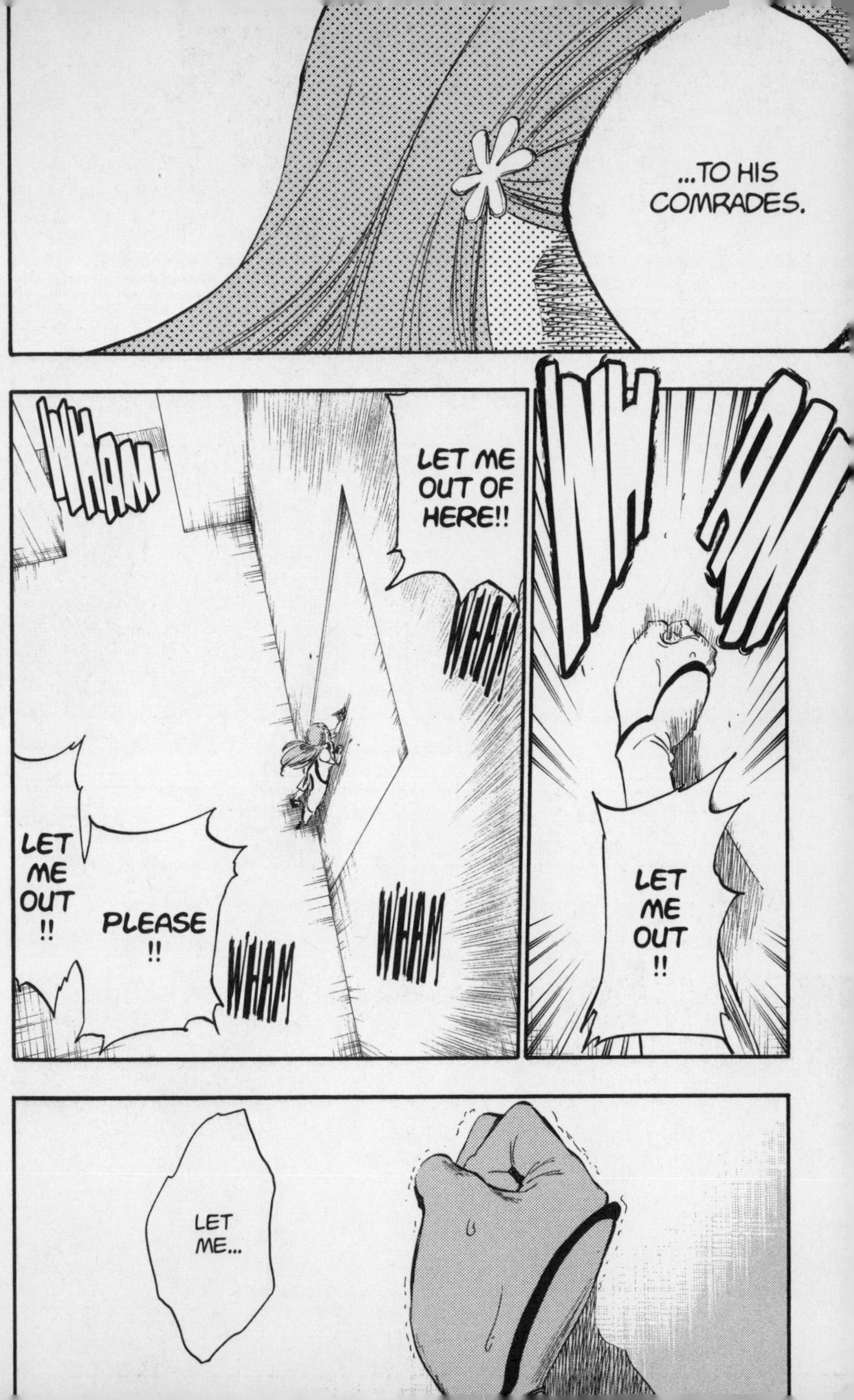
...TO HIS COMRADES.
WHAM
LET ME OUT !!
LET ME OUT OF HERE!!
WHAM
WHAM
WHAM
LET ME OUT !!
WHAM
PLEASE !!
WHAM
LET ME...

N...

NO...

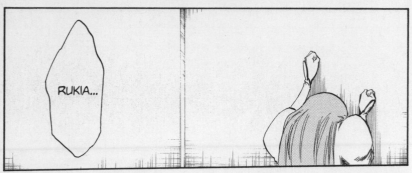

RUKIA...

TOM P

WHERE ARE YOU GOING?

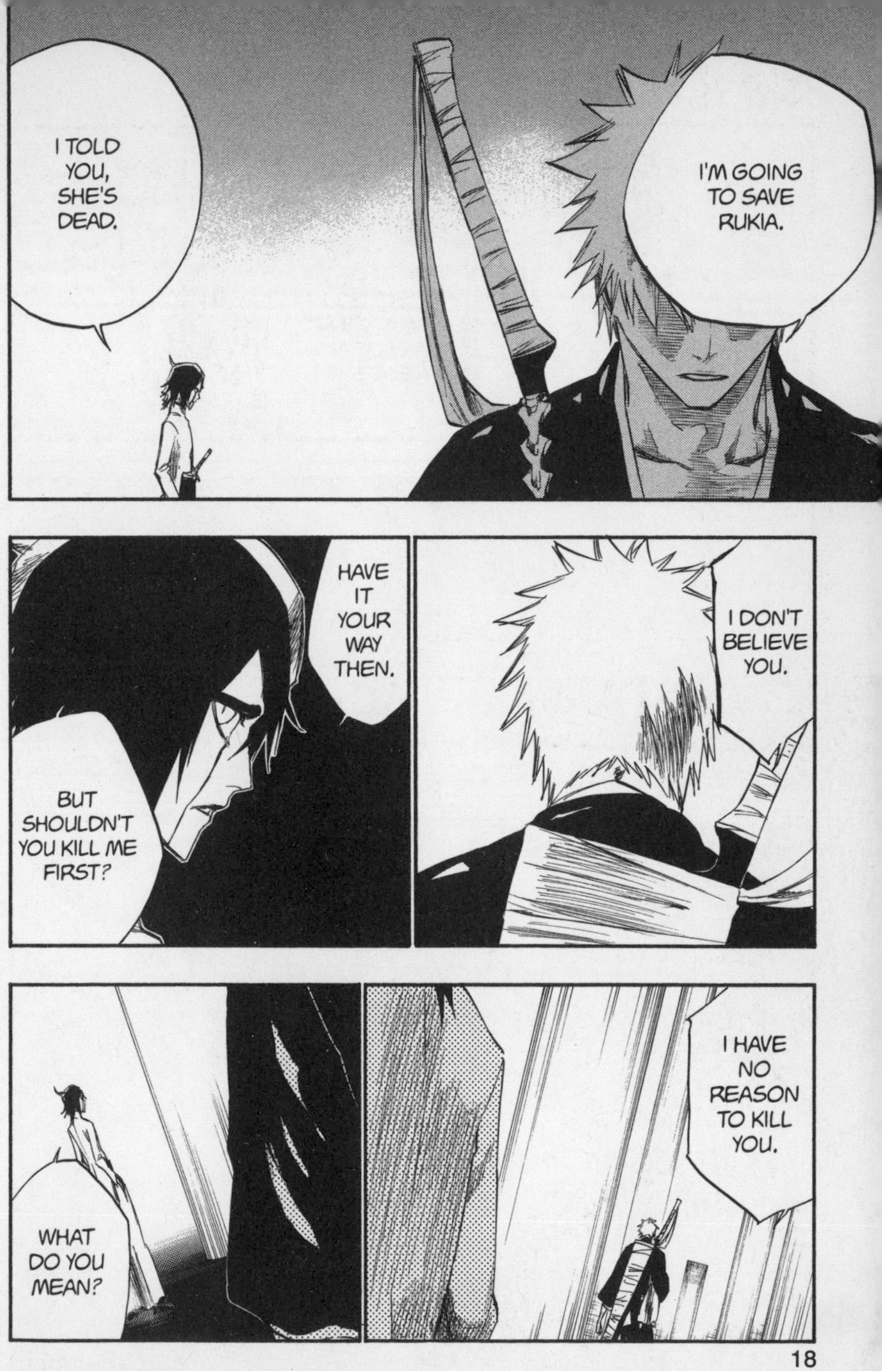
I'M GOING TO SAVE RUKIA.
I TOLD YOU, SHE'S DEAD.
I DON'T BELIEVE YOU.
HAVE IT YOUR WAY THEN.
BUT SHOULDN'T YOU KILL ME FIRST?
I HAVE NO REASON TO KILL YOU.
WHAT DO YOU MEAN?

READ THIS WAY

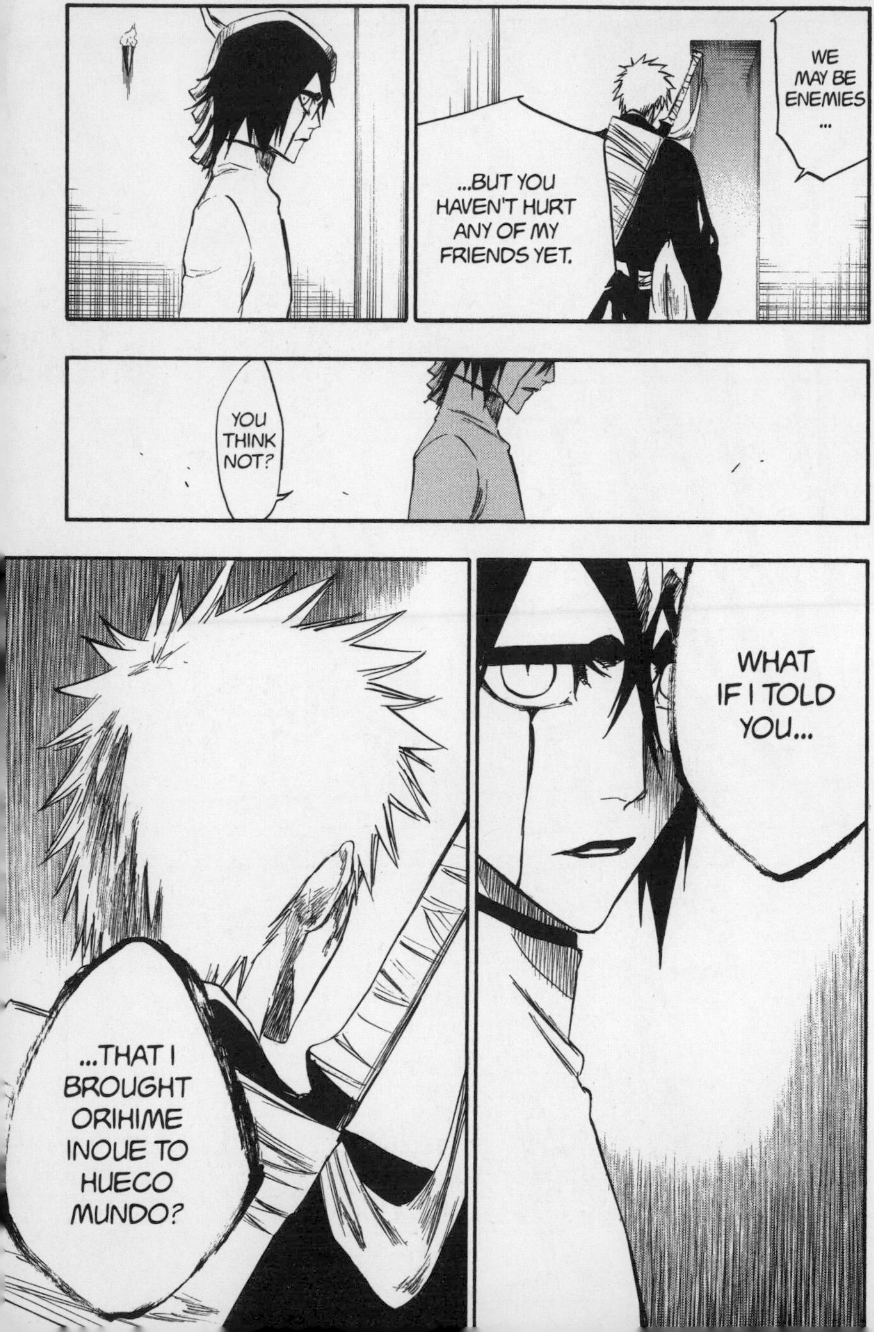
WE MAY BE ENEMIES ...
...BUT YOU HAVEN'T HURT ANY OF MY FRIENDS YET.
YOU THINK NOT?
WHAT IF I TOLD YOU...
...THAT I BROUGHT ORIHIME INOUE TO HUECO MUNDO?

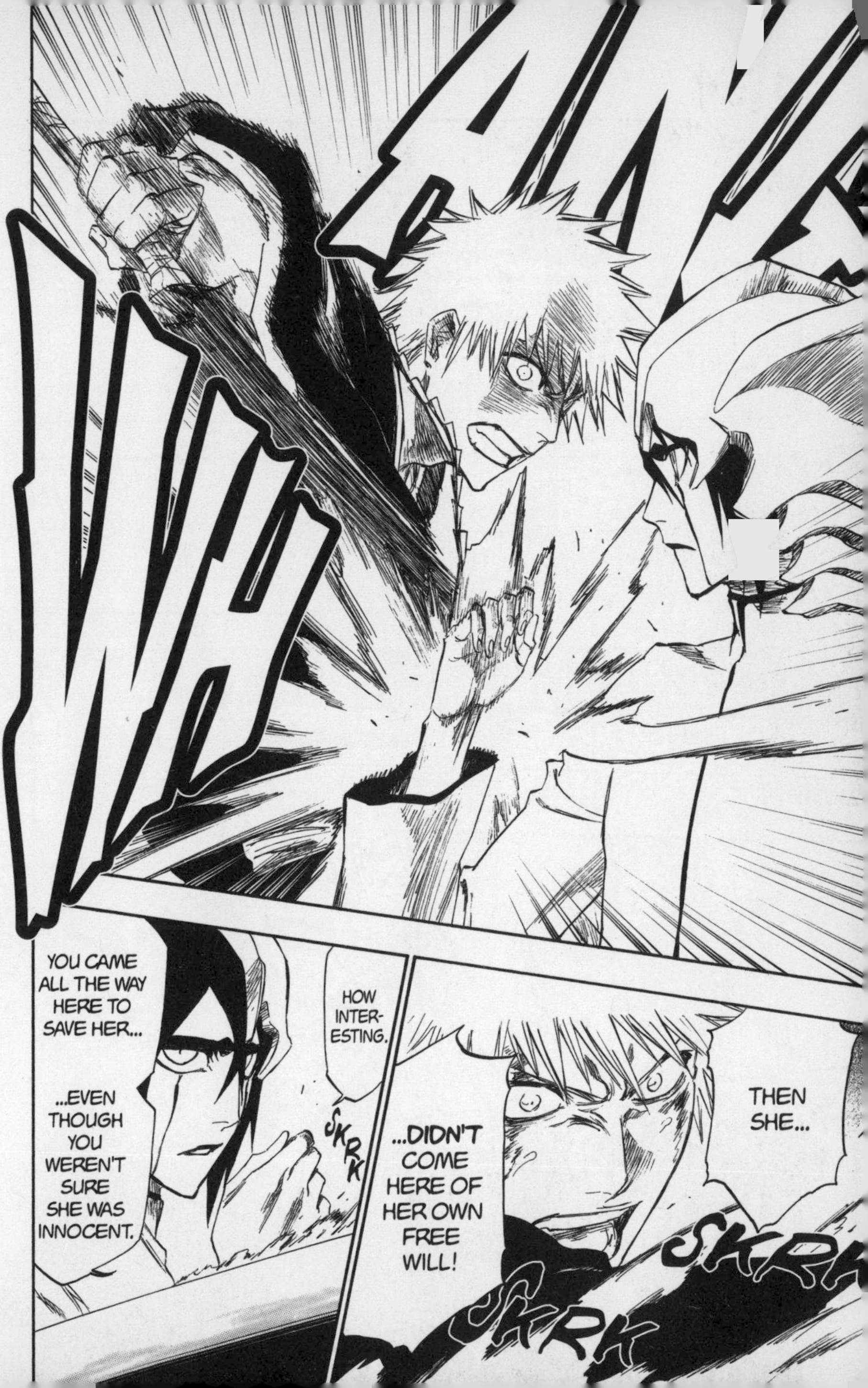
THEN SHE...
...DIDN'T COME HERE OF HER OWN FREE WILL!
SKRK
SKRK
HOW INTER-ESTING.
YOU CAME ALL THE WAY HERE TO SAVE HER...
...EVEN THOUGH YOU WEREN'T SURE SHE WAS INNOCENT.
SKRK

READ THIS WAY

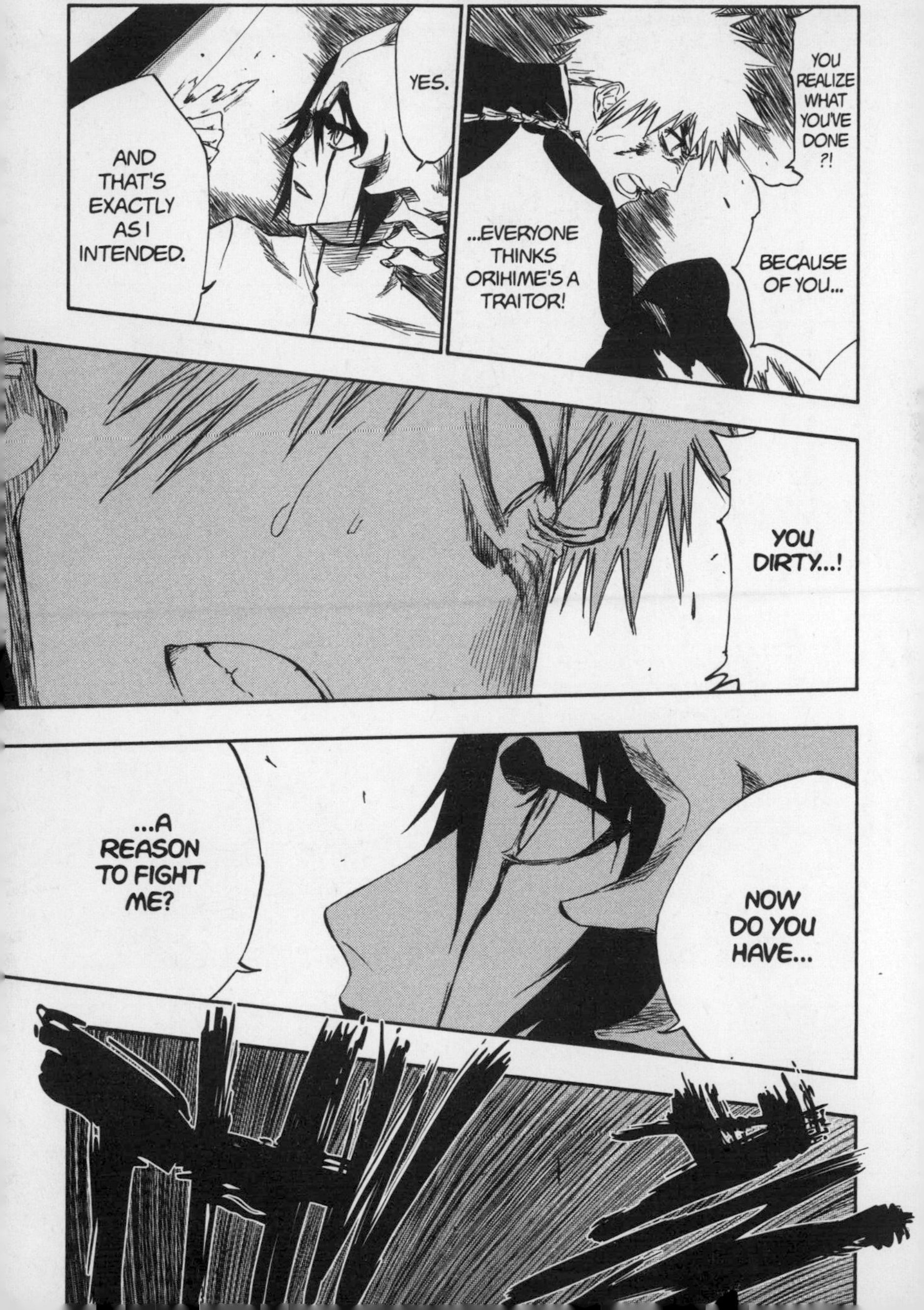
YOU REALIZE WHAT YOU'VE DONE ?!
BECAUSE OF YOU...
...EVERYONE THINKS ORIHIME'S A TRAITOR!
YES.
AND THAT'S EXACTLY AS I INTENDED.
YOU DIRTY...!
NOW DO YOU HAVE...
...A REASON TO FIGHT ME?

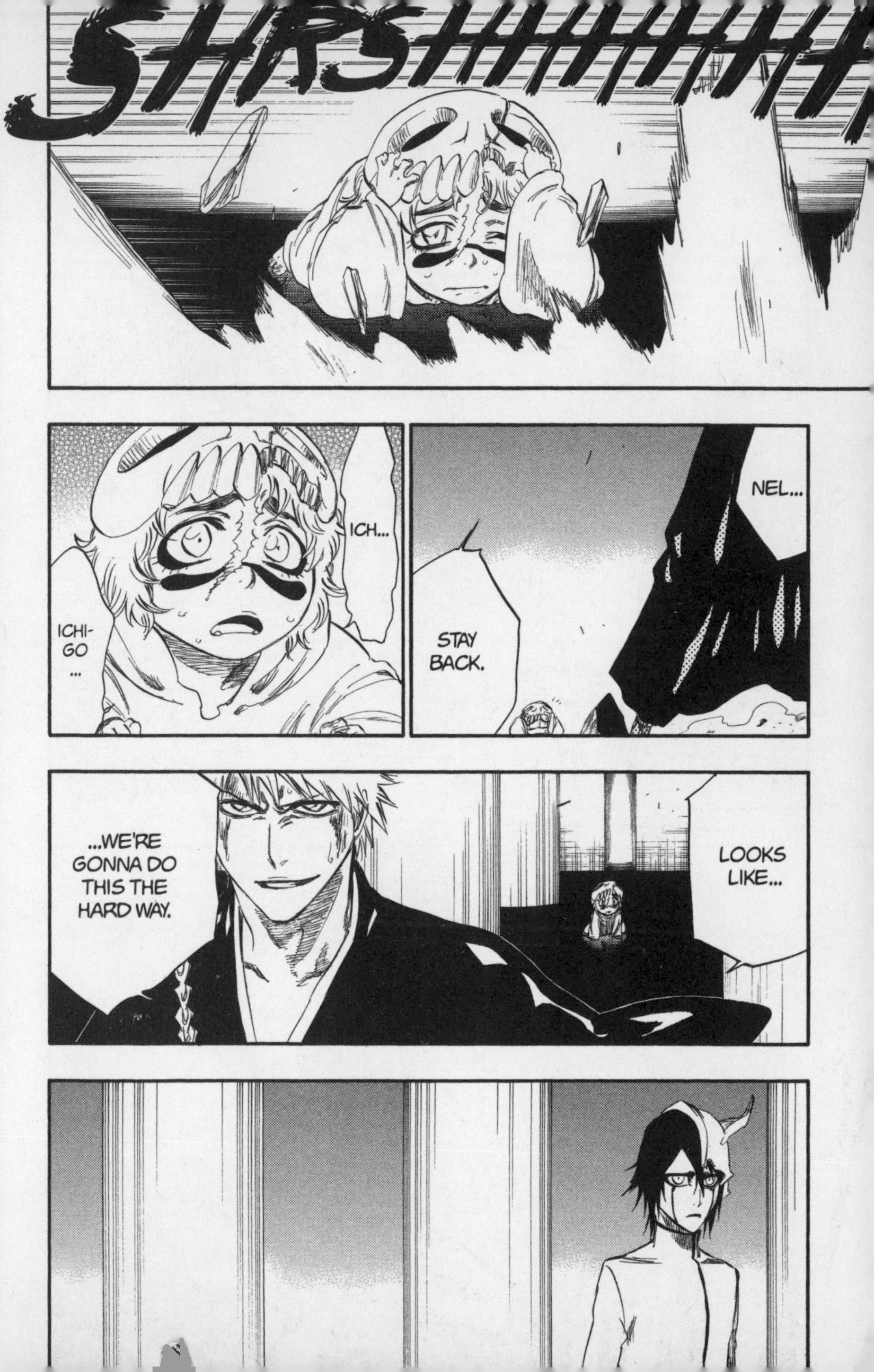
SHRSHHHHHHH
NEL...
STAY BACK.
ICH...
ICHI-GO ...
LOOKS LIKE...
...WE'RE GONNA DO THIS THE HARD WAY.

WMMM

SORRY...

BUT I'M IN A HURRY.

...HOLD BACK.

I WON'T...

SWUP

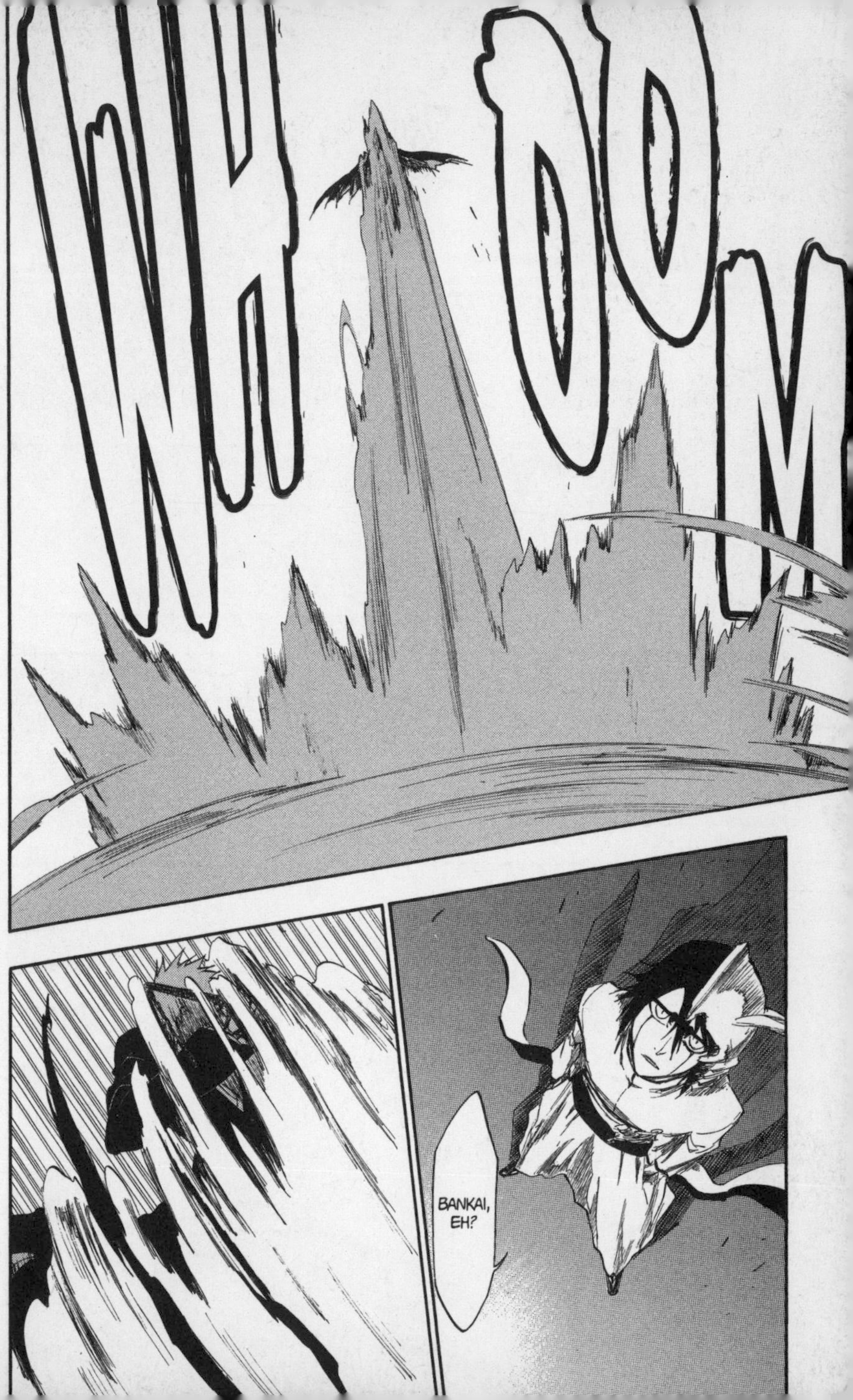
WHDOOM
BANKAI, EH?

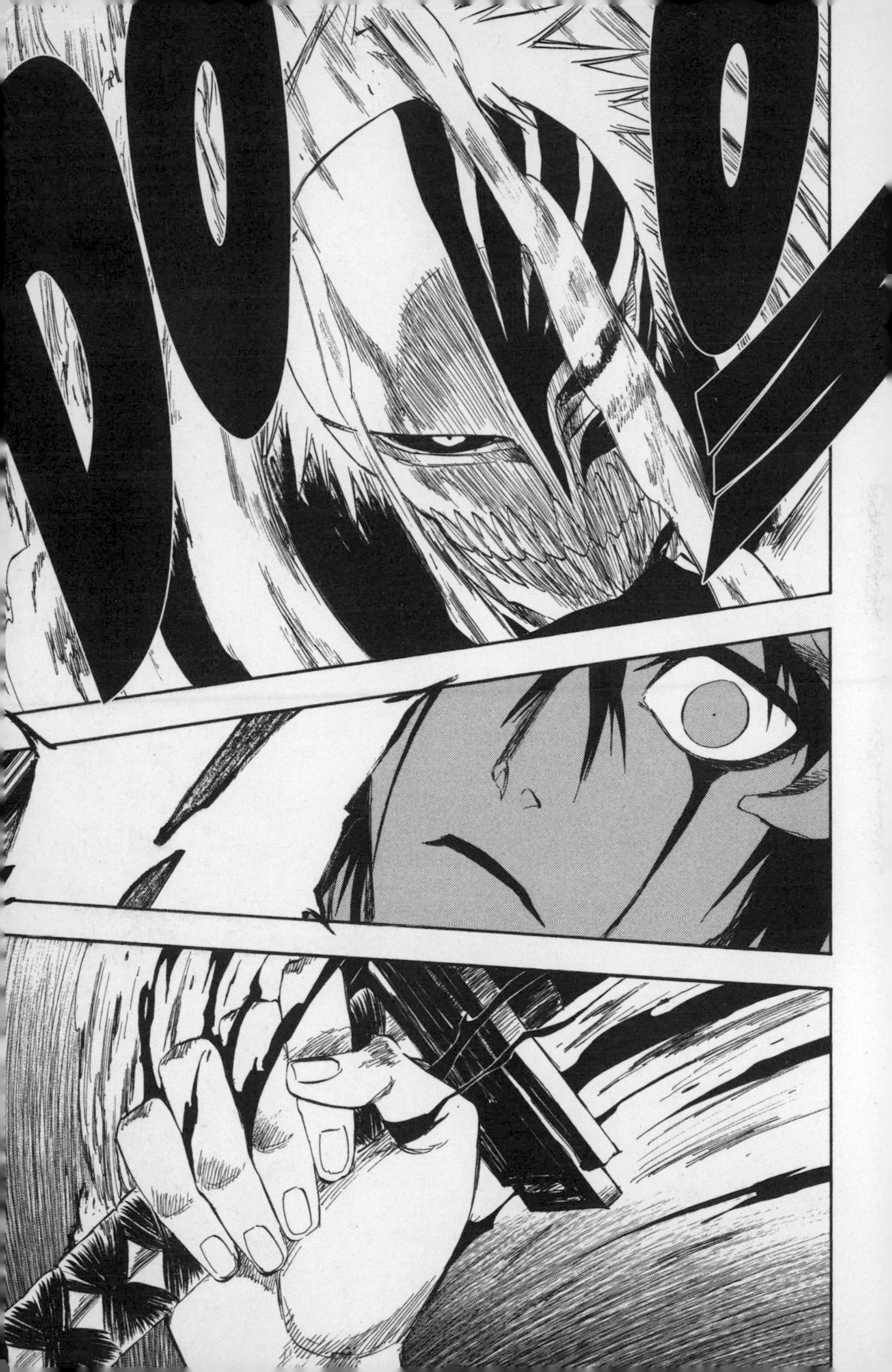
DOOM

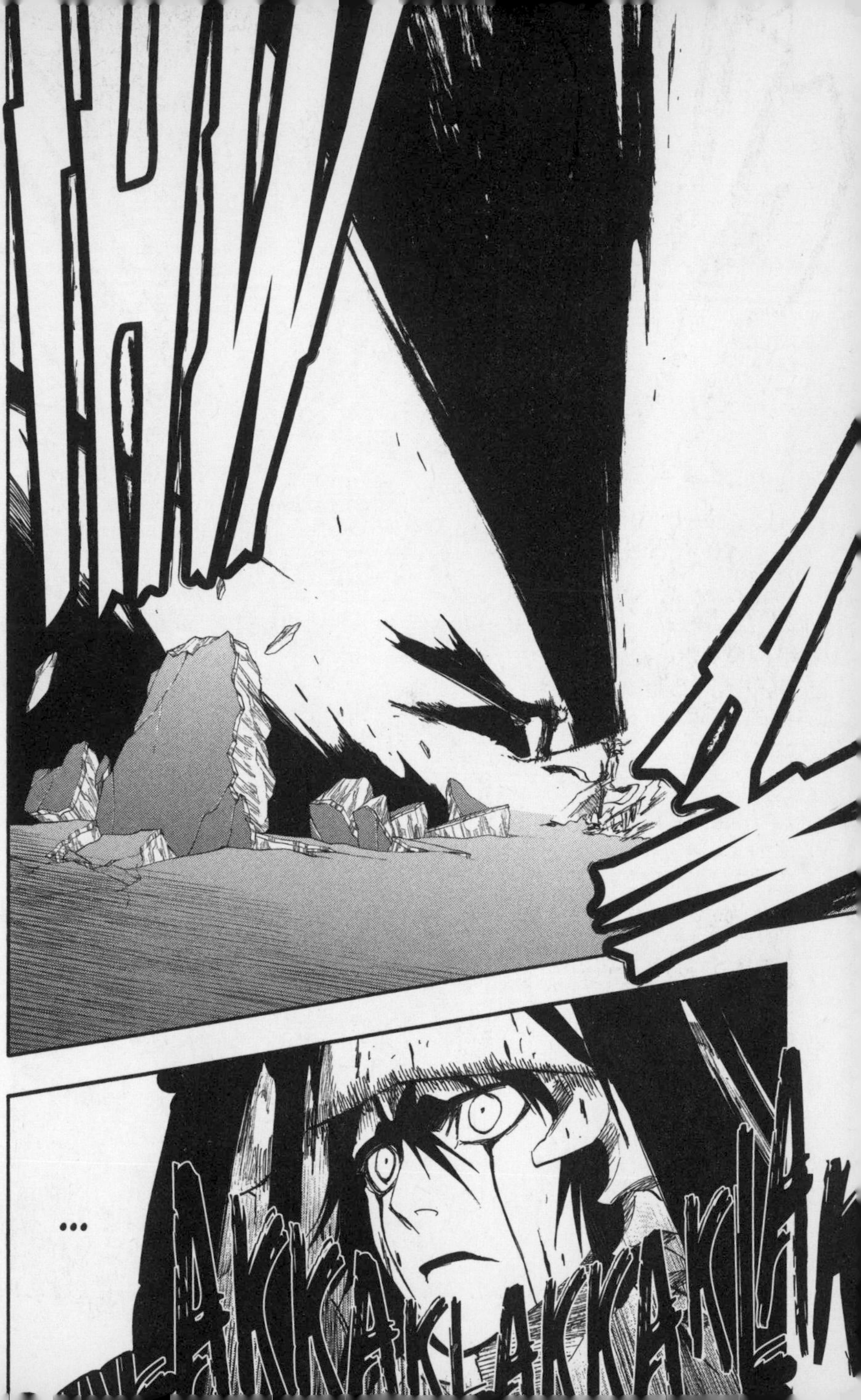
...

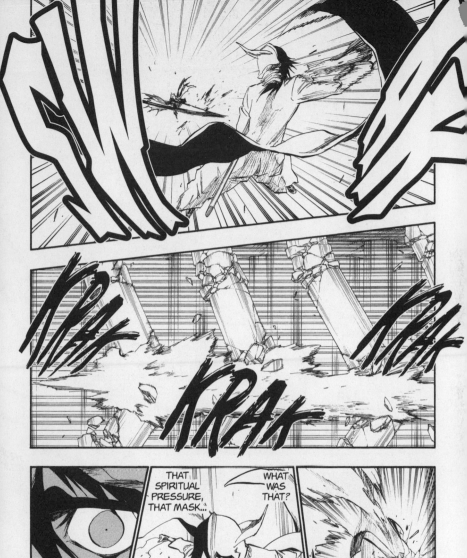

THAT SPIRITUAL PRESSURE, THAT MASK...

WHAT WAS THAT?

HE'S LIKE... ONE OF US!

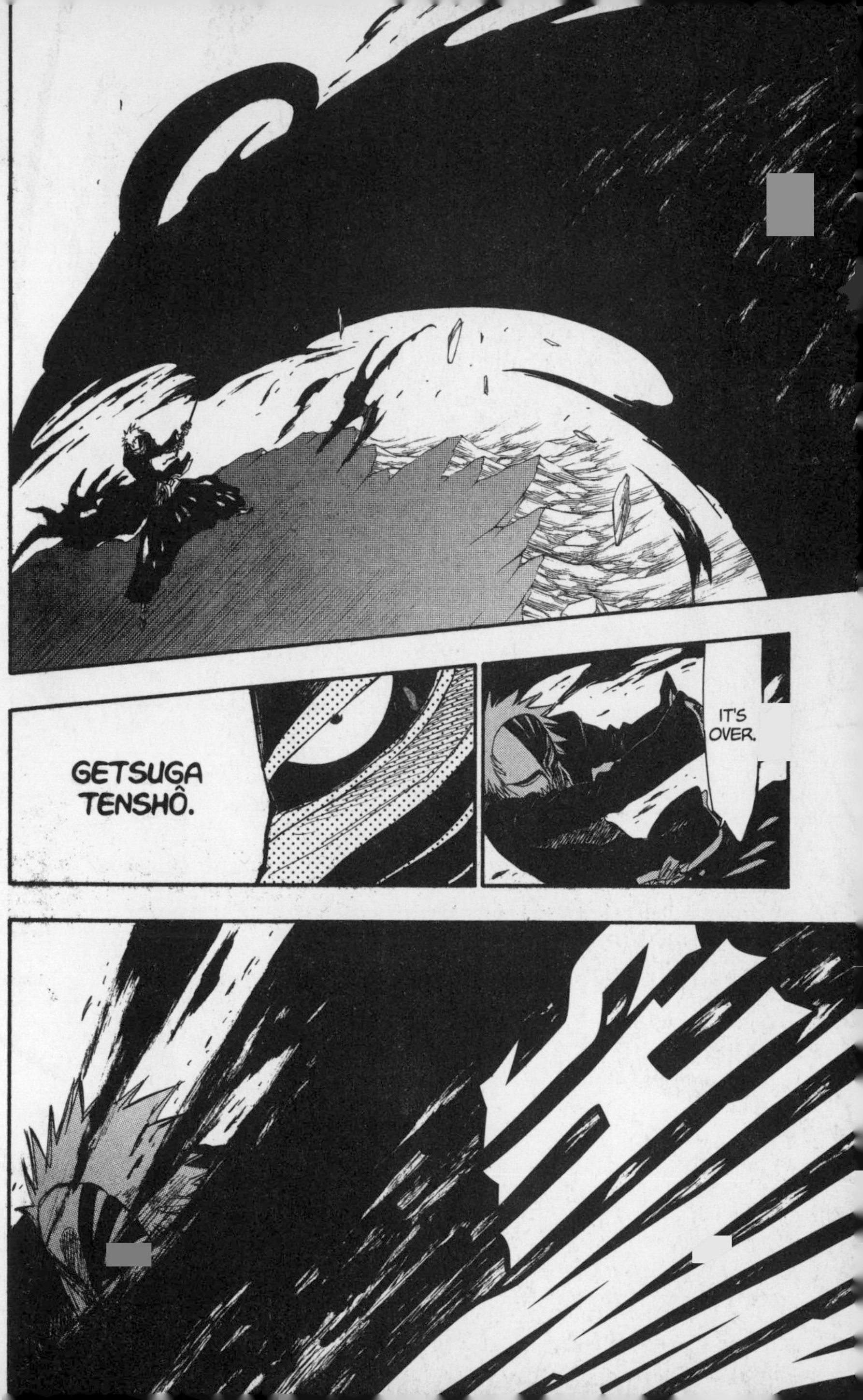
IT'S OVER.
GETSUGA TENSHÔ.

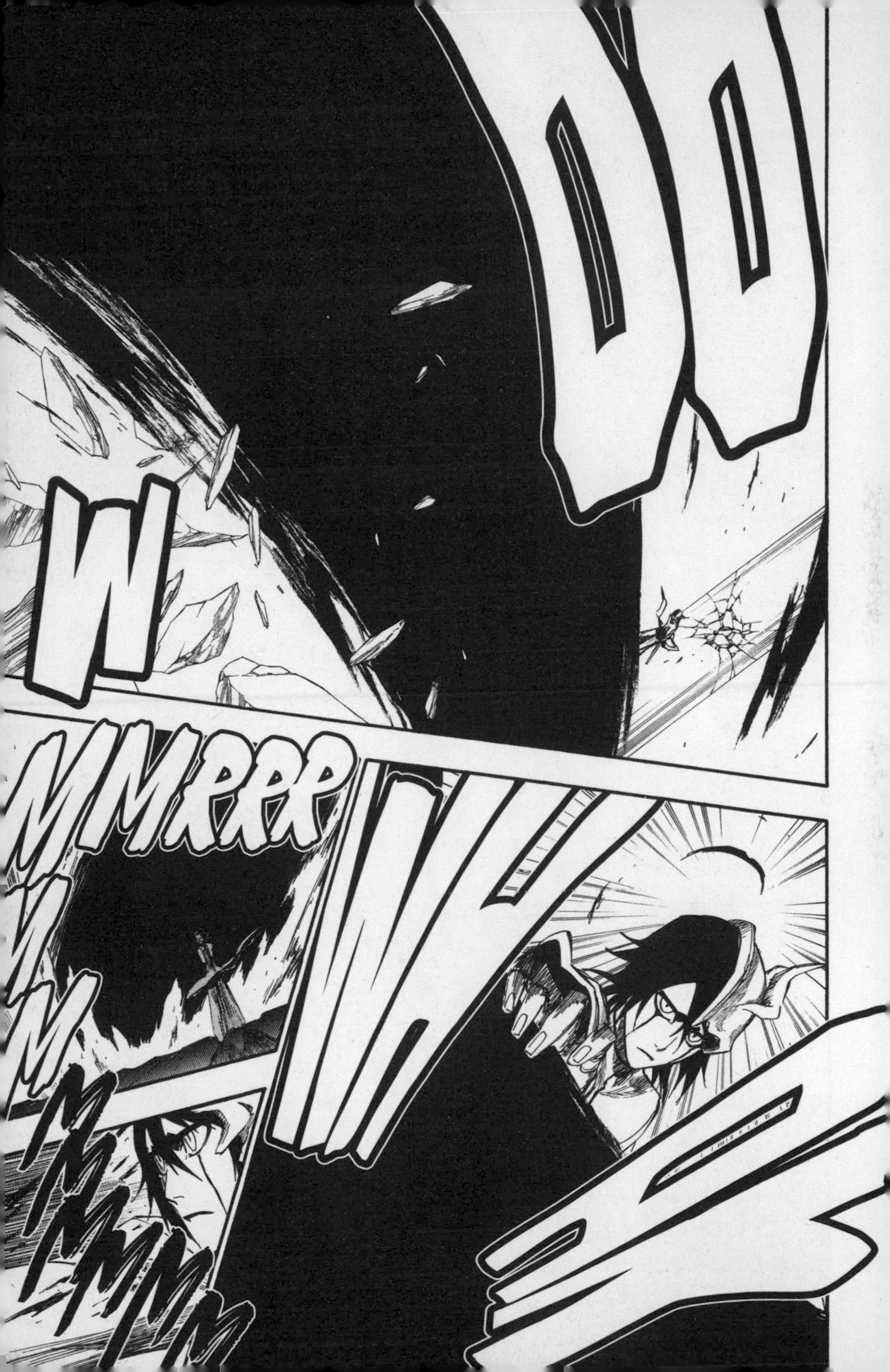

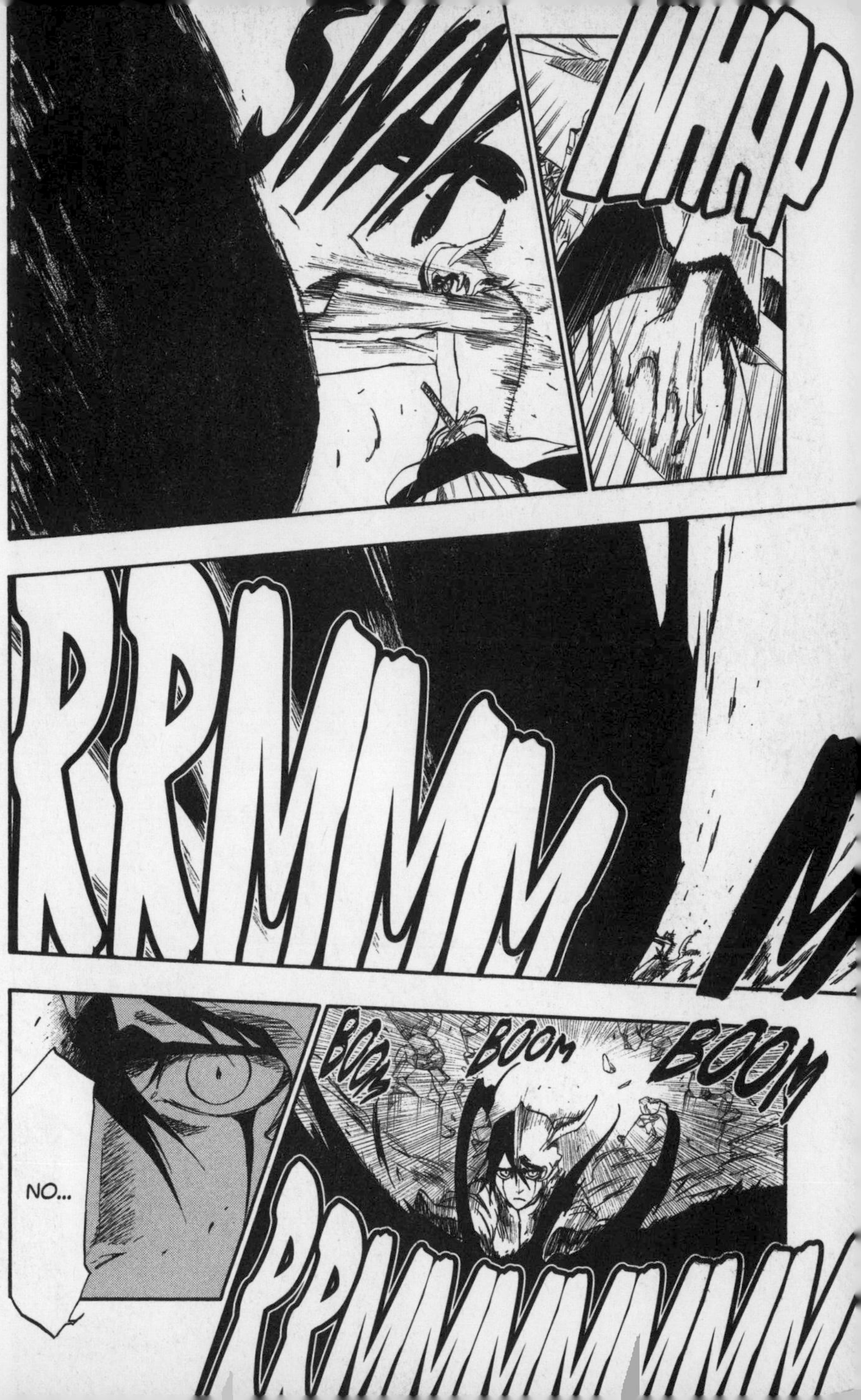
WHAP
SWA
RRMMMM
BOOM BOOM BOOM
PPMMMMMMMM
NO...

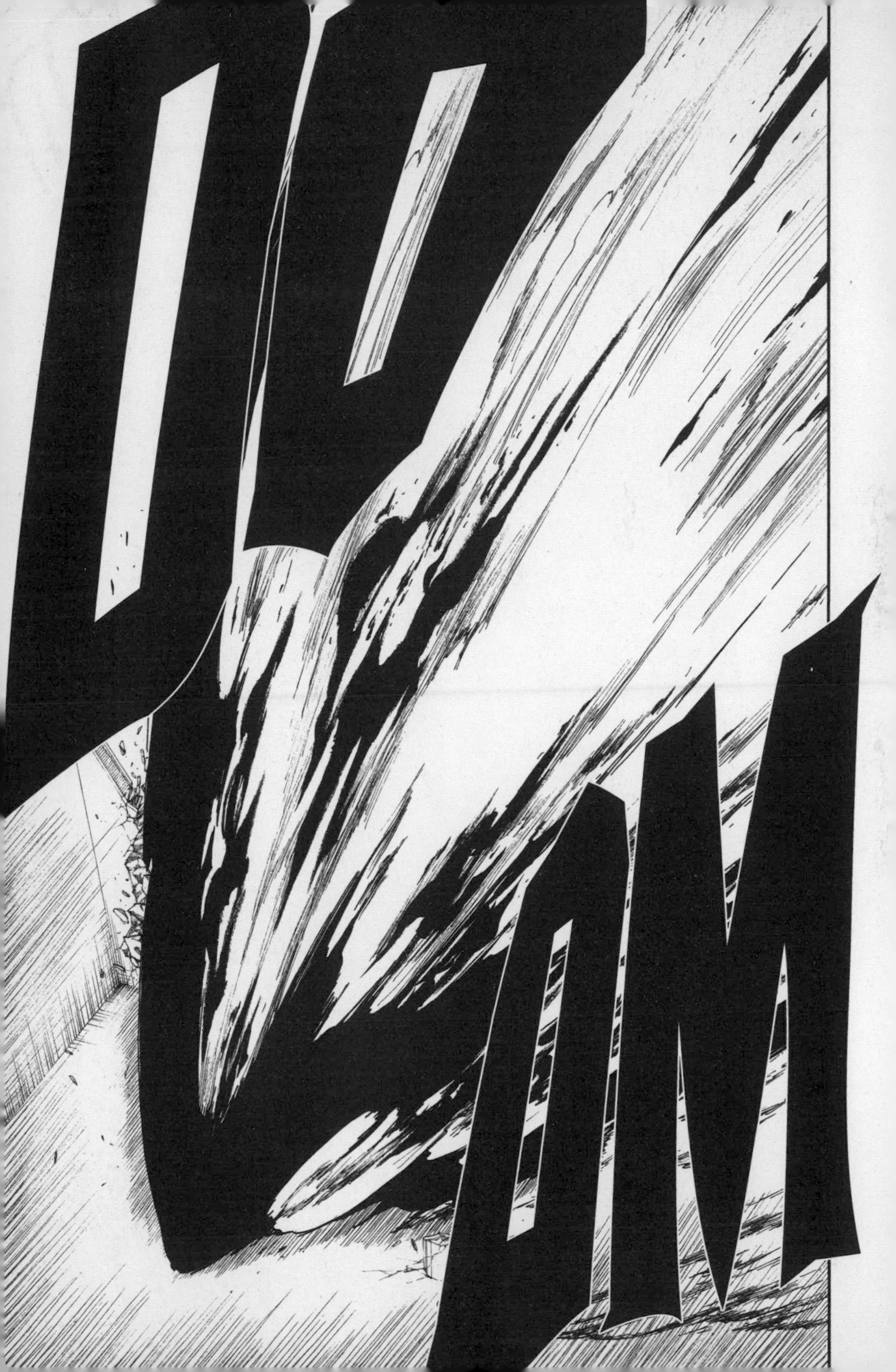

CHAKKA
BOOM
BOOM

CHAKKA
CHAKKA
BOOM

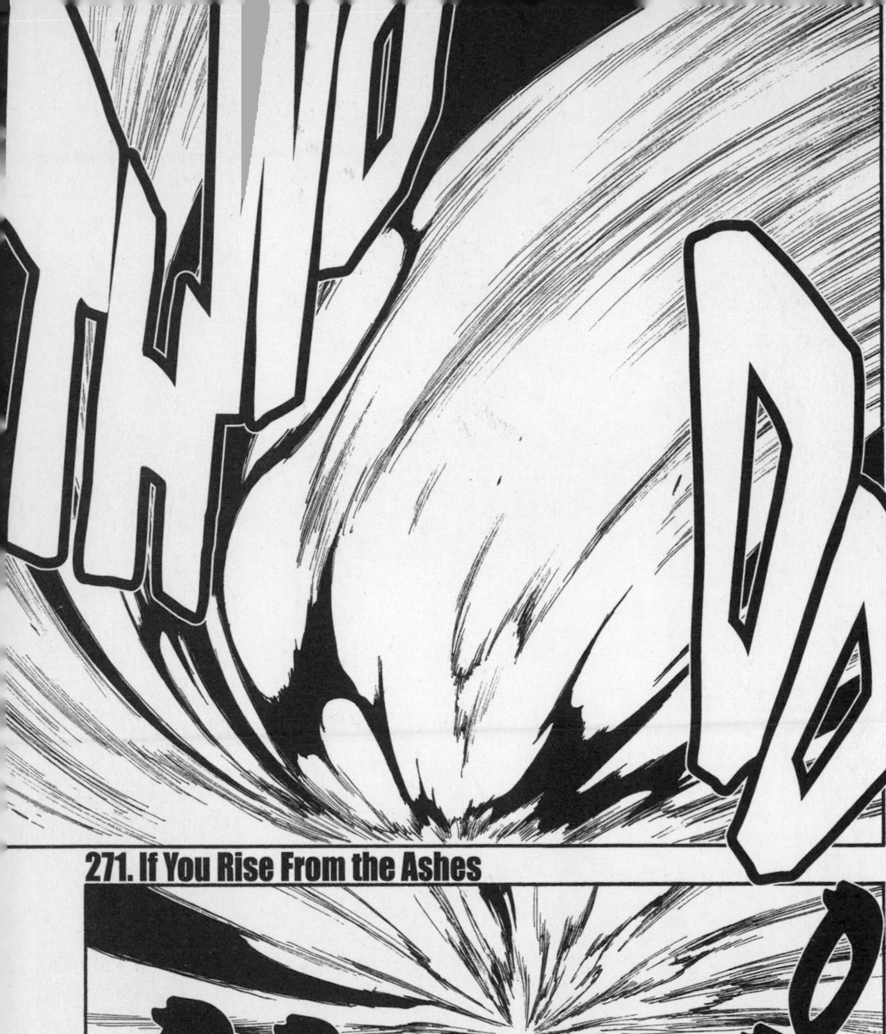

271. If You Rise From the Ashes

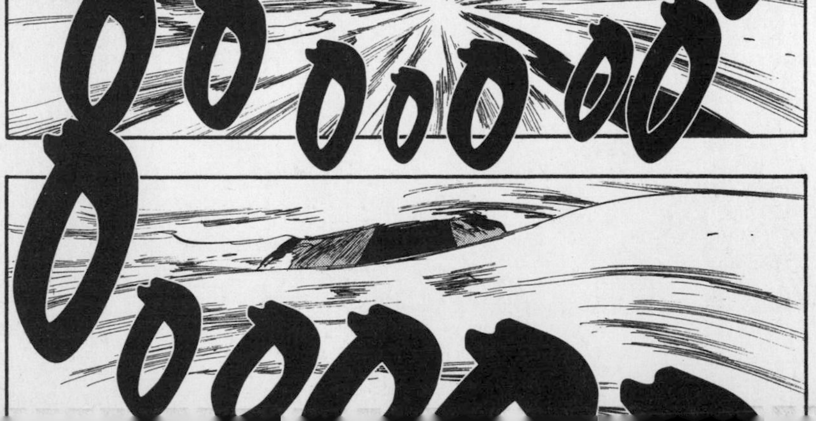

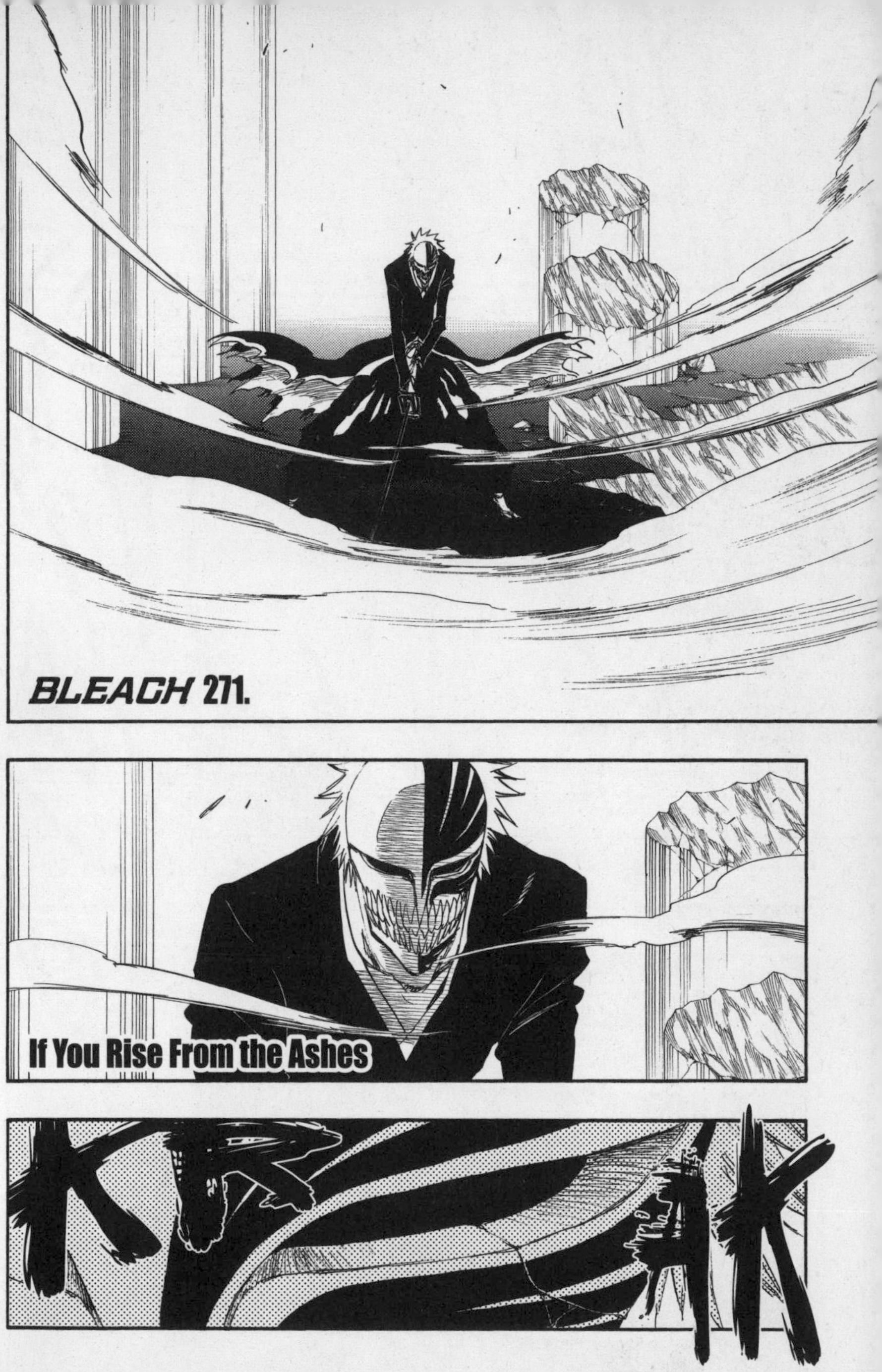
BLEACH 271.
If You Rise From the Ashes

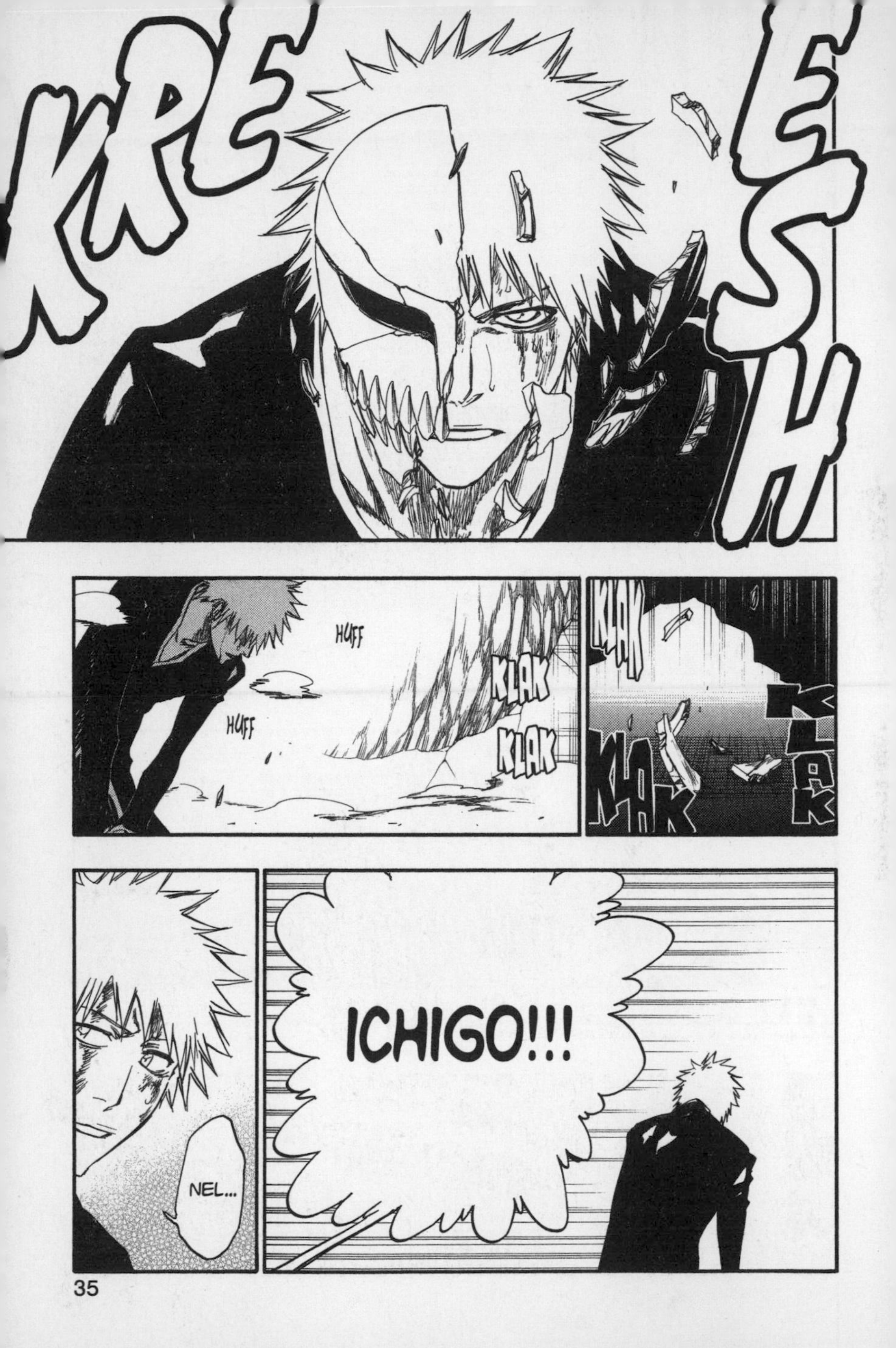
KRE
ESH
KLAK
KLAK
KLAK
HUFF
HUFF
KLAK
KLAK
ICHIGO!!!
NEL...

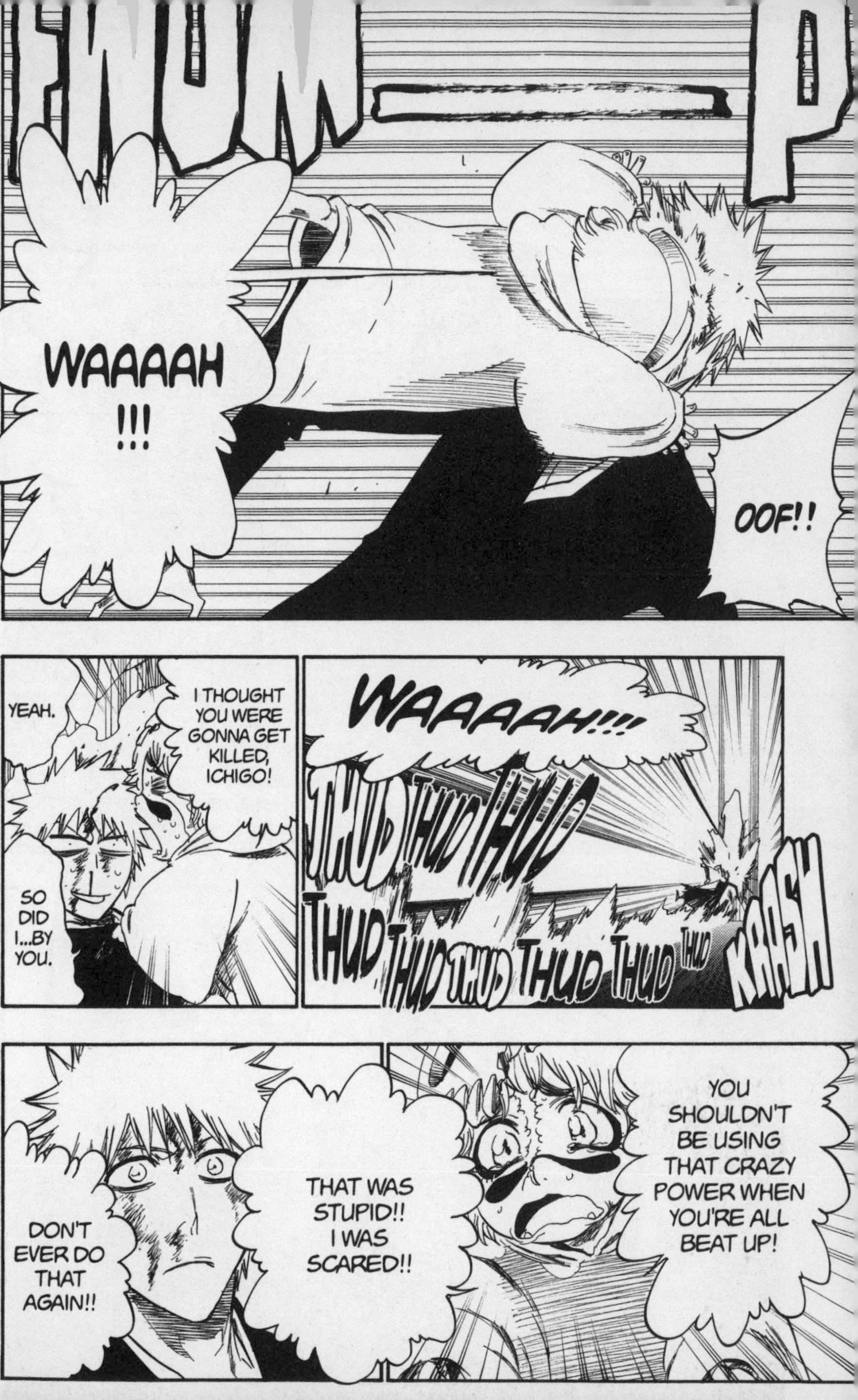
OOF!!
WAAAAH !!!
WAAAAH!!!
THUD THUD THUD
THUD THUD THUD THUD THUD THUD
KRASH
I THOUGHT YOU WERE GONNA GET KILLED, ICHIGO!
YEAH.
SO DID I...BY YOU.
YOU SHOULDN'T BE USING THAT CRAZY POWER WHEN YOU'RE ALL BEAT UP!
THAT WAS STUPID!! I WAS SCARED!!
DON'T EVER DO THAT AGAIN!!

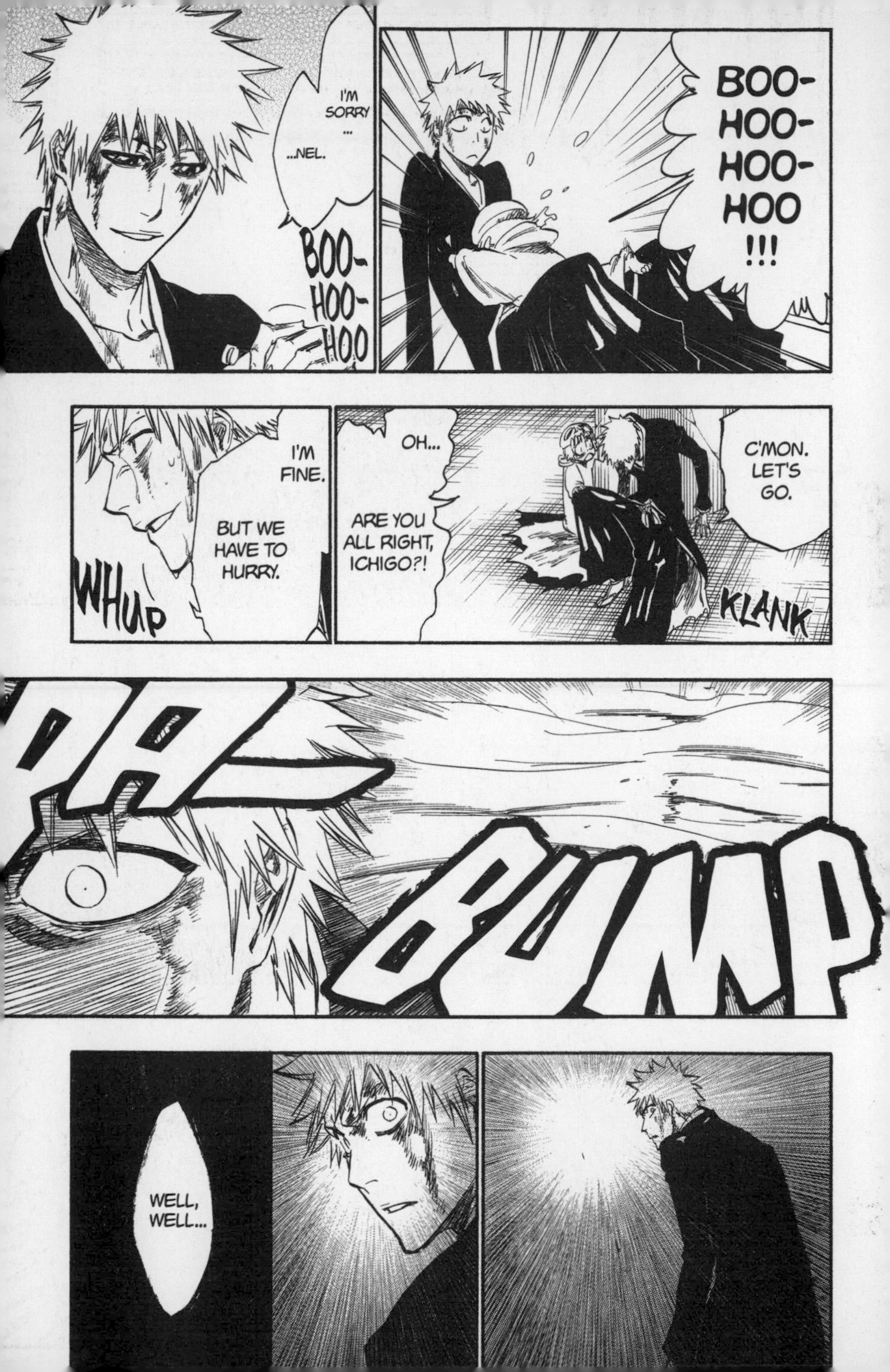
BOO-HOO-HOO-HOO!!!
I'M SORRY... ...NEL.
BOO-HOO-HOO
C'MON. LET'S GO.
KLANK
OH...
ARE YOU ALL RIGHT, ICHIGO?!
I'M FINE.
BUT WE HAVE TO HURRY.
WHUP
BA-BUMP
WELL, WELL...

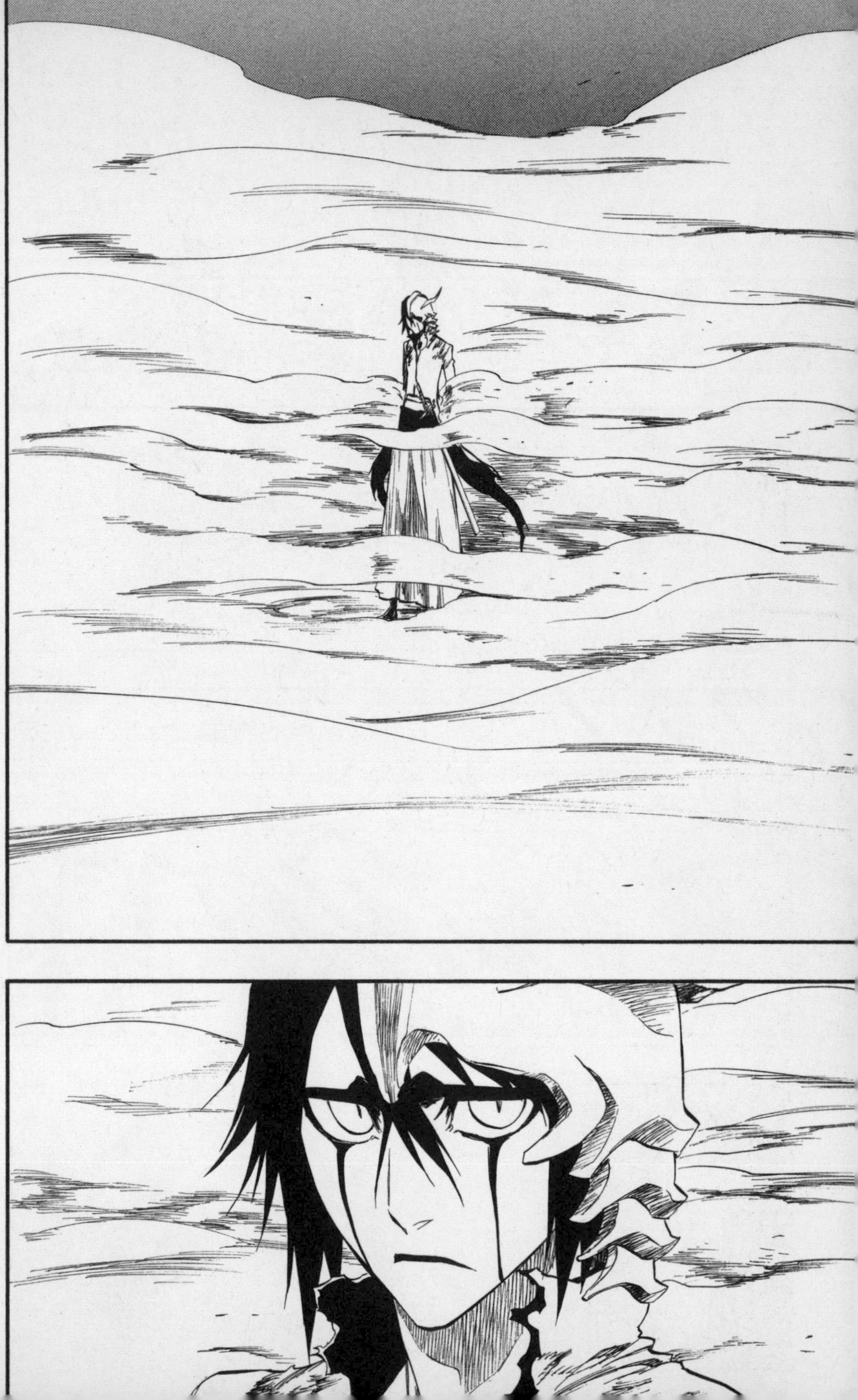

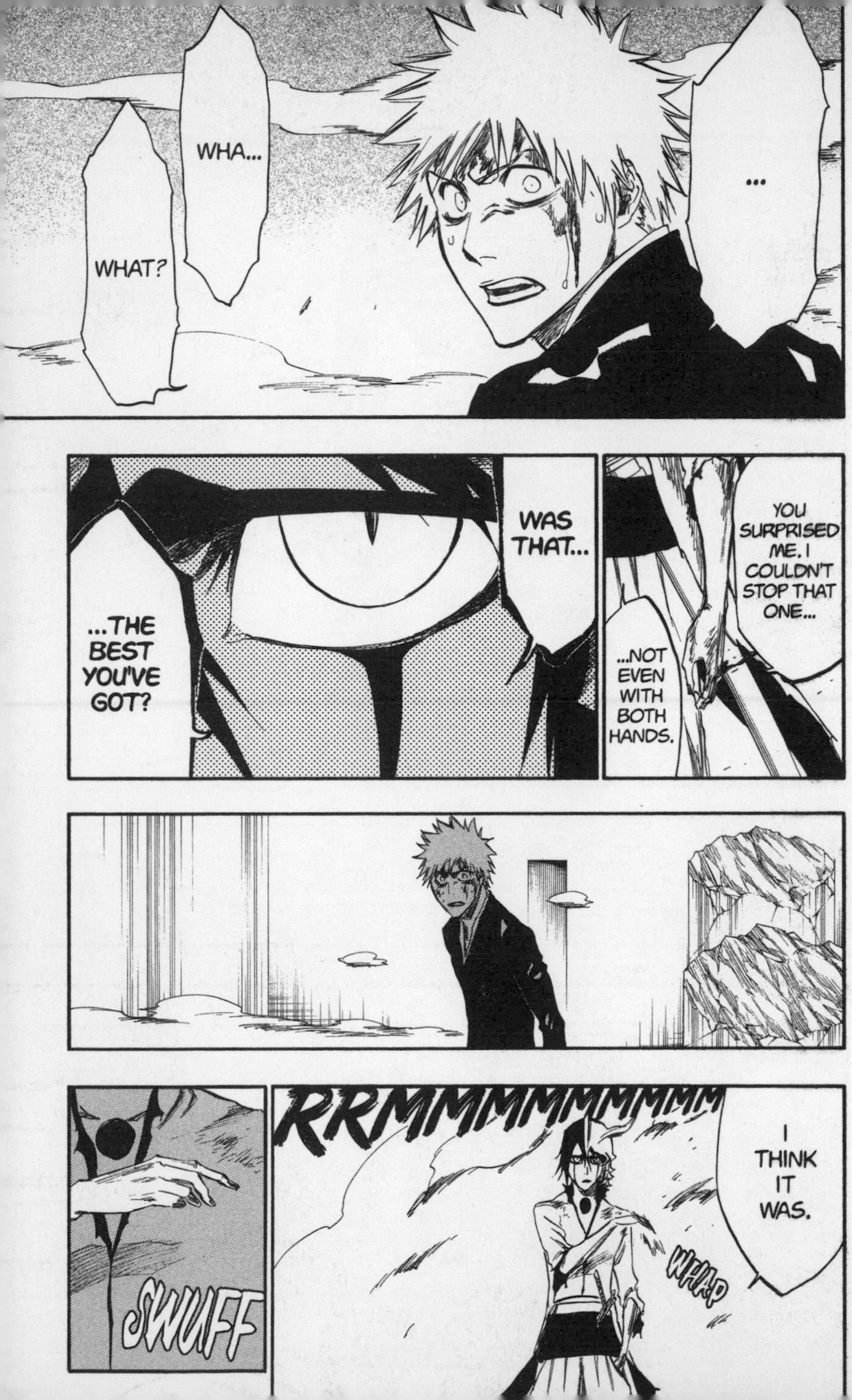
...
WHA...
WHAT?
YOU SURPRISED ME. I COULDN'T STOP THAT ONE...
...NOT EVEN WITH BOTH HANDS.
WAS THAT...
...THE BEST YOU'VE GOT?
I THINK IT WAS.
RRMMMMMMMMMM
WHAP
SWUFF

HOW UN-
FORTUNATE.

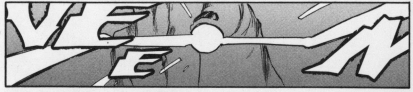

DOOM
BLAST
!!

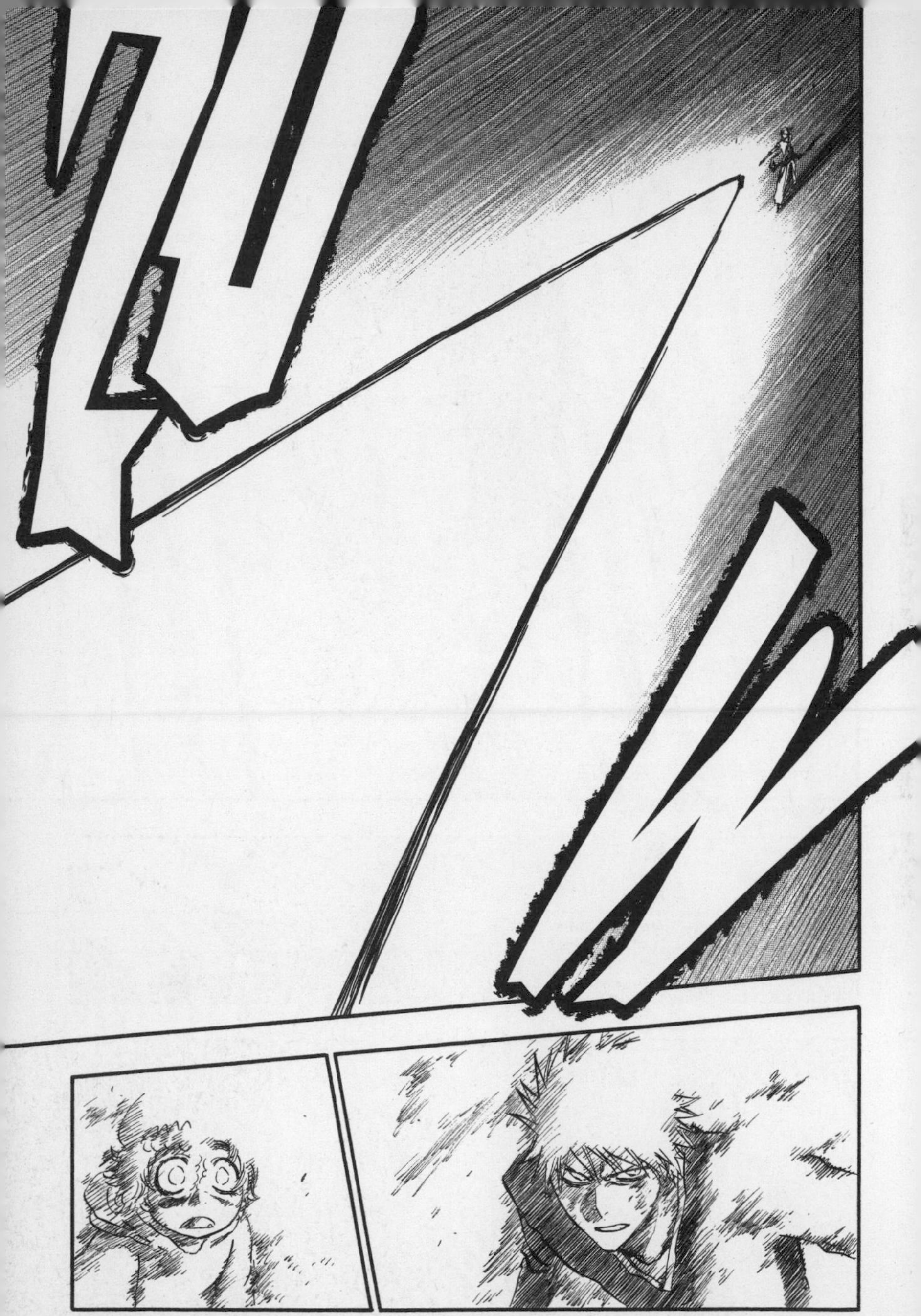

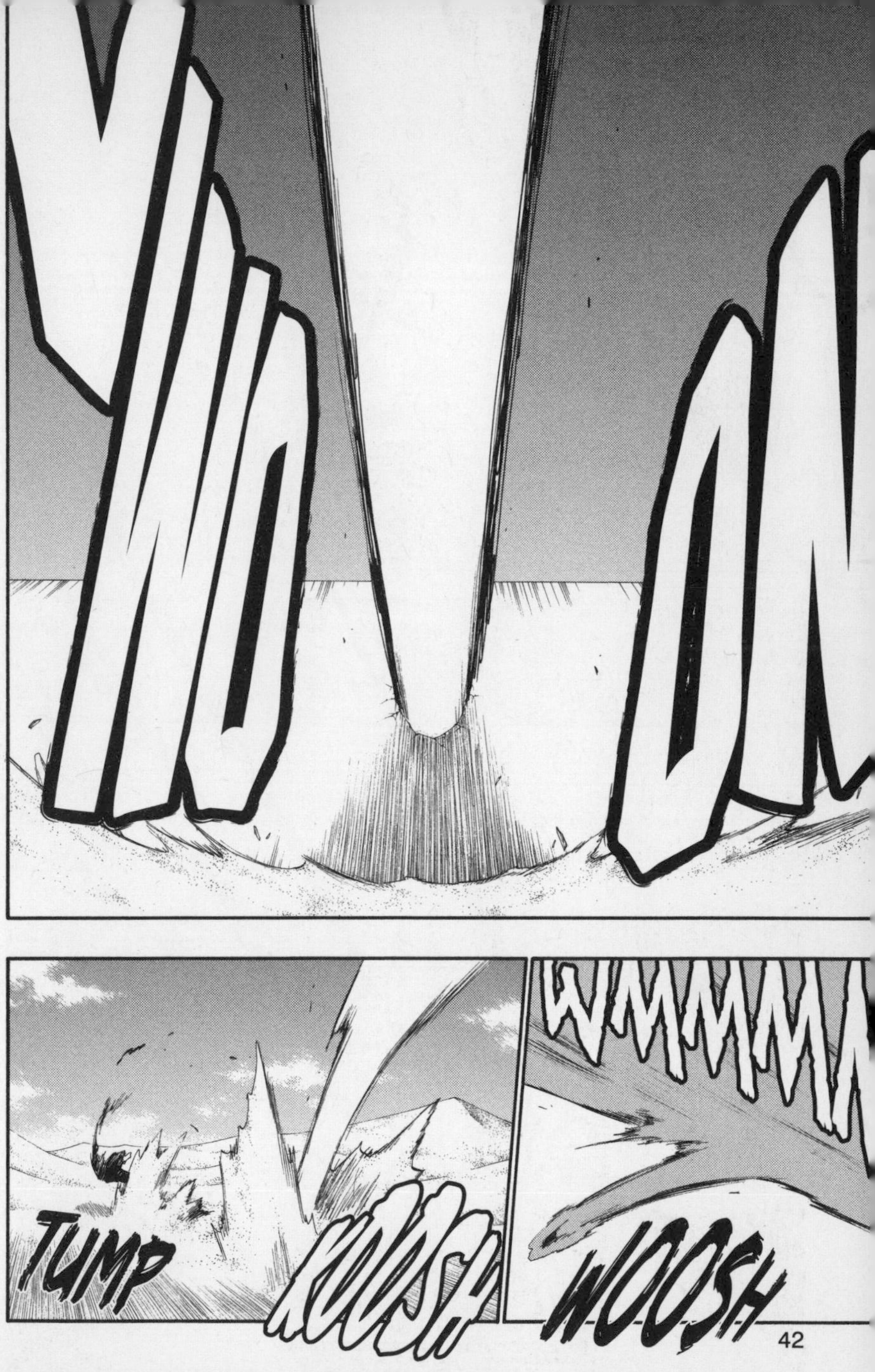
WOOSH
TUMP

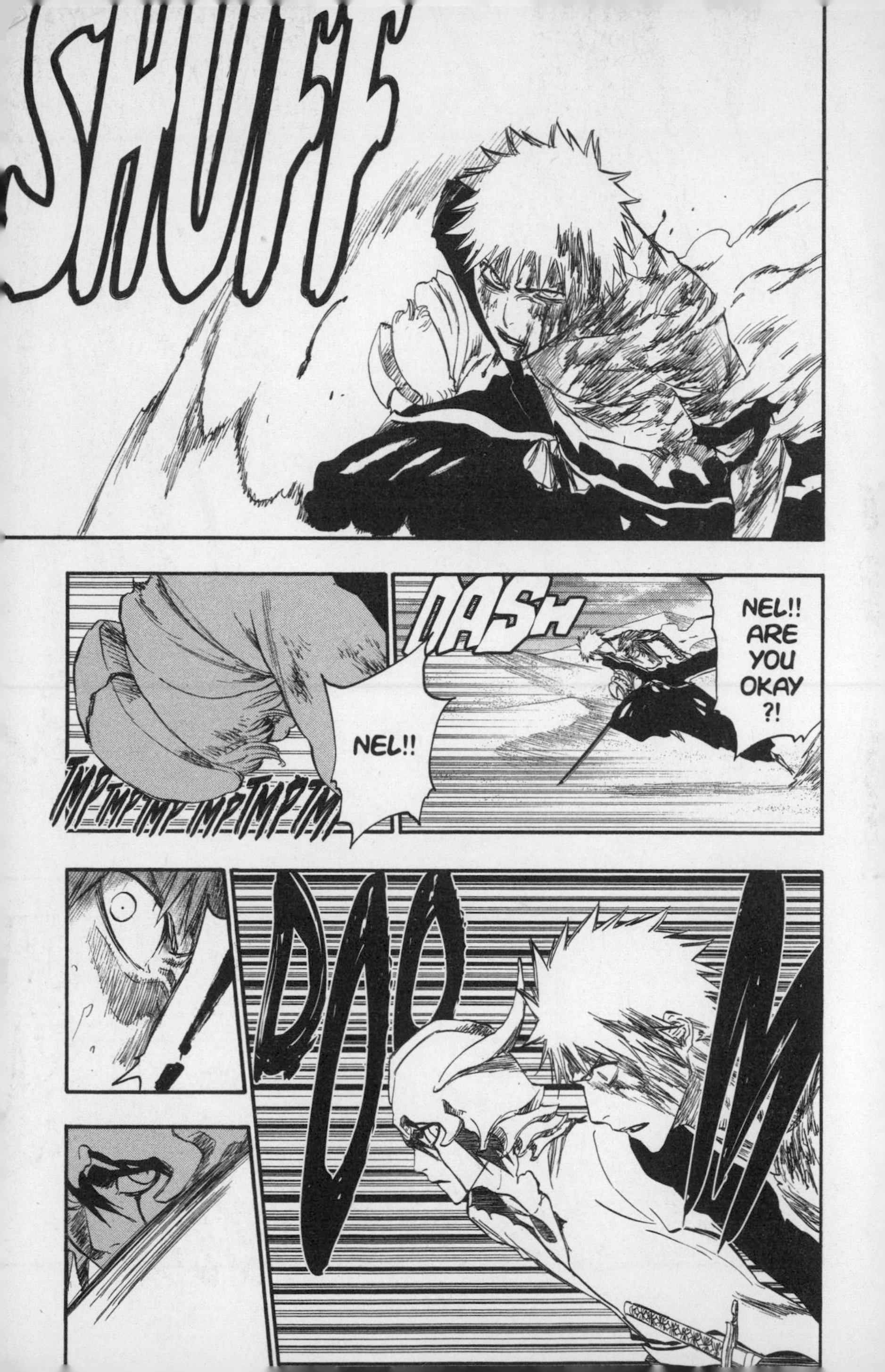
SHUFF
NEL!! ARE YOU OKAY ?!
DASH
NEL!!
TMP TMP TMP TMP TMP TM
DOOM

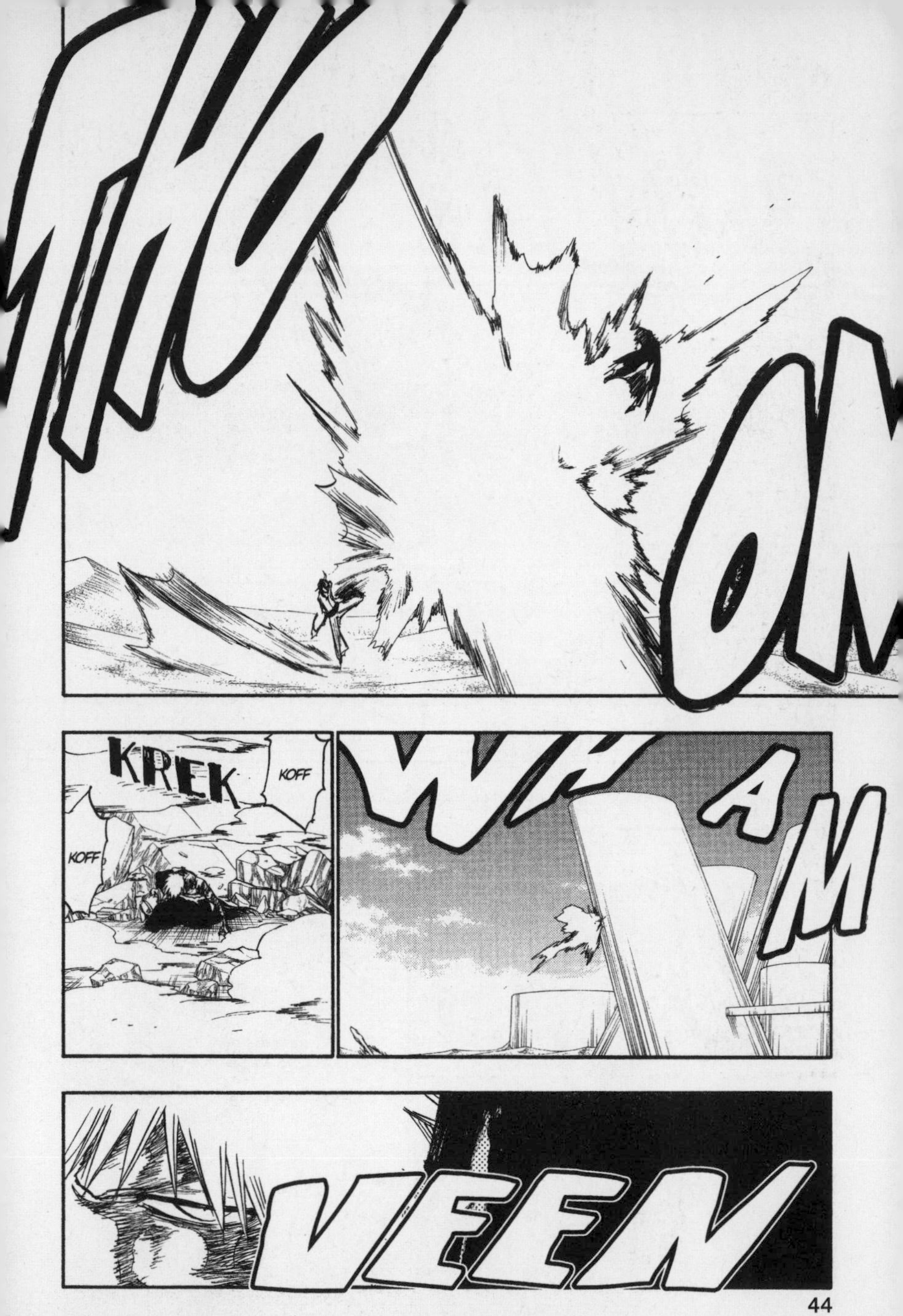
SHOOM
WHAM
KREK
KOFF
KOFF
VEEN

READ THIS WAY

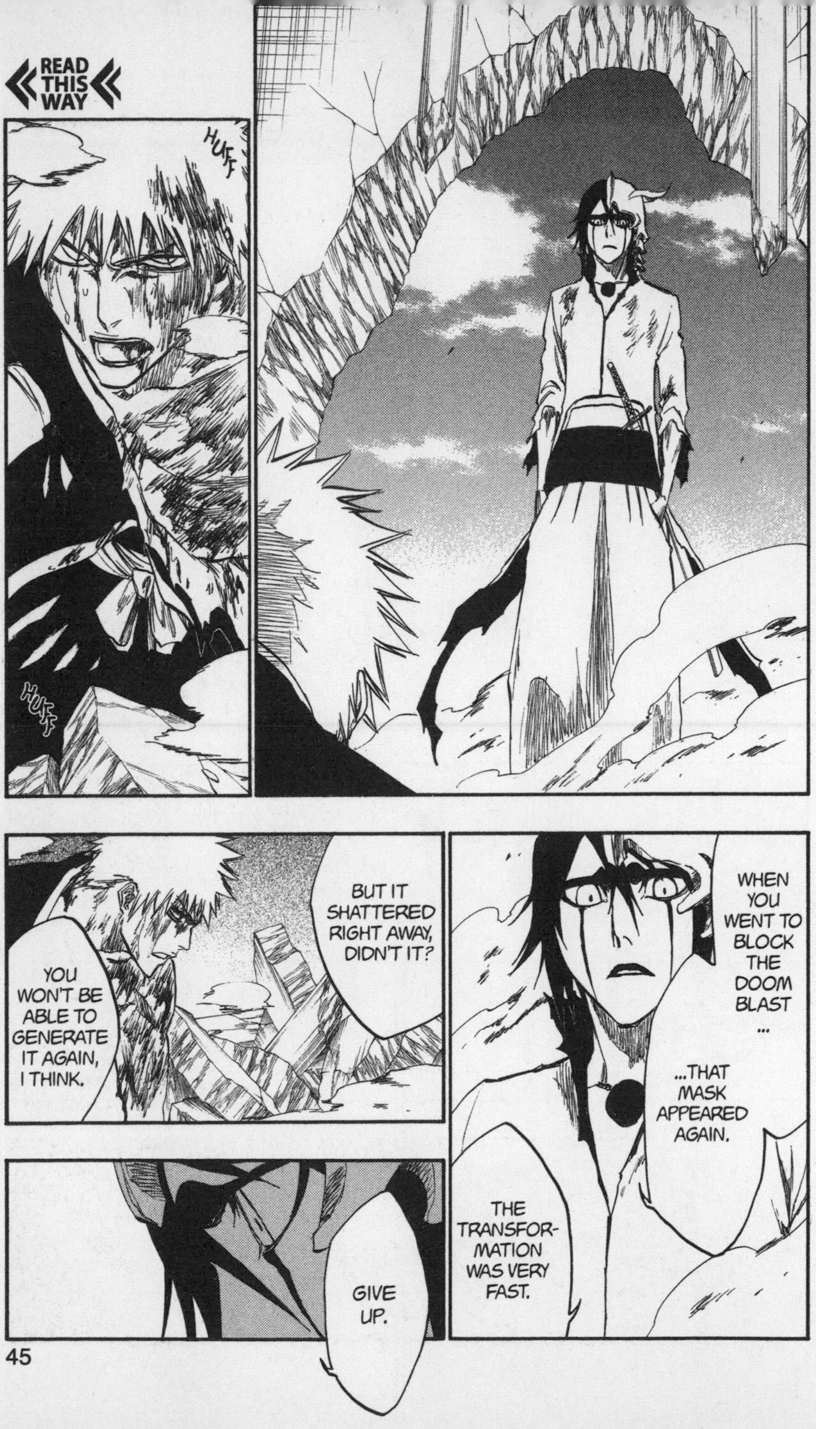
HUFF
HUFF
WHEN YOU WENT TO BLOCK THE DOOM BLAST ...
...THAT MASK APPEARED AGAIN.
THE TRANSFORMATION WAS VERY FAST.
BUT IT SHATTERED RIGHT AWAY, DIDN'T IT?
YOU WON'T BE ABLE TO GENERATE IT AGAIN, I THINK.
GIVE UP.

I DON'T
...

...GIVE
UP.

...AS GOOD AS WON!

YOU'RE THE LEADER OF THE ESPADAS, RIGHT?

SO IF I BEAT YOU, THIS WAR'S...

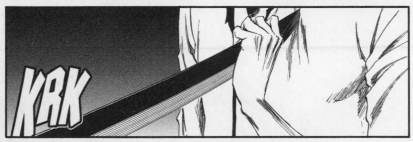

KRK

THAT'S UNFORTUNATE.

SHIK

I SEE.

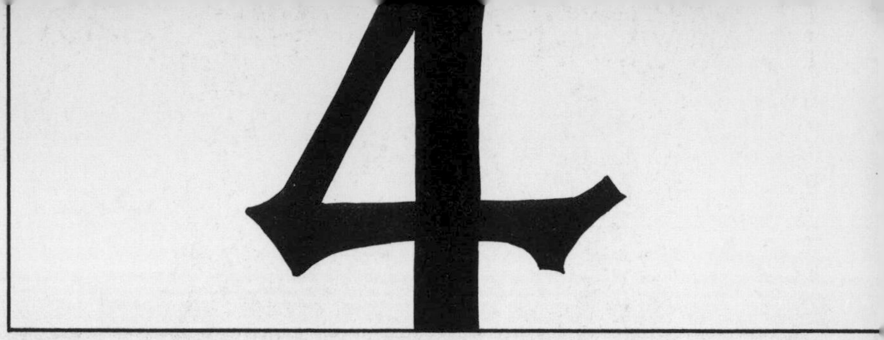
4
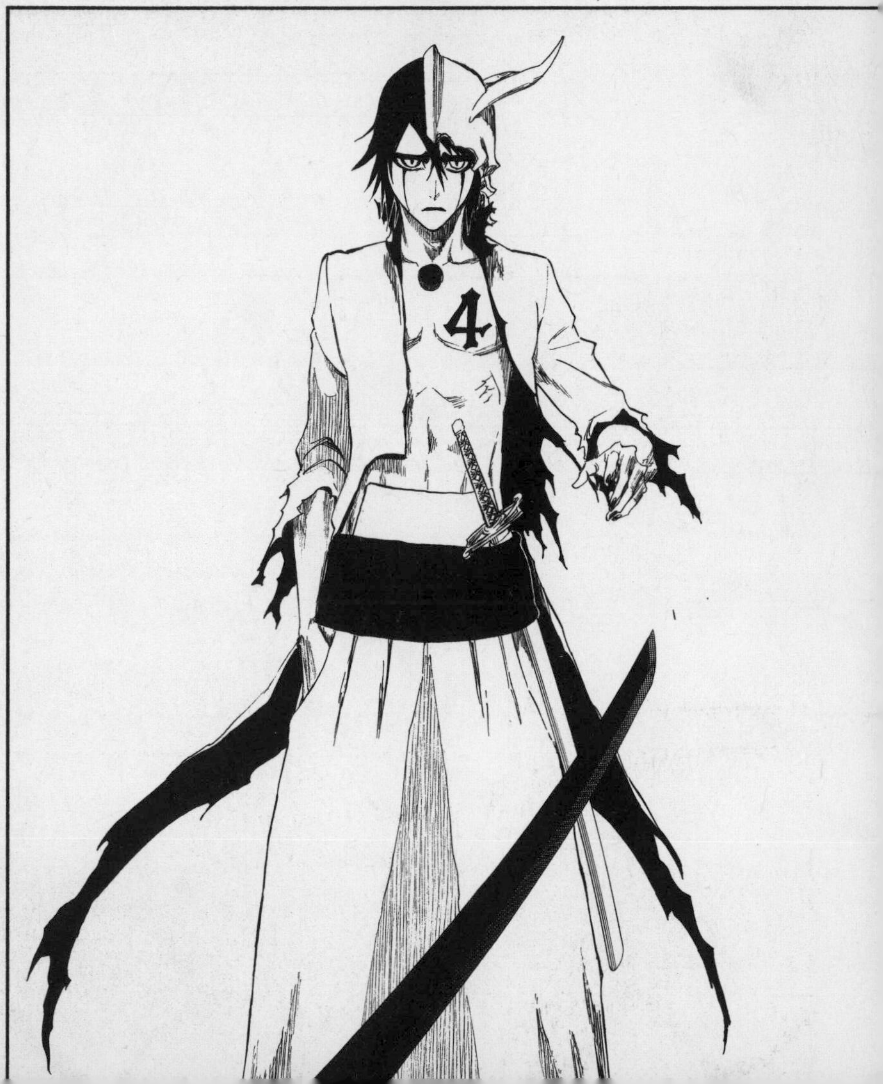
4

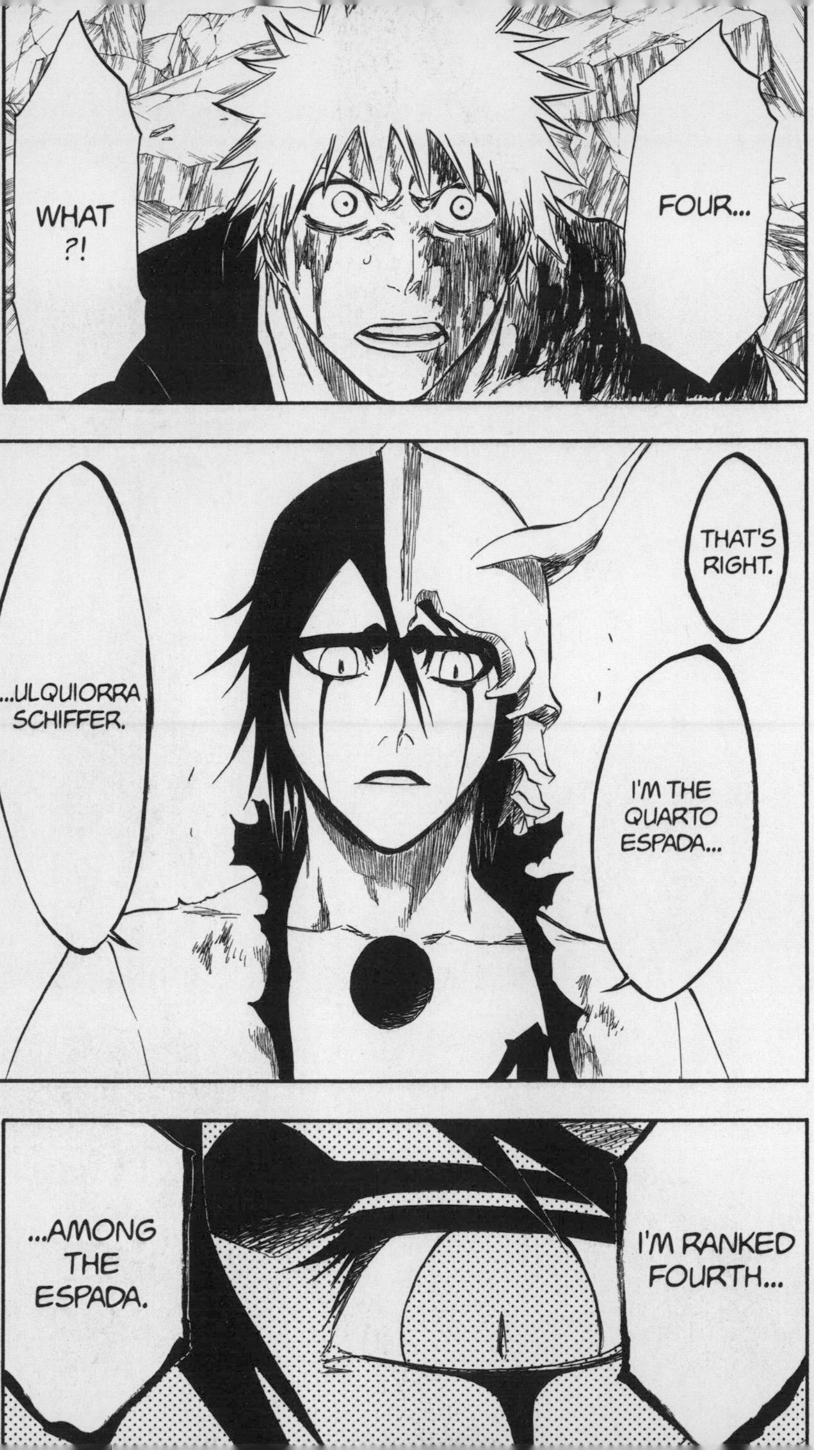
FOUR...
WHAT?!
THAT'S RIGHT.
I'M THE QUARTO ESPADA...
...ULQUIORRA SCHIFFER.
I'M RANKED FOURTH...
...AMONG THE ESPADA.

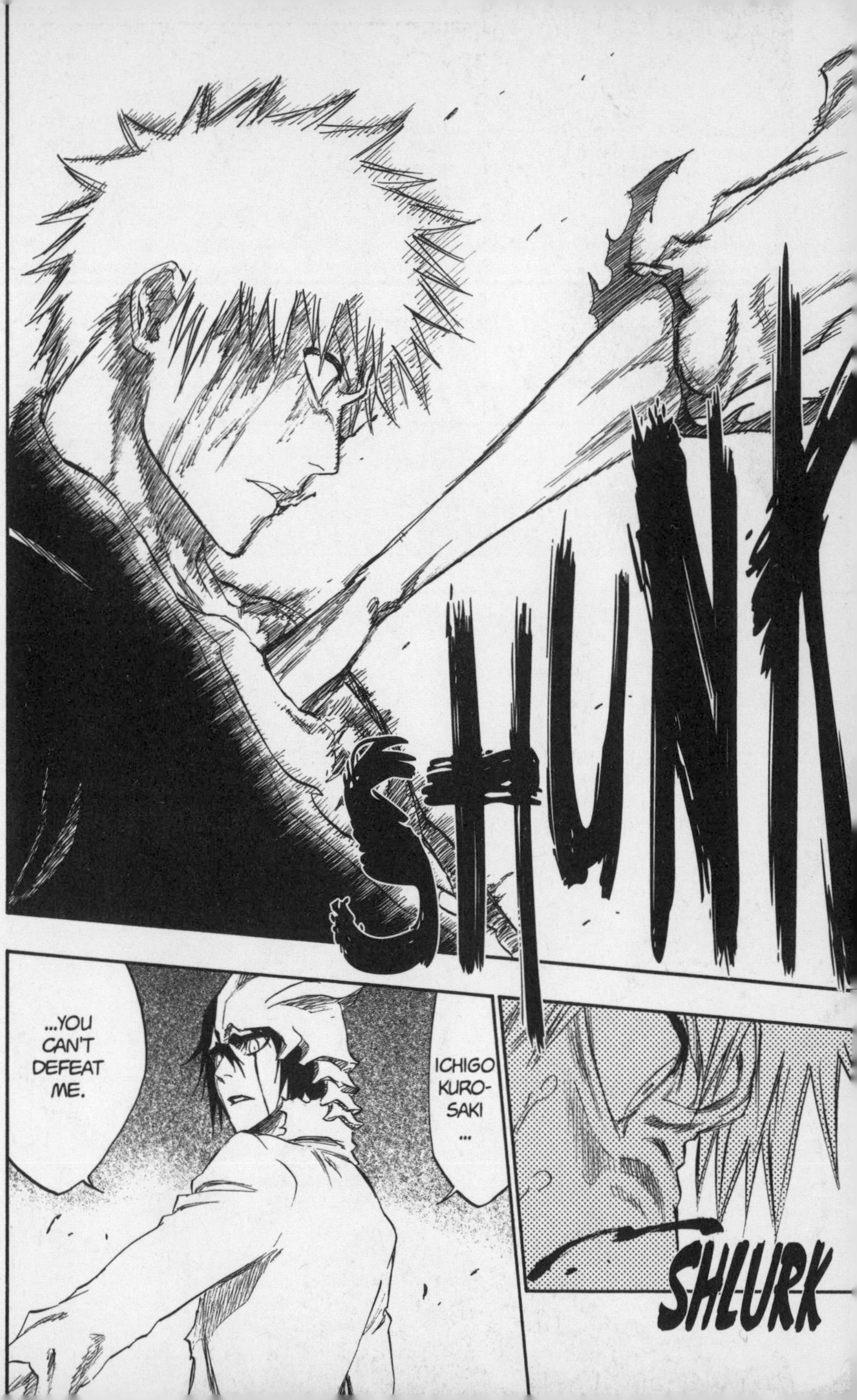
SHUNK
SHLURK
ICHIGO KURO-SAKI ...
...YOU CAN'T DEFEAT ME.

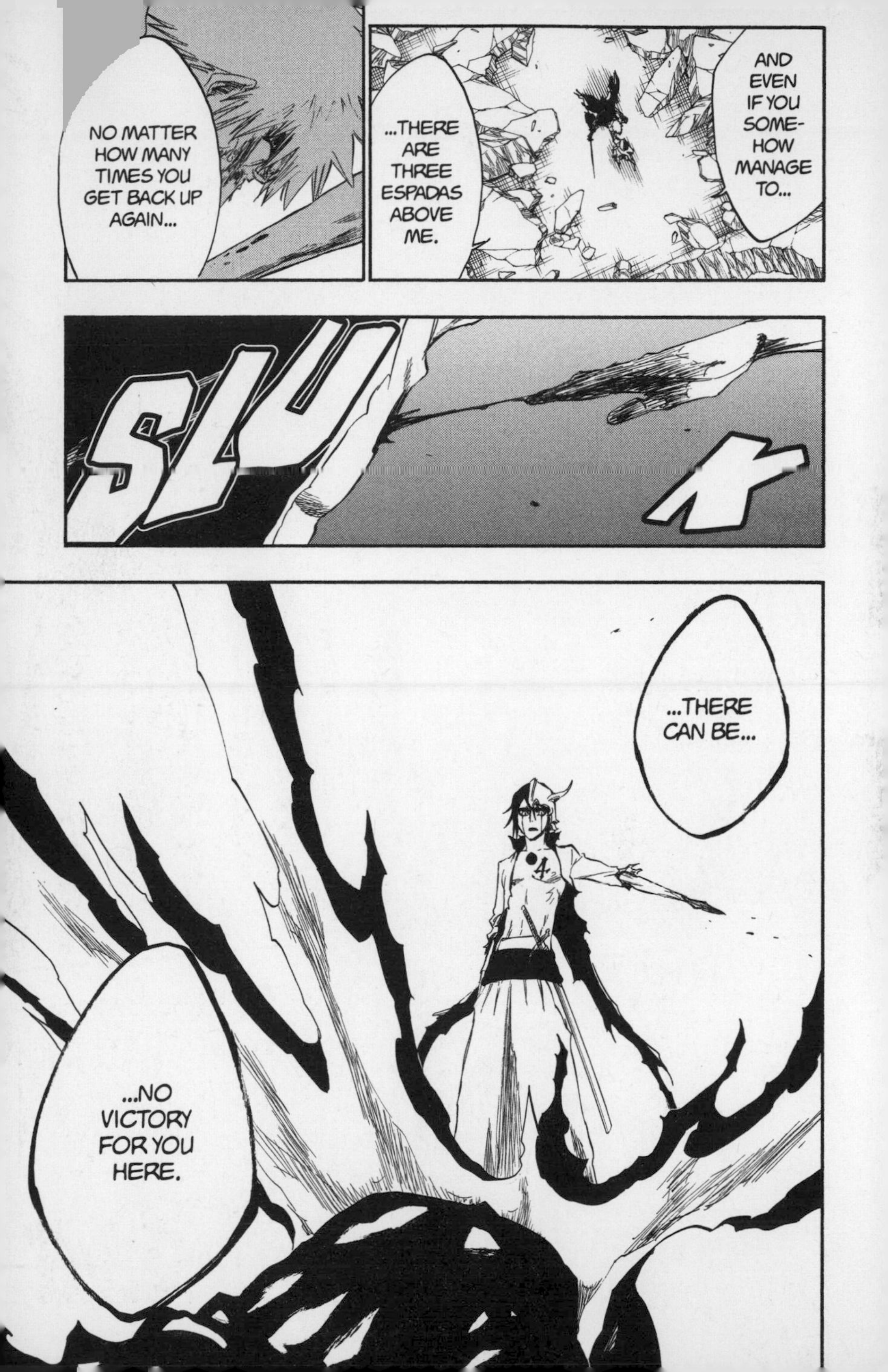

NO MATTER HOW MANY TIMES YOU GET BACK UP AGAIN...
...THERE ARE THREE ESPADAS ABOVE ME.
AND EVEN IF YOU SOME-HOW MANAGE TO...
SLUK
...THERE CAN BE...
...NO VICTORY FOR YOU HERE.

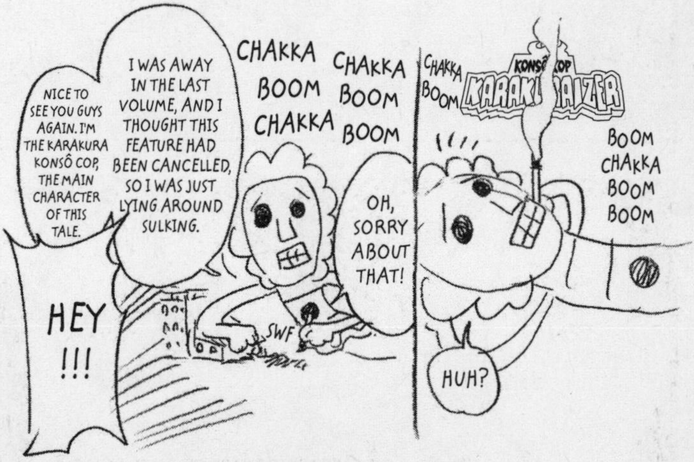

CHAKKA BOOM
BOOM CHAKKA BOOM BOOM
HUH?
CHAKKA BOOM CHAKKA BOOM
CHAKKA BOOM CHAKKA
OH, SORRY ABOUT THAT!
I WAS AWAY IN THE LAST VOLUME, AND I THOUGHT THIS FEATURE HAD BEEN CANCELLED, SO I WAS JUST LYING AROUND SULKING.
NICE TO SEE YOU GUYS AGAIN. I'M THE KARAKURA KONSÔ COP, THE MAIN CHARACTER OF THIS TALE.
SWF
HEY !!!

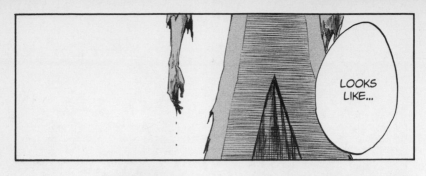

LOOKS LIKE...

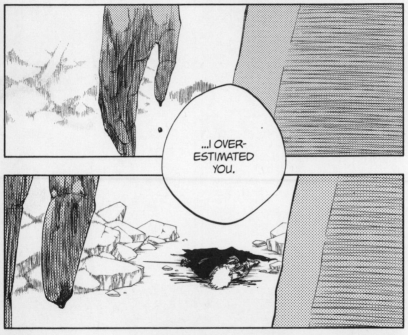

...I OVER-ESTIMATED YOU.

YOU'RE NOT AS STRONG AS I THOUGHT.

272. Don't Kill My Volupture

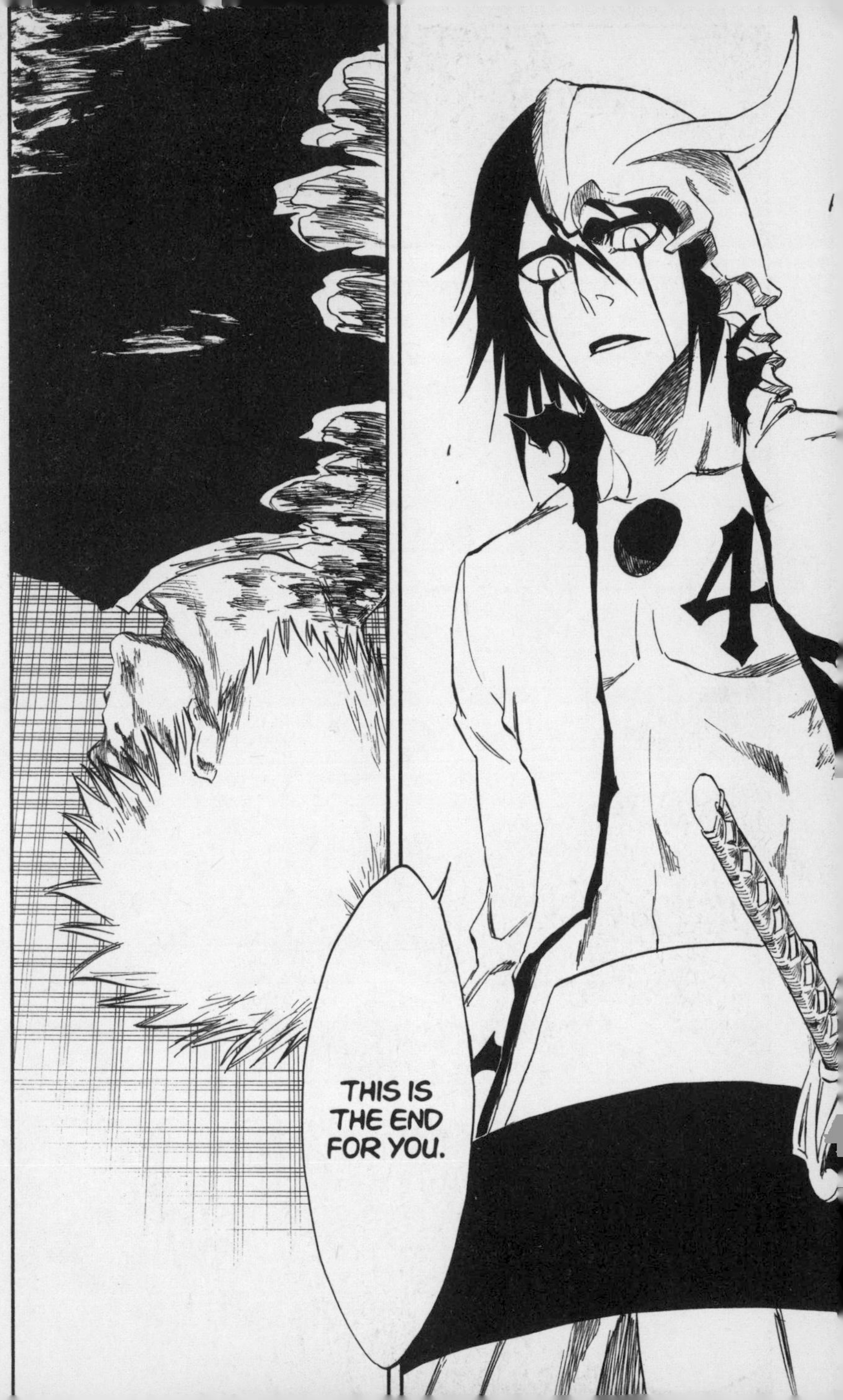
THIS IS THE END FOR YOU.

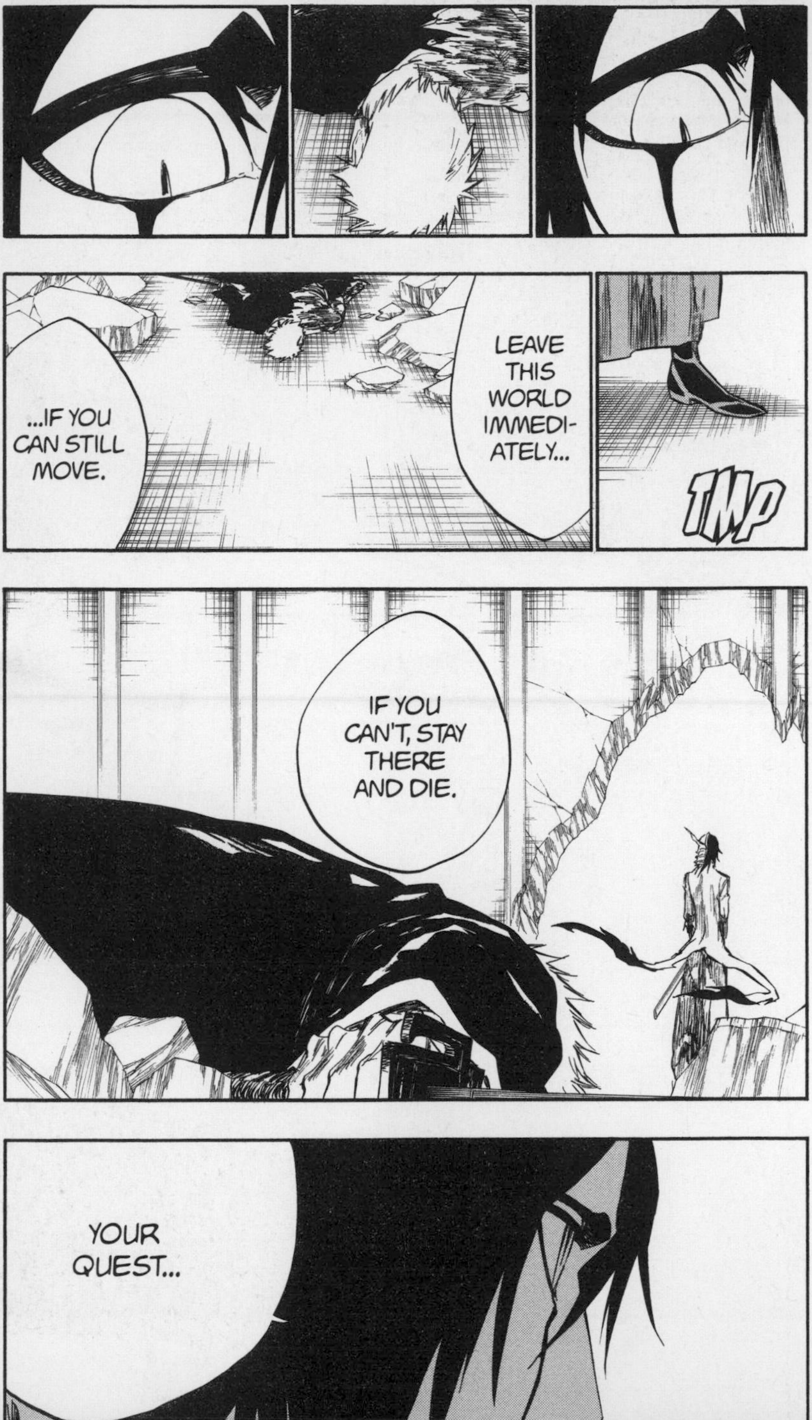
TMP
LEAVE THIS WORLD IMMEDI-ATELY...
...IF YOU CAN STILL MOVE.
IF YOU CAN'T, STAY THERE AND DIE.
YOUR QUEST...

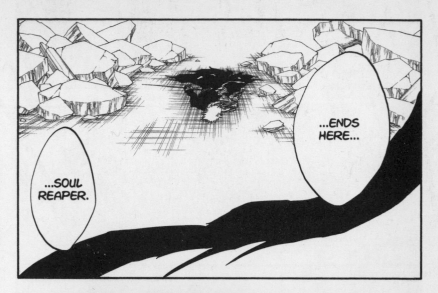

...ENDS HERE...

...SOUL REAPER.

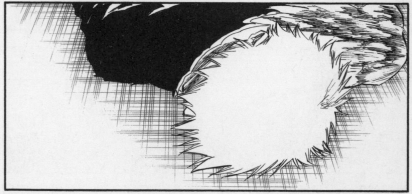

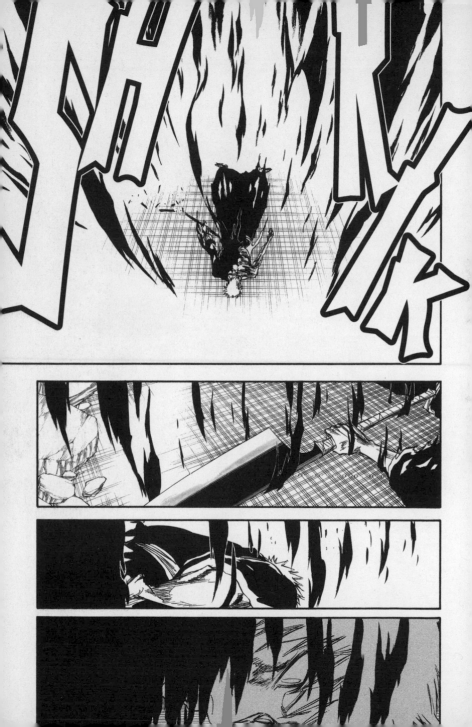

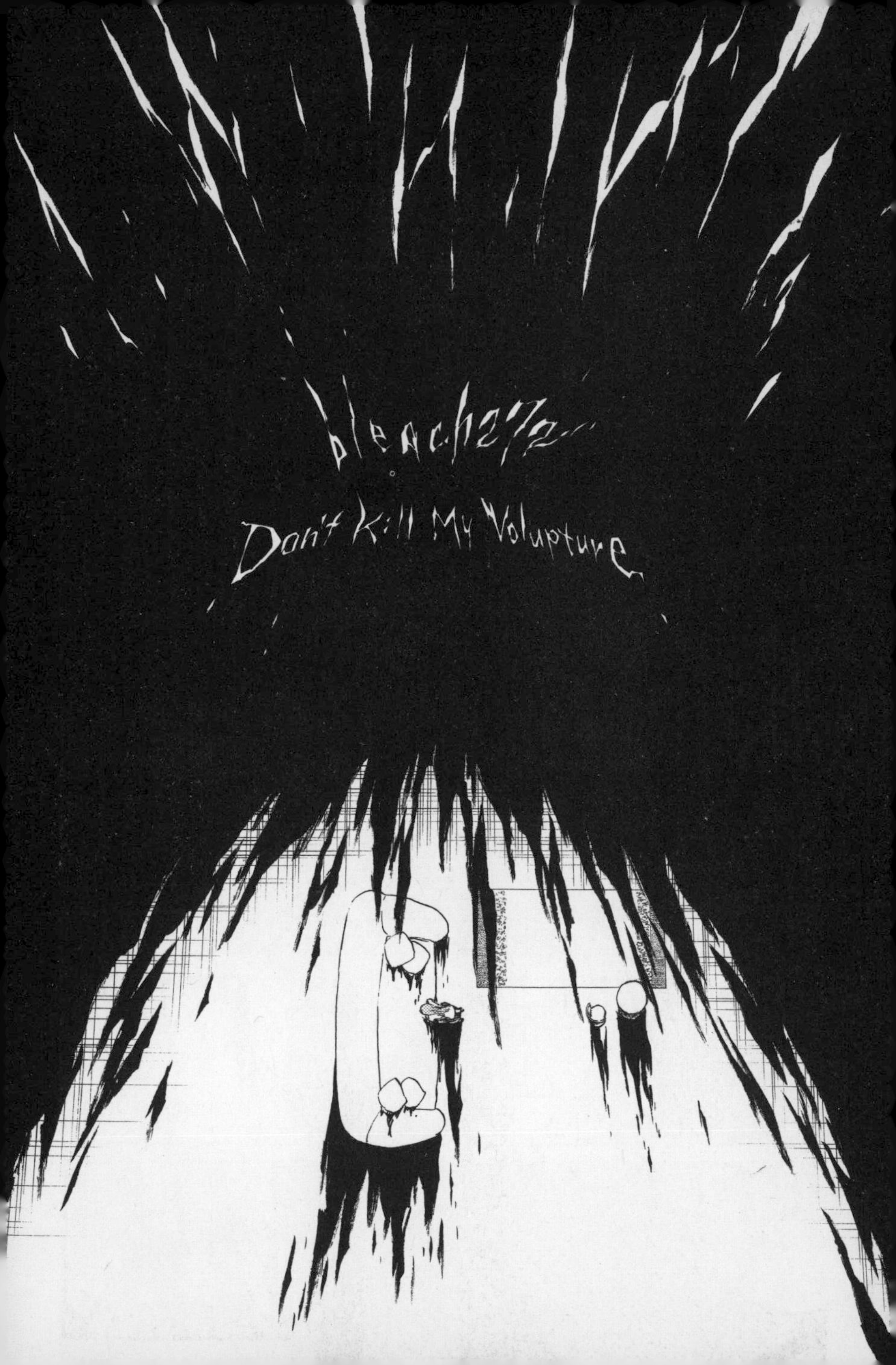
bleach 272.
Don't Kill My Volupture

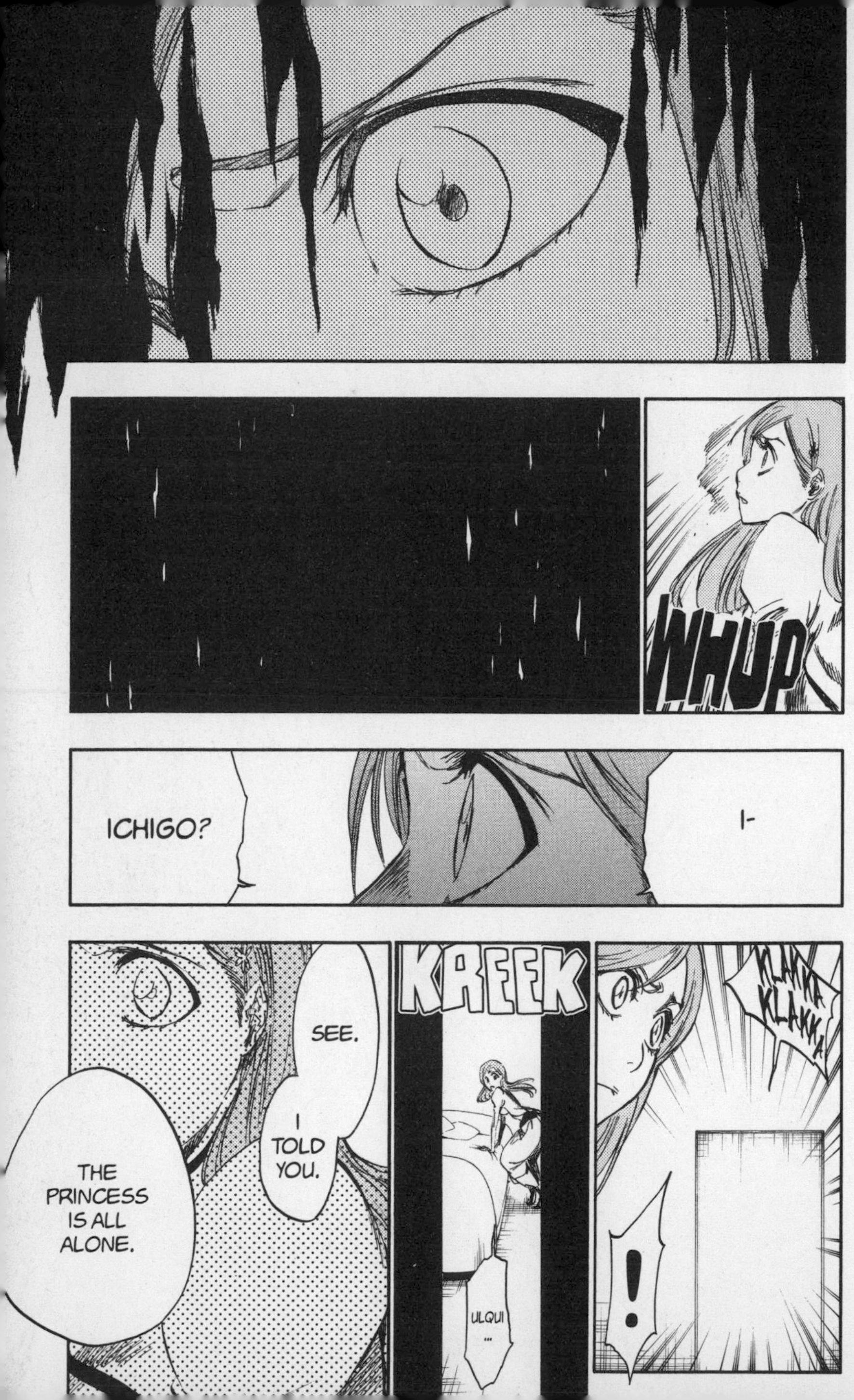
WHUP
I-
ICHIGO?
KLAKKA KLAKKA
!
KREEK
ULQUI...
SEE.
I TOLD YOU.
THE PRINCESS IS ALL ALONE.

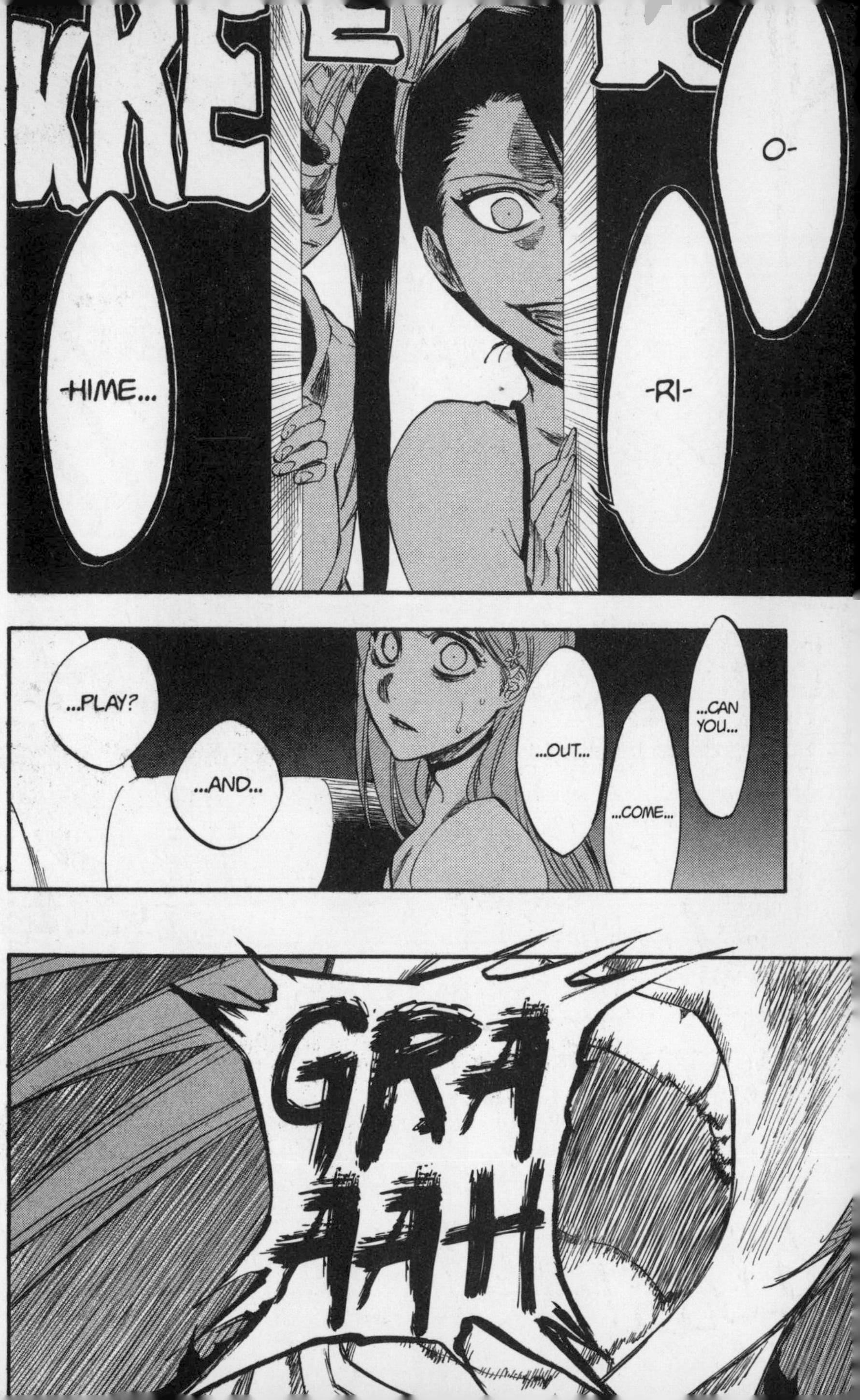
KRE
O-
-RI-
-HIME...
...CAN YOU...
...COME...
...OUT...
...AND...
...PLAY?
GRAAAH

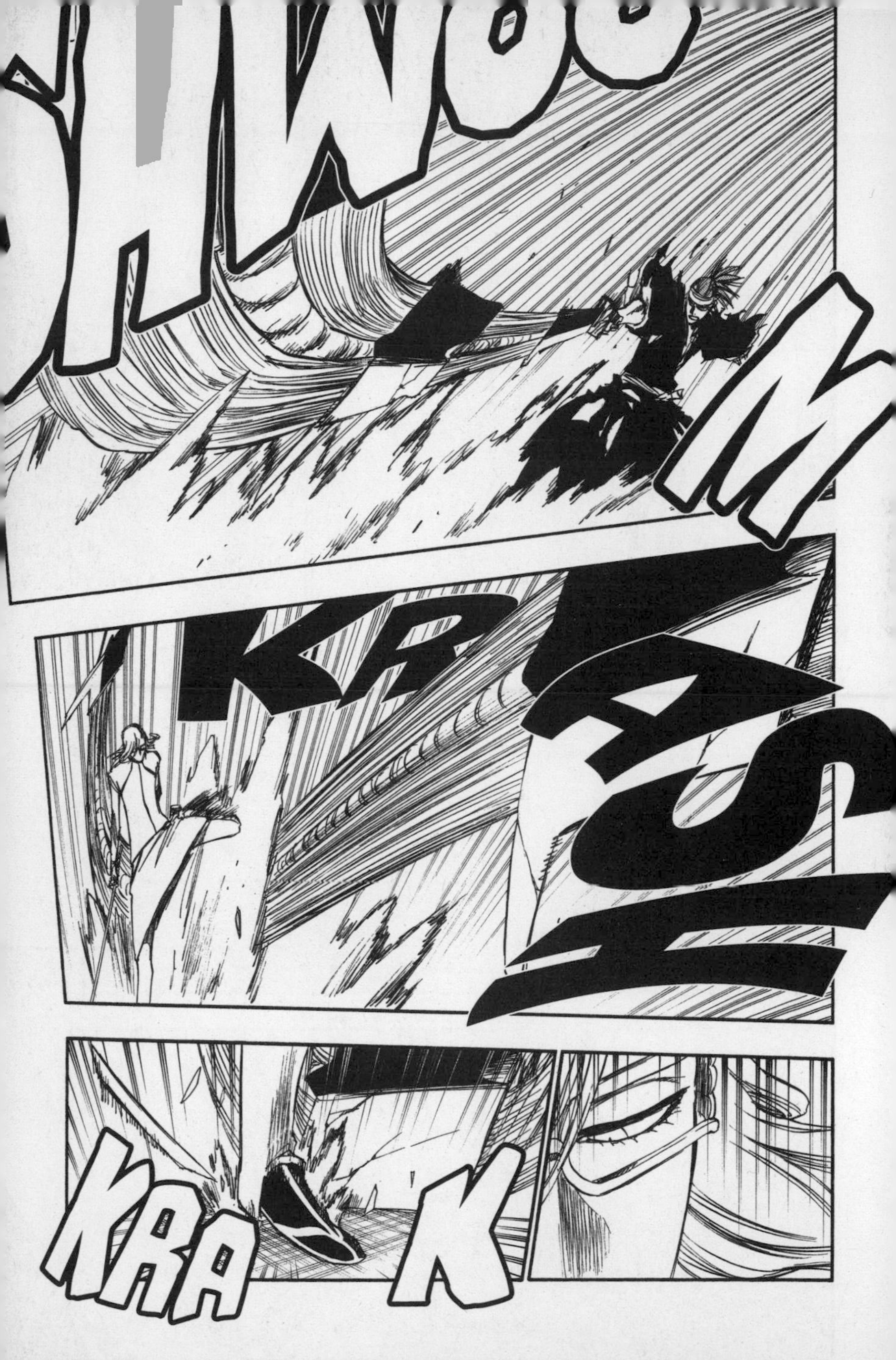
SHWOOM
KRASH
KRAK

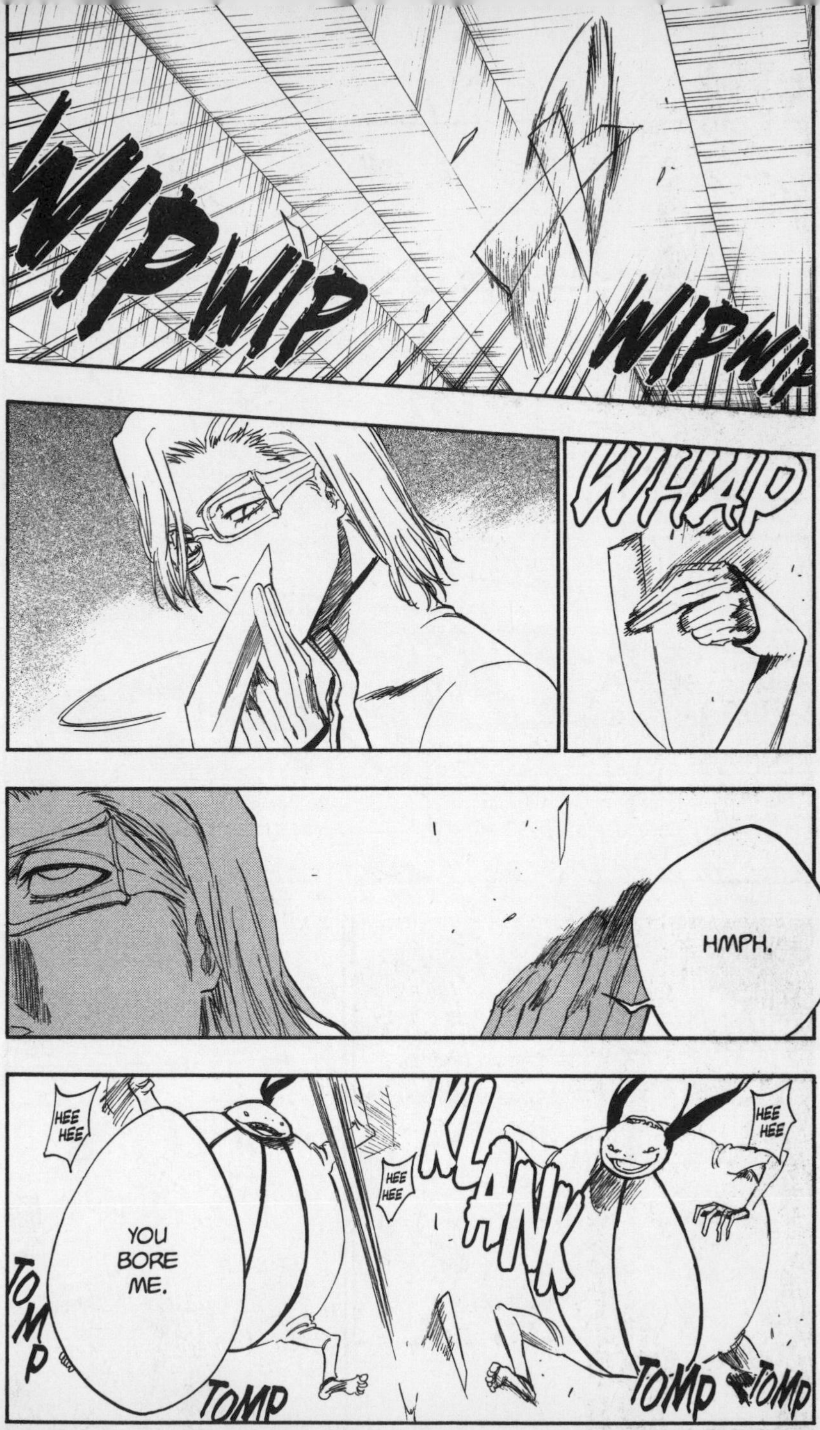
WIPWIP
WIPWIP
WHAP
HMPH.
HEE HEE
KLANK
HEE HEE
HEE HEE
YOU BORE ME.
TOMP
TOMP
TOMP
TOMP
TOMP

READ THIS WAY

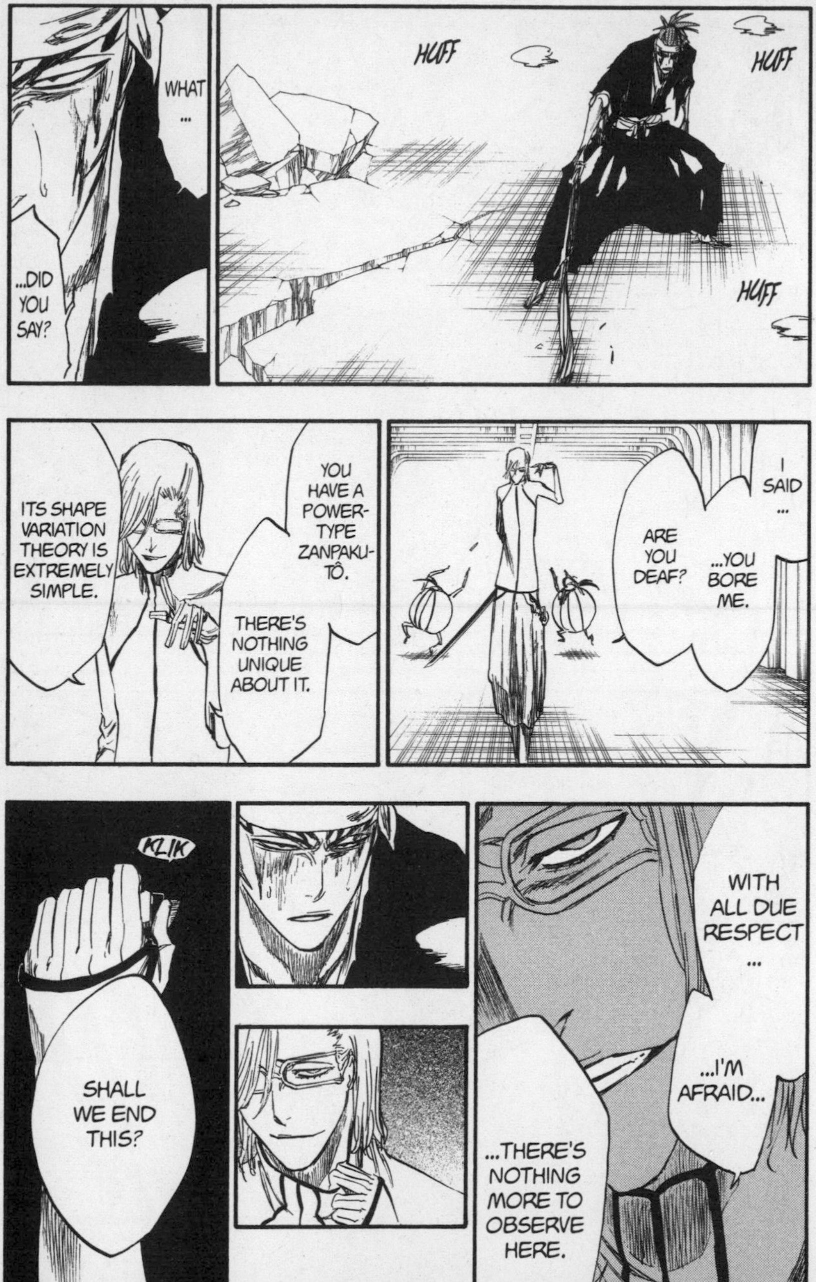
HUFF
HUFF
HUFF
WHAT...
...DID YOU SAY?
I SAID...
...YOU BORE ME.
ARE YOU DEAF?
YOU HAVE A POWER-TYPE ZANPAKU-TÔ.
THERE'S NOTHING UNIQUE ABOUT IT.
ITS SHAPE VARIATION THEORY IS EXTREMELY SIMPLE.
WITH ALL DUE RESPECT...
...I'M AFRAID...
...THERE'S NOTHING MORE TO OBSERVE HERE.
KLIK
SHALL WE END THIS?

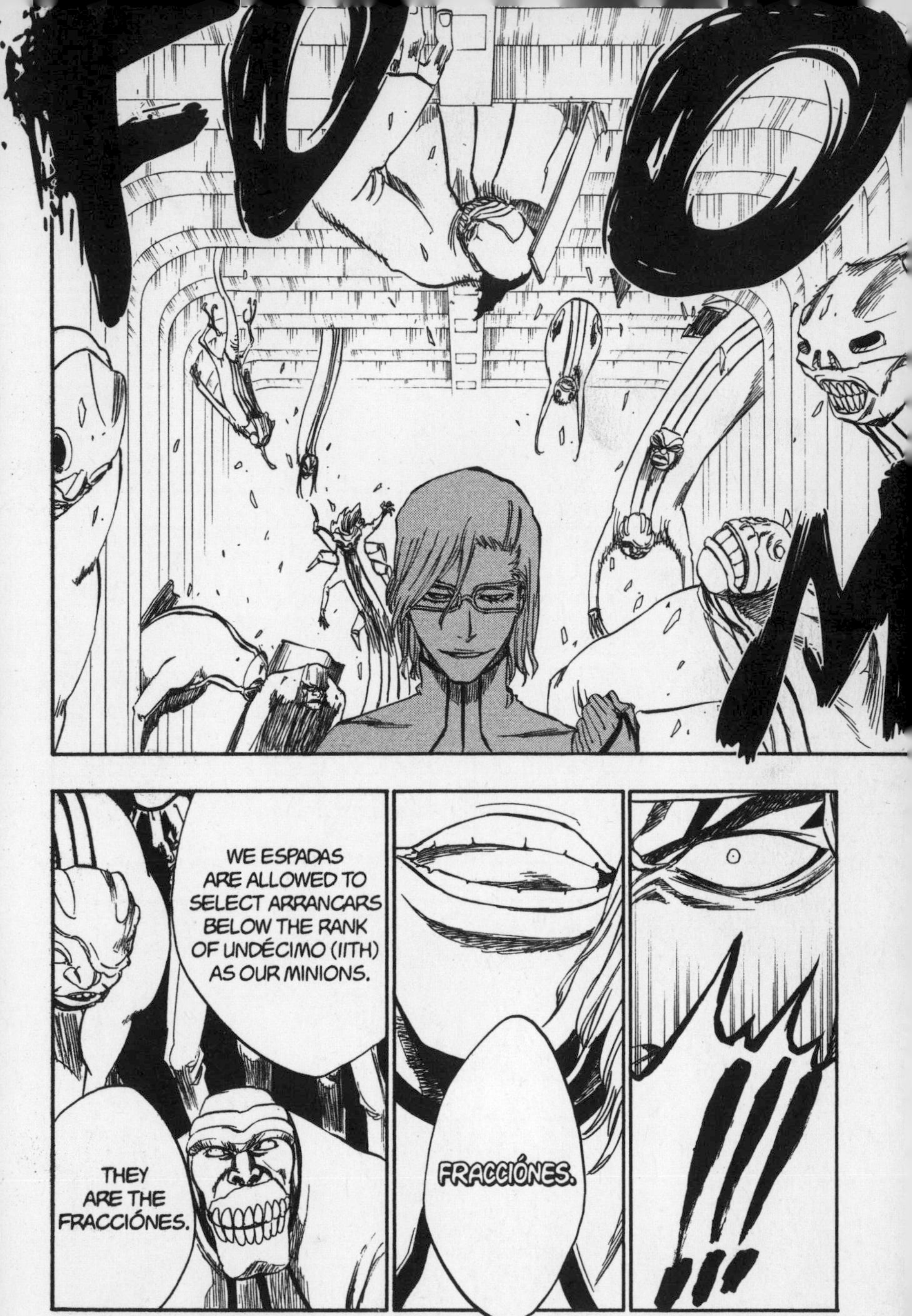
FOOOM
!!!
FRACCIÓNES.
WE ESPADAS ARE ALLOWED TO SELECT ARRANCARS BELOW THE RANK OF UNDÉCIMO (11TH) AS OUR MINIONS.
THEY ARE THE FRACCIÓNES.

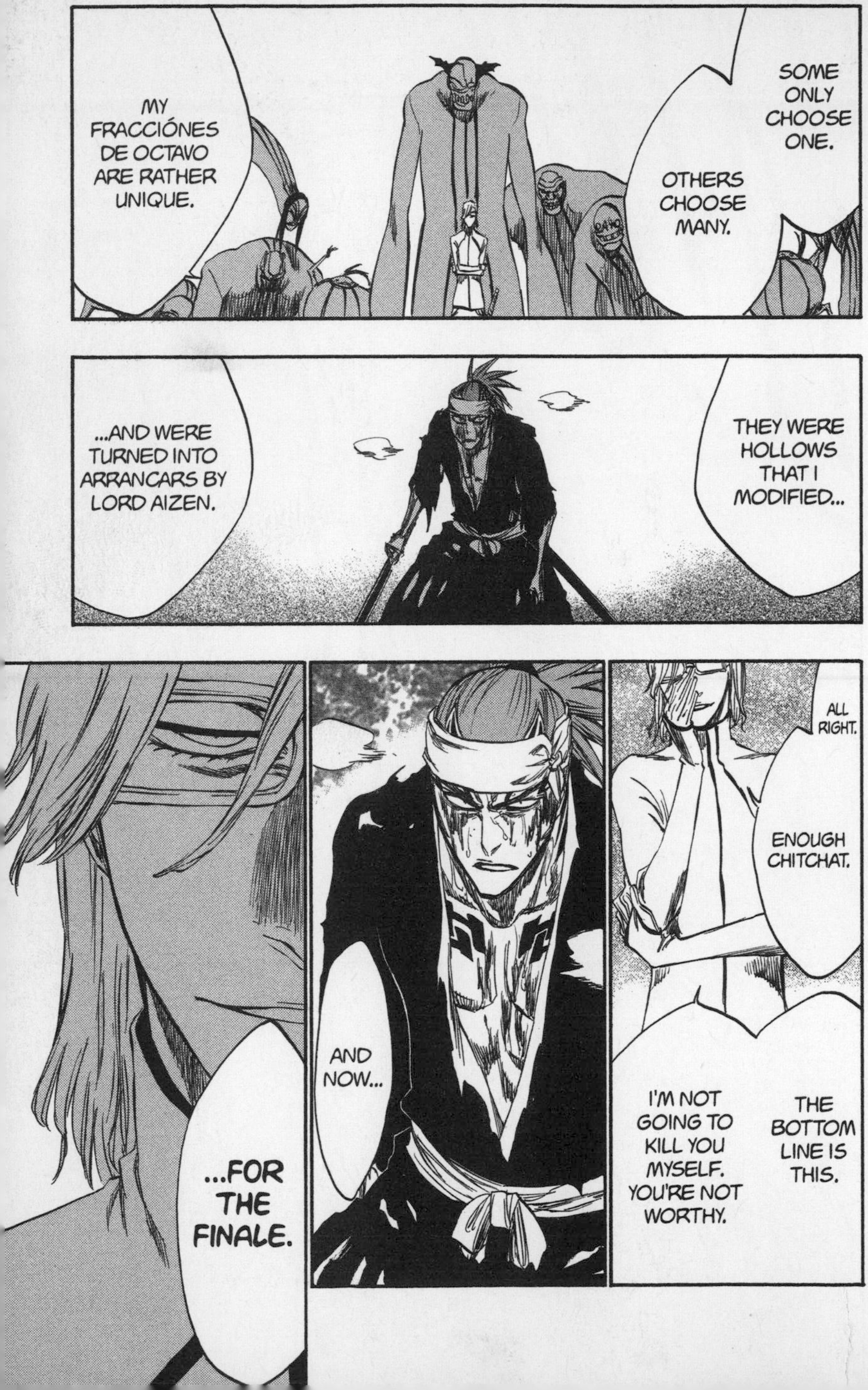
SOME ONLY CHOOSE ONE.
OTHERS CHOOSE MANY.
MY FRACCIÓNES DE OCTAVO ARE RATHER UNIQUE.
THEY WERE HOLLOWS THAT I MODIFIED...
...AND WERE TURNED INTO ARRANCARS BY LORD AIZEN.
ALL RIGHT.
ENOUGH CHITCHAT.
THE BOTTOM LINE IS THIS.
I'M NOT GOING TO KILL YOU MYSELF. YOU'RE NOT WORTHY.
AND NOW...
...FOR THE FINALE.

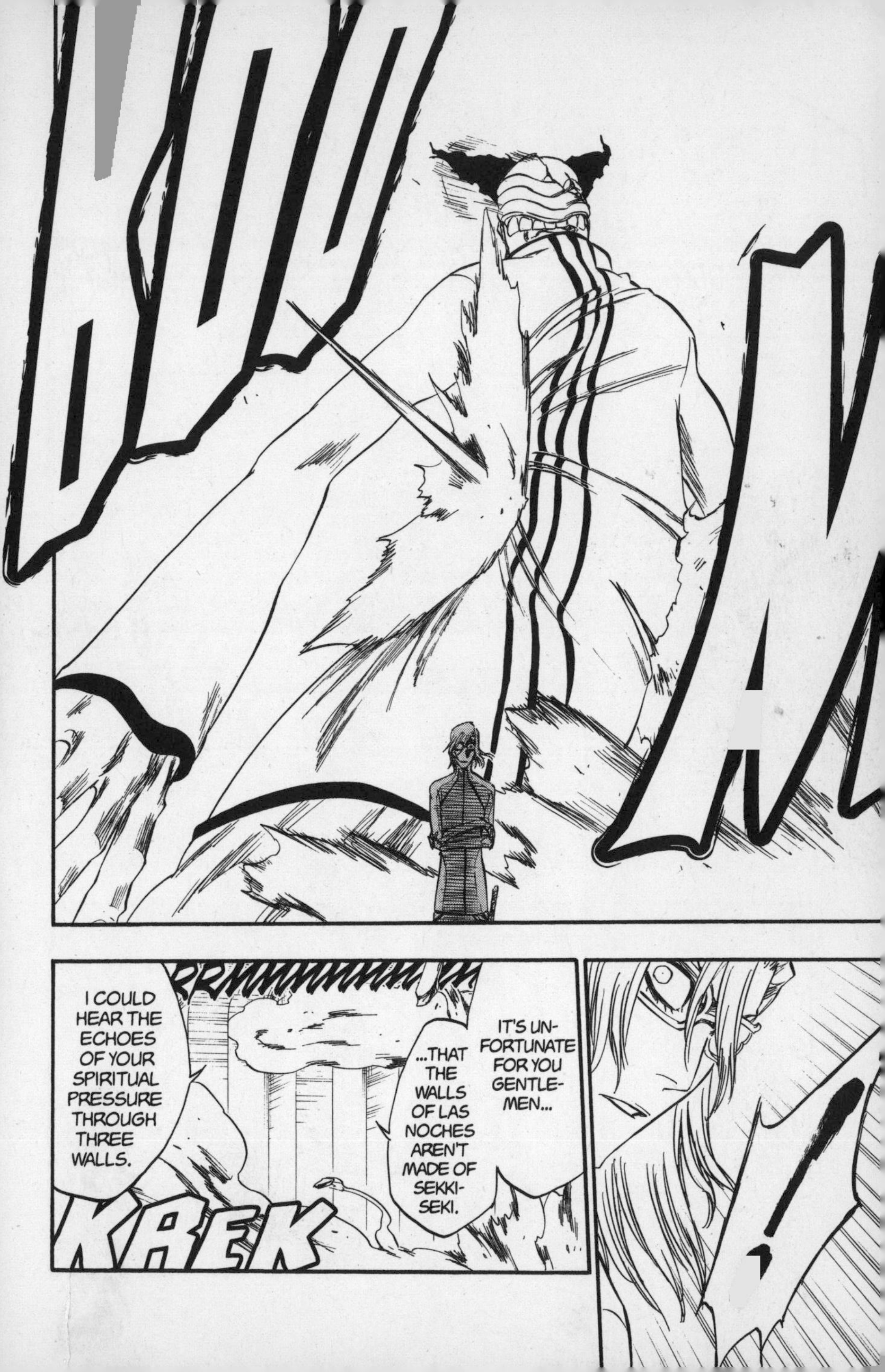
IT'S UN-FORTUNATE FOR YOU GENTLE-MEN...
...THAT THE WALLS OF LAS NOCHES AREN'T MADE OF SEKKI-SEKI.
I COULD HEAR THE ECHOES OF YOUR SPIRITUAL PRESSURE THROUGH THREE WALLS.
KREK

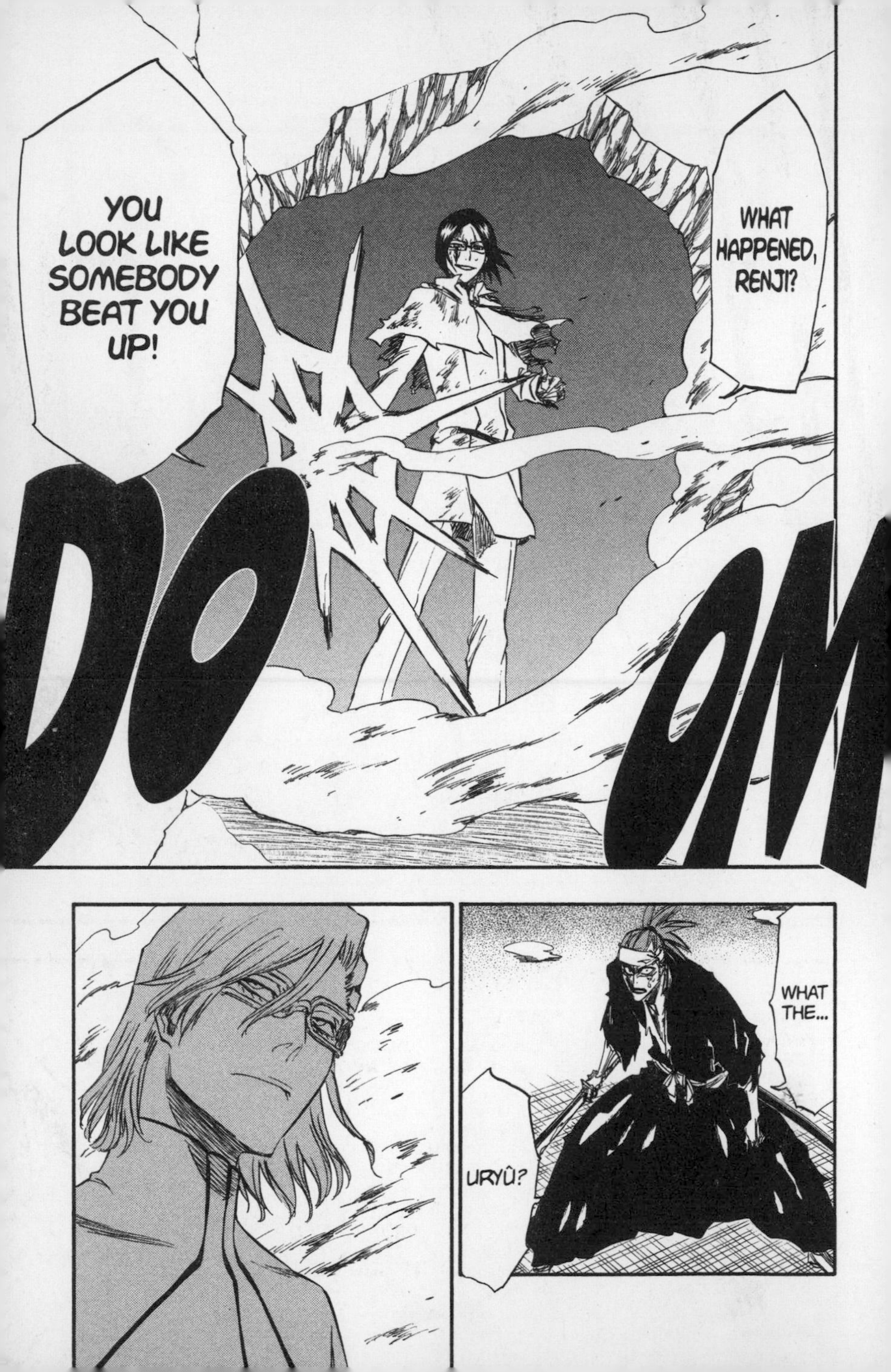
WHAT HAPPENED, RENJI?
YOU LOOK LIKE SOMEBODY BEAT YOU UP!
DOOM
WHAT THE...
URYÛ?

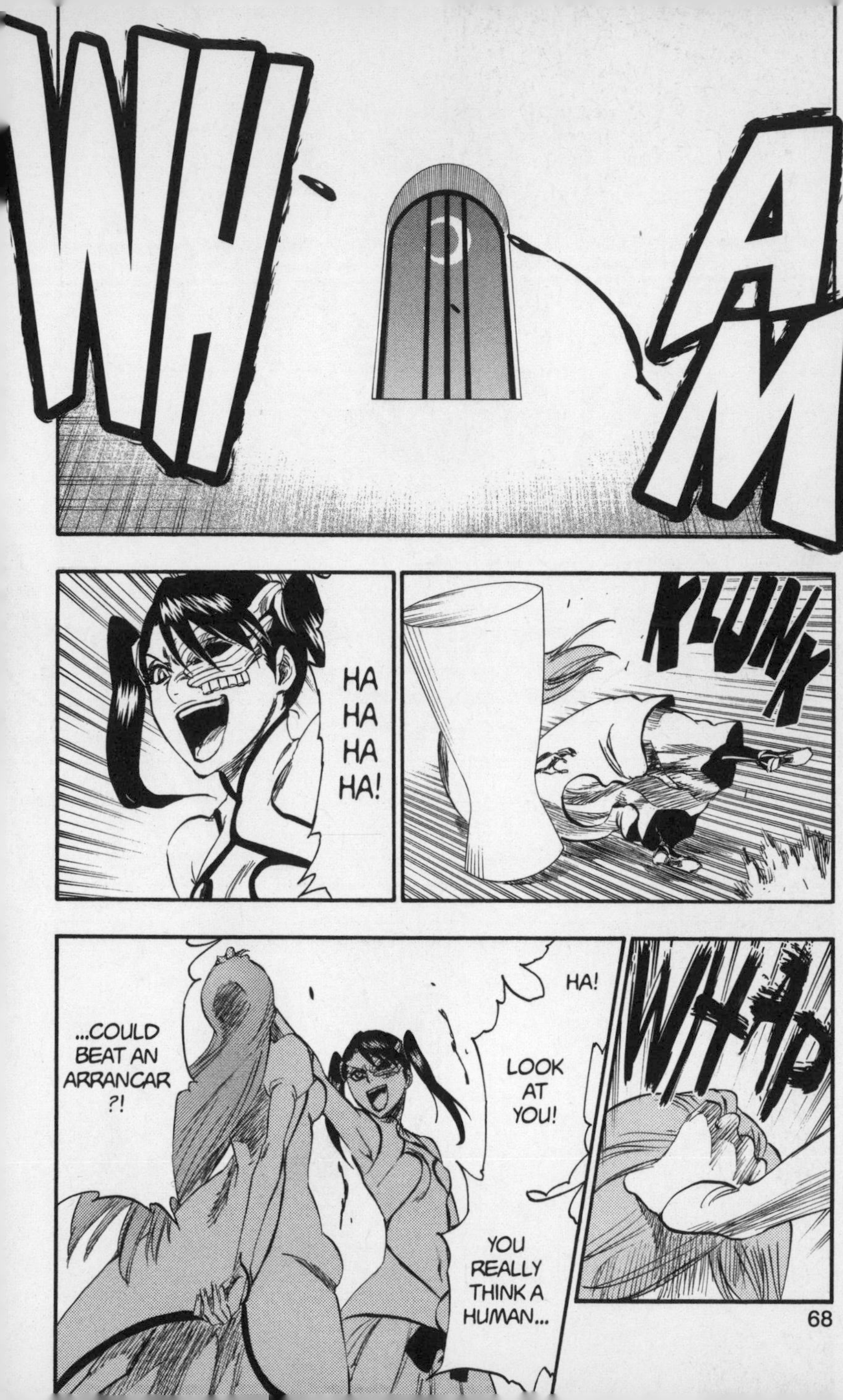
WH-AM
KLUNK
HA HA HA HA!
WHAP
HA!
LOOK AT YOU!
YOU REALLY THINK A HUMAN...
...COULD BEAT AN ARRANCAR?!

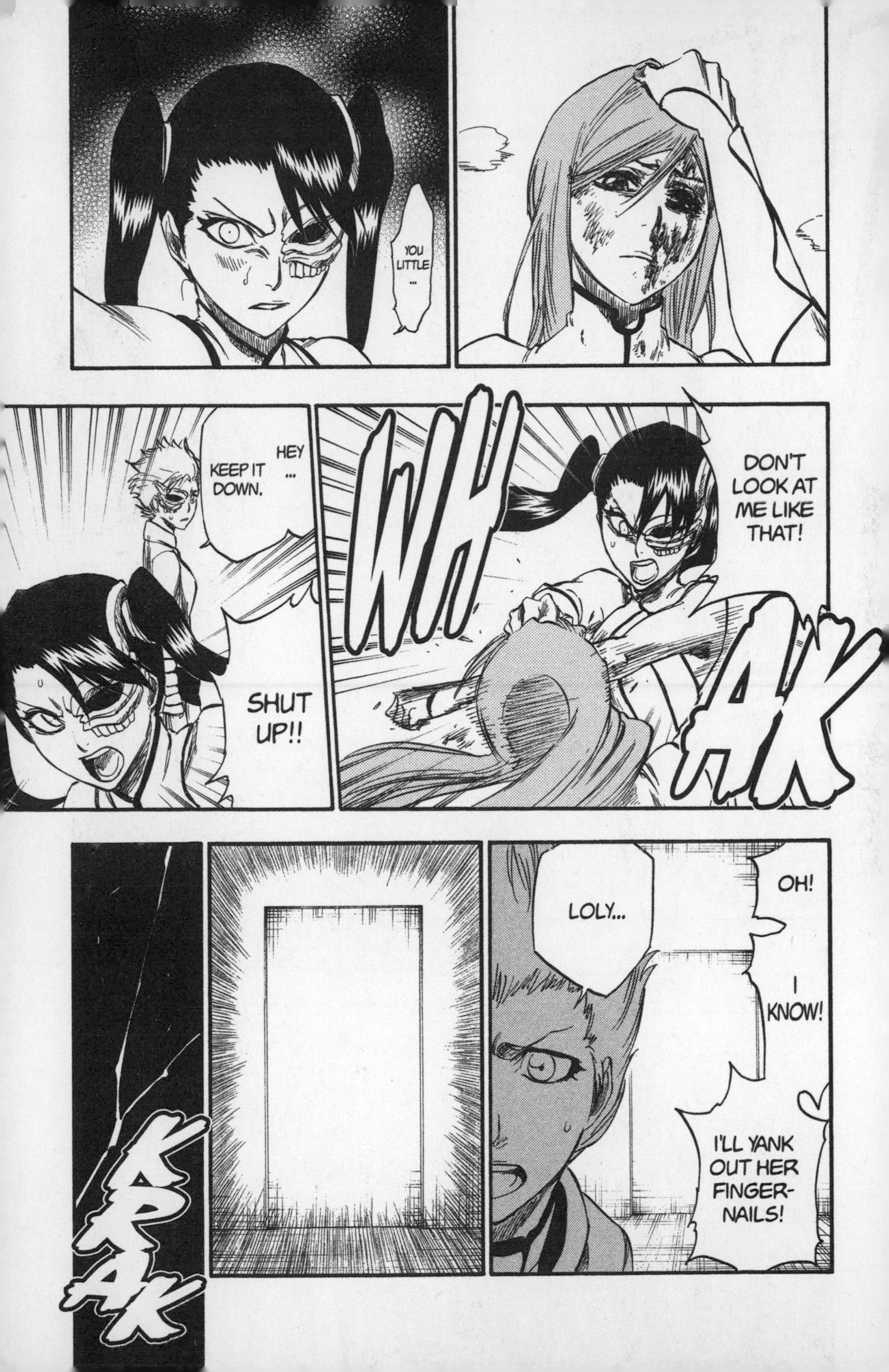
YOU LITTLE ...
DON'T LOOK AT ME LIKE THAT!
WH
AK
HEY ... KEEP IT DOWN.
SHUT UP!!
OH! I KNOW!
LOLY...
I'LL YANK OUT HER FINGER-NAILS!
KRAK

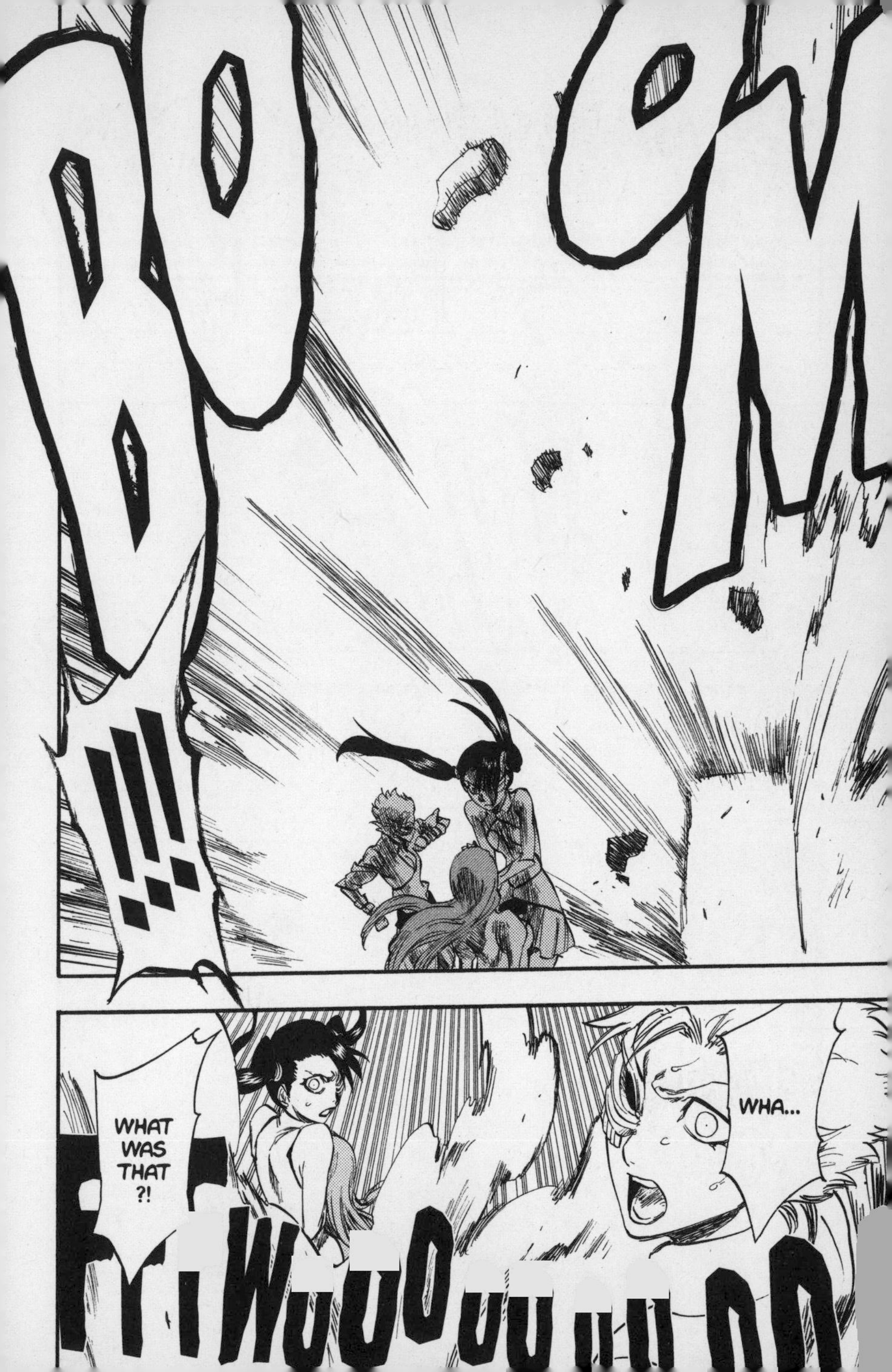
!!!
WHA...
WHAT WAS THAT ?!

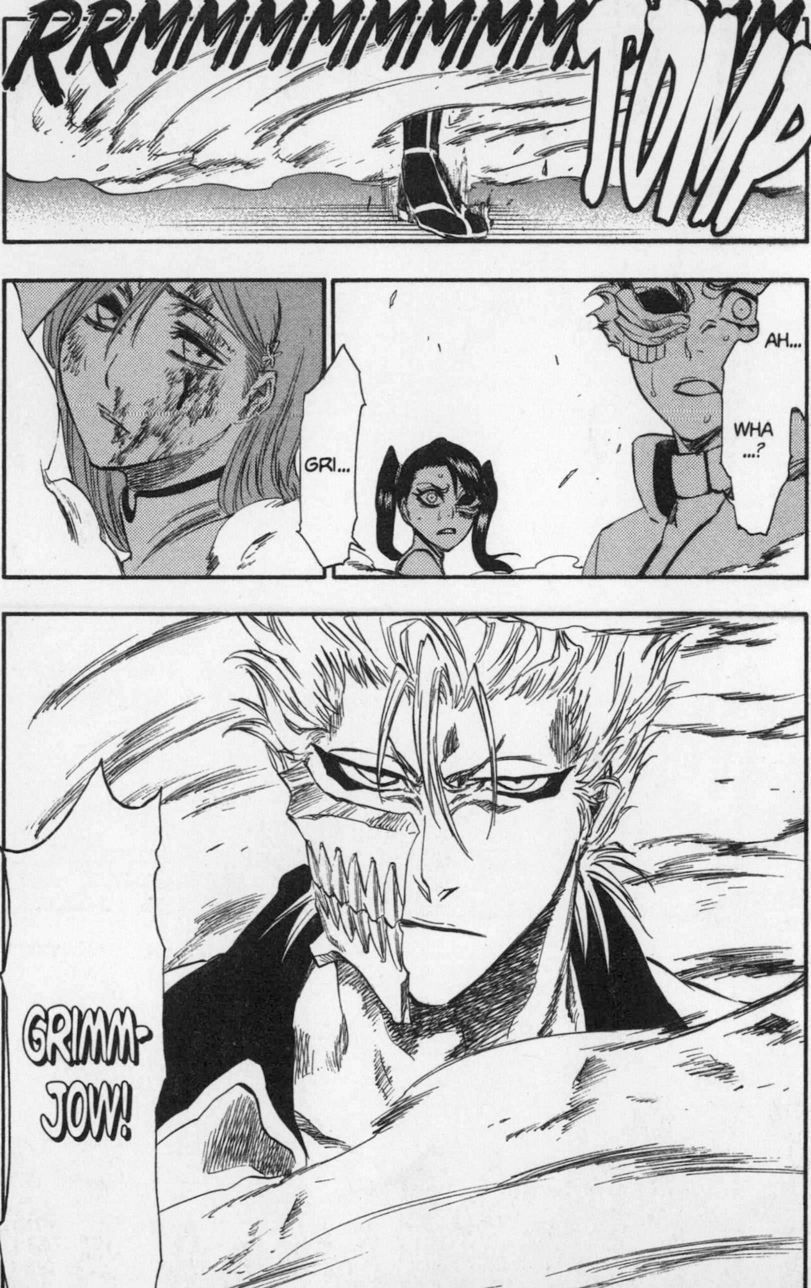
RRMMMMMMMMMM
TOMP
AH...
WHA ...?
GRI...
GRIMM-JOW!

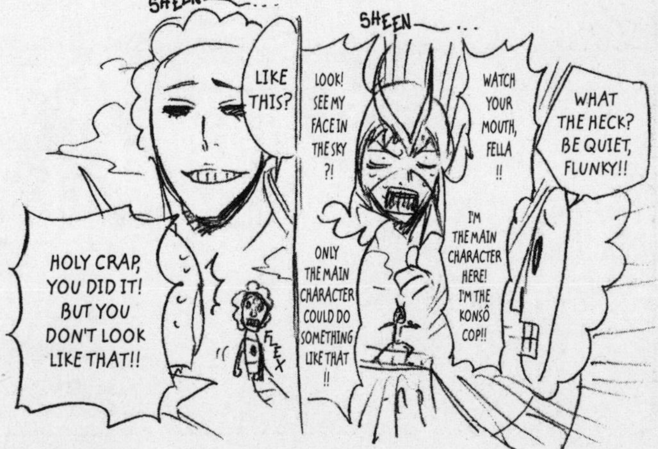
WHAT THE HECK? BE QUIET, FLUNKY!!
SHEEN...
WATCH YOUR MOUTH, FELLA!!
LOOK! SEE MY FACE IN THE SKY?!
I'M THE MAIN CHARACTER HERE! I'M THE KONSÔ COP!!
ONLY THE MAIN CHARACTER COULD DO SOMETHING LIKE THAT!!
SHEEN...
LIKE THIS?
HOLY CRAP, YOU DID IT! BUT YOU DON'T LOOK LIKE THAT!!
FLEX

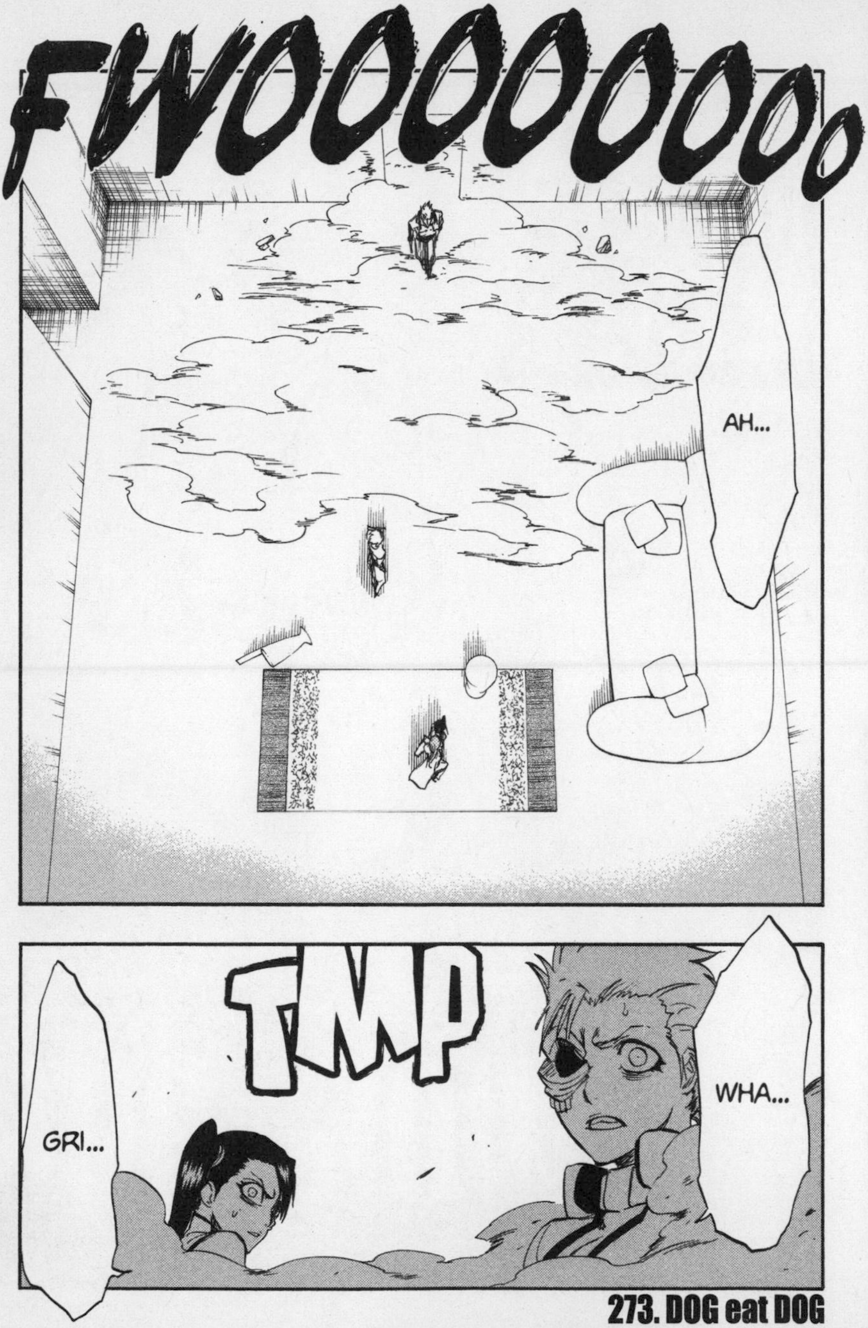
FWOOOOOOOO
AH...
WHA...
TMP
GRI...

273. DOG eat DOG

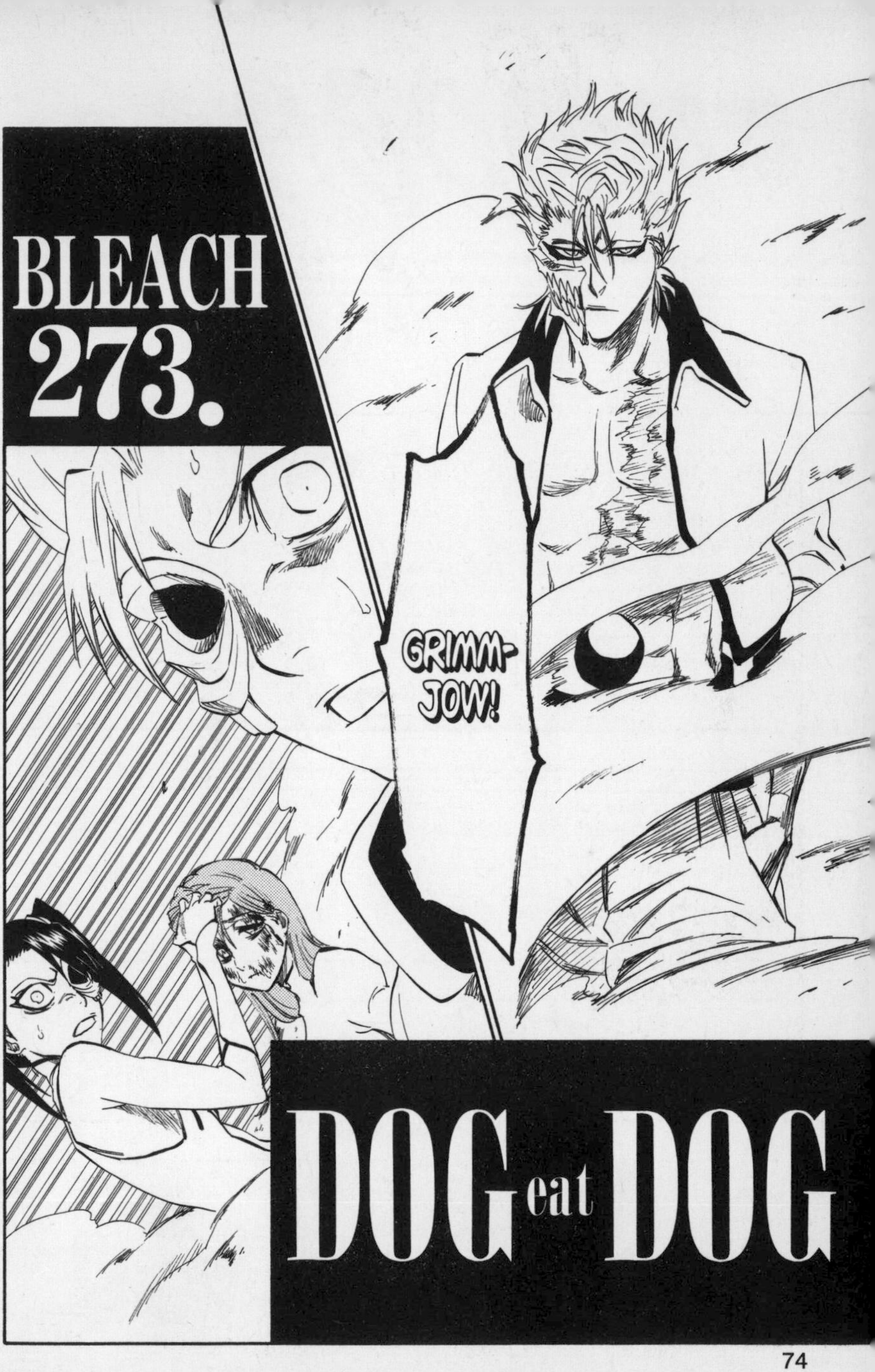
BLEACH
273.
GRIMM-JOW!
DOG eat DOG

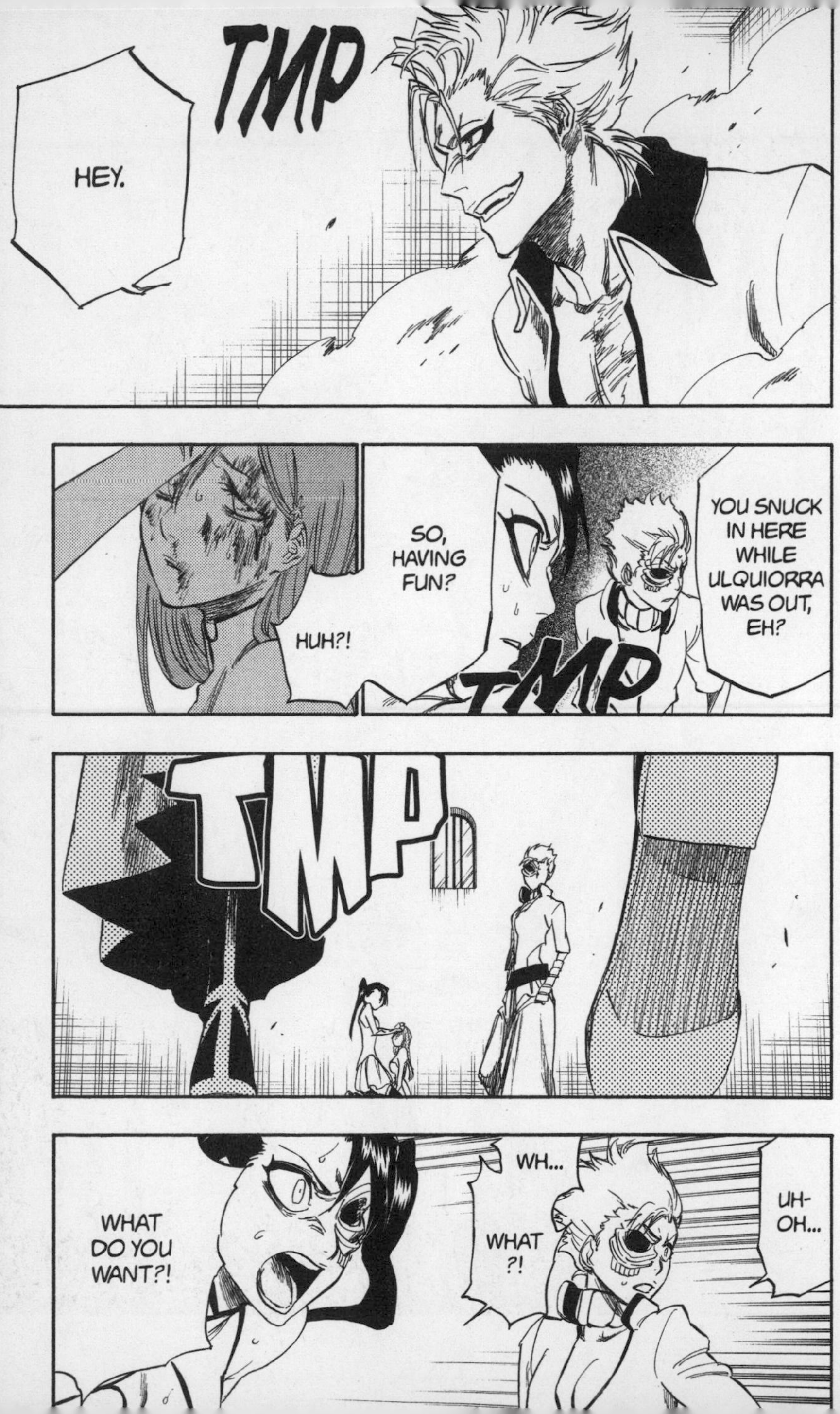
TMP
HEY.
YOU SNUCK IN HERE WHILE ULQUIORRA WAS OUT, EH?
SO, HAVING FUN?
TMP
HUH?!
TMP
UH-OH...
WH...
WHAT?!
WHAT DO YOU WANT?!

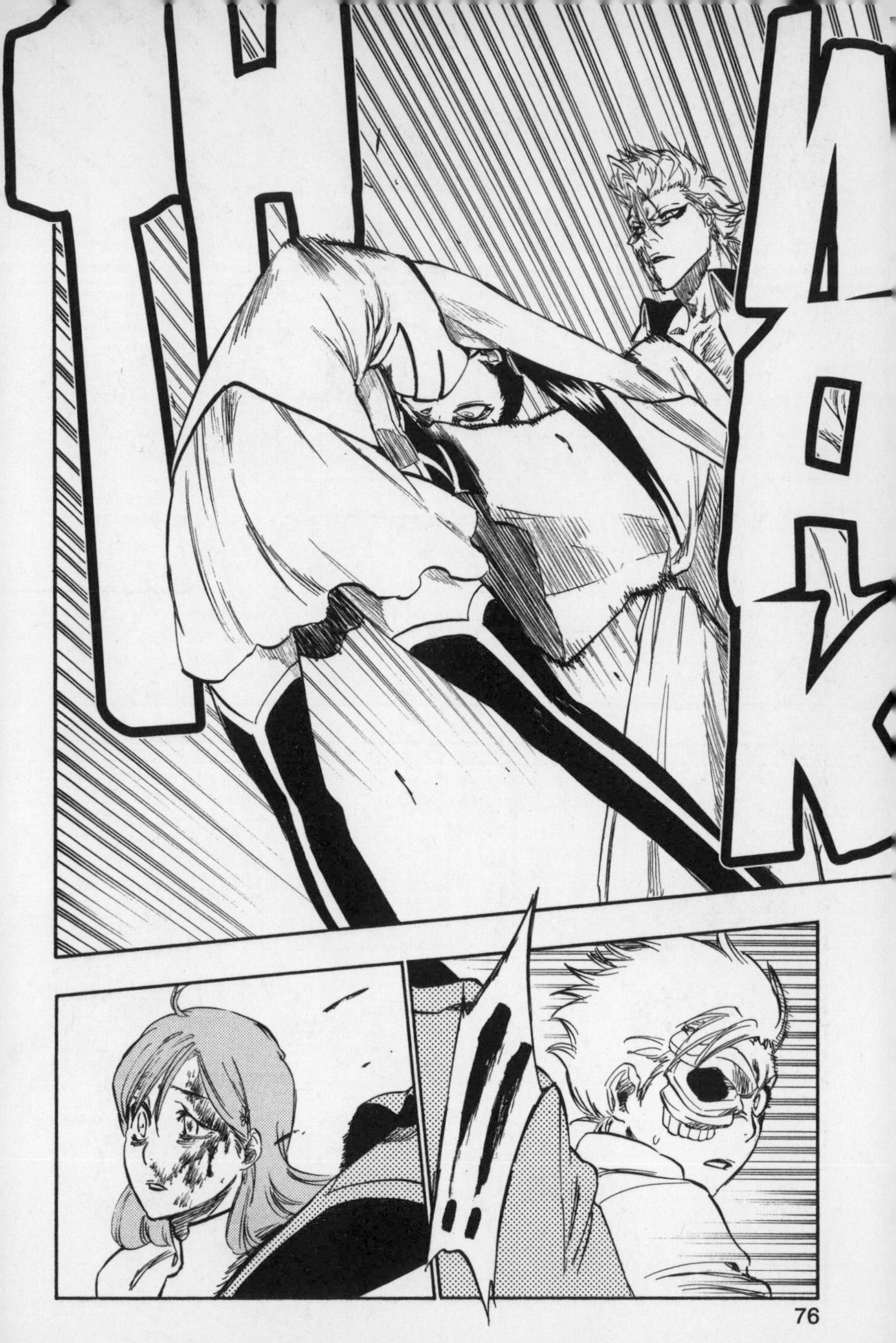

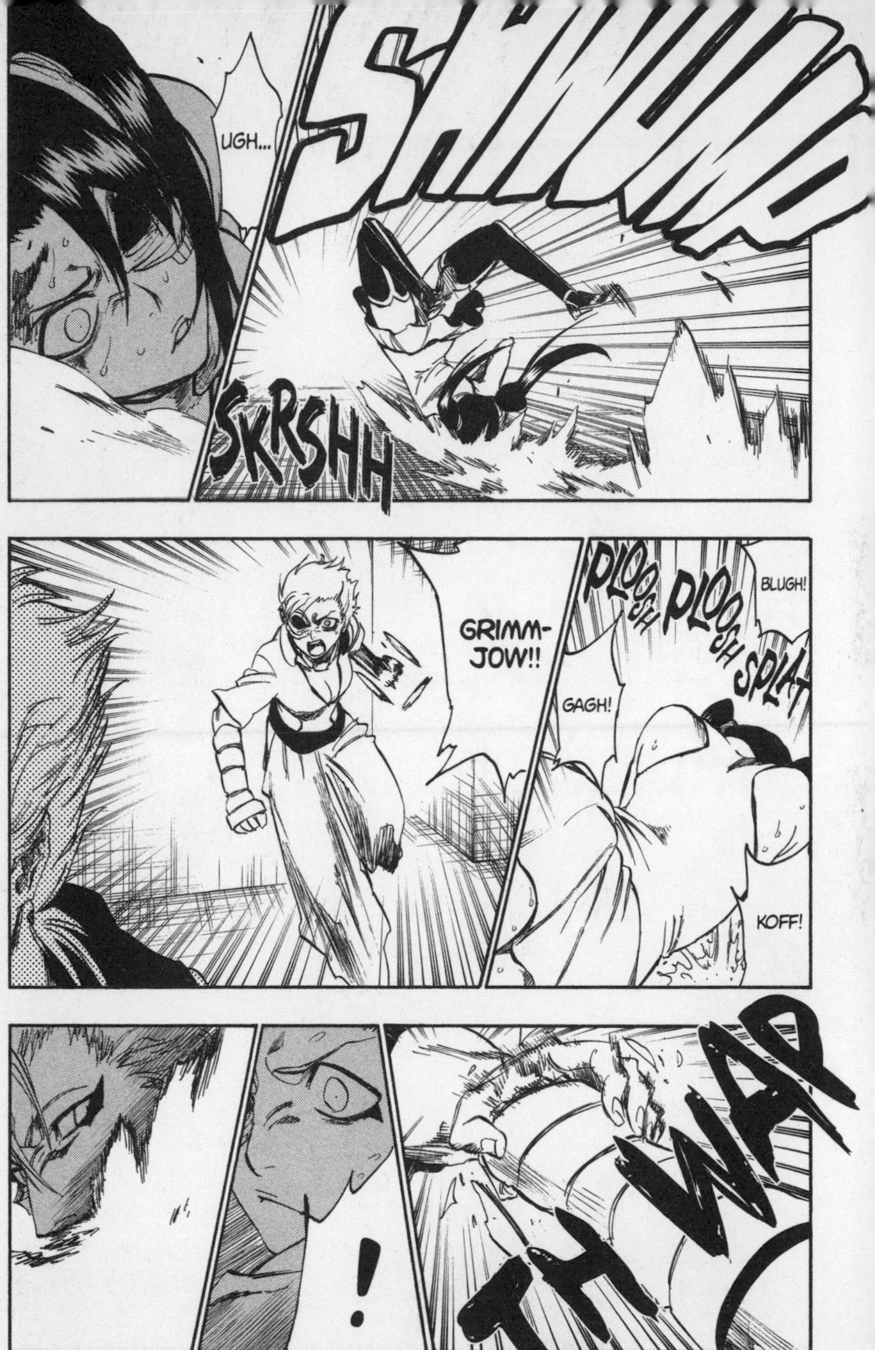
SKRSHH
UGH...
PLOOSH PLOOSH SPLAT
BLUGH!
GAGH!
KOFF!
GRIMM-JOW!!
THWAP
!

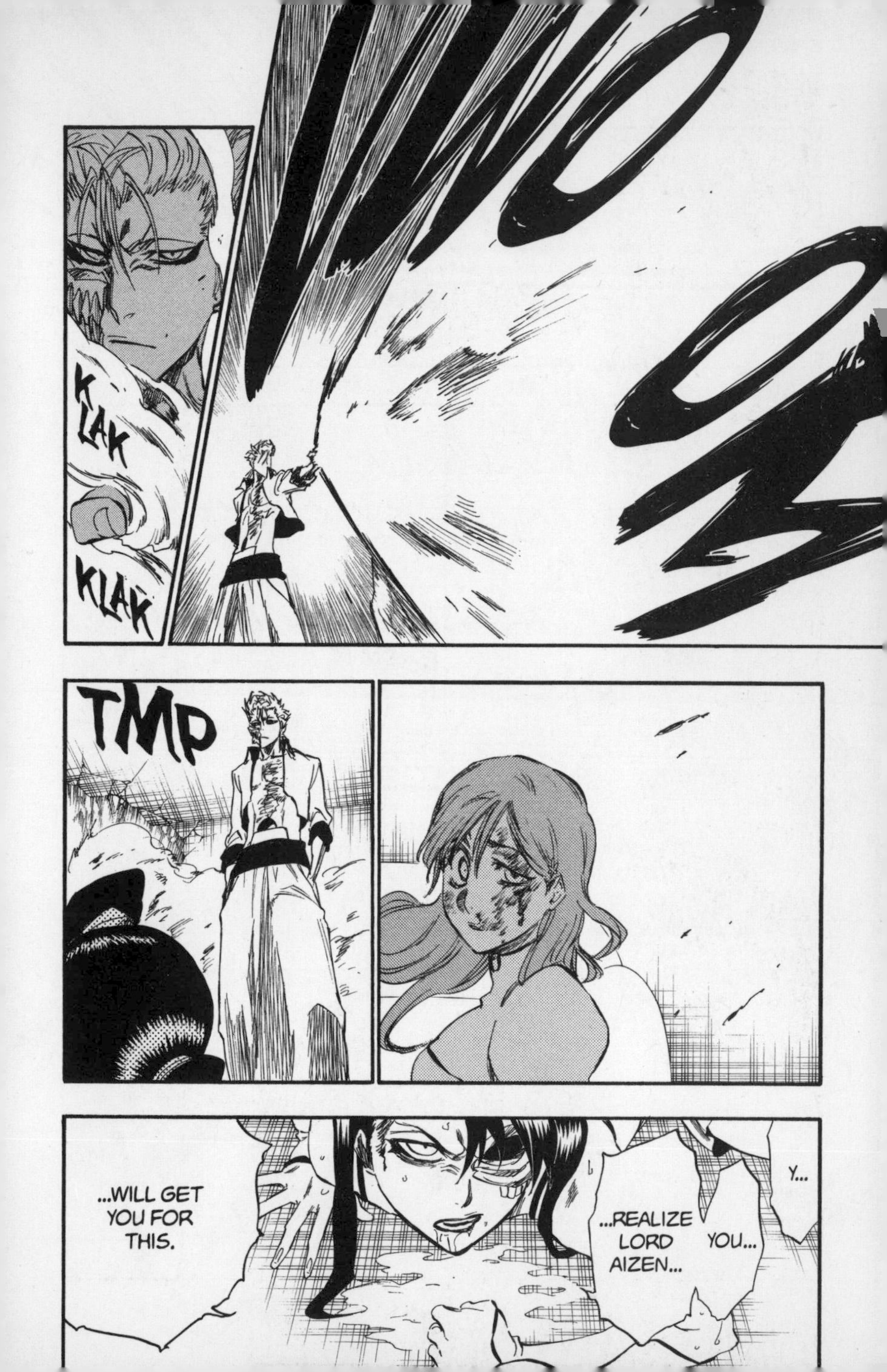
VWOOM
KLAK
KLAK
TMP
Y...
YOU...
...REALIZE LORD AIZEN...
...WILL GET YOU FOR THIS.

WH AP

YOU'RE JUST A...

HEY!

WAIT! WHAT ARE YOU...

HUH?

AAH!!

PLEASE DON'T!! I...

I WON'T TELL ANYONE !!

STOP !!

STOP!! NO!!

STOP !!

NO!

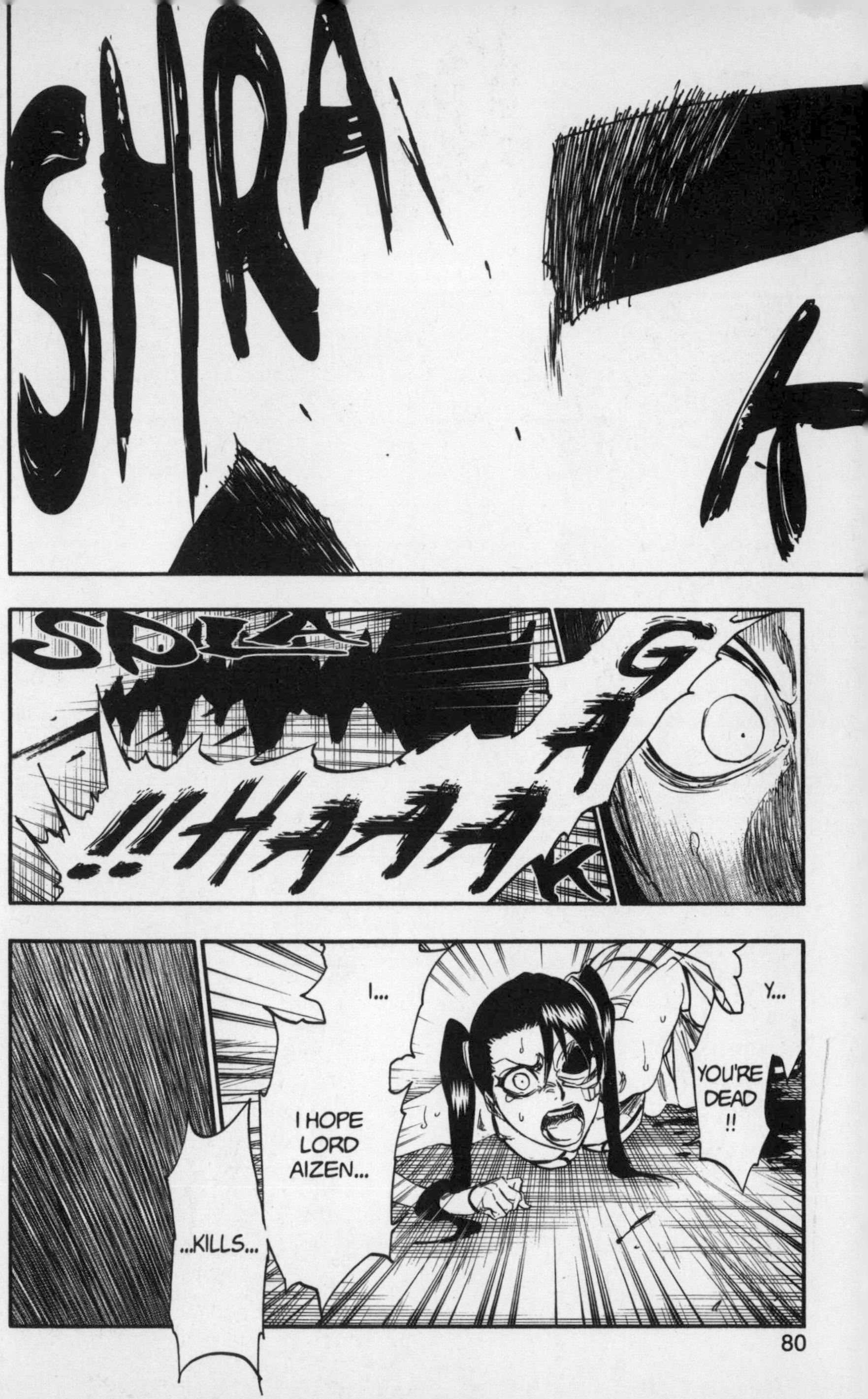
Y...
YOU'RE DEAD !!
I...
I HOPE LORD AIZEN...
...KILLS...

READ THIS WAY

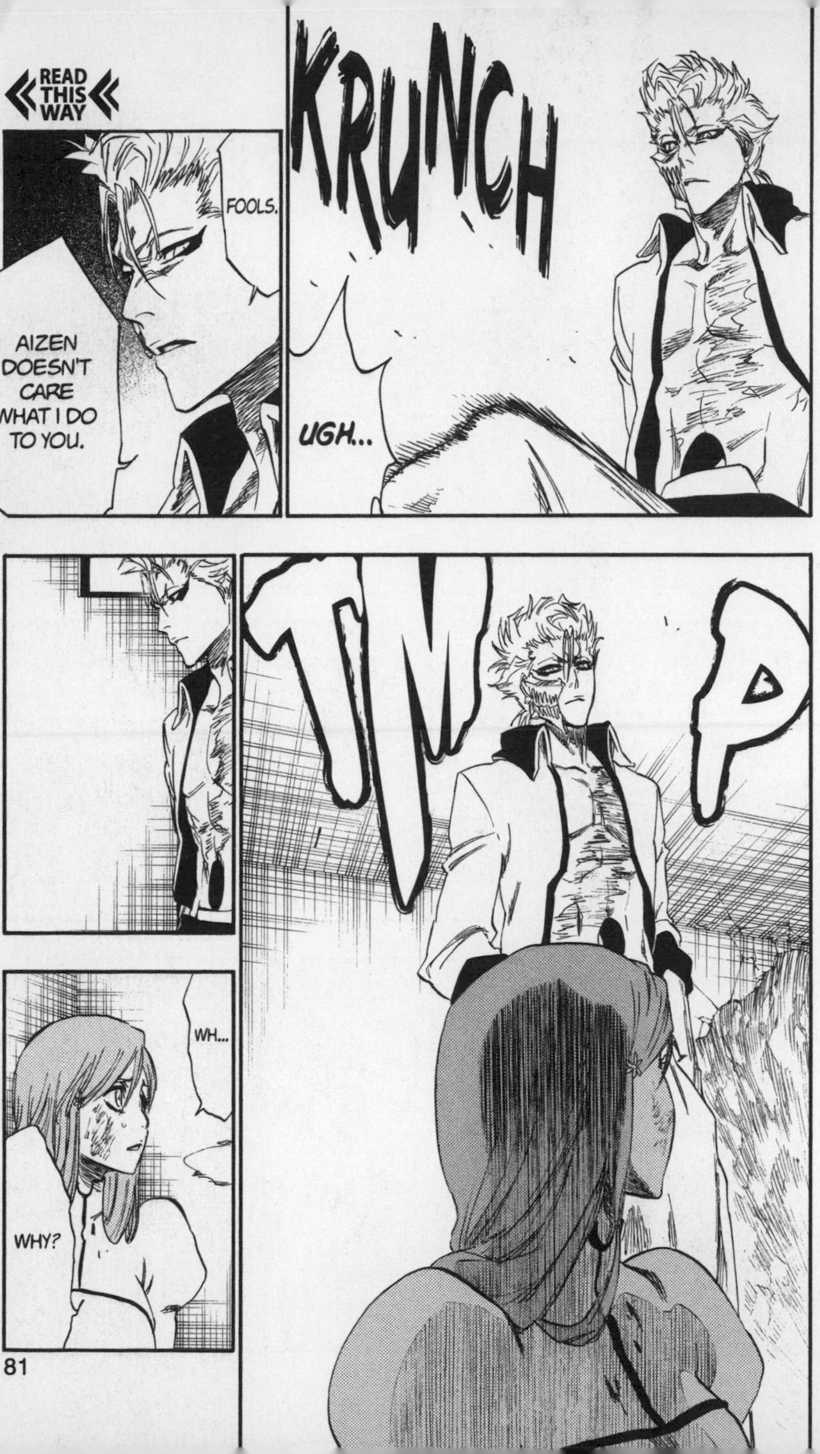

KRUNCH
UGH...
FOOLS.
AIZEN DOESN'T CARE WHAT I DO TO YOU.
WH...
WHY?

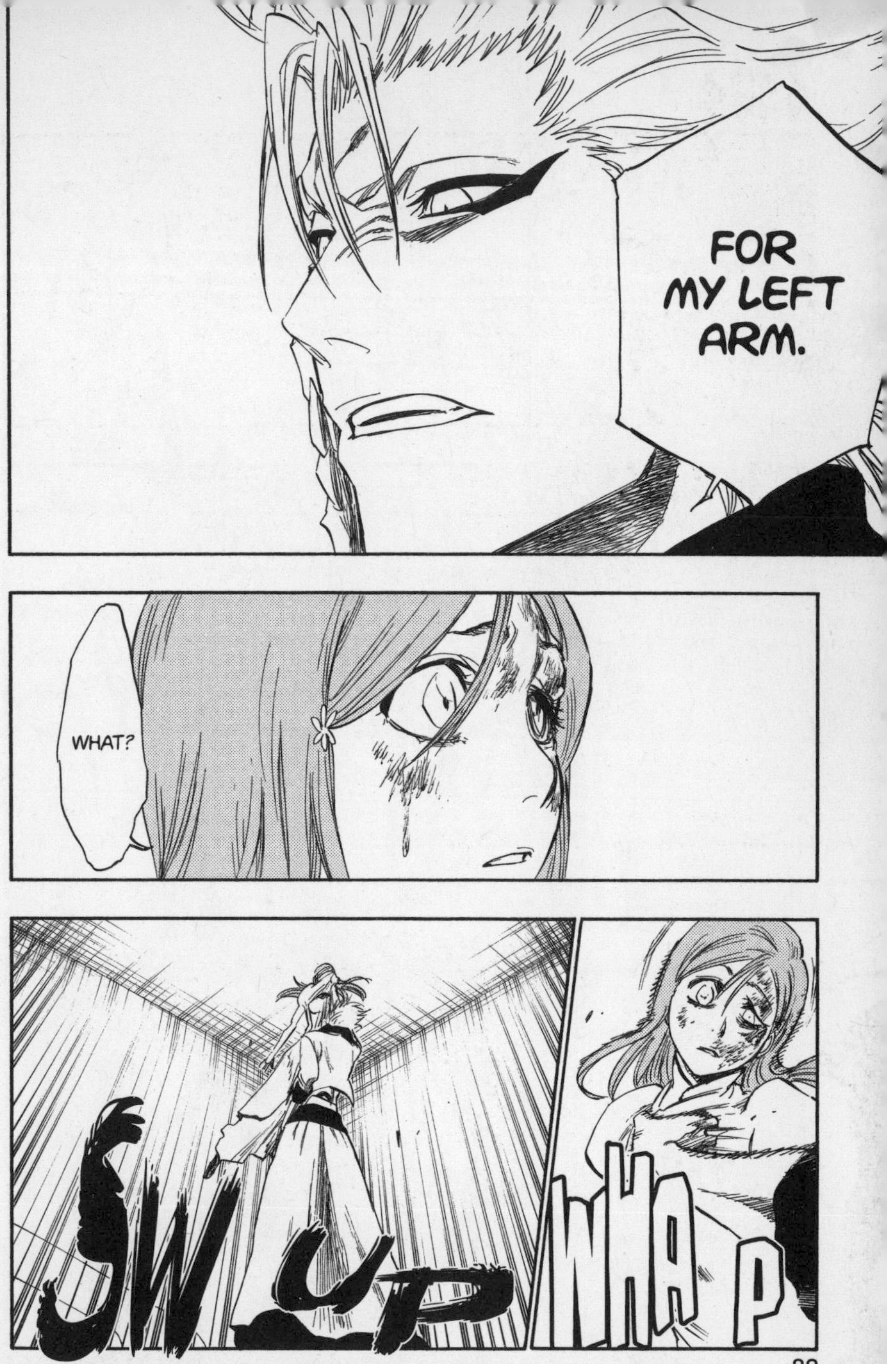
FOR MY LEFT ARM.
WHAT?
WHAP
SWUP

READ THIS WAY

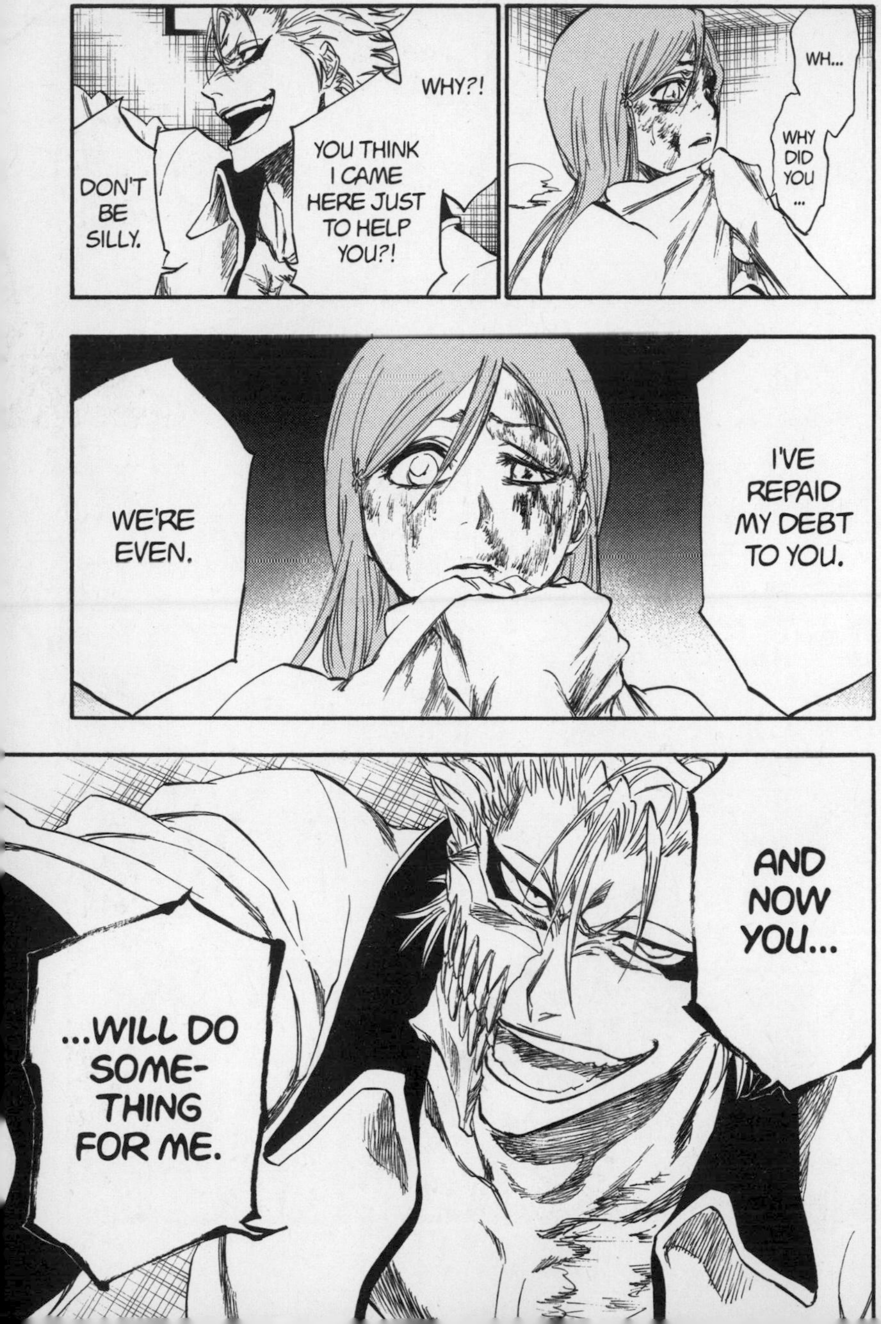
WH...
WHY DID YOU ...
WHY?!
YOU THINK I CAME HERE JUST TO HELP YOU?!
DON'T BE SILLY.
I'VE REPAID MY DEBT TO YOU.
WE'RE EVEN.
AND NOW YOU...
...WILL DO SOME-THING FOR ME.

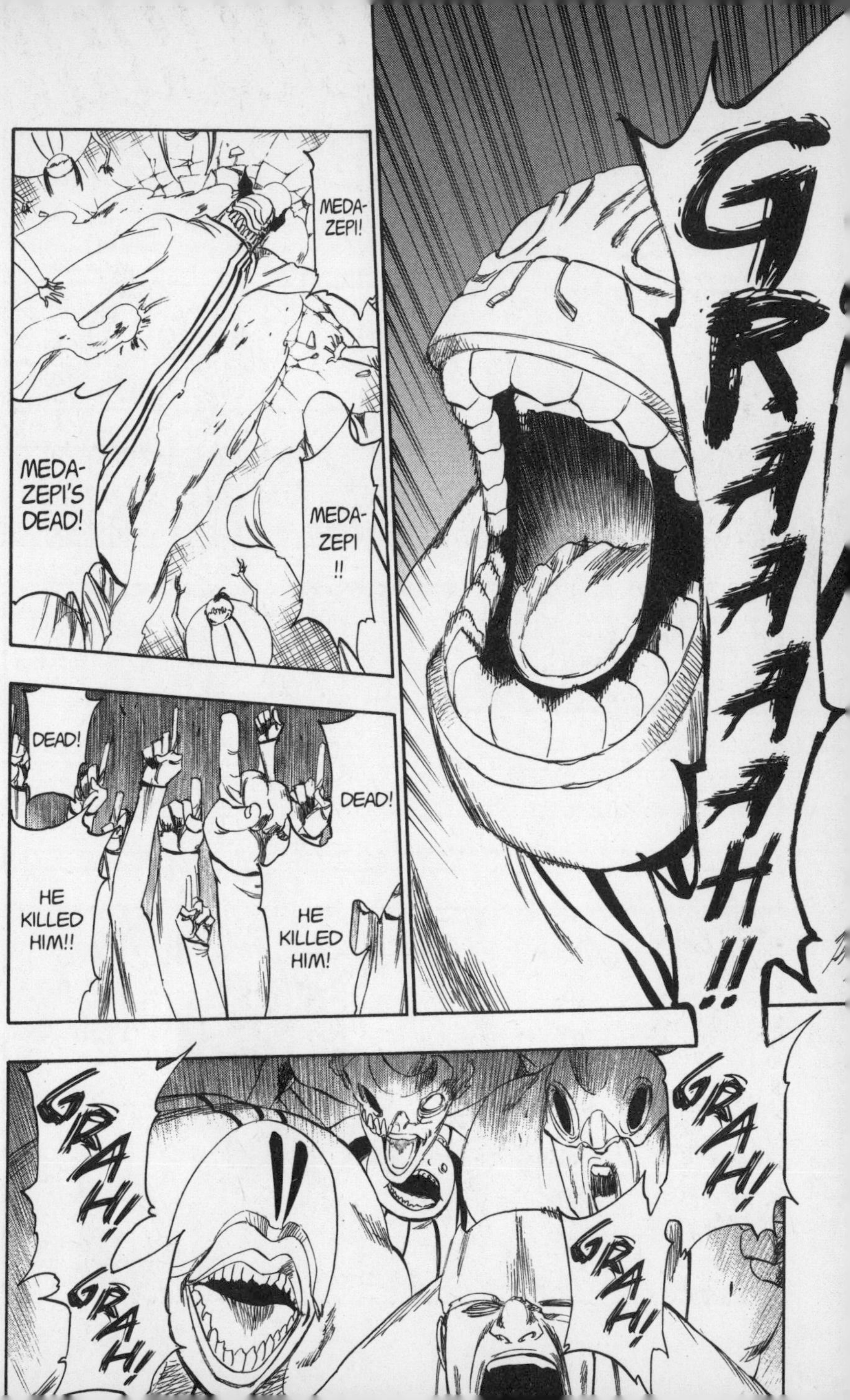

GRAAAAH!!
MEDA-ZEPI!
MEDA-ZEPI!!
MEDA-ZEPI'S DEAD!
DEAD!
DEAD!
HE KILLED HIM!
HE KILLED HIM!!
GRAH!
GRAH!
GRAH!
GRAH!

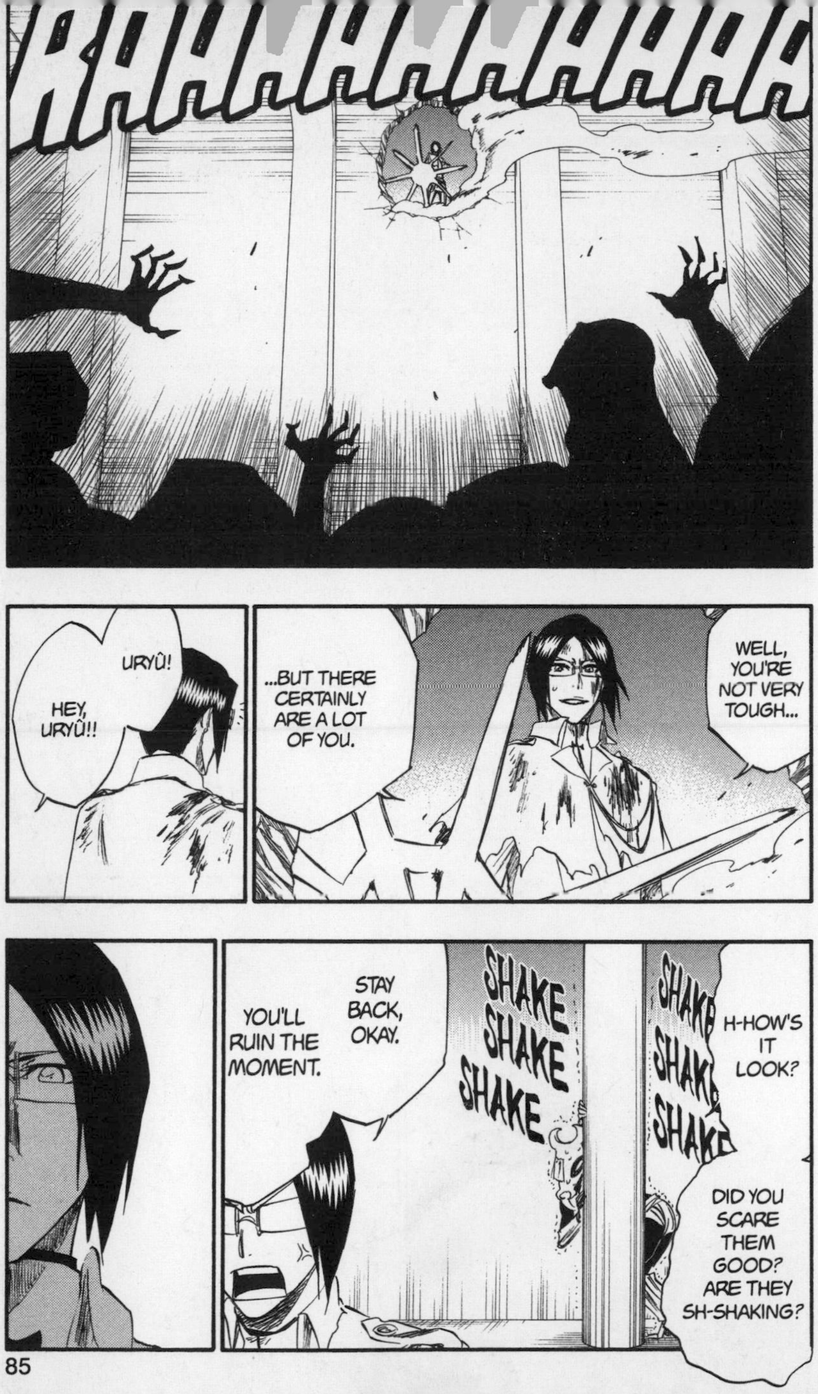
RAAAAAAAAAA
WELL, YOU'RE NOT VERY TOUGH...
...BUT THERE CERTAINLY ARE A LOT OF YOU.
URYÛ!
HEY, URYÛ!!
SHAKE SHAKE SHAKE
H-HOW'S IT LOOK?
SHAKE SHAKE SHAKE
DID YOU SCARE THEM GOOD? ARE THEY SH-SHAKING?
STAY BACK, OKAY.
YOU'LL RUIN THE MOMENT.

WOOOOOOOOOOOOOOO

WWAAAAAAA

!!

SILENCE!!

SO LET'S HEAR HIM OUT.

OUR GUEST HAS SOMETHING HE WISHES TO SAY.

...AN ESPADA?

ARE YOU...

SORRY TO GET RIGHT TO THE POINT, BUT I NEED TO CONFIRM ONE THING.

THAT'S VERY KIND OF YOU.

OCTAVO...

...SZAYELAPORRO GRANTZ.

I AM THE OCTAVO ESPADA...

YES.

THE EIGHTH.

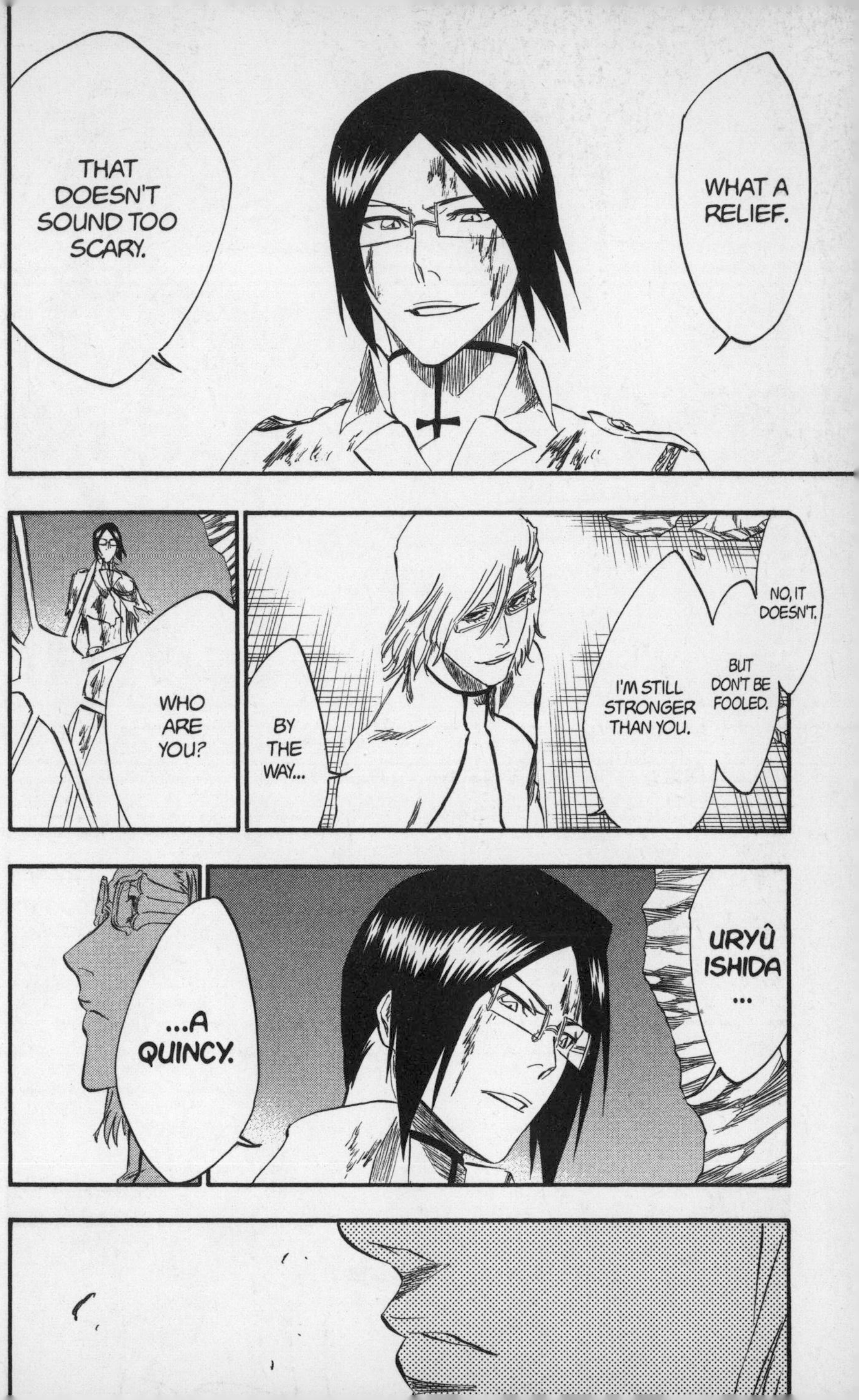
WHAT A RELIEF.
THAT DOESN'T SOUND TOO SCARY.
NO, IT DOESN'T.
BUT DON'T BE FOOLED.
I'M STILL STRONGER THAN YOU.
BY THE WAY...
WHO ARE YOU?
URYÛ ISHIDA ...
...A QUINCY.

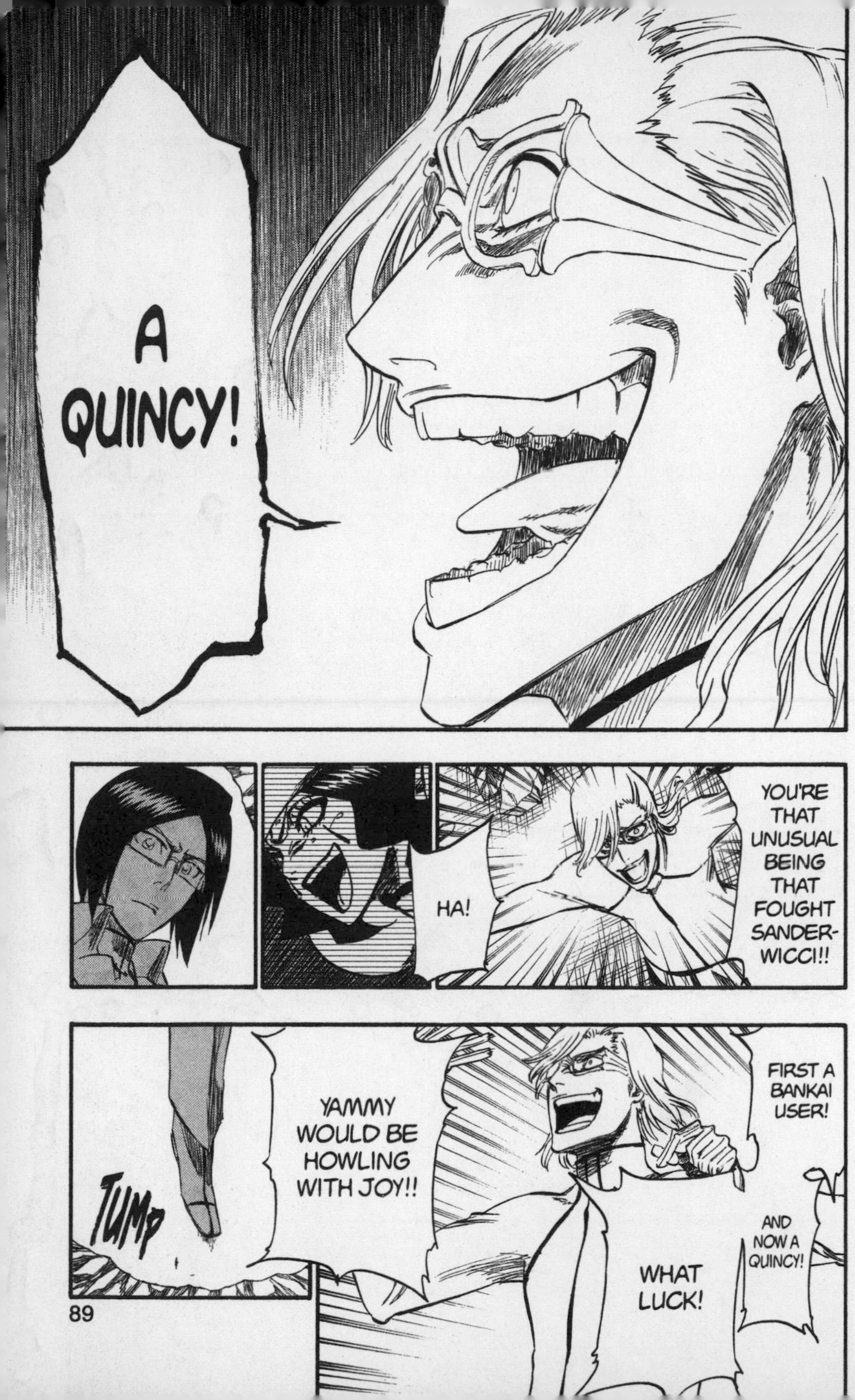
A QUINCY!
YOU'RE THAT UNUSUAL BEING THAT FOUGHT SANDER-WICCI!!
HA!
FIRST A BANKAI USER!
AND NOW A QUINCY!
WHAT LUCK!
YAMMY WOULD BE HOWLING WITH JOY!!
TUMP

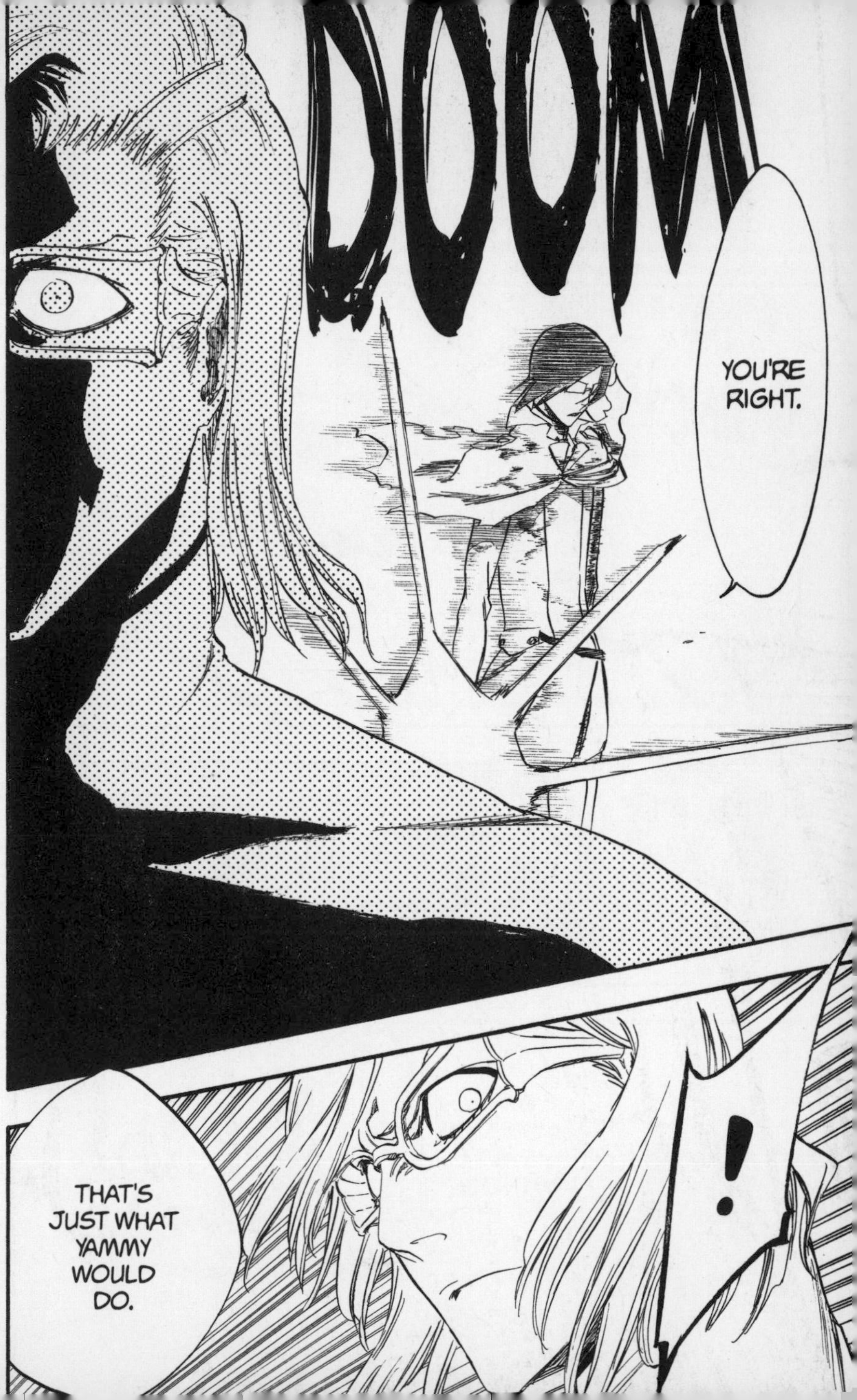
DOOM
YOU'RE RIGHT.
!
THAT'S JUST WHAT YAMMY WOULD DO.

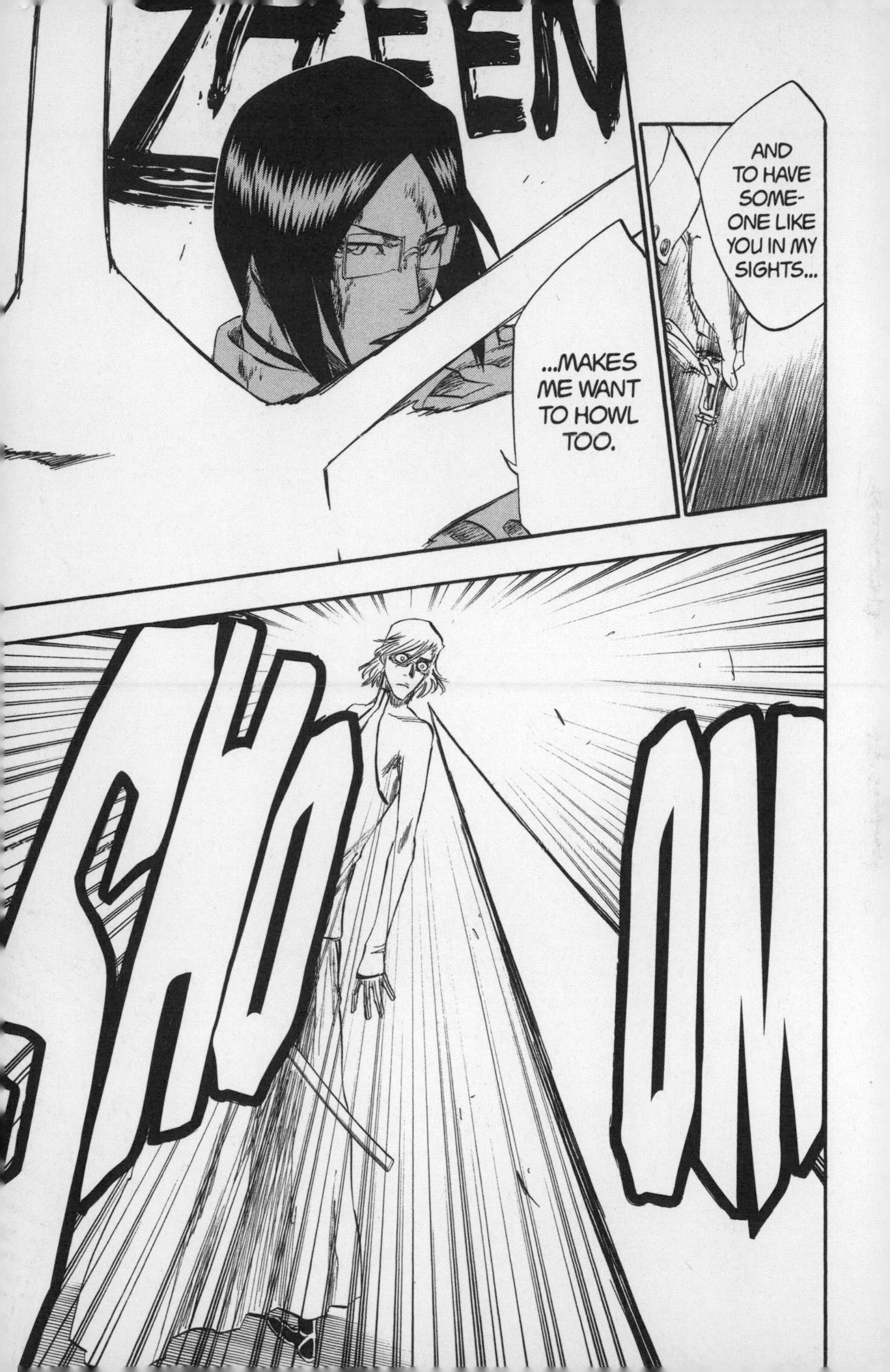
AND TO HAVE SOME-ONE LIKE YOU IN MY SIGHTS...
ZZEEN
...MAKES ME WANT TO HOWL TOO.
SHOOM

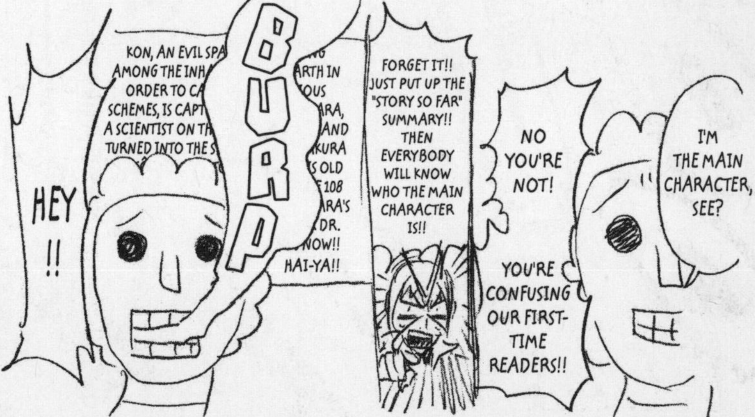
I'M THE MAIN CHARACTER, SEE?
NO YOU'RE NOT!
YOU'RE CONFUSING OUR FIRST-TIME READERS!!
FORGET IT!! JUST PUT UP THE "STORY SO FAR" SUMMARY!! THEN EVERYBODY WILL KNOW WHO THE MAIN CHARACTER IS!!
HAI-YA!!
BURP
HEY !!

274. The Monster

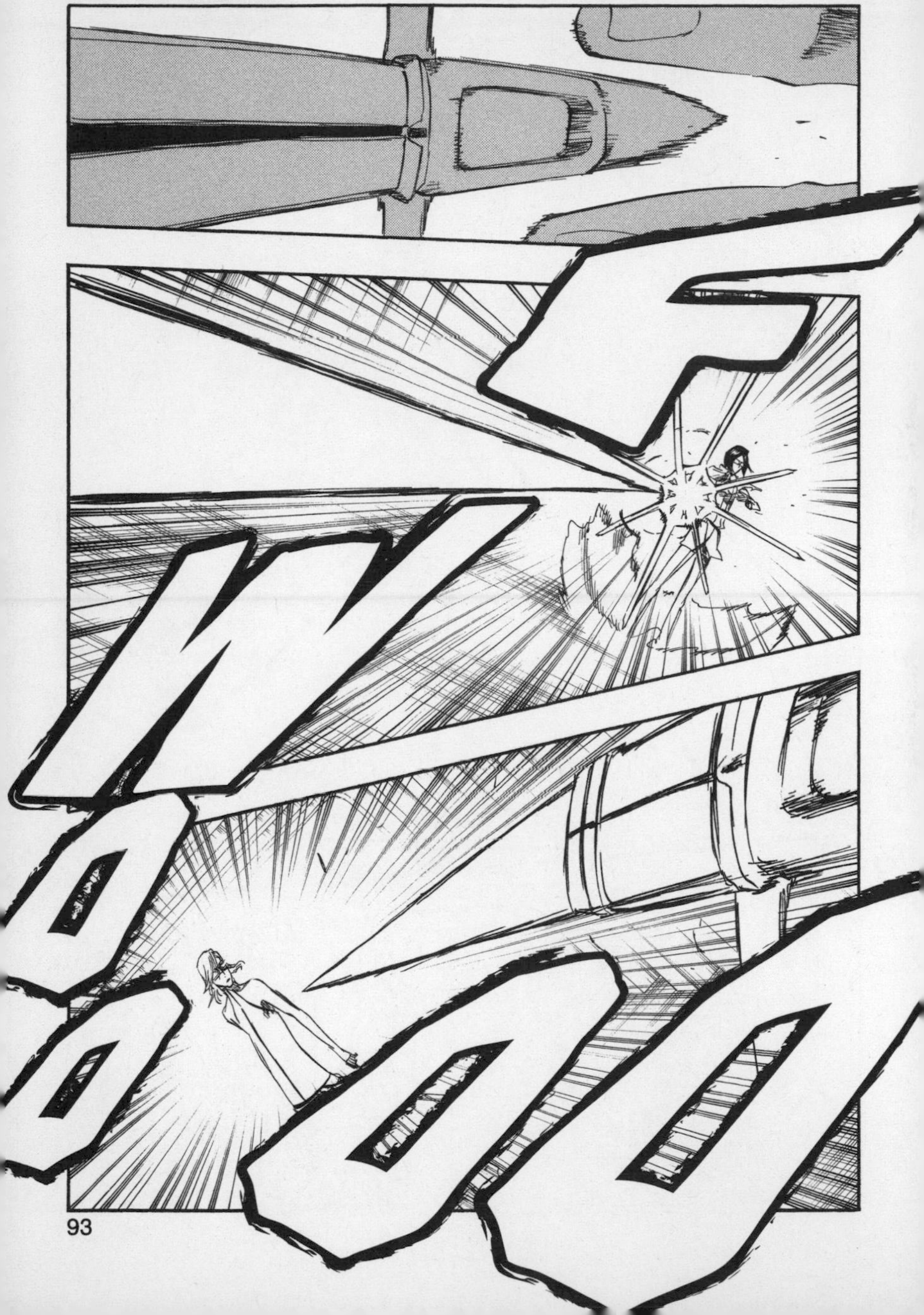

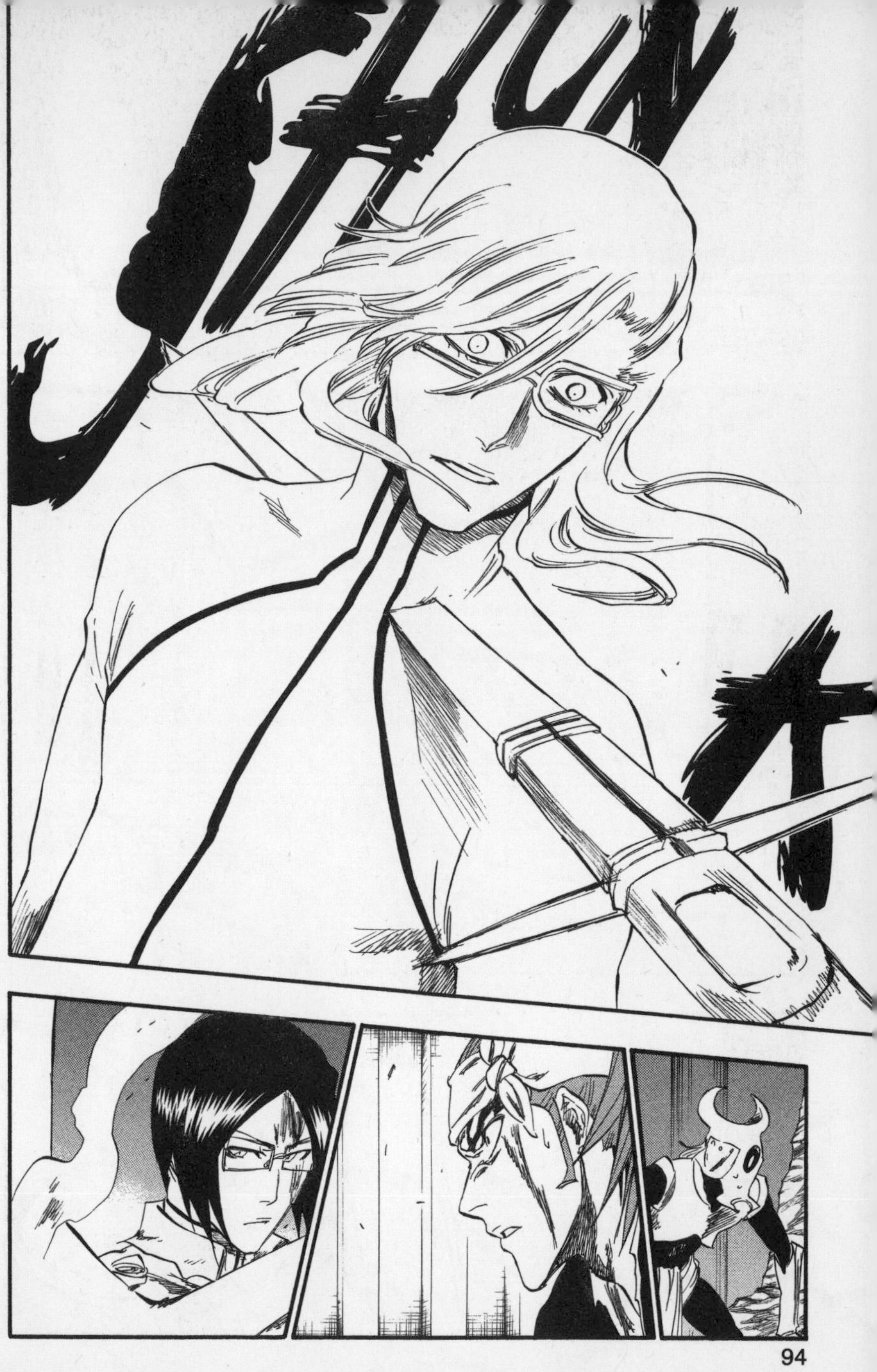
SHUN

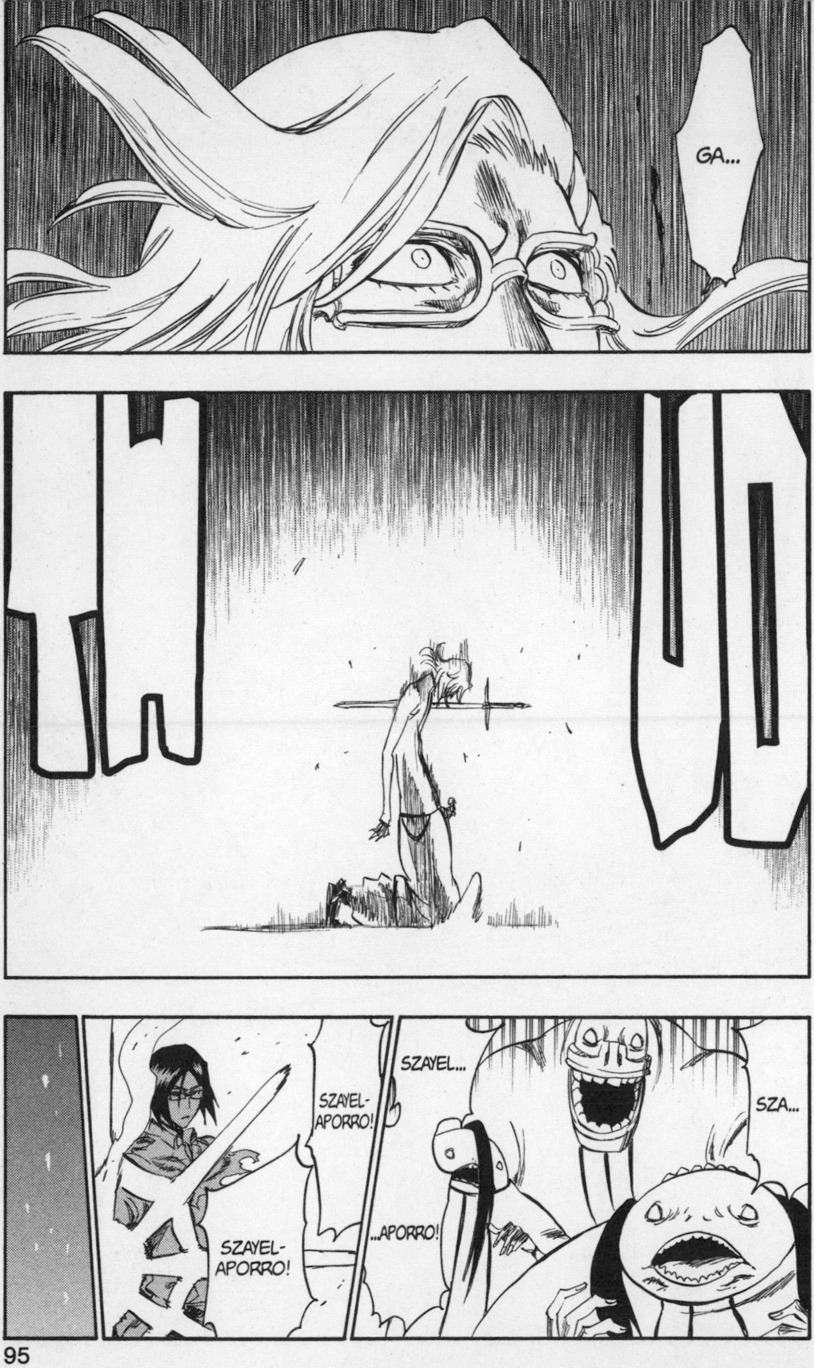
GA...
SZA...
SZAYEL...
...APORRO!
SZAYEL-APORRO!
SZAYEL-APORRO!

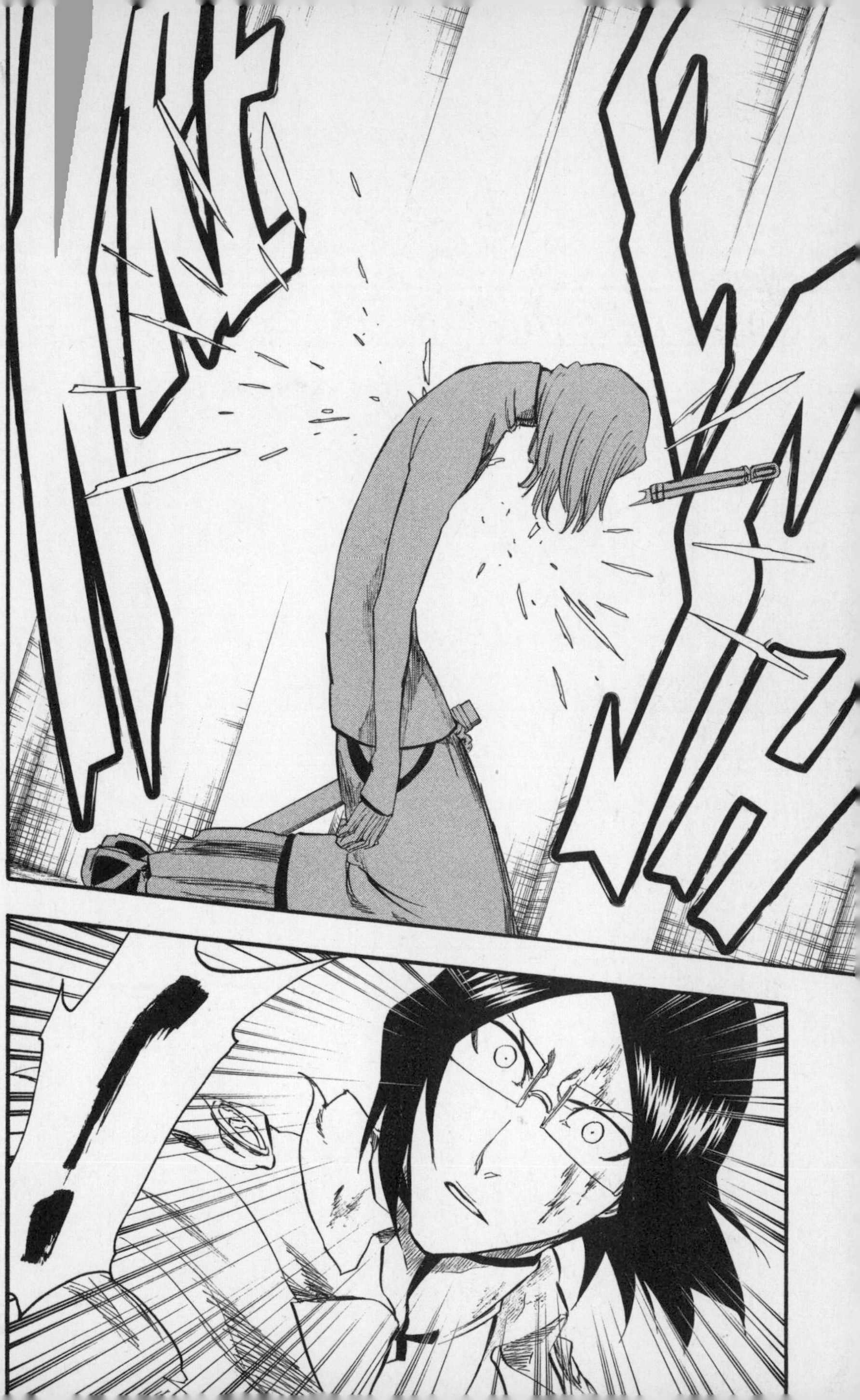

READ THIS WAY

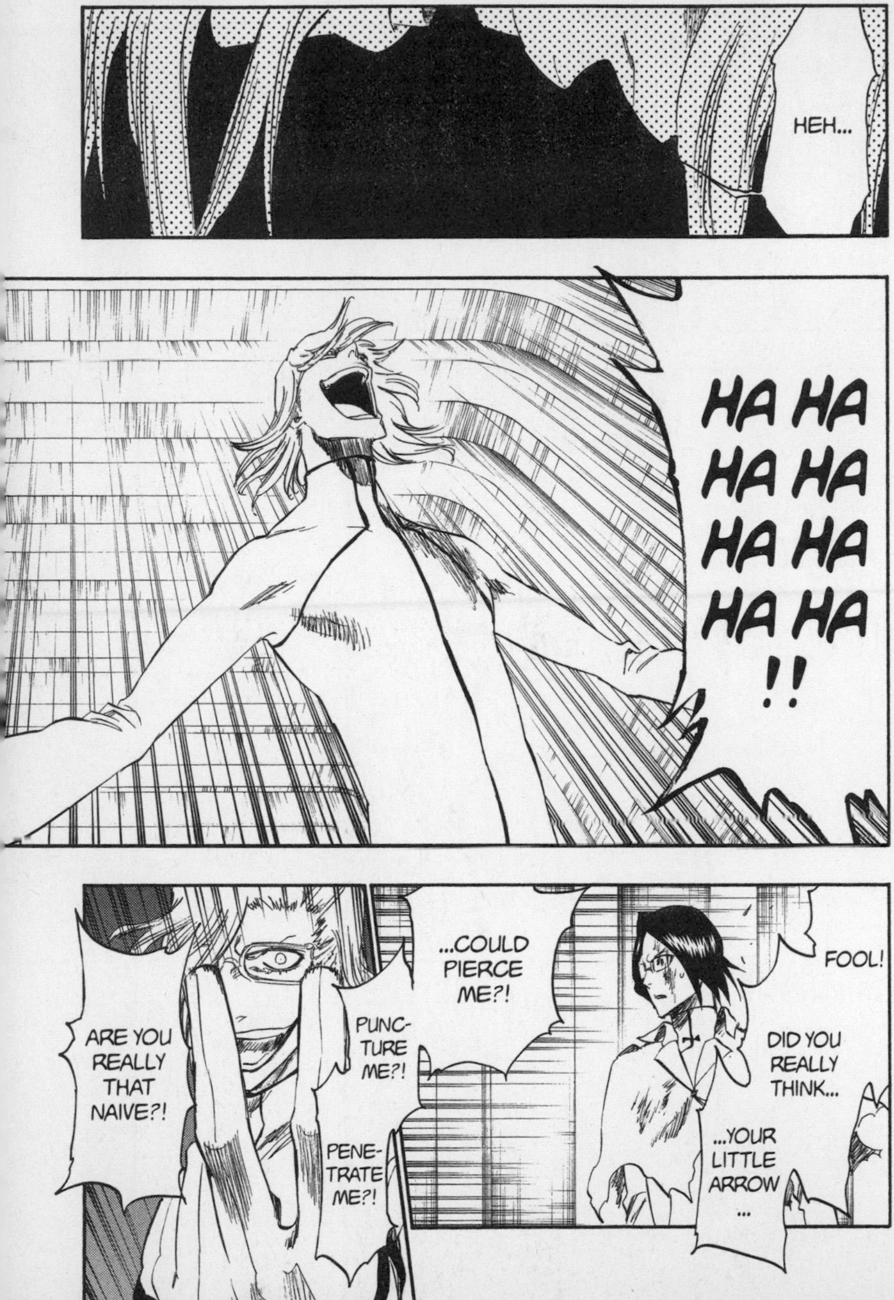
HEH...
HA HA HA HA HA HA HA HA !!
FOOL!
DID YOU REALLY THINK...
...YOUR LITTLE ARROW ...
...COULD PIERCE ME?!
PUNC-TURE ME?!
PENE-TRATE ME?!
ARE YOU REALLY THAT NAIVE?!

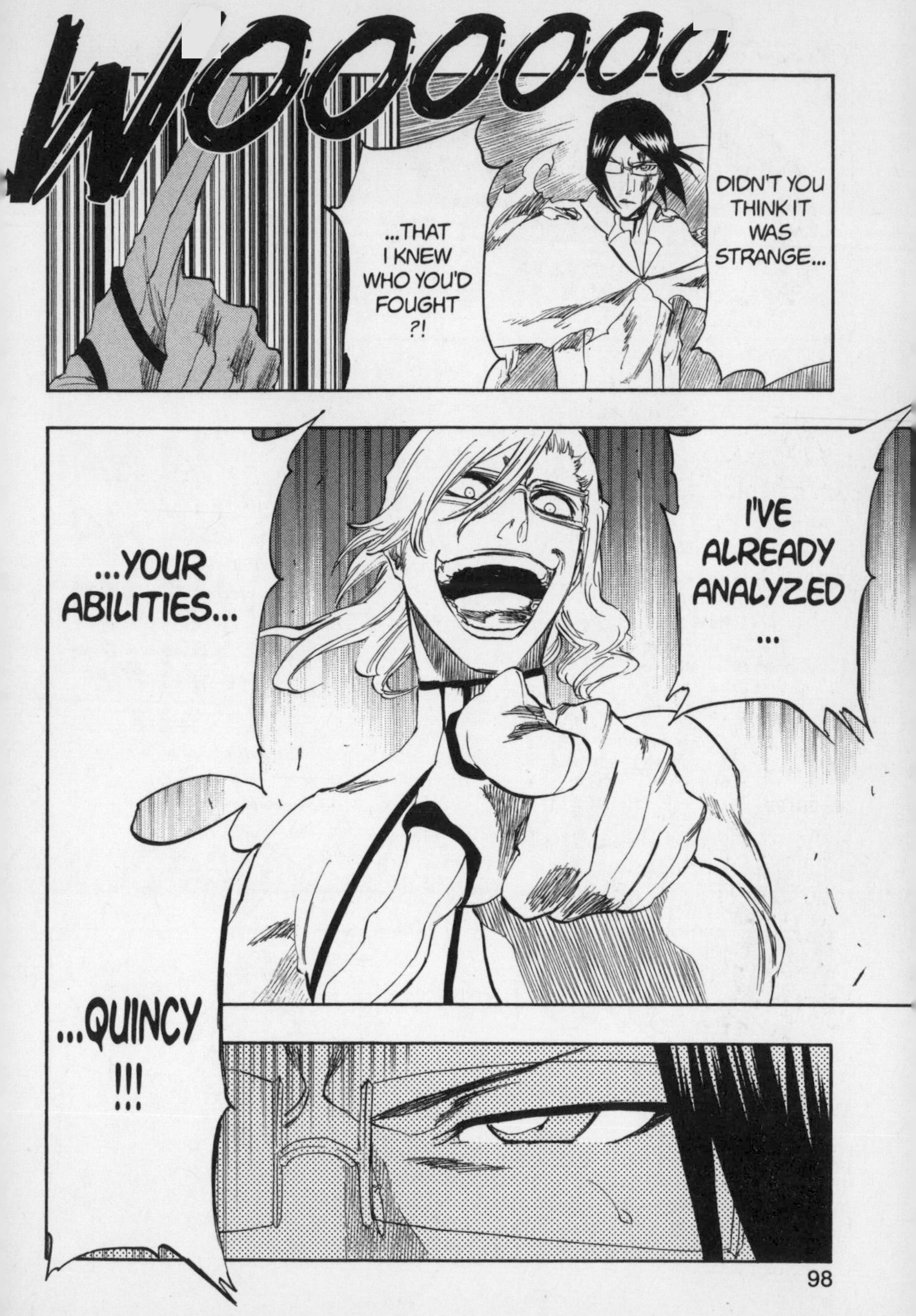
WOOOOO
DIDN'T YOU THINK IT WAS STRANGE...
...THAT I KNEW WHO YOU'D FOUGHT ?!
I'VE ALREADY ANALYZED ...
...YOUR ABILITIES...
...QUINCY !!!

BLEACH.274. The Monster

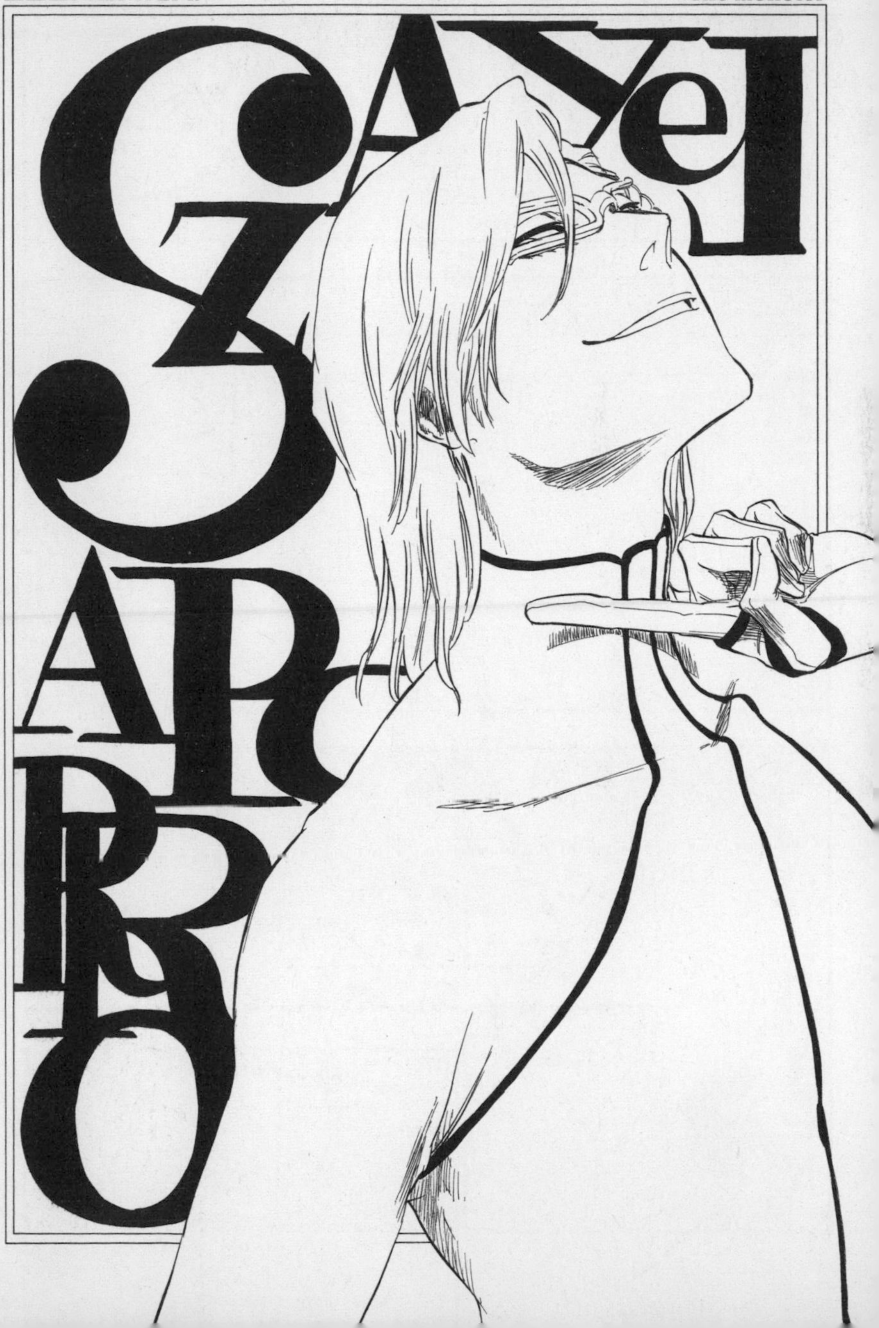

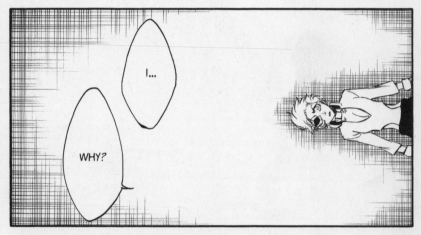

I...

WHY?

IT WAS HER.

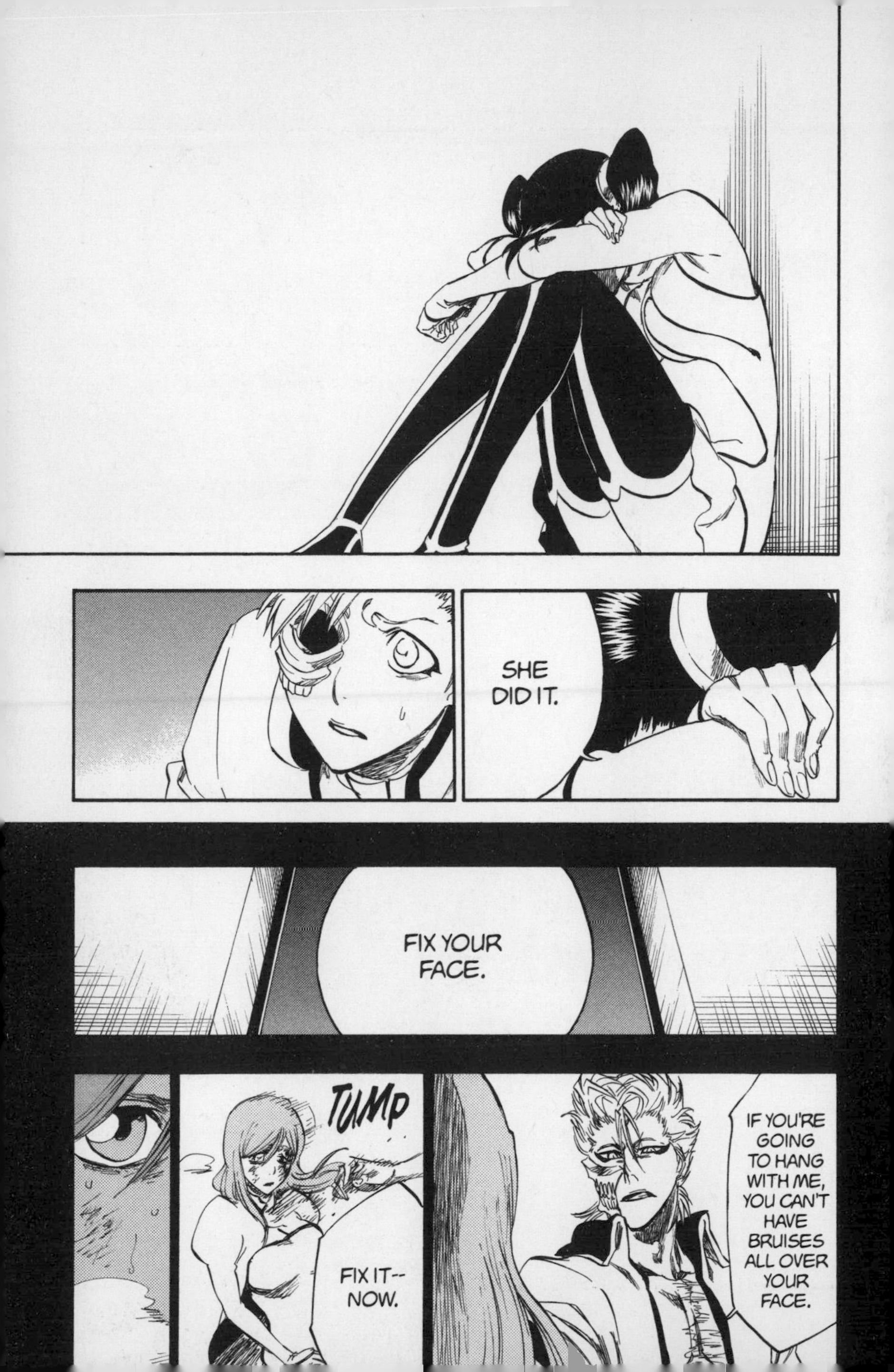
SHE DID IT.
FIX YOUR FACE.
IF YOU'RE GOING TO HANG WITH ME, YOU CAN'T HAVE BRUISES ALL OVER YOUR FACE.
TUMP
FIX IT-- NOW.

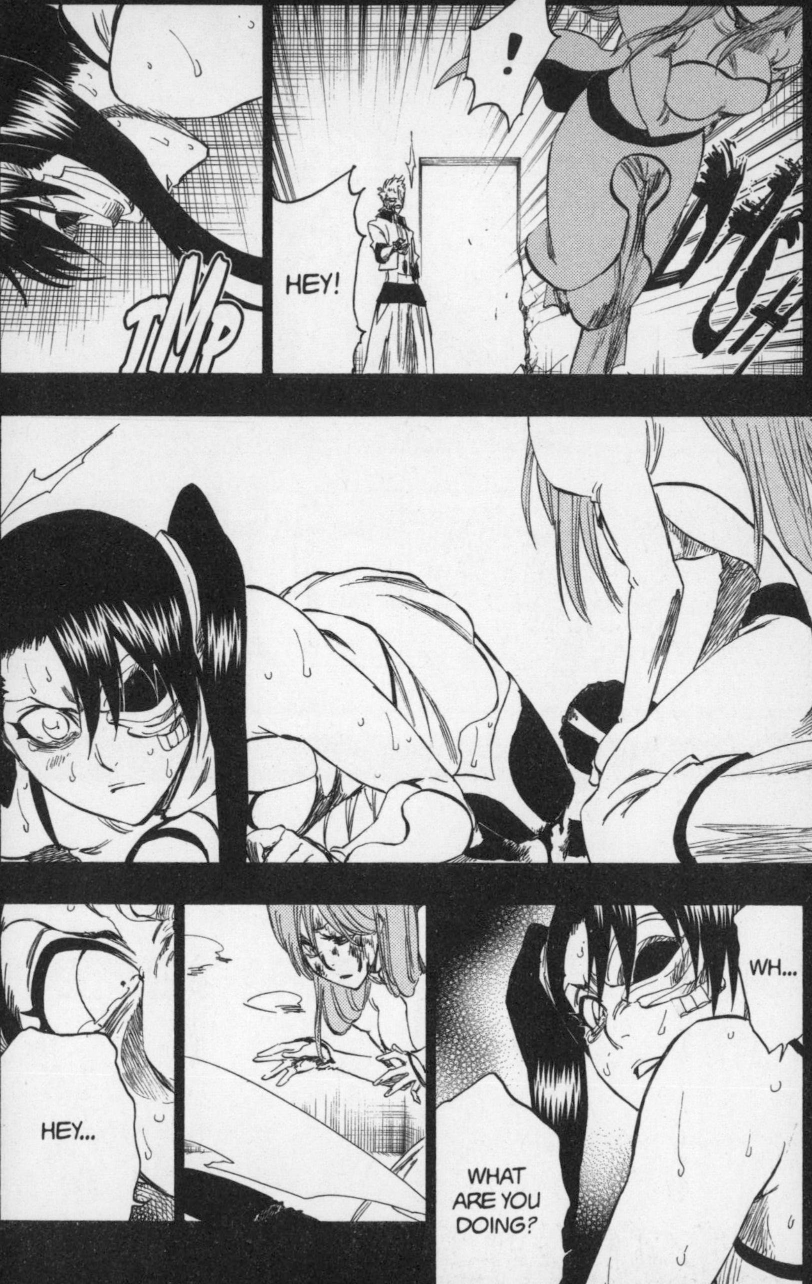
!
HEY!
TMP
WH...
WHAT ARE YOU DOING?
HEY...

DON'T TOUCH ME!!

WHAT ARE YOU DOING?!

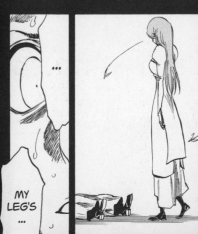

...

MY LEG'S ...

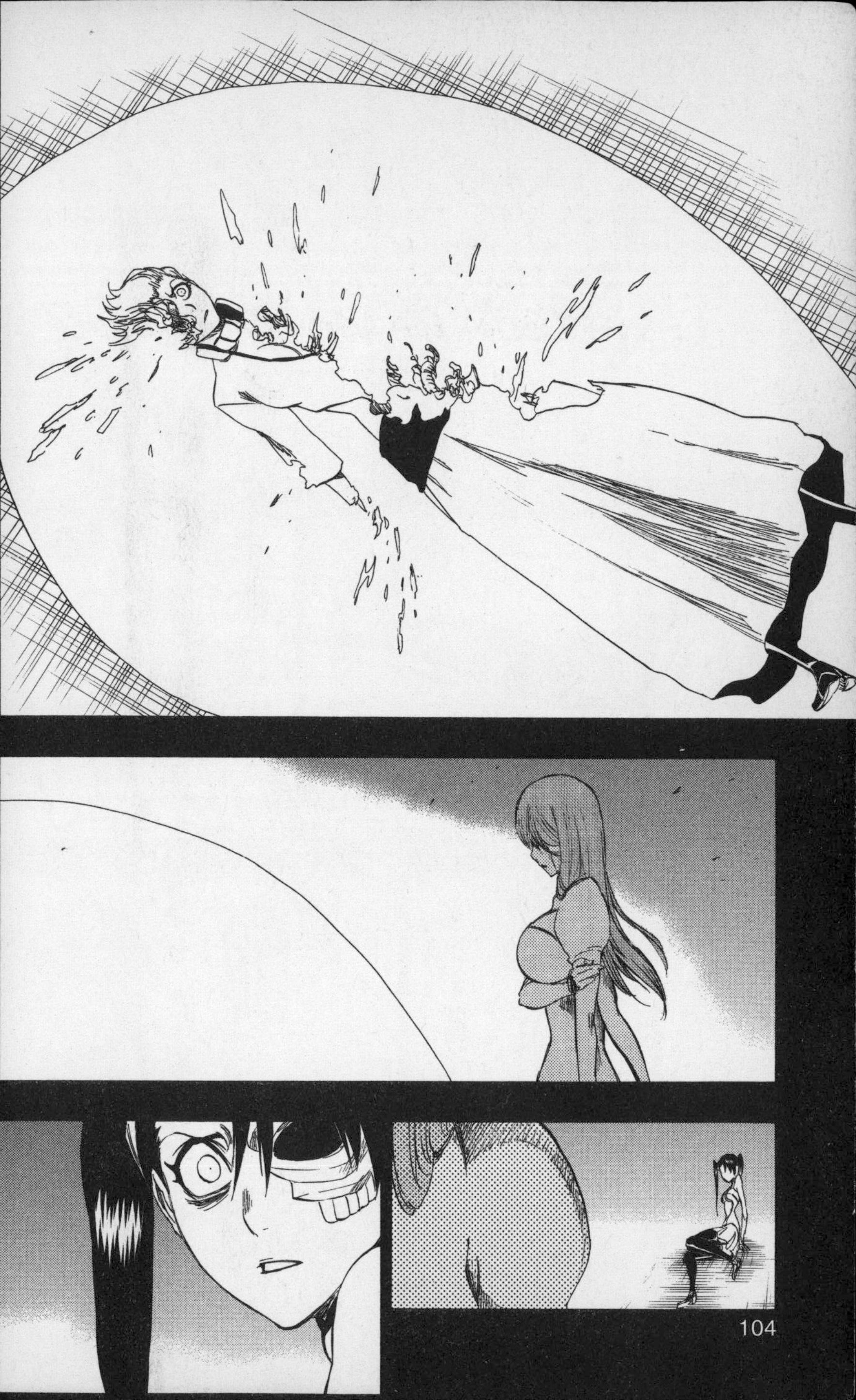

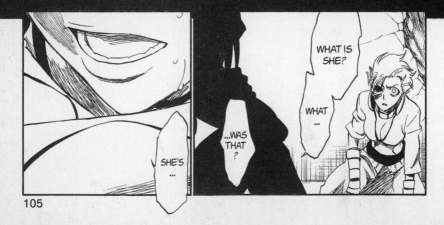

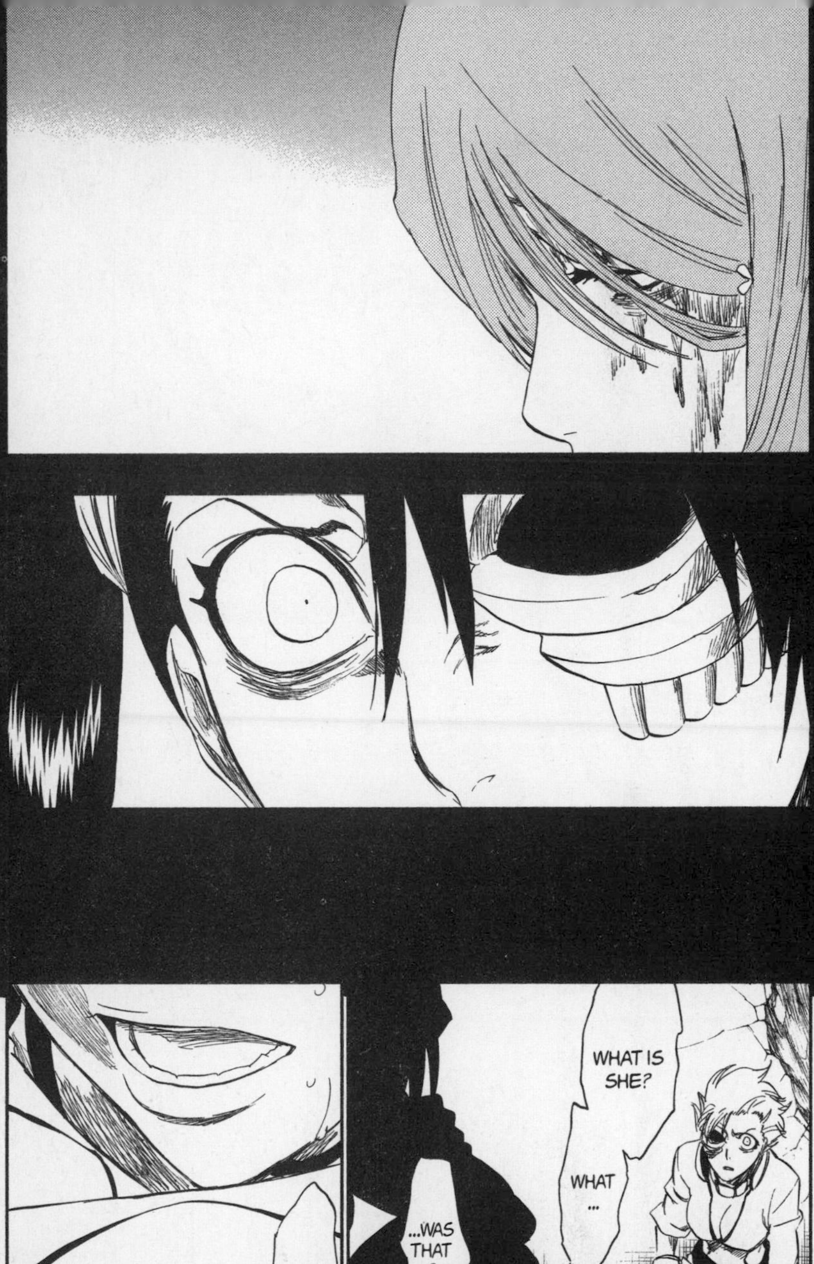
WHAT IS SHE?
WHAT ...
...WAS THAT ?
SHE'S ...

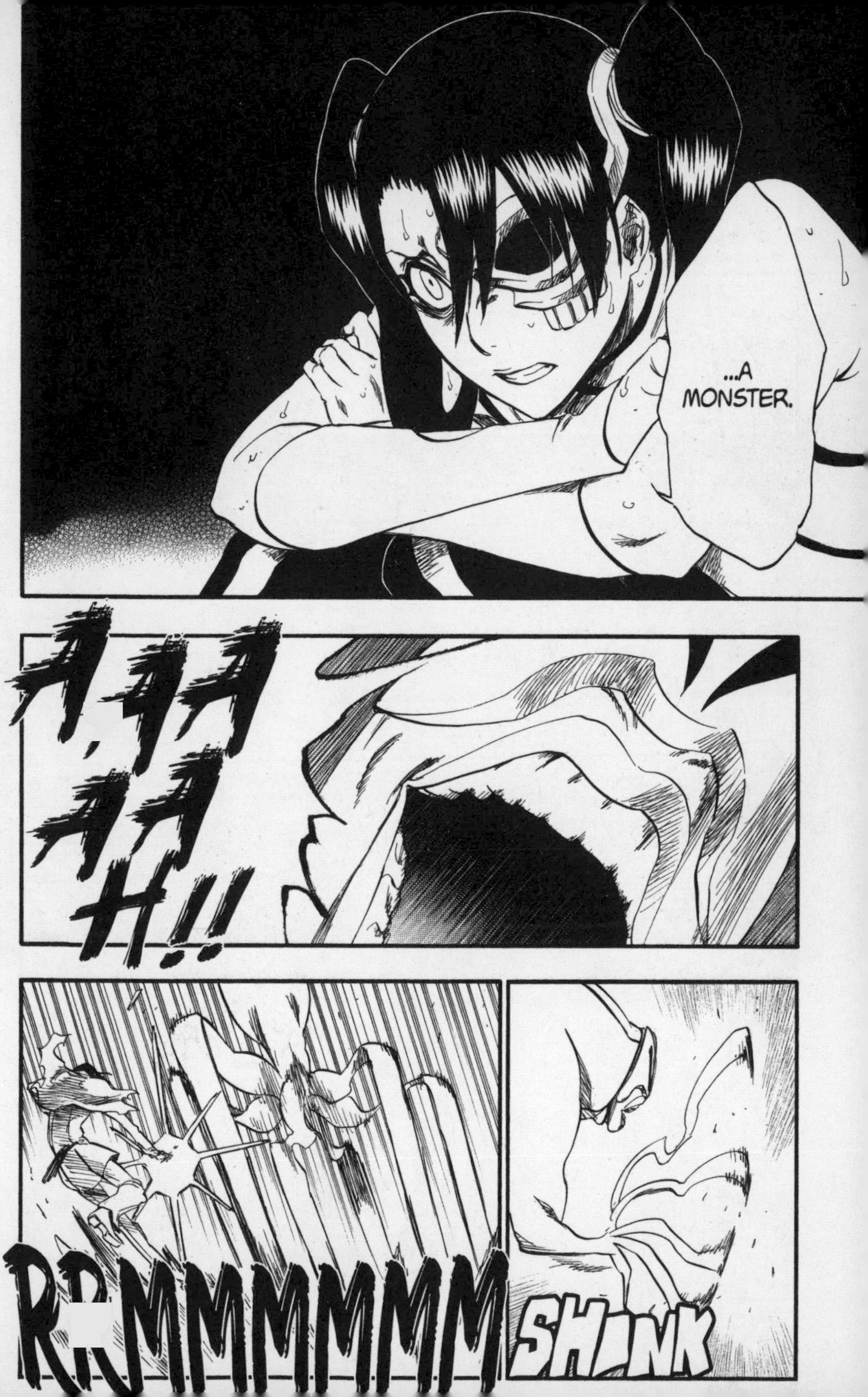
...A
MONSTER.

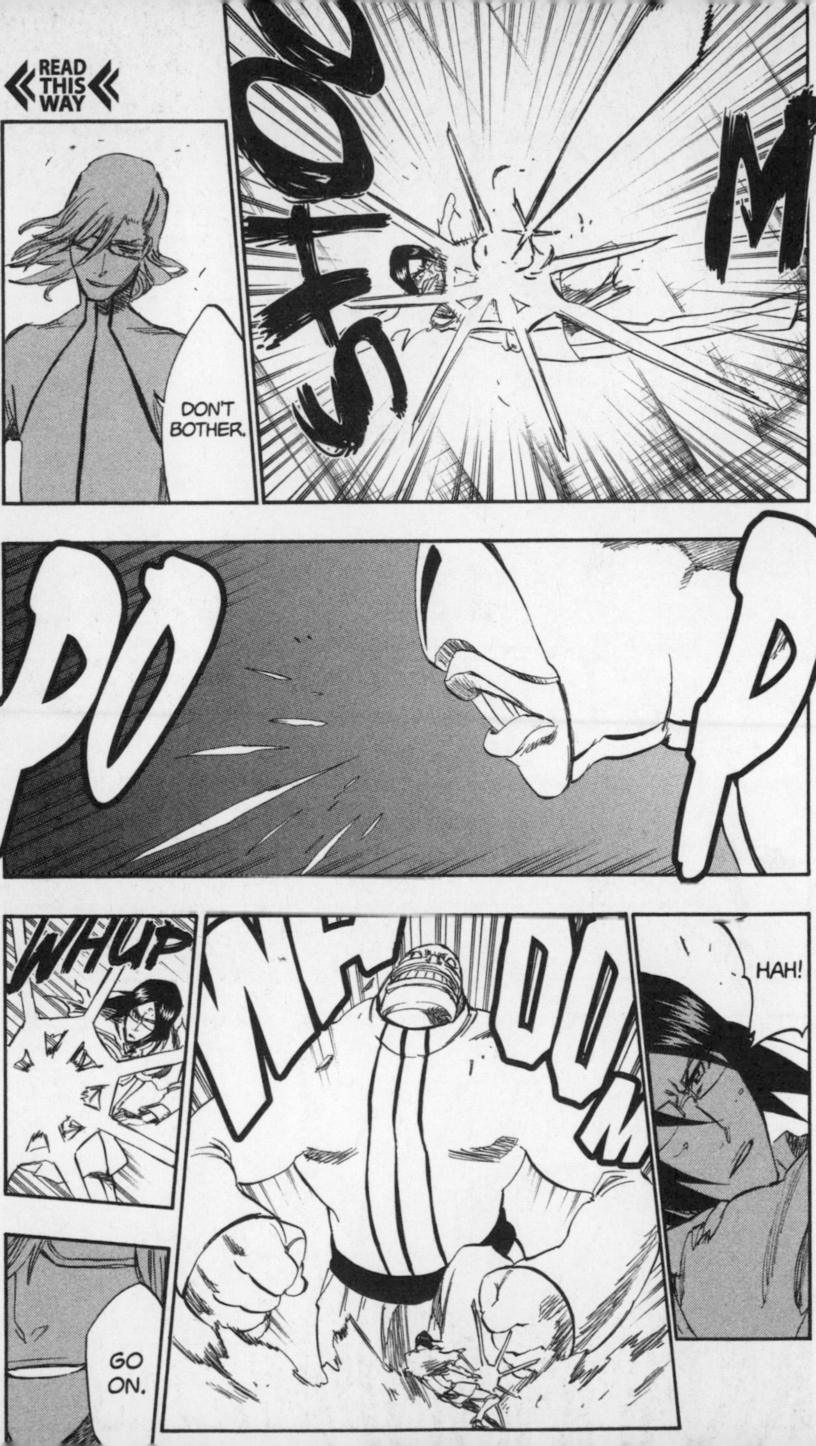
READ THIS WAY
DON'T BOTHER.
HAH!
WHUP
GO ON.

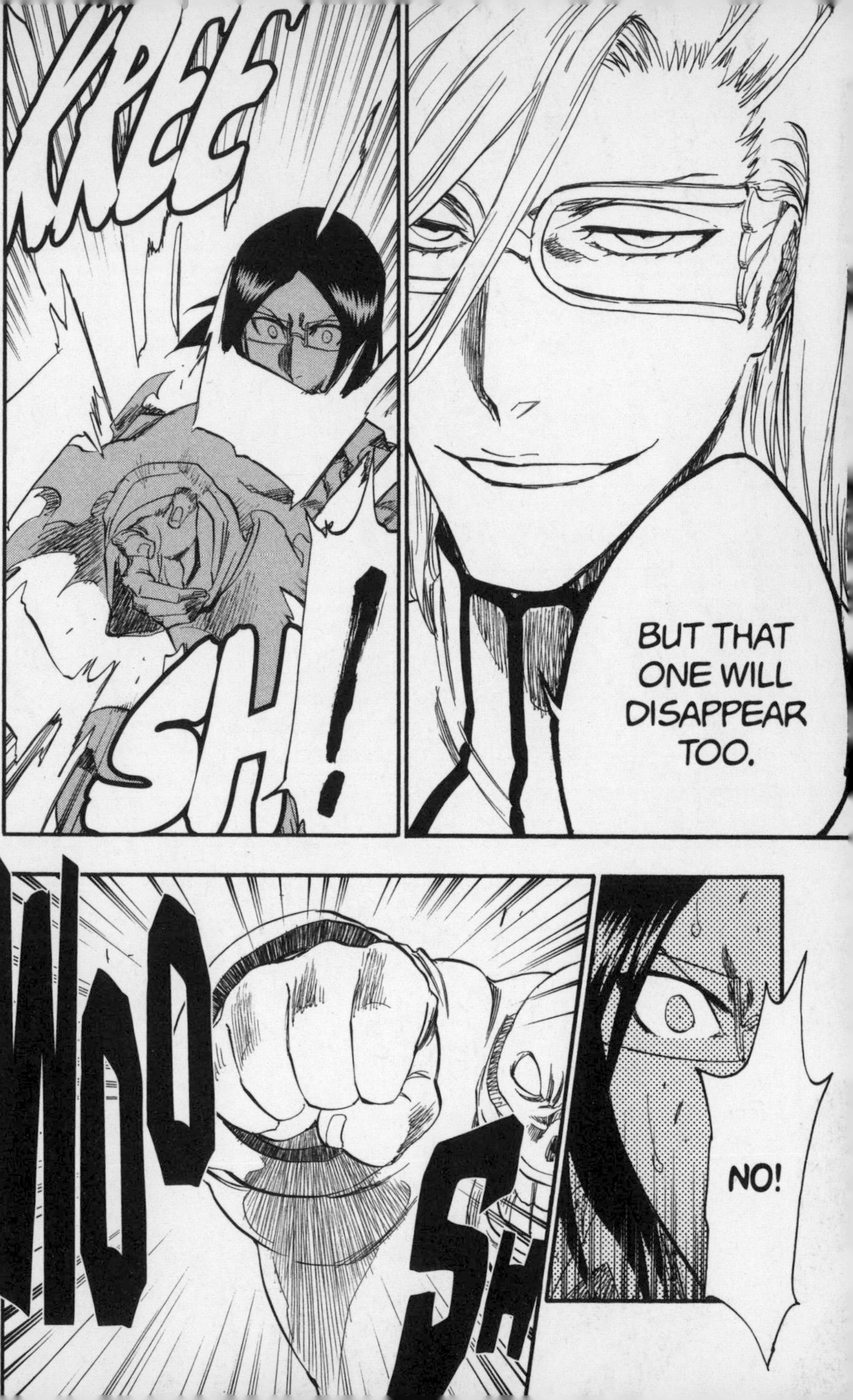
BUT THAT ONE WILL DISAPPEAR TOO.
NO!

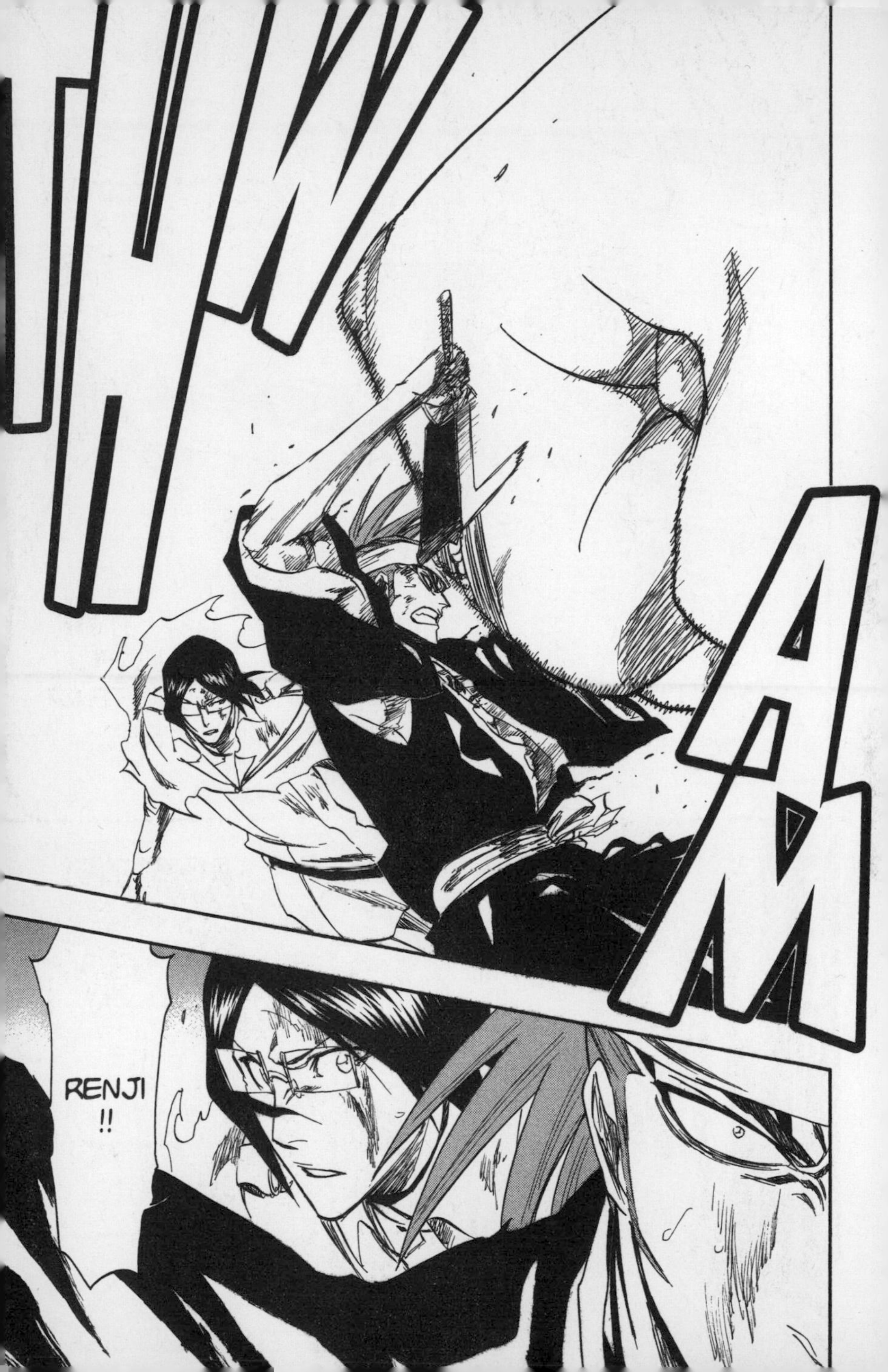
THWAM
RENJI !!

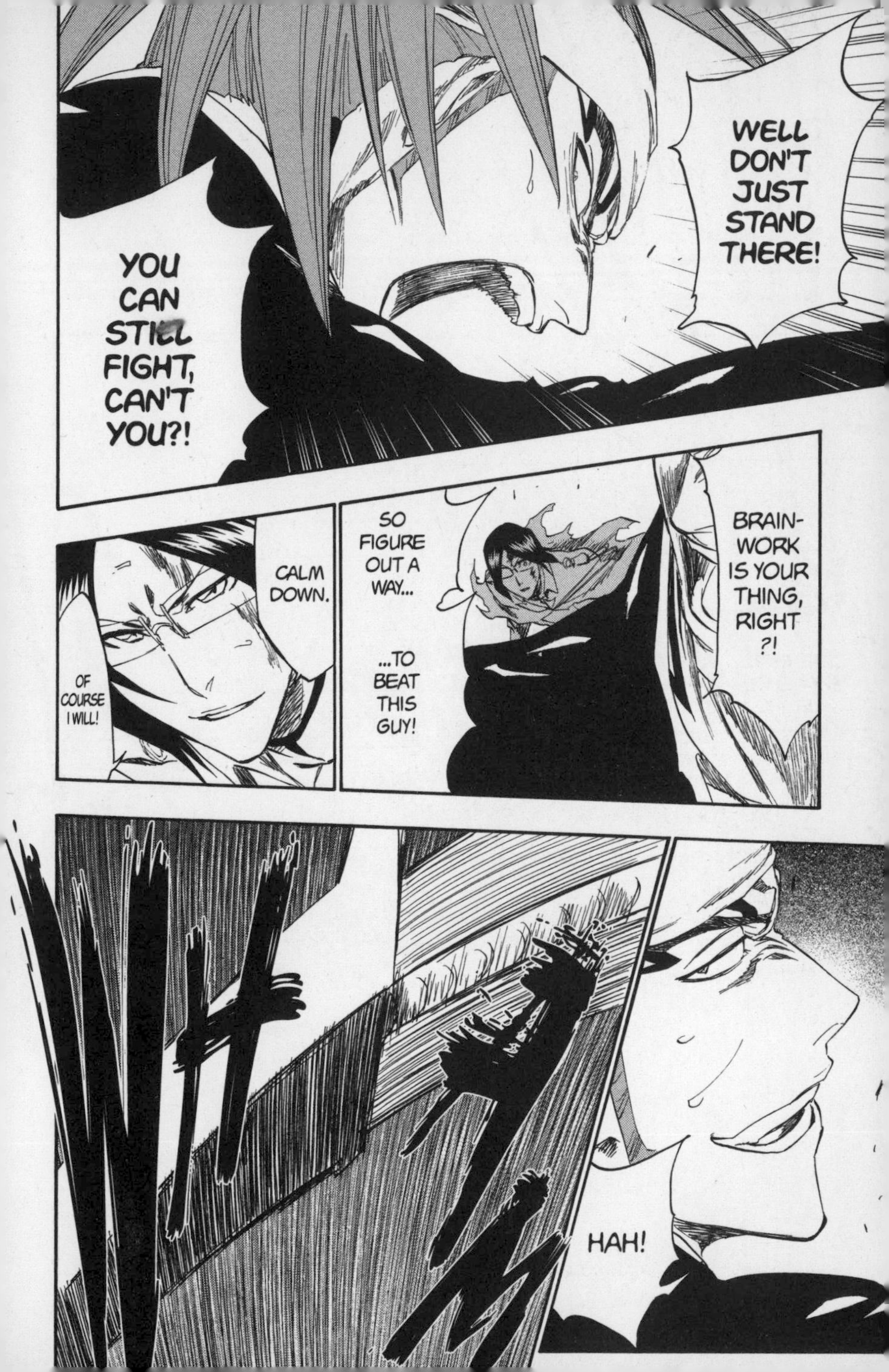
WELL DON'T JUST STAND THERE!
YOU CAN STILL FIGHT, CAN'T YOU?!
BRAIN-WORK IS YOUR THING, RIGHT?!
SO FIGURE OUT A WAY...
...TO BEAT THIS GUY!
CALM DOWN.
OF COURSE I WILL!
HAH!

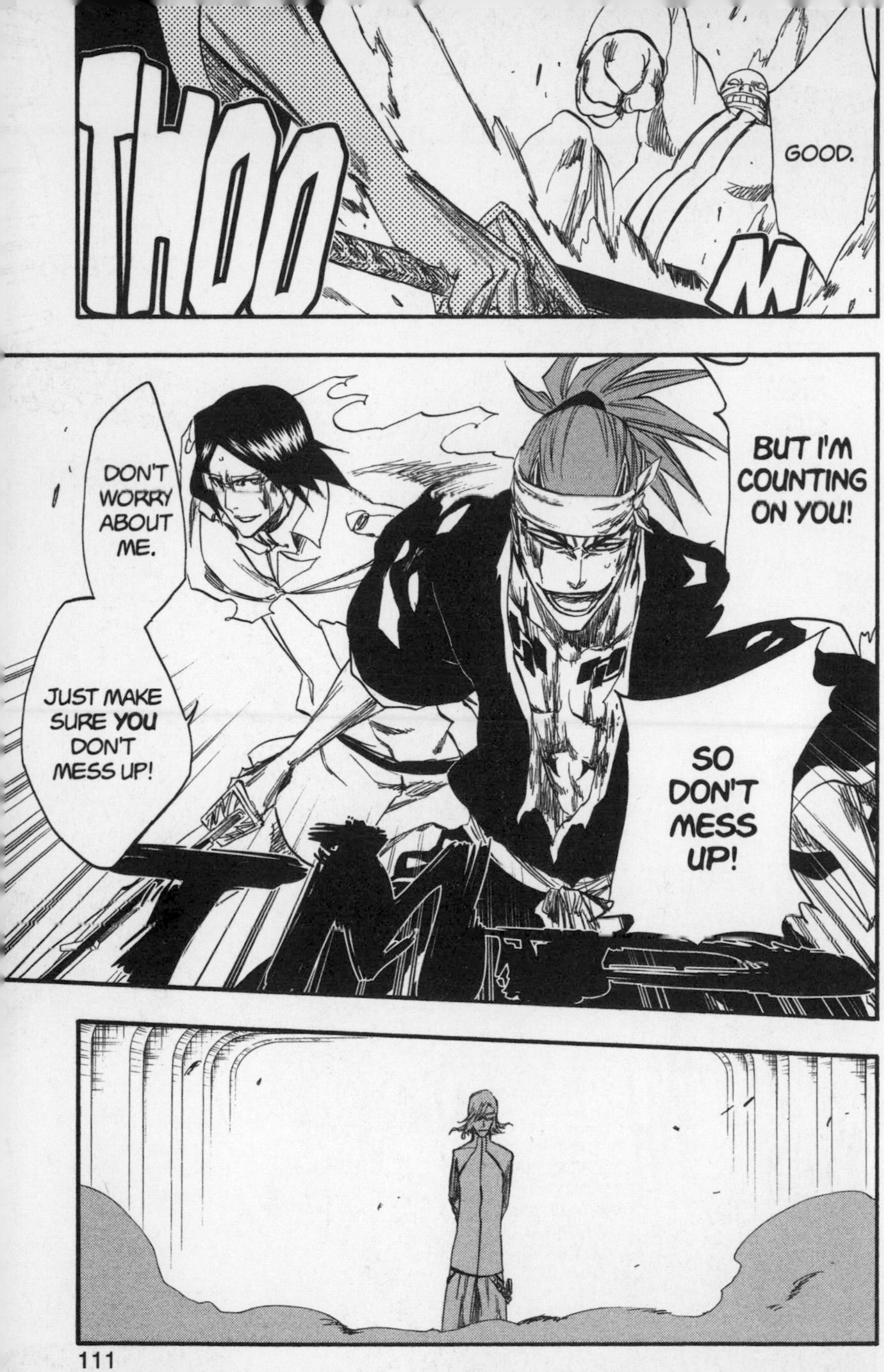

GOOD.
THOOM
BUT I'M COUNTING ON YOU!
SO DON'T MESS UP!
DON'T WORRY ABOUT ME.
JUST MAKE SURE YOU DON'T MESS UP!

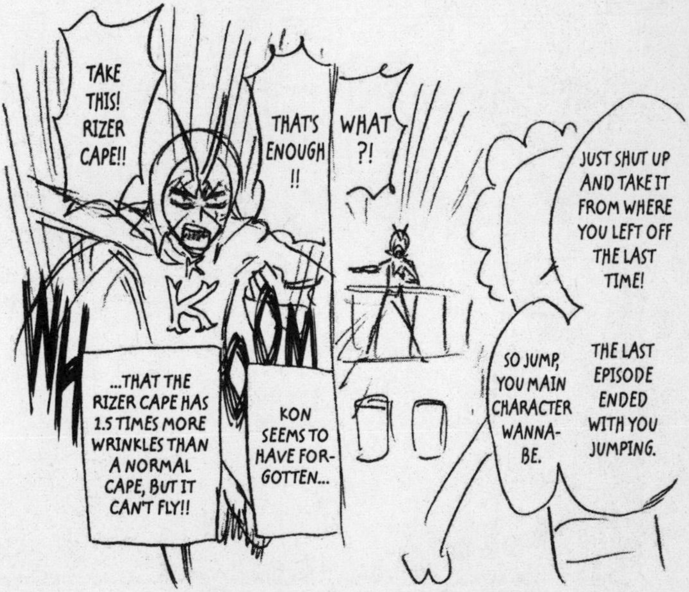
JUST SHUT UP AND TAKE IT FROM WHERE YOU LEFT OFF THE LAST TIME!
THE LAST EPISODE ENDED WITH YOU JUMPING.
SO JUMP, YOU MAIN CHARACTER WANNA-BE.
WHAT?!
THAT'S ENOUGH!!
TAKE THIS! RIZER CAPE!!
WHOOM
KON SEEMS TO HAVE FORGOTTEN...
...THAT THE RIZER CAPE HAS 1.5 TIMES MORE WRINKLES THAN A NORMAL CAPE, BUT IT CAN'T FLY!!

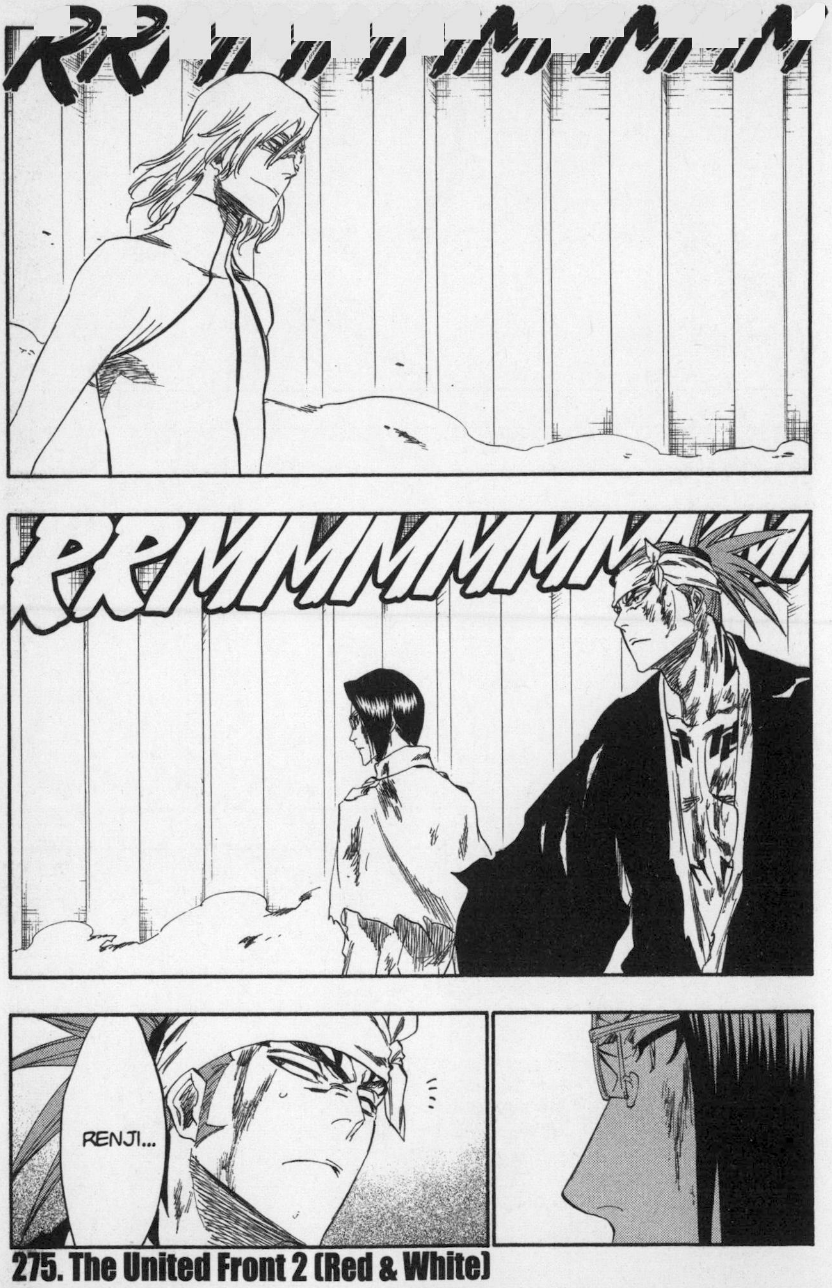
RENJI...

275. The United Front 2 (Red & White)

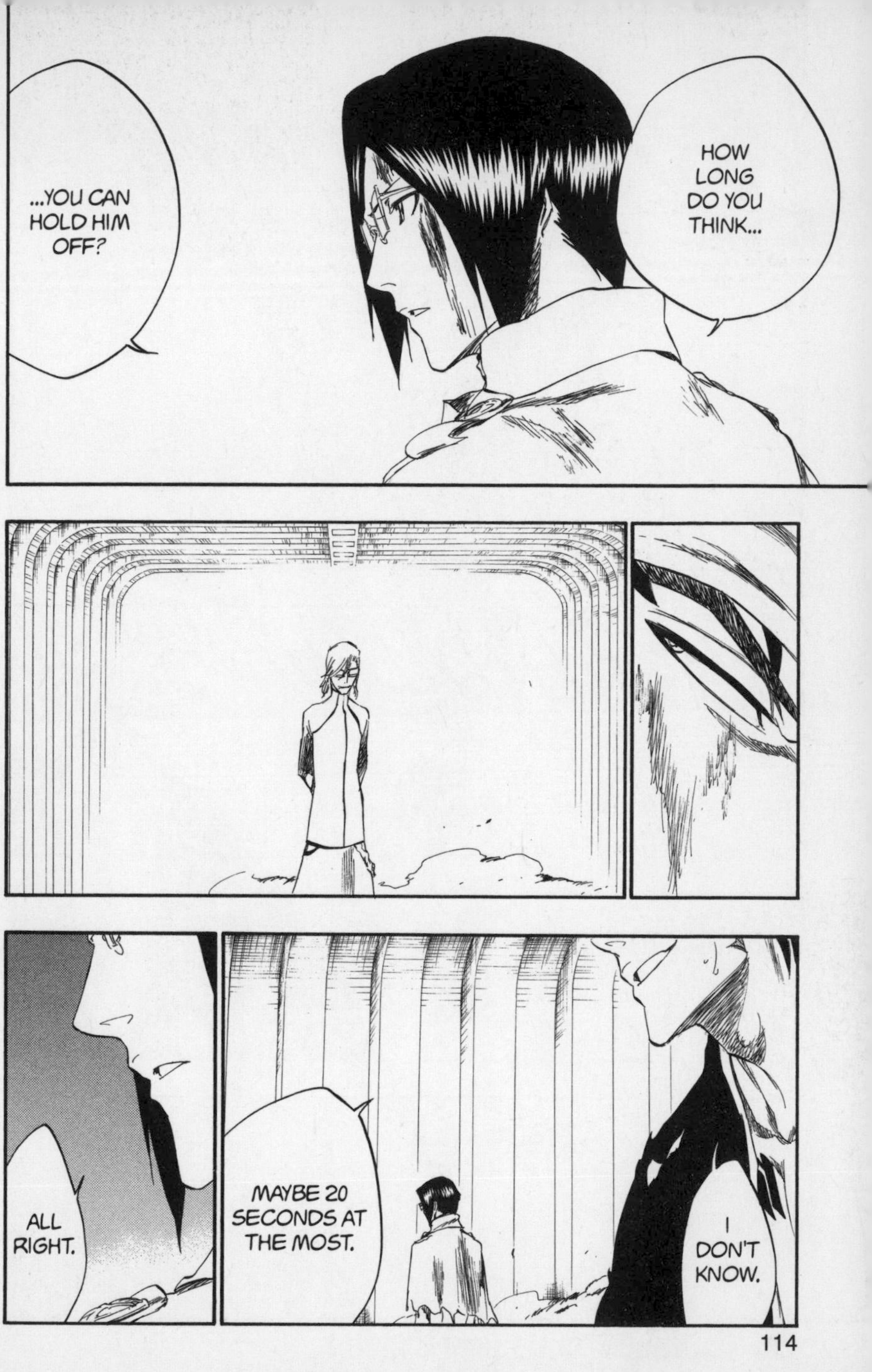
HOW LONG DO YOU THINK...
...YOU CAN HOLD HIM OFF?
I DON'T KNOW.
MAYBE 20 SECONDS AT THE MOST.
ALL RIGHT.

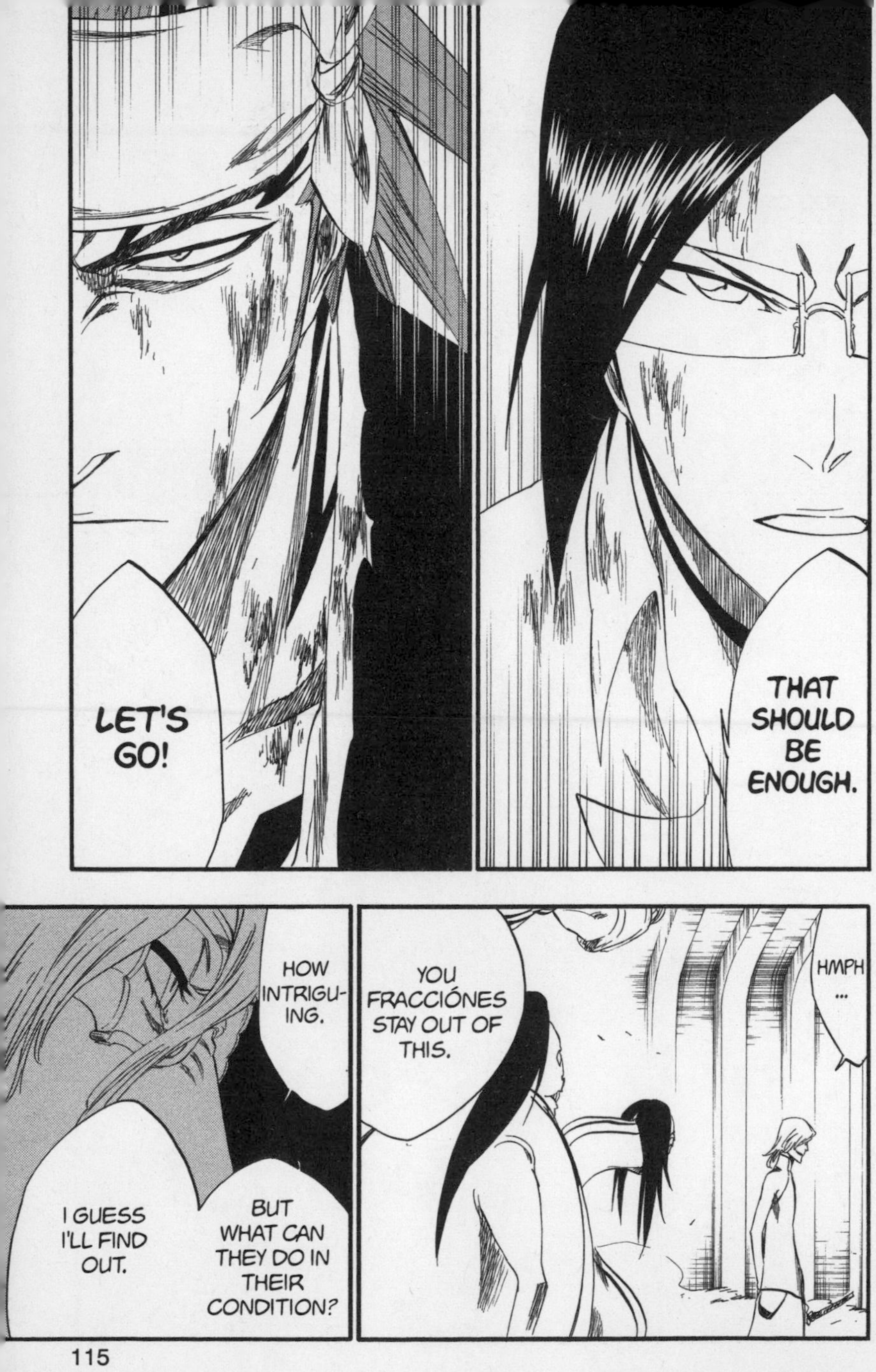
THAT SHOULD BE ENOUGH.
LET'S GO!
HMPH ...
YOU FRACCIÓNES STAY OUT OF THIS.
HOW INTRIGU-ING.
BUT WHAT CAN THEY DO IN THEIR CONDITION?
I GUESS I'LL FIND OUT.

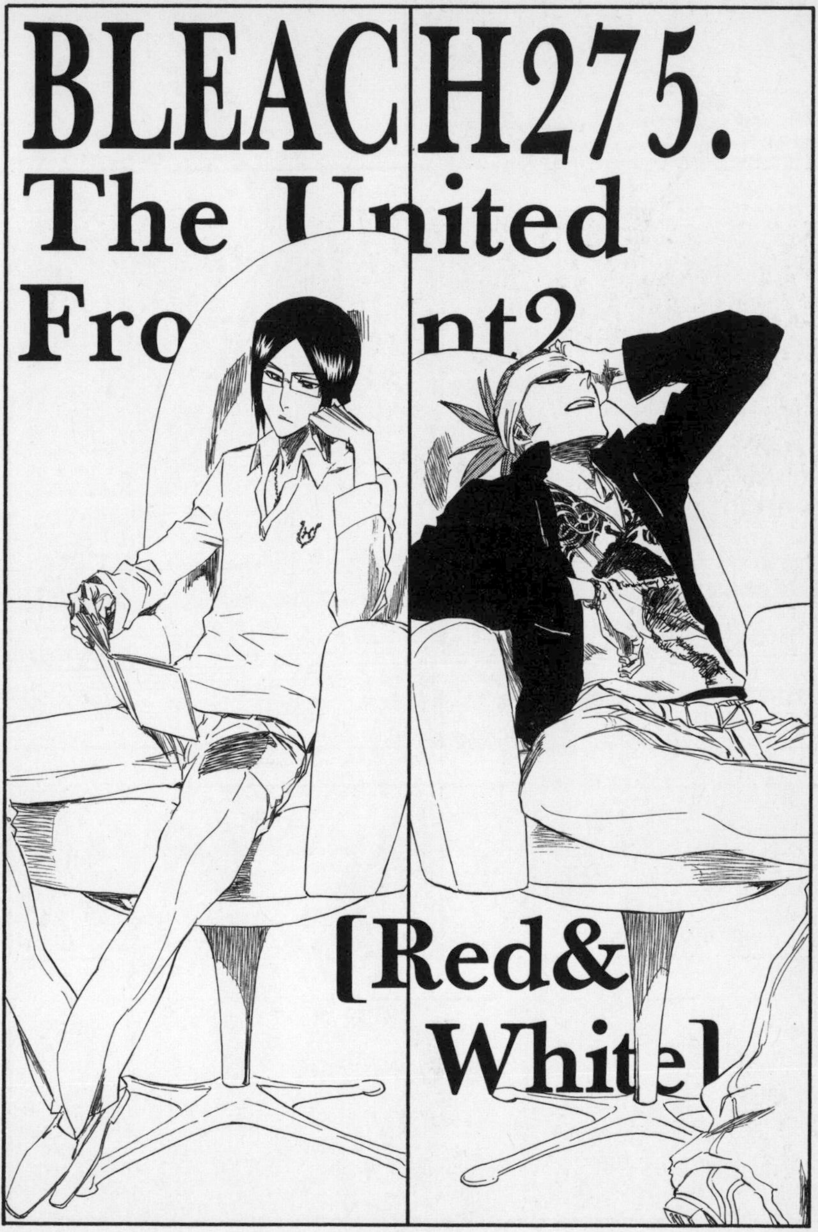
BLEACH275.
The United
Fro nt2
[Red&
White]

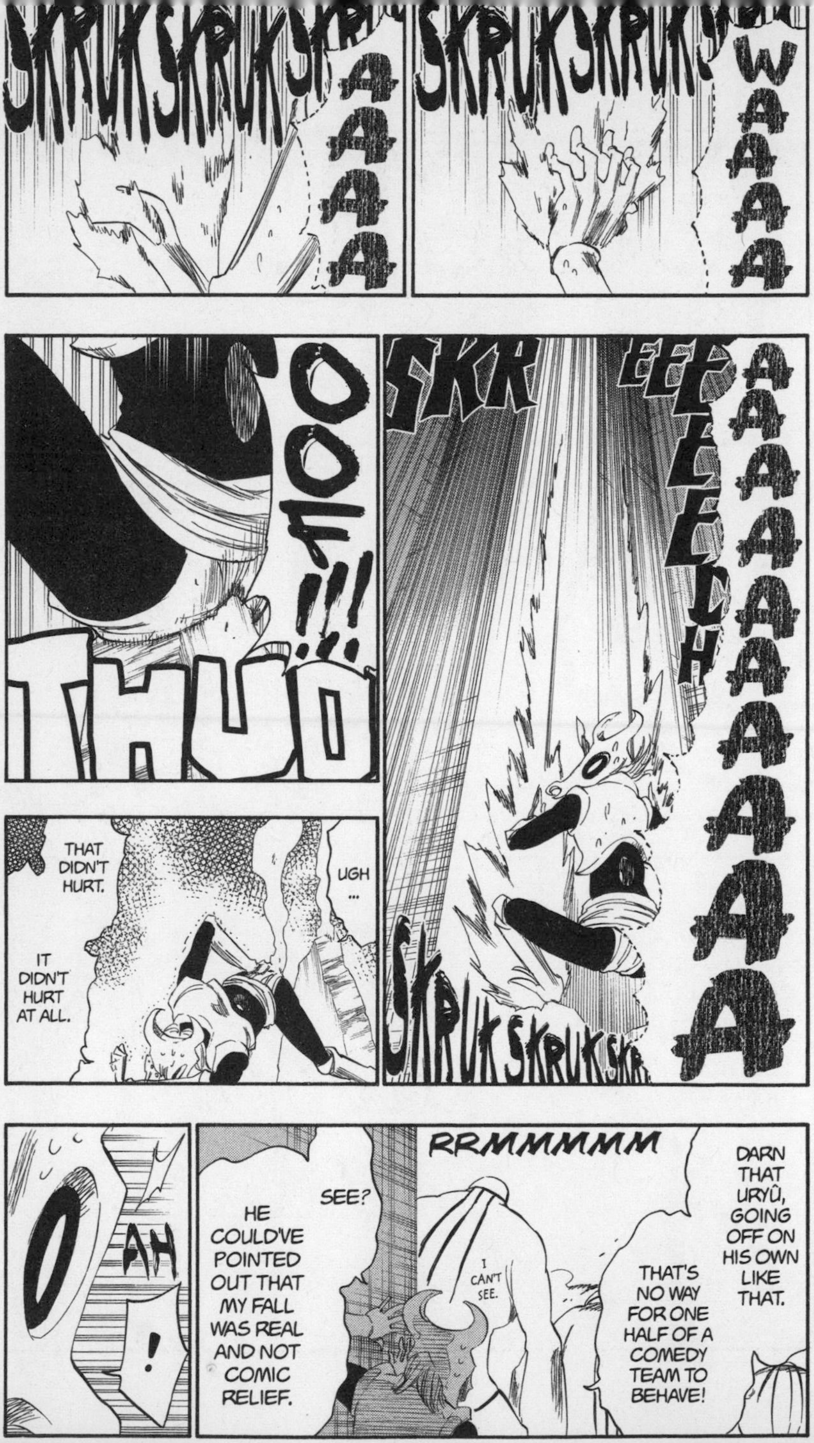
SKRUKSKRUKSKR
WAAAAAA
SKRUKSKRUKSKR
AAAA
SKR
EEEEEEH
AAAAAAAAAAAA
SKRUK SKRUK SKR
OOOF!!!
THUD
THAT DIDN'T HURT.
UGH...
IT DIDN'T HURT AT ALL.
RRMMMMMM
DARN THAT URYÛ, GOING OFF ON HIS OWN LIKE THAT.
THAT'S NO WAY FOR ONE HALF OF A COMEDY TEAM TO BEHAVE!
I CAN'T SEE.
SEE?
HE COULD'VE POINTED OUT THAT MY FALL WAS REAL AND NOT COMIC RELIEF.
O
AH
!

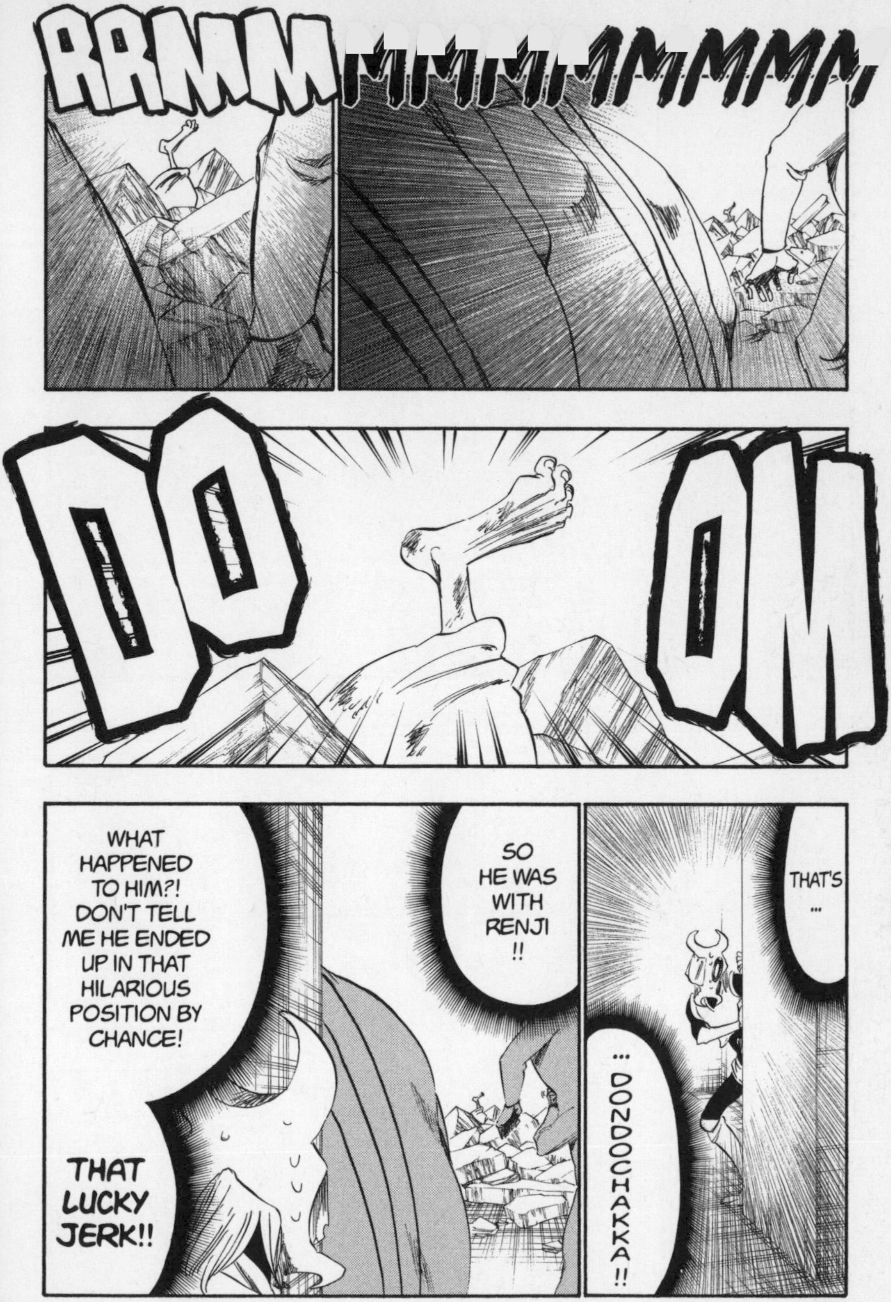
RRMMMMMMMMMMMMM
DOOM
THAT'S ...
... DONDOCHAKKA!!
SO HE WAS WITH RENJI !!
WHAT HAPPENED TO HIM?! DON'T TELL ME HE ENDED UP IN THAT HILARIOUS POSITION BY CHANCE!
THAT LUCKY JERK!!

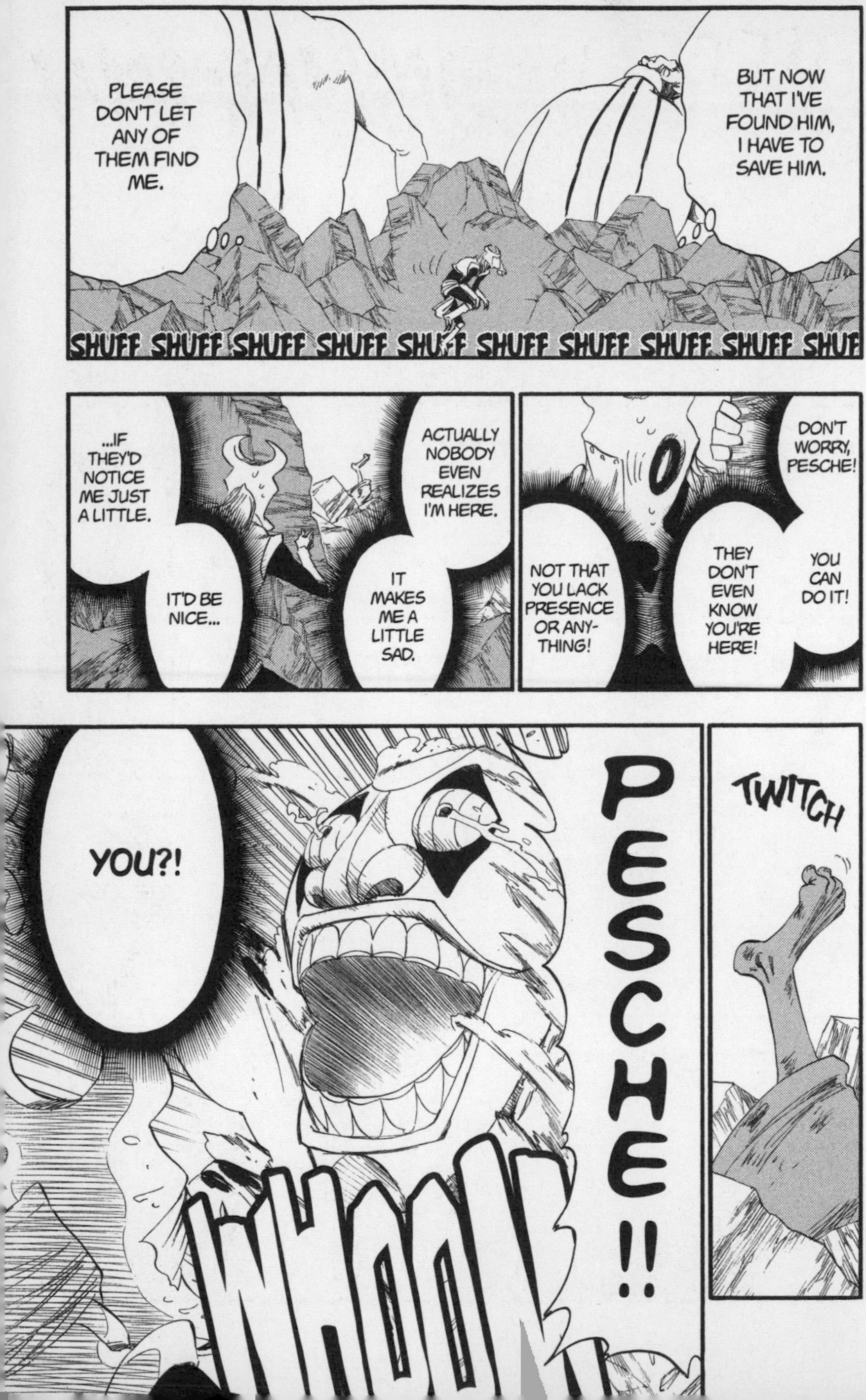
BUT NOW THAT I'VE FOUND HIM, I HAVE TO SAVE HIM.
PLEASE DON'T LET ANY OF THEM FIND ME.
SHUFF SHUFF SHUFF SHUFF SHUFF SHUFF SHUFF SHUFF SHUFF SHUF
DON'T WORRY, PESCHE!
YOU CAN DO IT!
THEY DON'T EVEN KNOW YOU'RE HERE!
NOT THAT YOU LACK PRESENCE OR ANY-THING!
ACTUALLY NOBODY EVEN REALIZES I'M HERE.
IT MAKES ME A LITTLE SAD.
...IF THEY'D NOTICE ME JUST A LITTLE.
IT'D BE NICE...
TWITCH
PESCHE!!
YOU?!
WHOOM

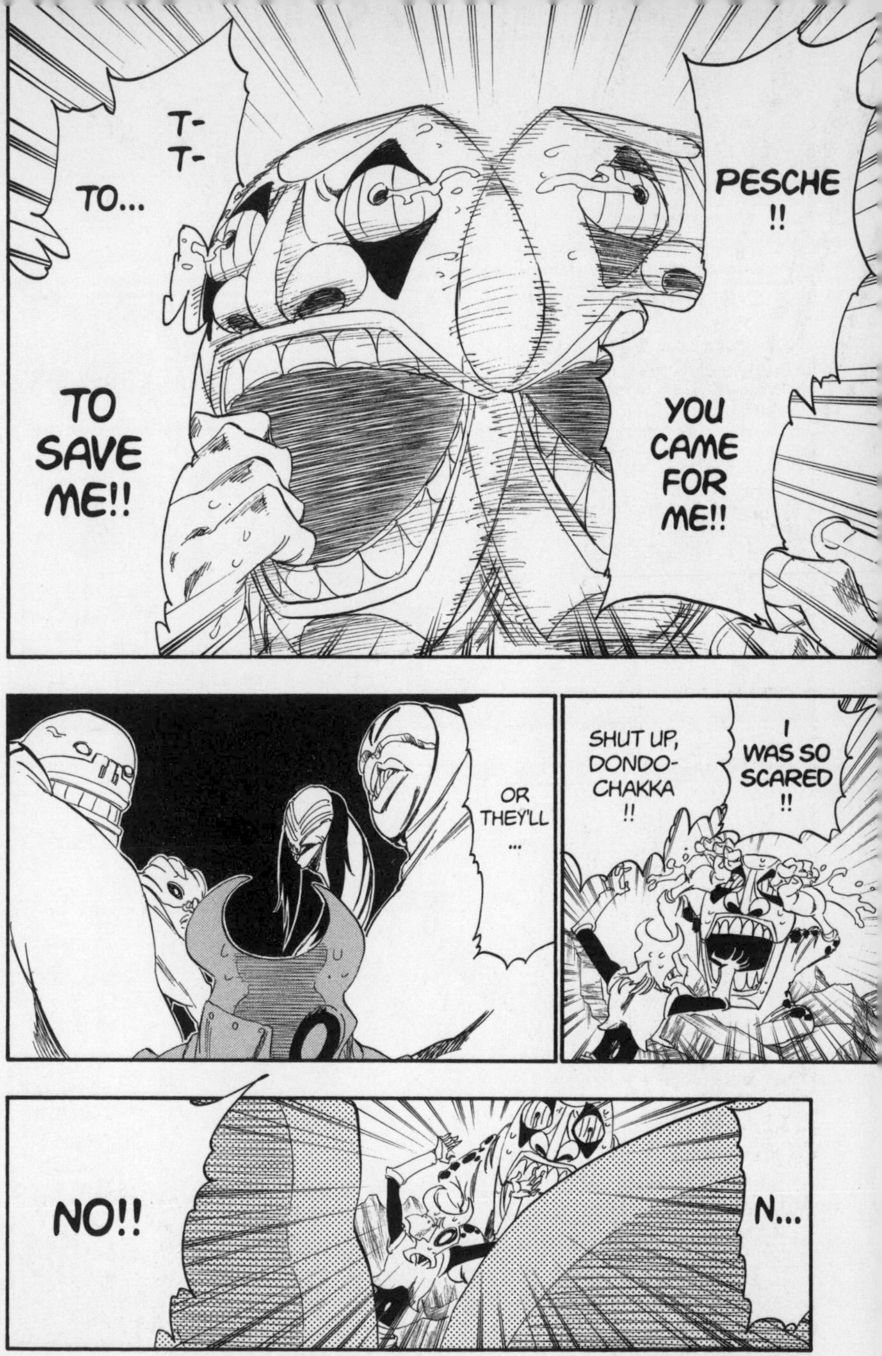
PESCHE!!
YOU CAME FOR ME!!
T-T-TO...
TO SAVE ME!!
I WAS SO SCARED!!
SHUT UP, DONDO-CHAKKA!!
OR THEY'LL...
N...
NO!!

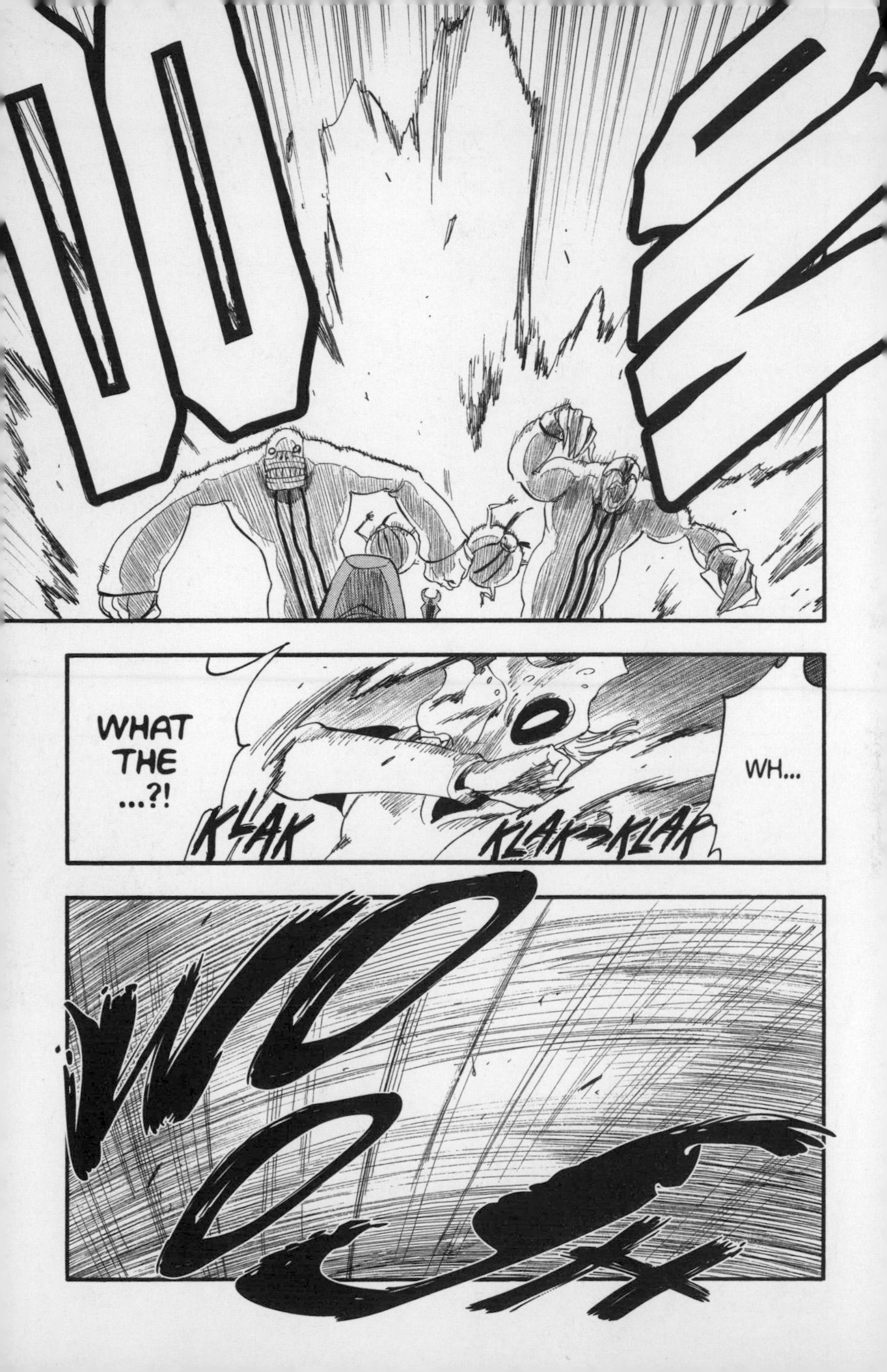
WH...
WHAT THE ...?!
KLAK KLAK
KLAK

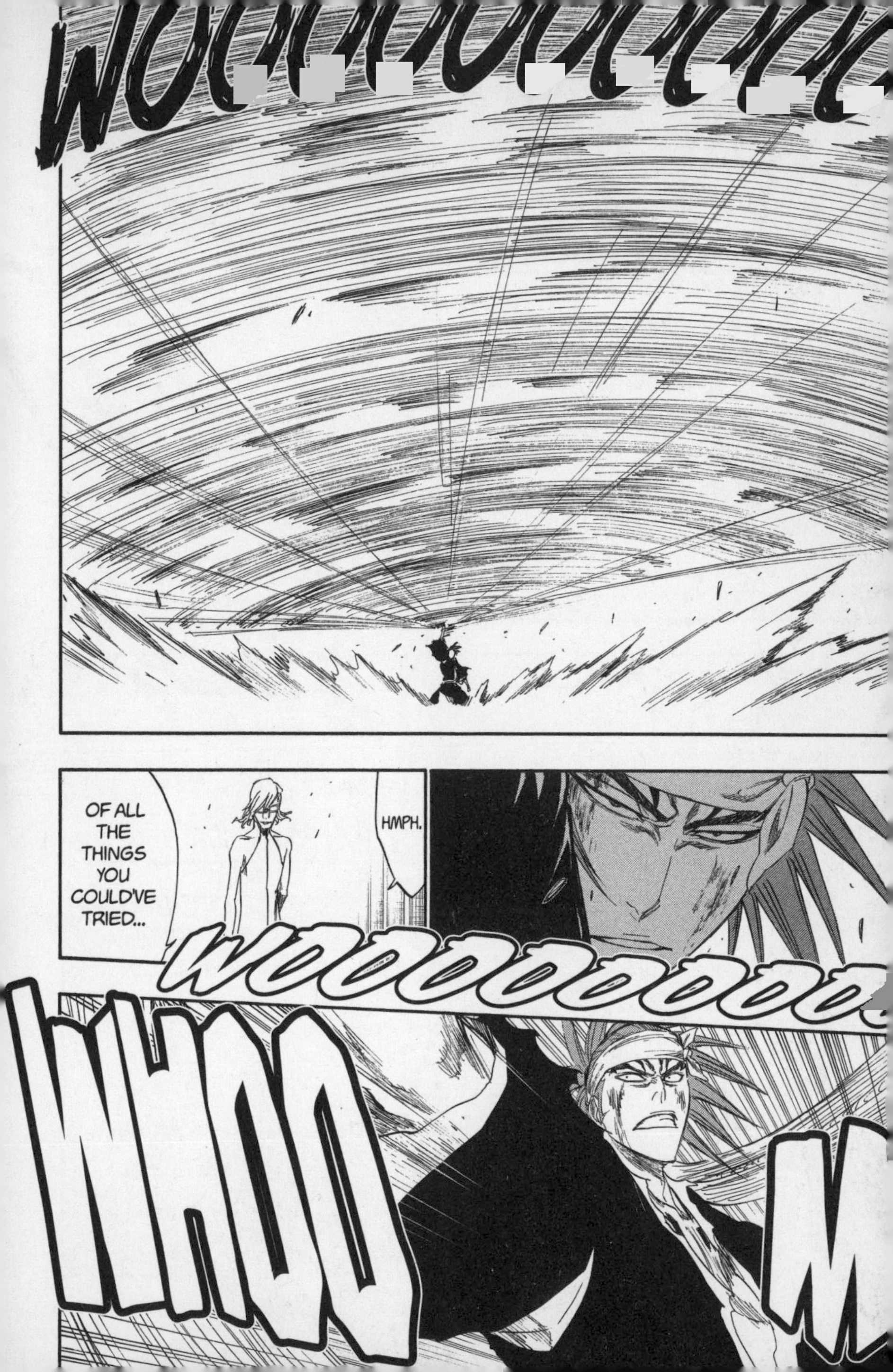
HMPH.
OF ALL THE THINGS YOU COULD'VE TRIED...
WHOOM

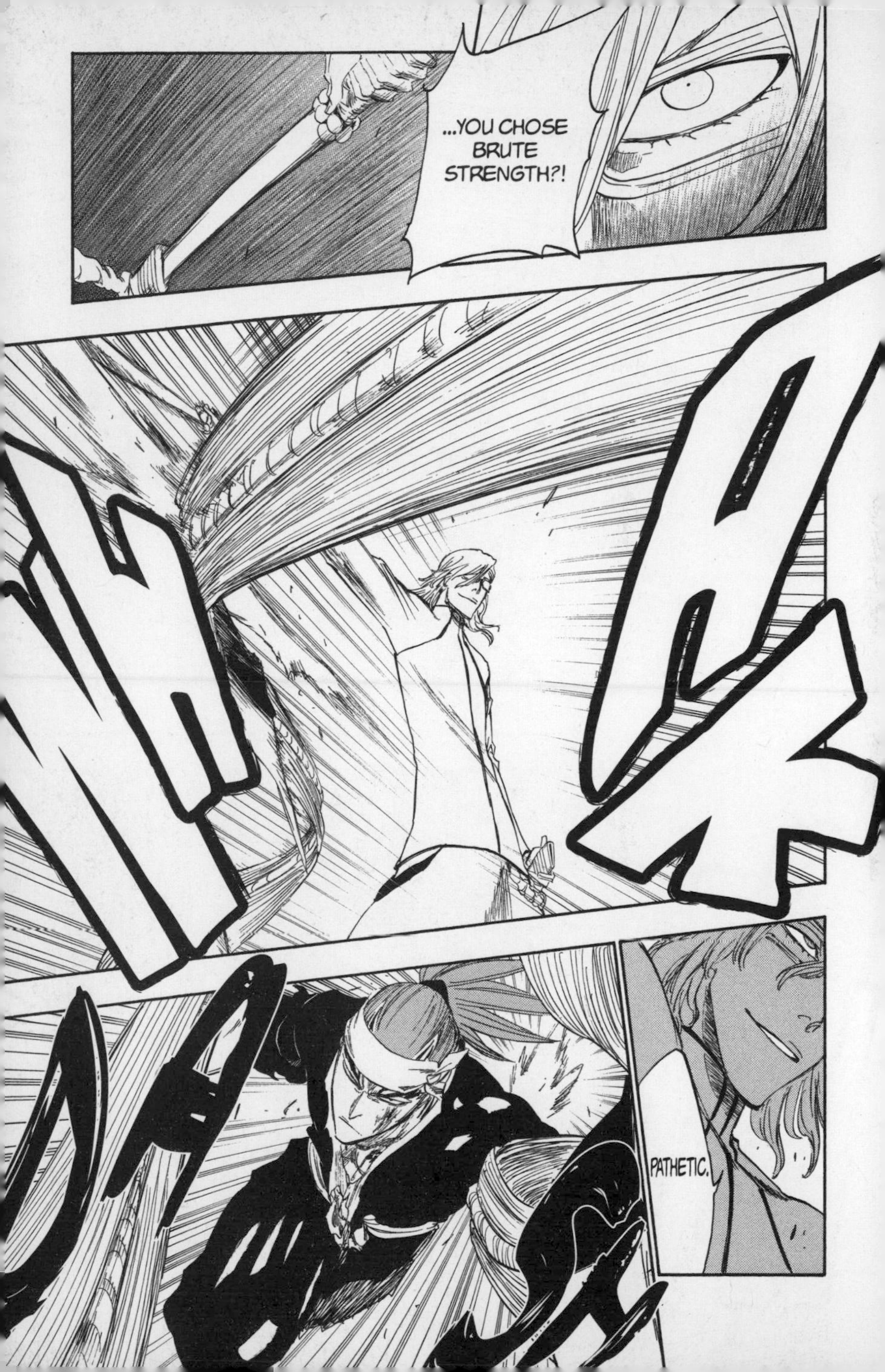
...YOU CHOSE BRUTE STRENGTH?!
PATHETIC.

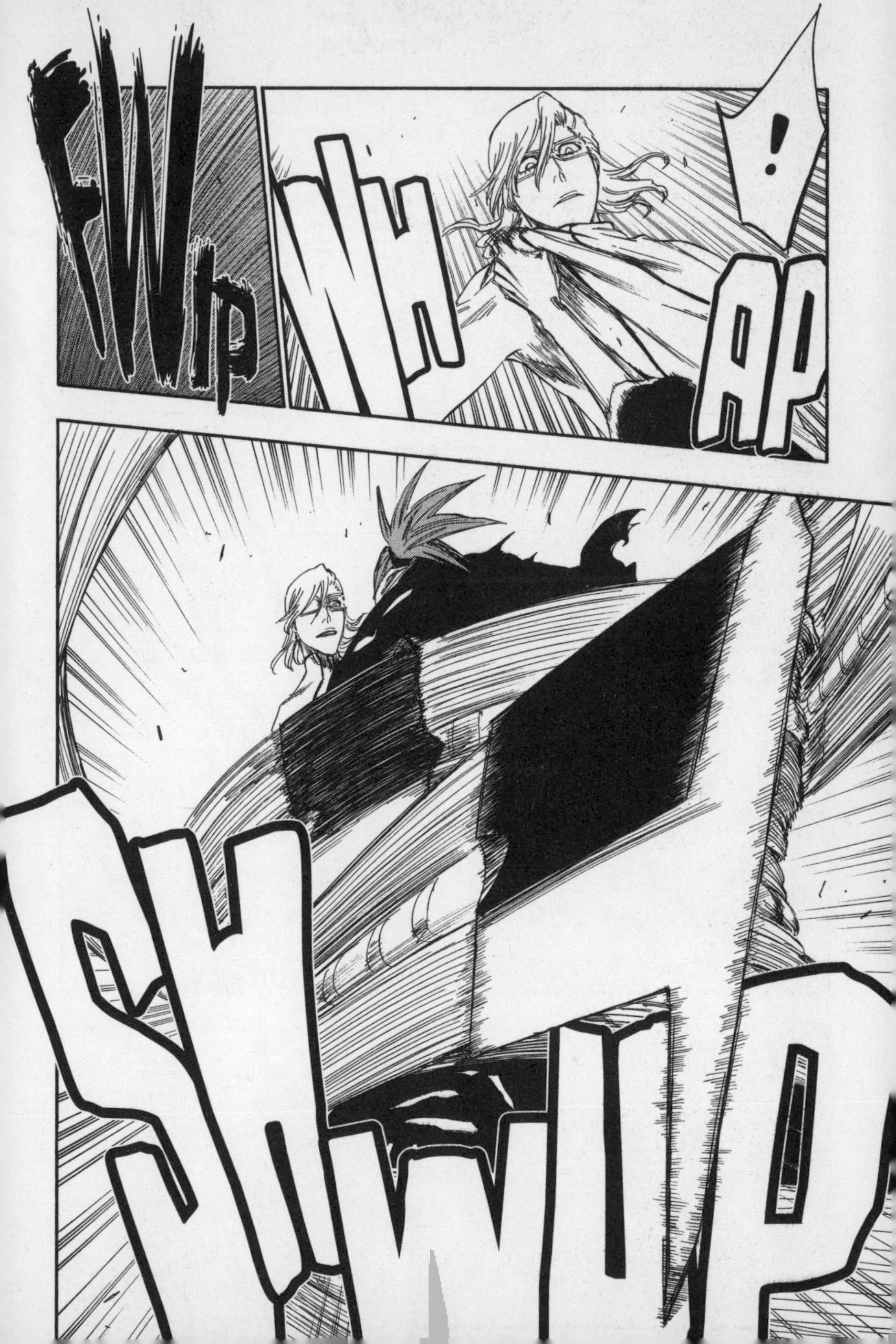
!
WHAP

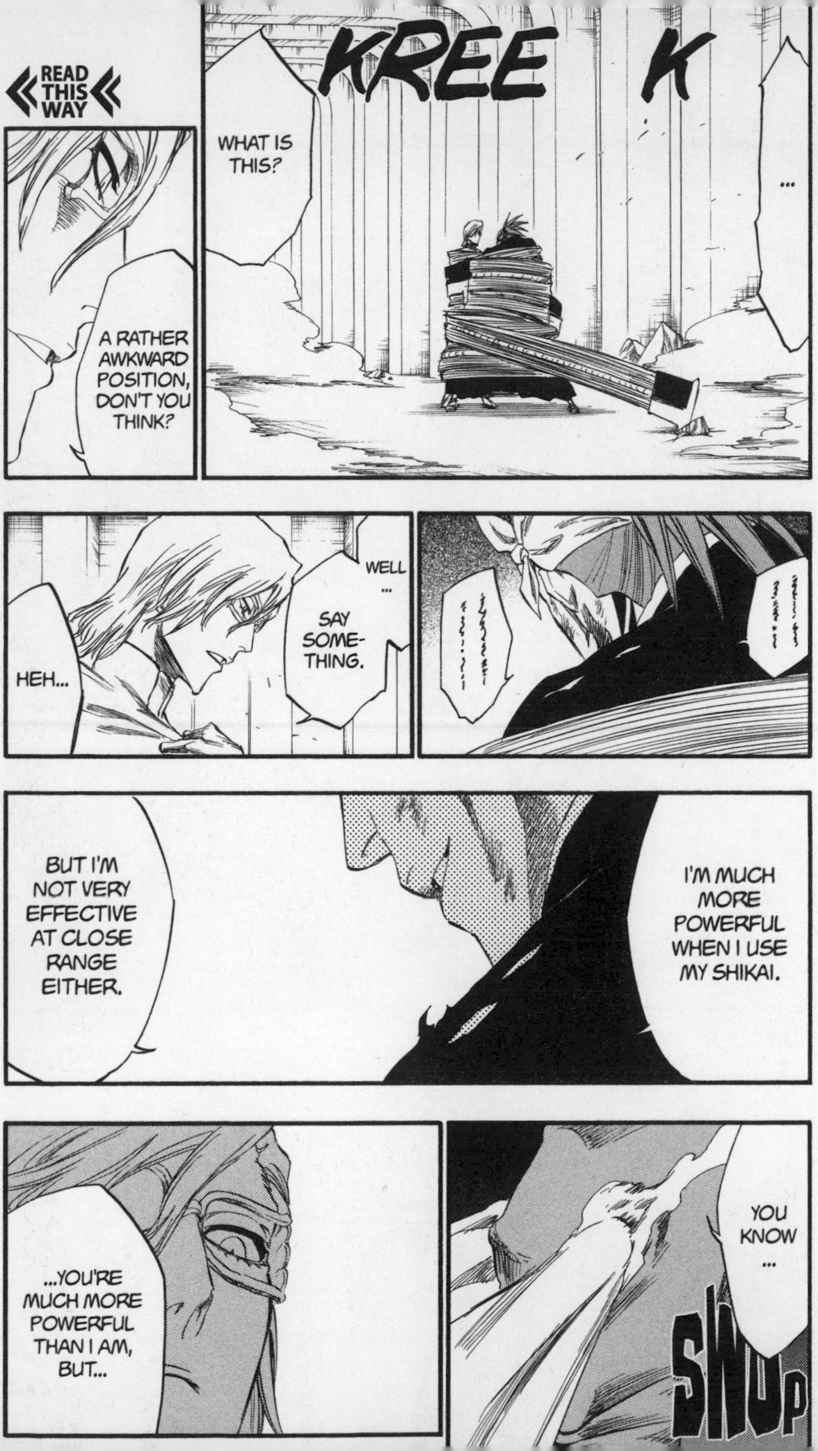
READ THIS WAY
KREE K
...
WHAT IS THIS?
A RATHER AWKWARD POSITION, DON'T YOU THINK?
WELL ...
SAY SOME-THING.
HEH...
I'M MUCH MORE POWERFUL WHEN I USE MY SHIKAI.
BUT I'M NOT VERY EFFECTIVE AT CLOSE RANGE EITHER.
YOU KNOW ...
SNUP
...YOU'RE MUCH MORE POWERFUL THAN I AM, BUT...

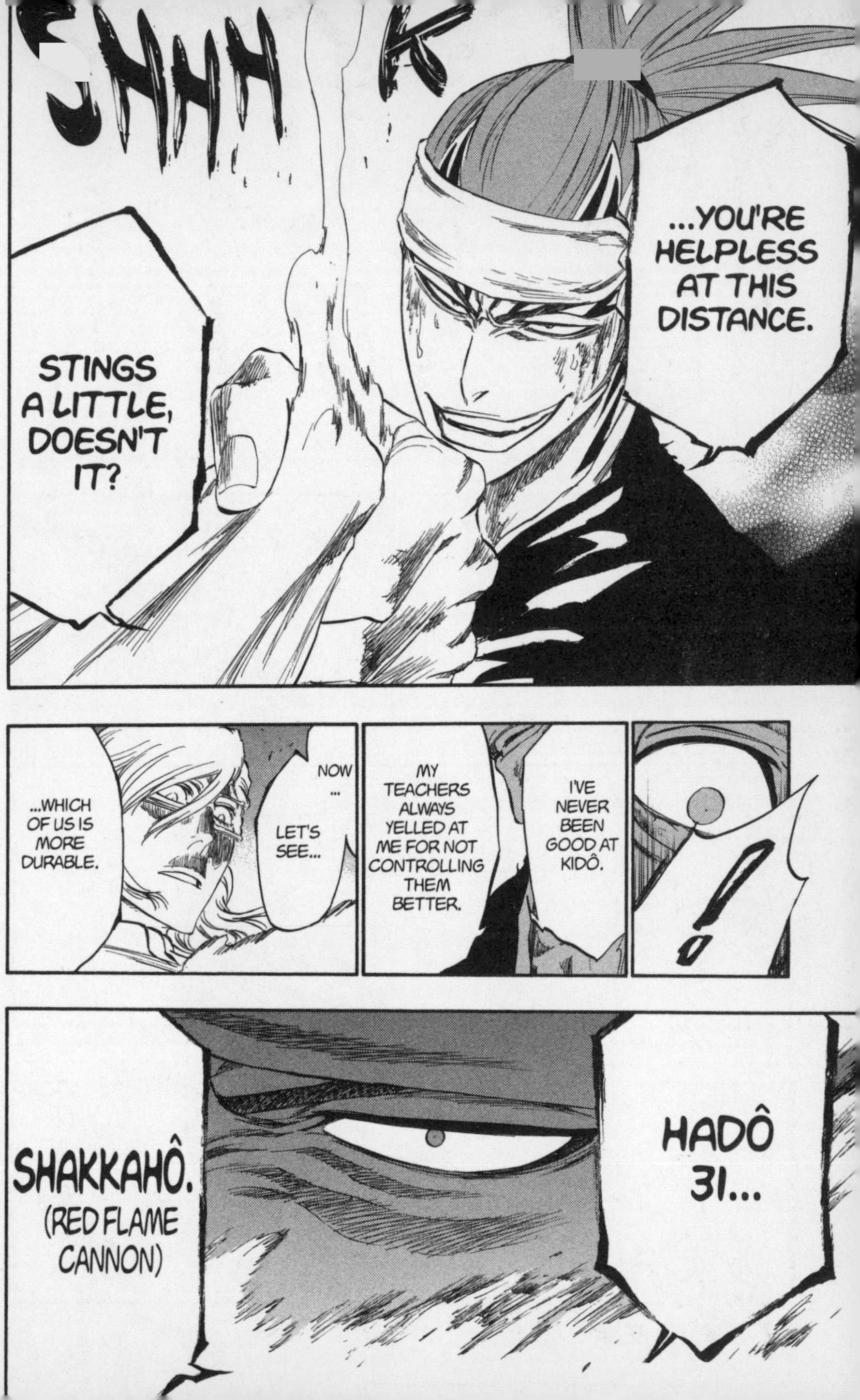
SHHHK
...YOU'RE HELPLESS AT THIS DISTANCE.
STINGS A LITTLE, DOESN'T IT?
!
I'VE NEVER BEEN GOOD AT KIDÔ.
MY TEACHERS ALWAYS YELLED AT ME FOR NOT CONTROLLING THEM BETTER.
NOW... LET'S SEE...
...WHICH OF US IS MORE DURABLE.
HADÔ 31...
SHAKKAHÔ.
(RED FLAME CANNON)

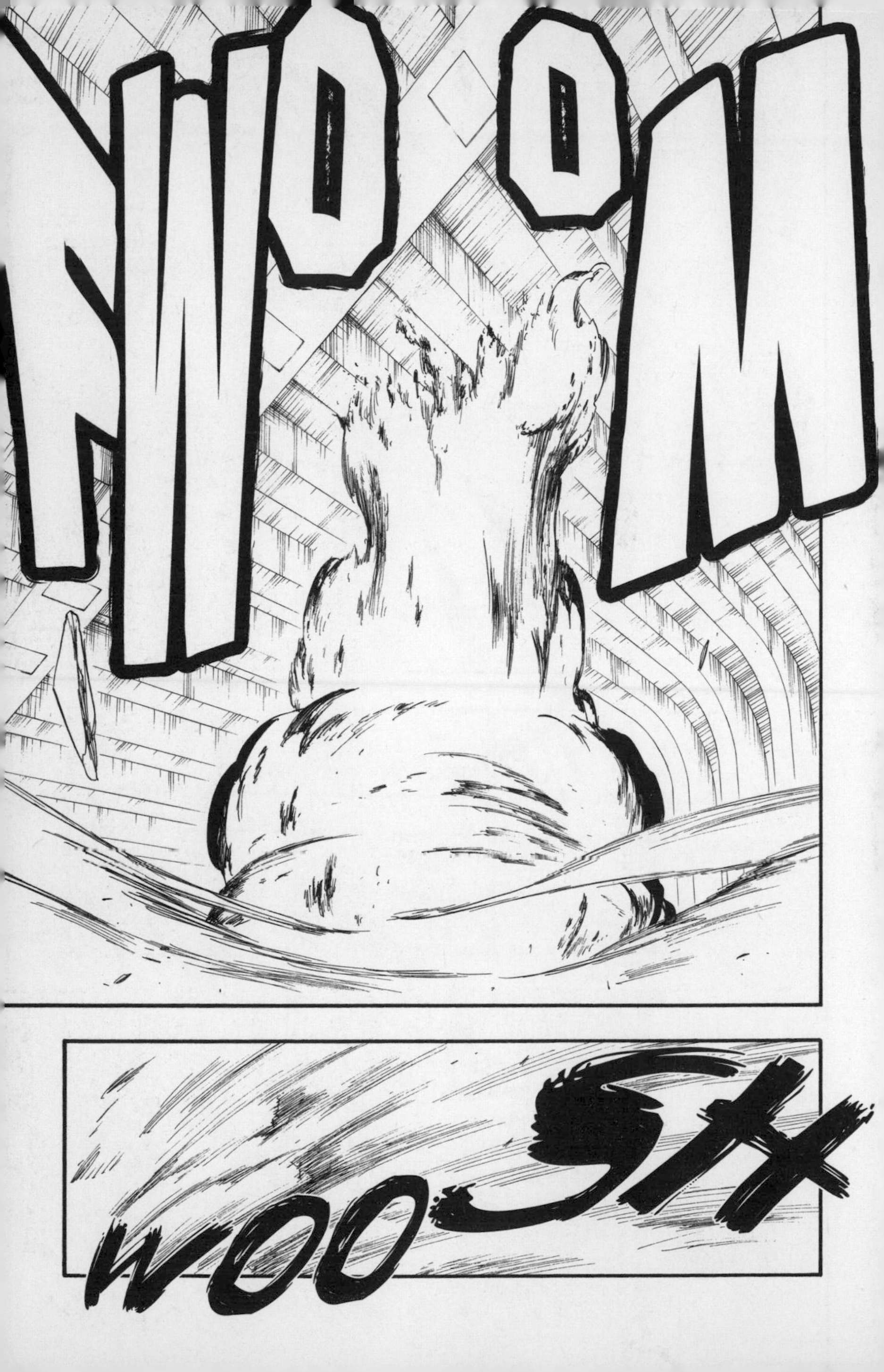
FWOOM
WOOSH

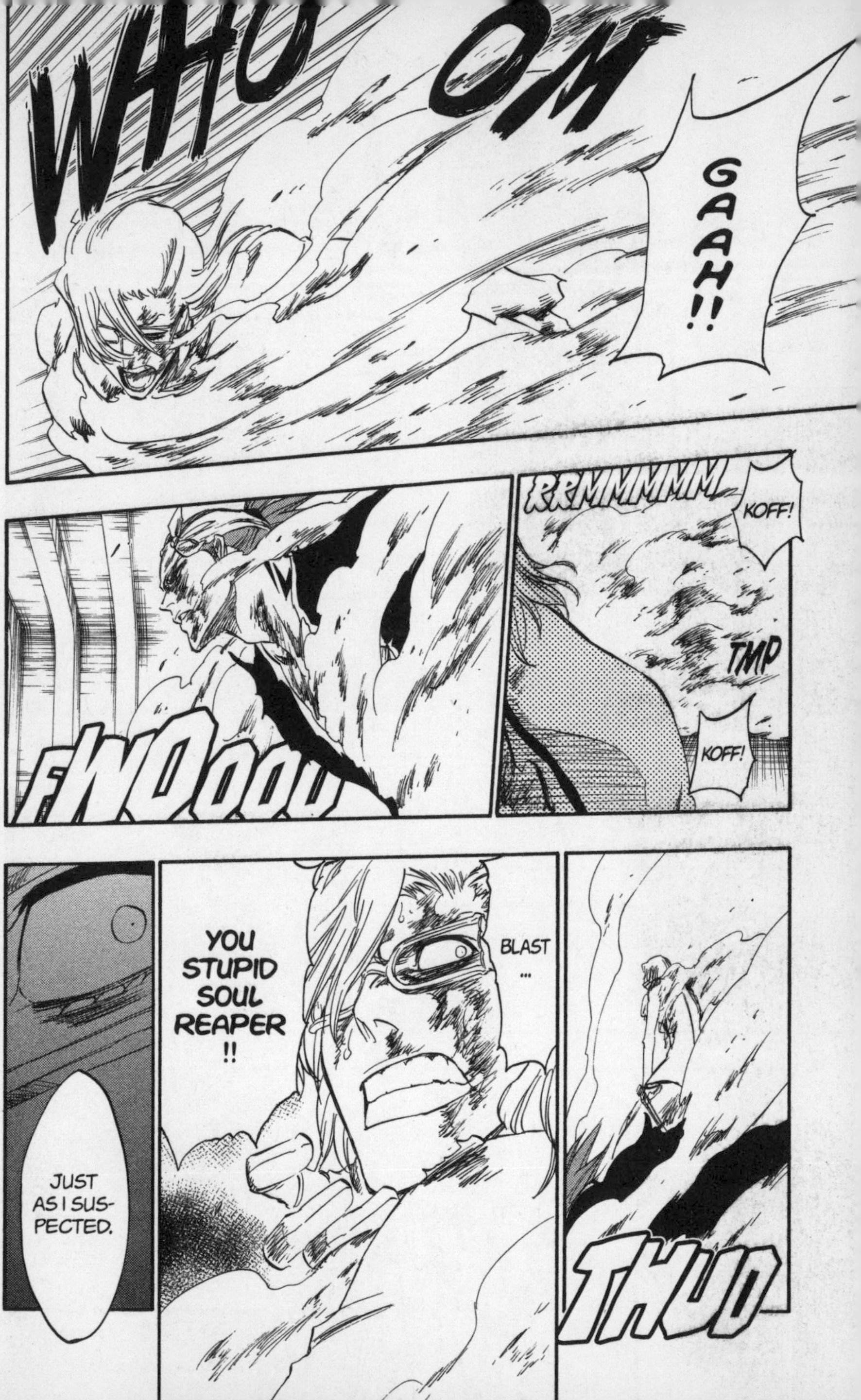
WHOOM
GAAH!!
RRMMMMM
KOFF!
TMP
KOFF!
FWOOOO
THUD
BLAST...
YOU STUPID SOUL REAPER!!
JUST AS I SUSPECTED.

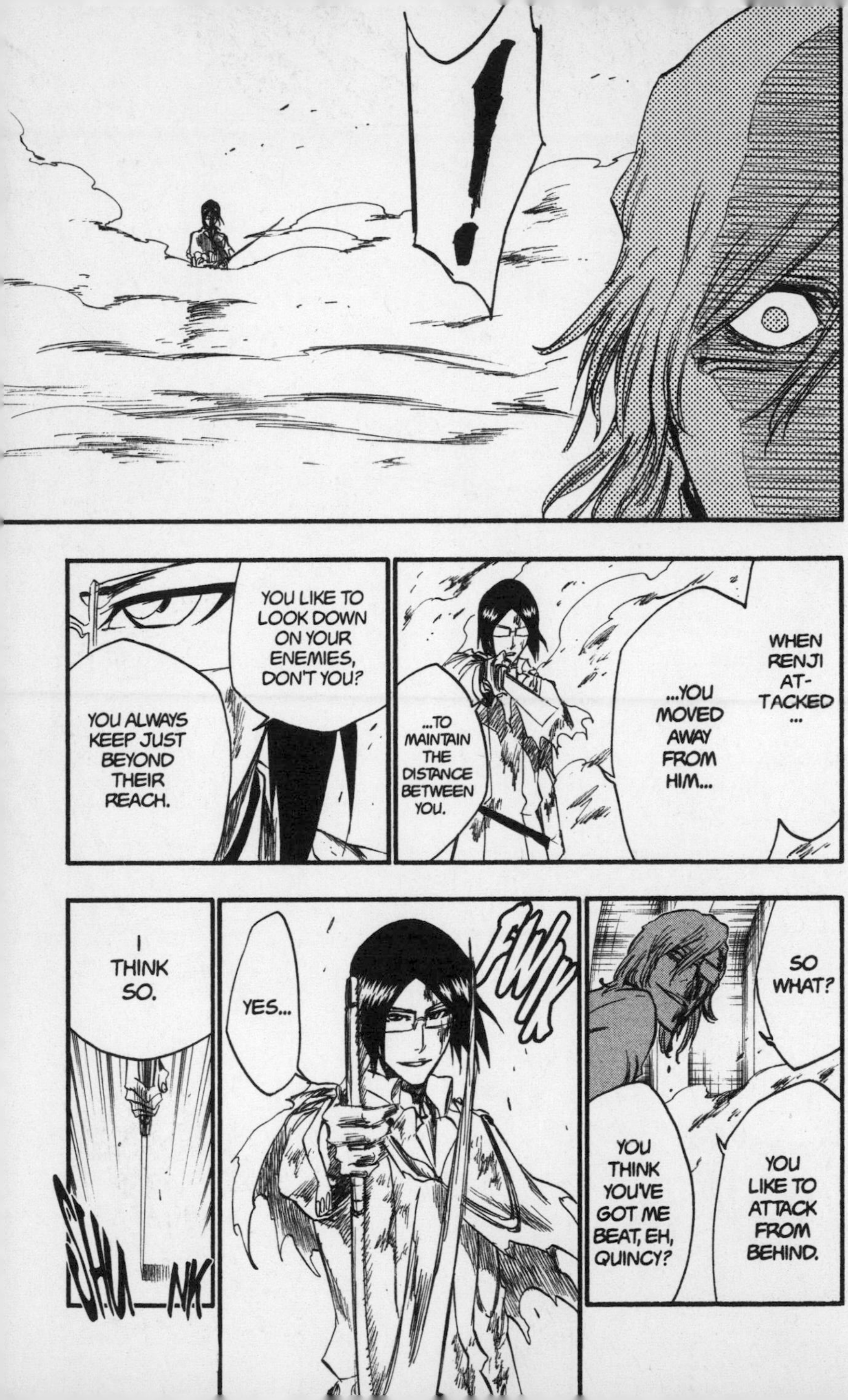
!
WHEN RENJI AT-TACKED...
...YOU MOVED AWAY FROM HIM...
...TO MAINTAIN THE DISTANCE BETWEEN YOU.
YOU LIKE TO LOOK DOWN ON YOUR ENEMIES, DON'T YOU?
YOU ALWAYS KEEP JUST BEYOND THEIR REACH.
SO WHAT?
YOU LIKE TO ATTACK FROM BEHIND.
YOU THINK YOU'VE GOT ME BEAT, EH, QUINCY?
YES...
I THINK SO.
SHUNK

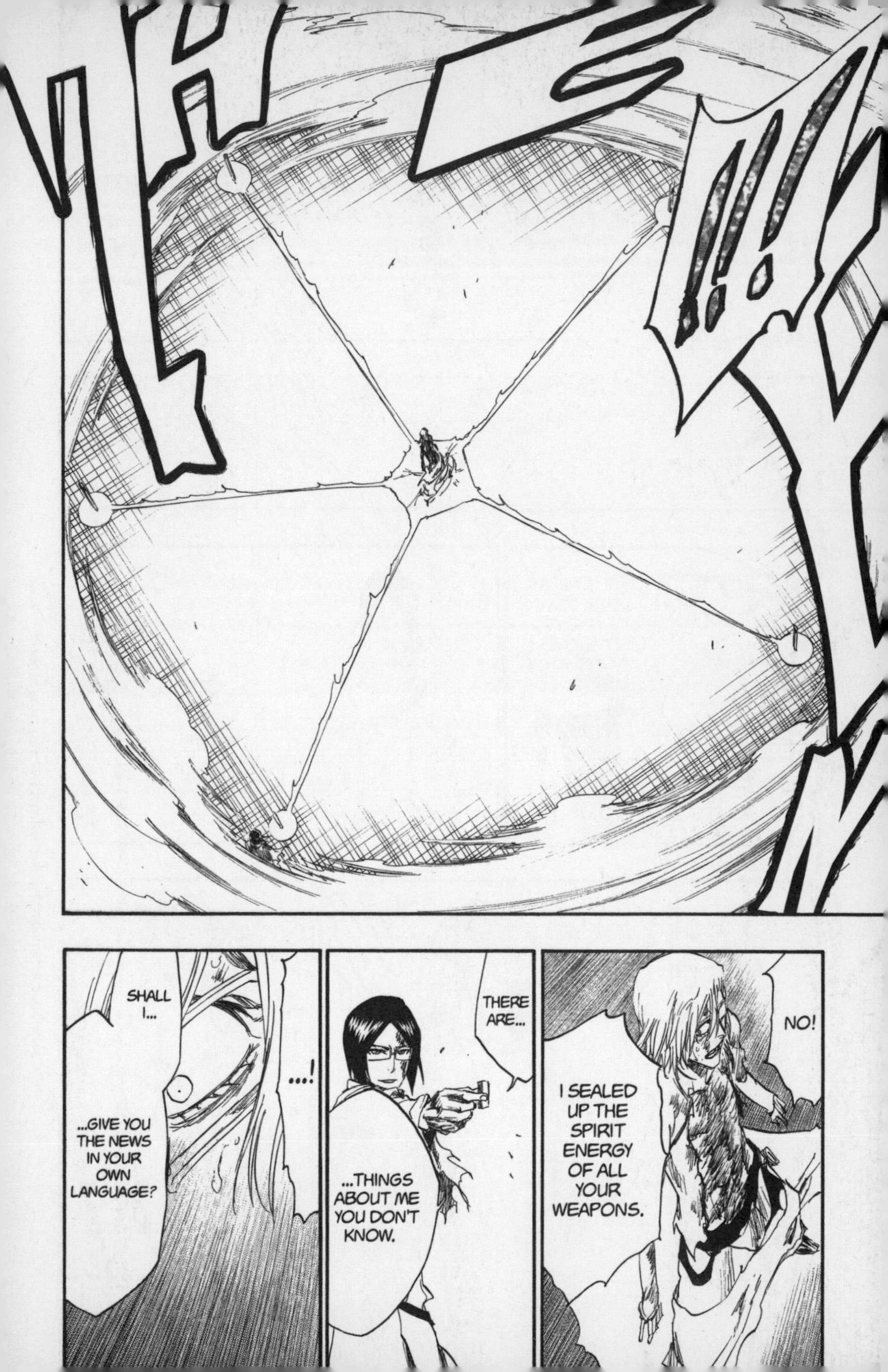
NO!
I SEALED UP THE SPIRIT ENERGY OF ALL YOUR WEAPONS.
THERE ARE...
...!
...THINGS ABOUT ME YOU DON'T KNOW.
SHALL I...
...GIVE YOU THE NEWS IN YOUR OWN LANGUAGE?

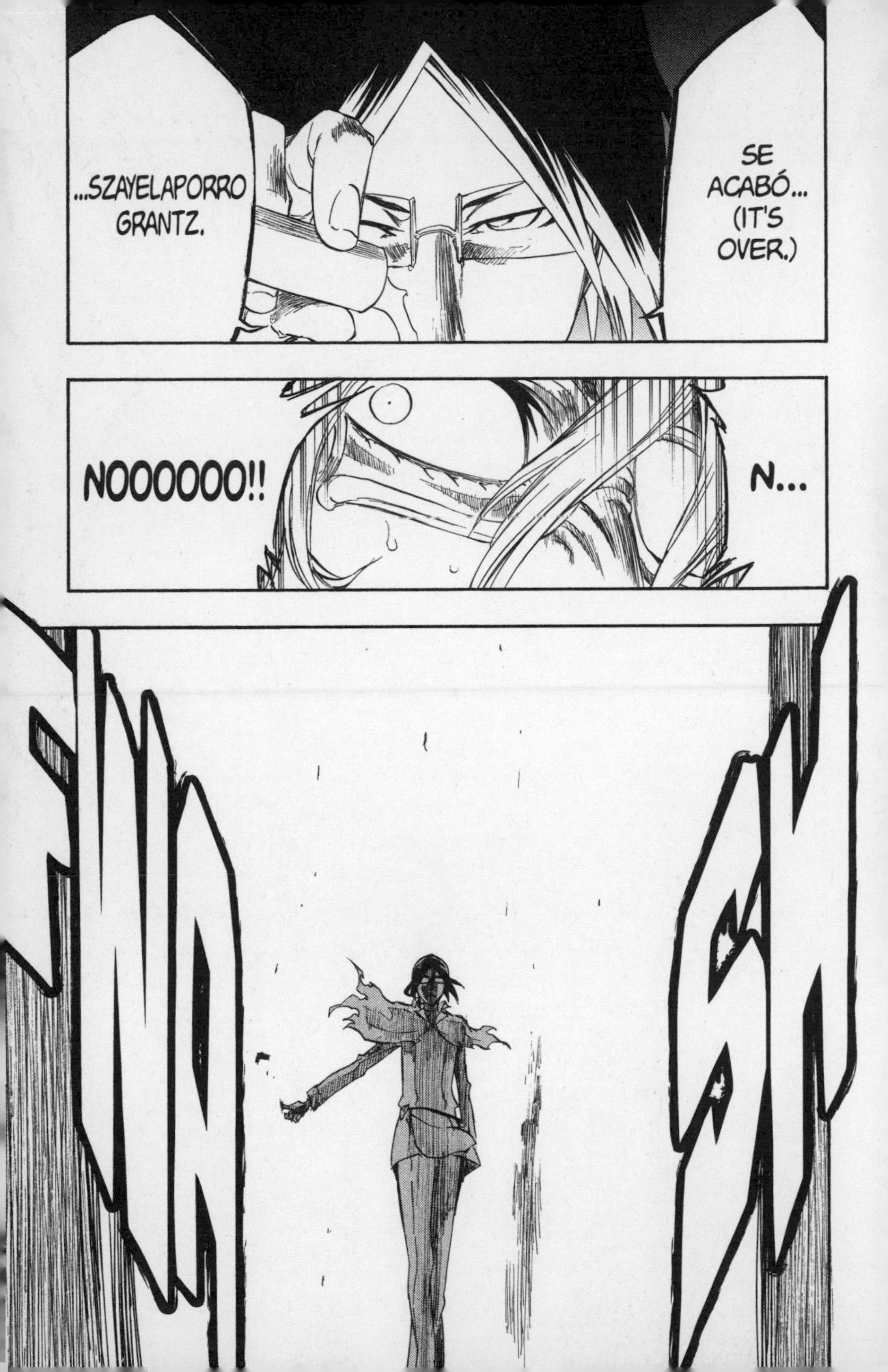
SE ACABÓ... (IT'S OVER.)
...SZAYELAPORRO GRANTZ.
N...
NOOOOOO!!

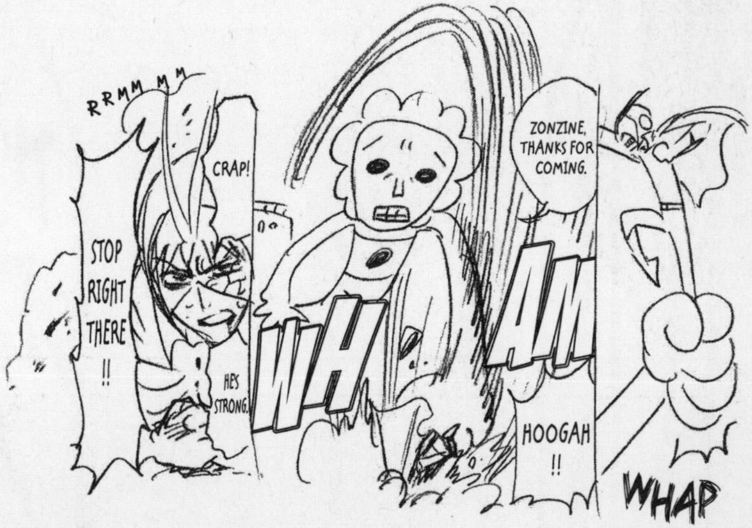
WHAP
ZONZINE, THANKS FOR COMING.
HOOGAH !!
WHAM
CRAP!
HE'S STRONG.
RRMMMMM
STOP RIGHT THERE !!

276. Blockin' Beast

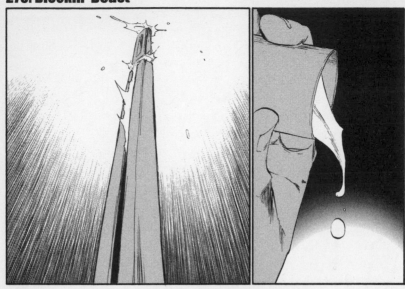

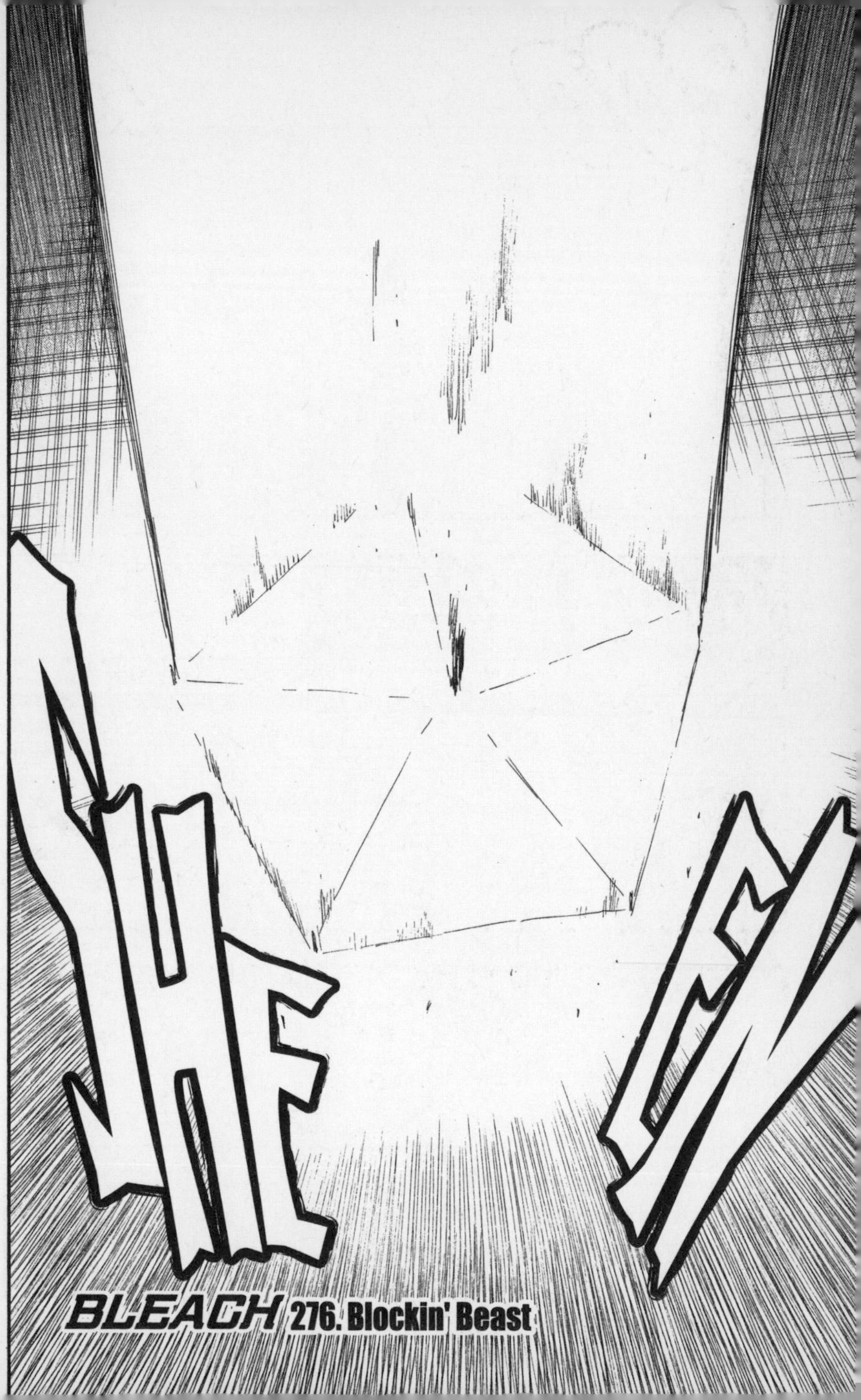
BLEACH 276. Blockin' Beast

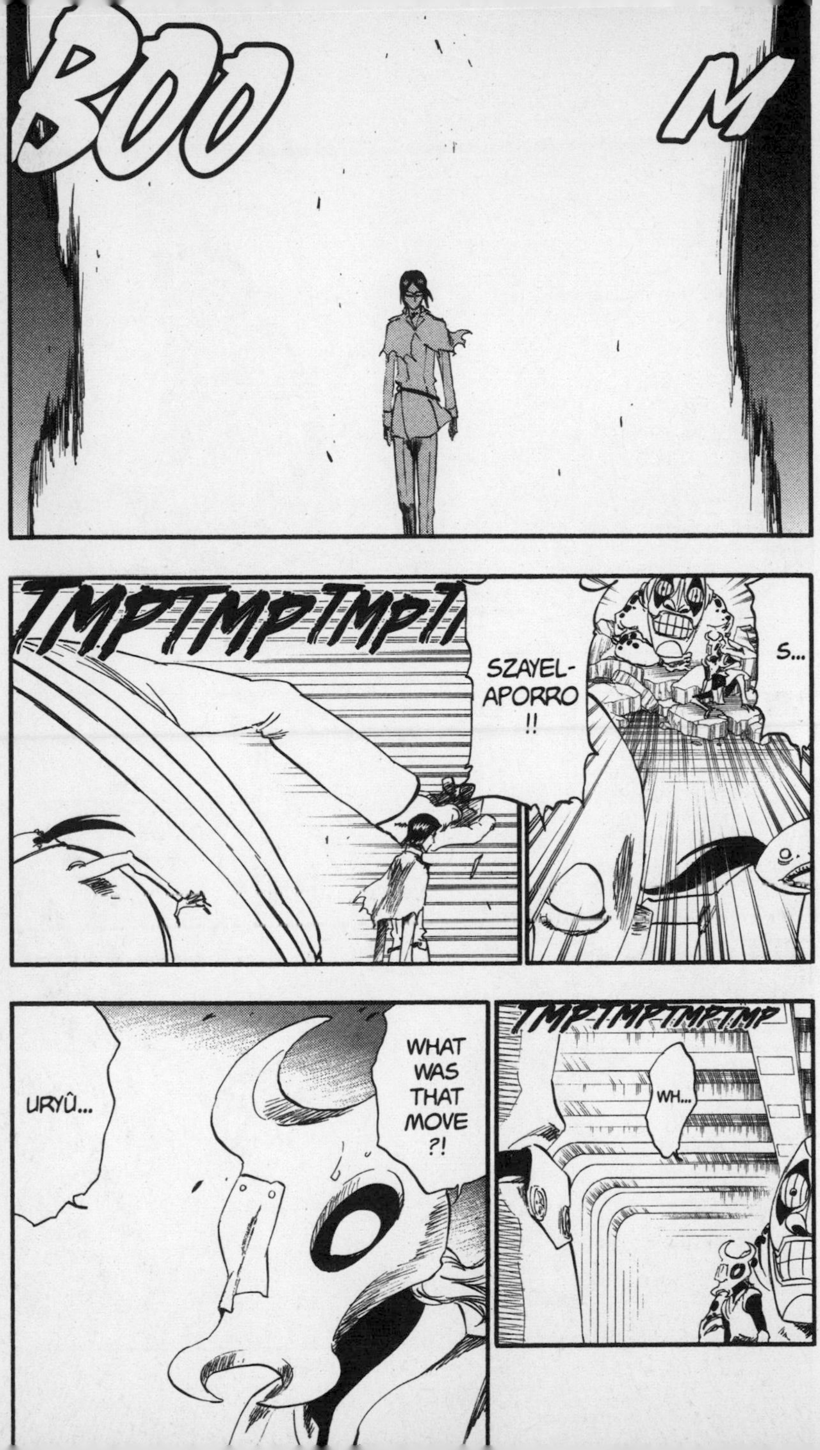
BOOM
S...
SZAYEL-APORRO !!
TMPTMPTMPT
TMPTMPTMPTMP
WH...
WHAT WAS THAT MOVE ?!
URYÛ...

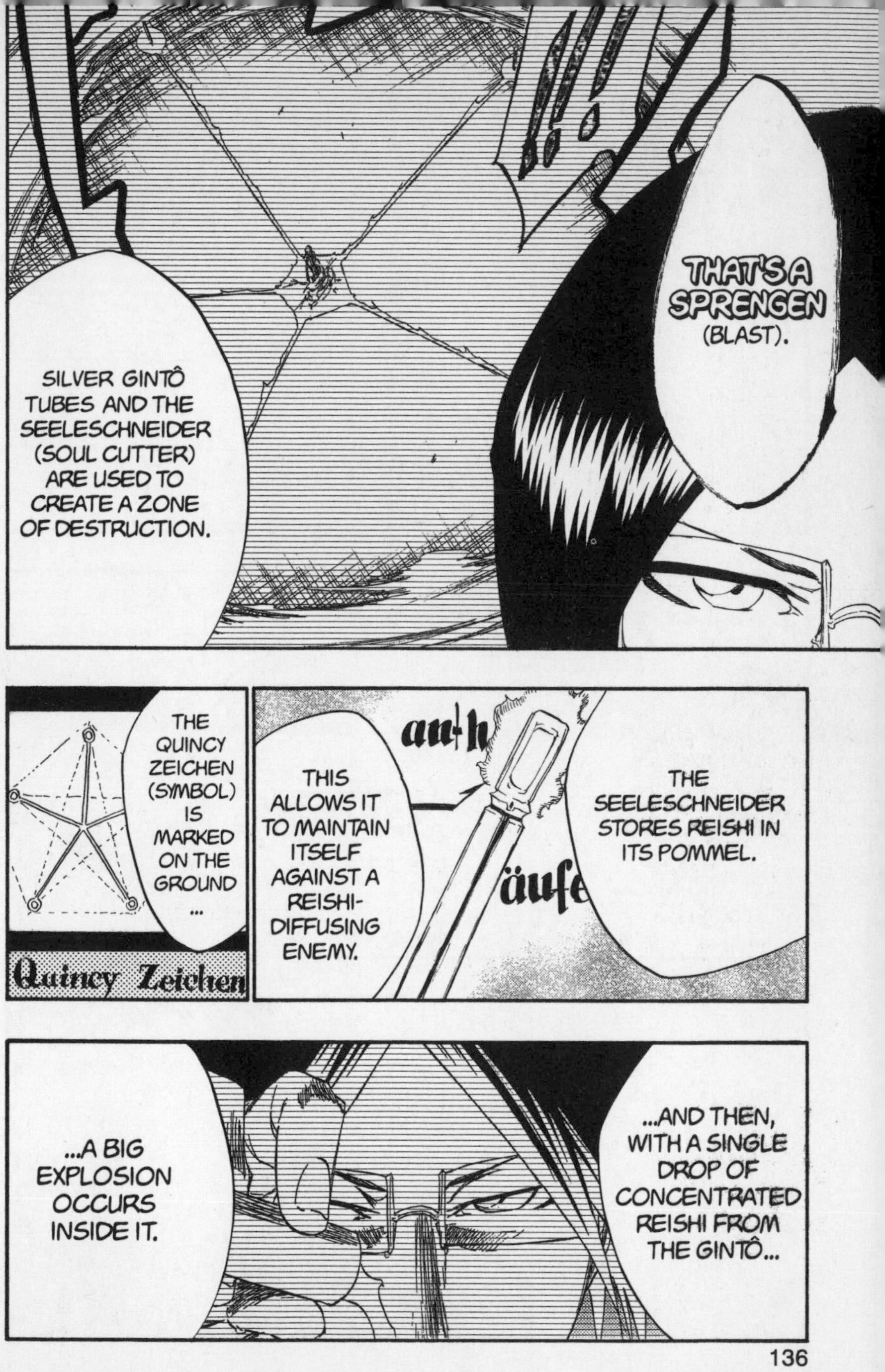
THAT'S A SPRENGEN (BLAST).
SILVER GINTÔ TUBES AND THE SEELESCHNEIDER (SOUL CUTTER) ARE USED TO CREATE A ZONE OF DESTRUCTION.
THE SEELESCHNEIDER STORES REISHI IN ITS POMMEL.
THIS ALLOWS IT TO MAINTAIN ITSELF AGAINST A REISHI-DIFFUSING ENEMY.
THE QUINCY ZEICHEN (SYMBOL) IS MARKED ON THE GROUND ...
Quincy Zeichen
...AND THEN, WITH A SINGLE DROP OF CONCENTRATED REISHI FROM THE GINTÔ...
...A BIG EXPLOSION OCCURS INSIDE IT.

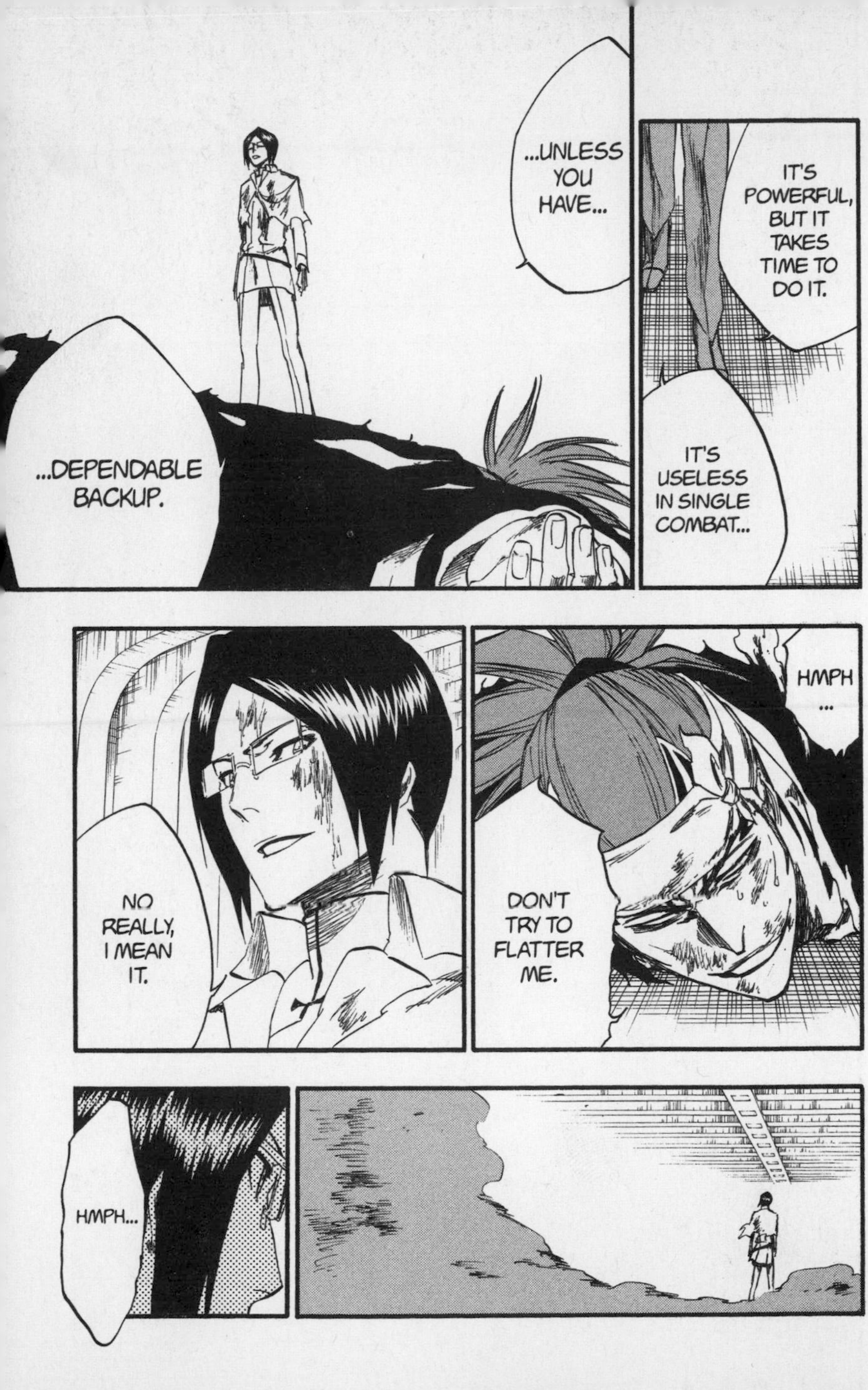
IT'S POWERFUL, BUT IT TAKES TIME TO DO IT.
IT'S USELESS IN SINGLE COMBAT...
...UNLESS YOU HAVE...
...DEPENDABLE BACKUP.
HMPH...
DON'T TRY TO FLATTER ME.
NO REALLY, I MEAN IT.
HMPH...

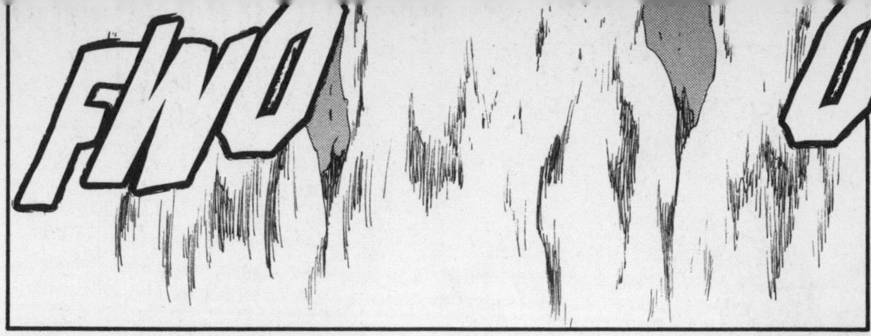
FWOO
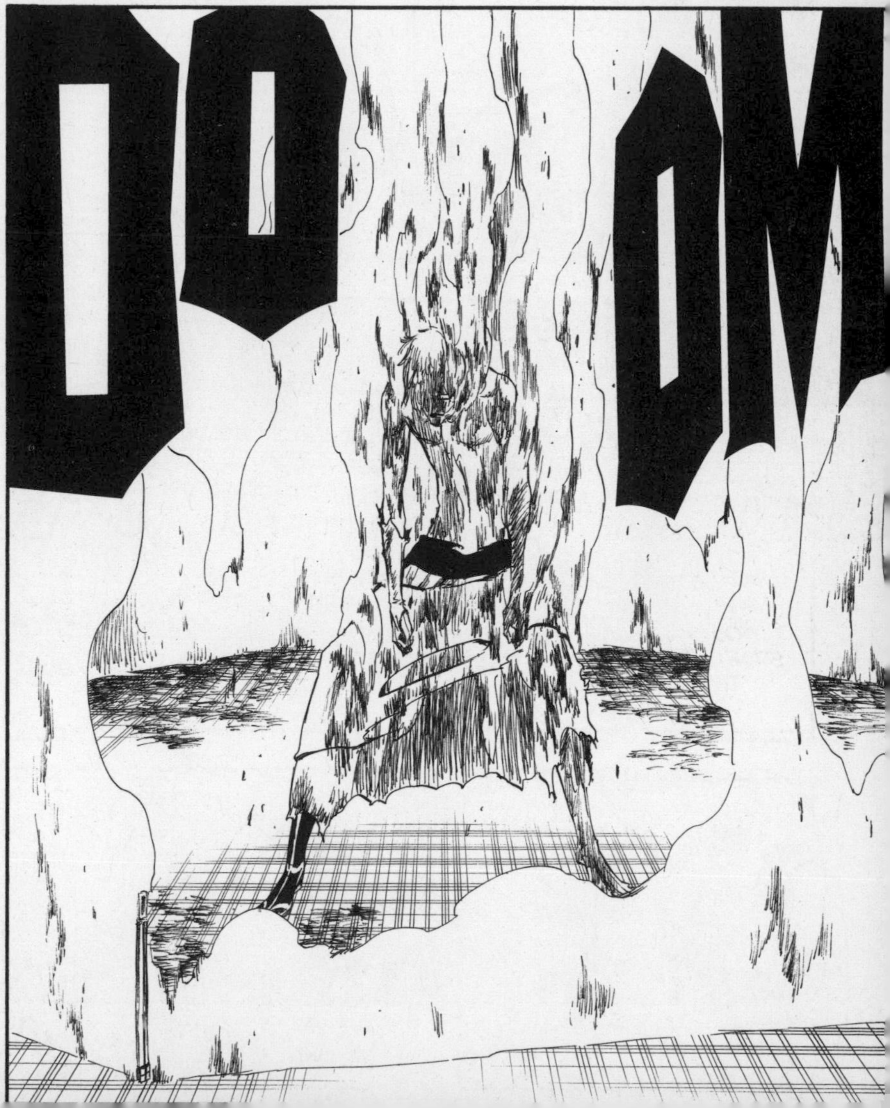
DOOM

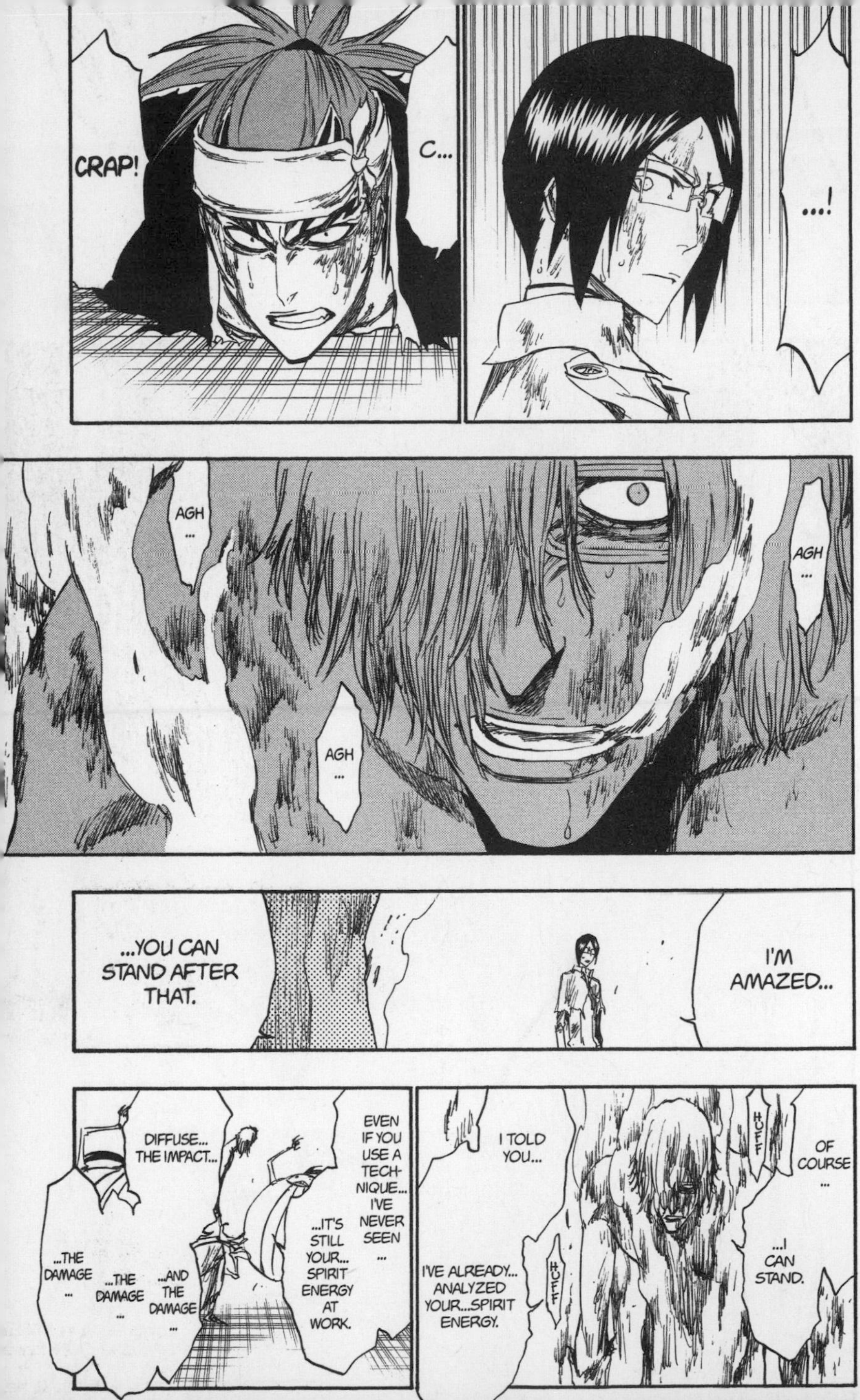
...!
C...
CRAP!
AGH...
AGH...
AGH...
I'M AMAZED...
...YOU CAN STAND AFTER THAT.
OF COURSE...
HUFF
...I CAN STAND.
I TOLD YOU...
HUFF
I'VE ALREADY... ANALYZED YOUR...SPIRIT ENERGY.
EVEN IF YOU USE A TECHNIQUE... I'VE NEVER SEEN...
...IT'S STILL YOUR... SPIRIT ENERGY AT WORK.
DIFFUSE... THE IMPACT...
...AND THE DAMAGE...
...THE DAMAGE...
...THE DAMAGE...

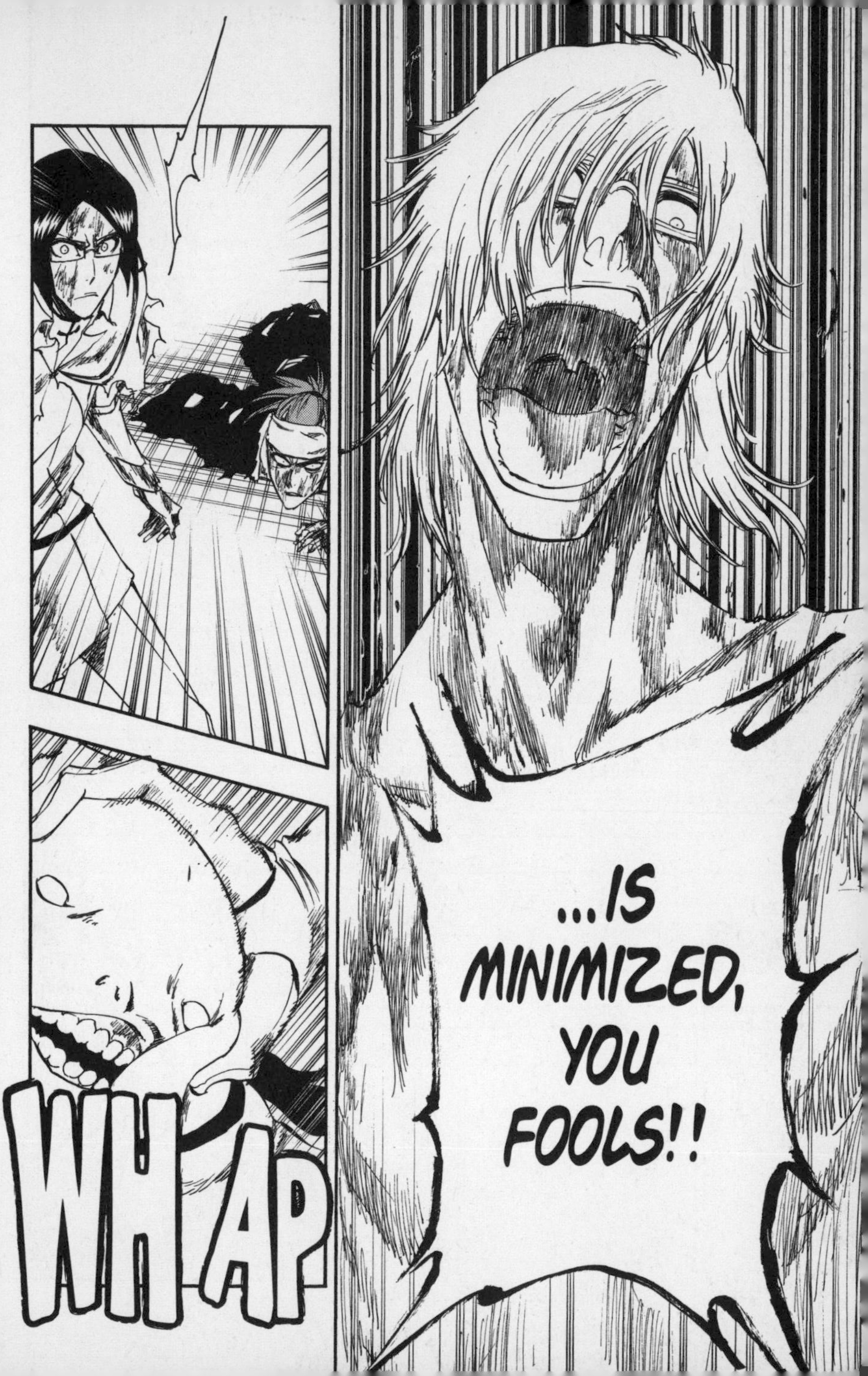
...IS MINIMIZED, YOU FOOLS!!
WHAP

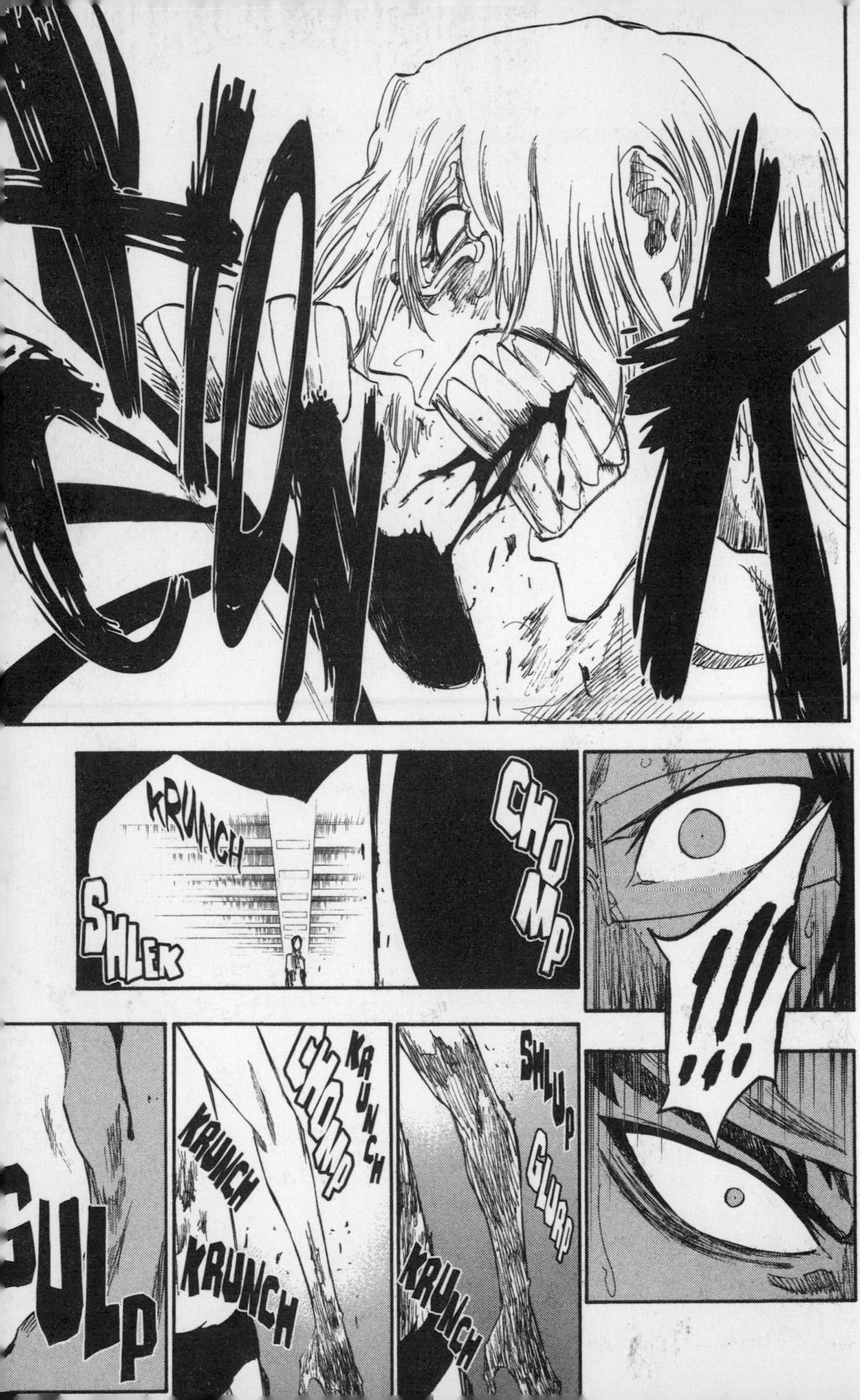

!!!
CHOMP
KRUNCH
SHLEK
SHLUP
GLURP
KRUNCH
KRUNCH
CHOMP
KRUNCH
KRUNCH
GULP

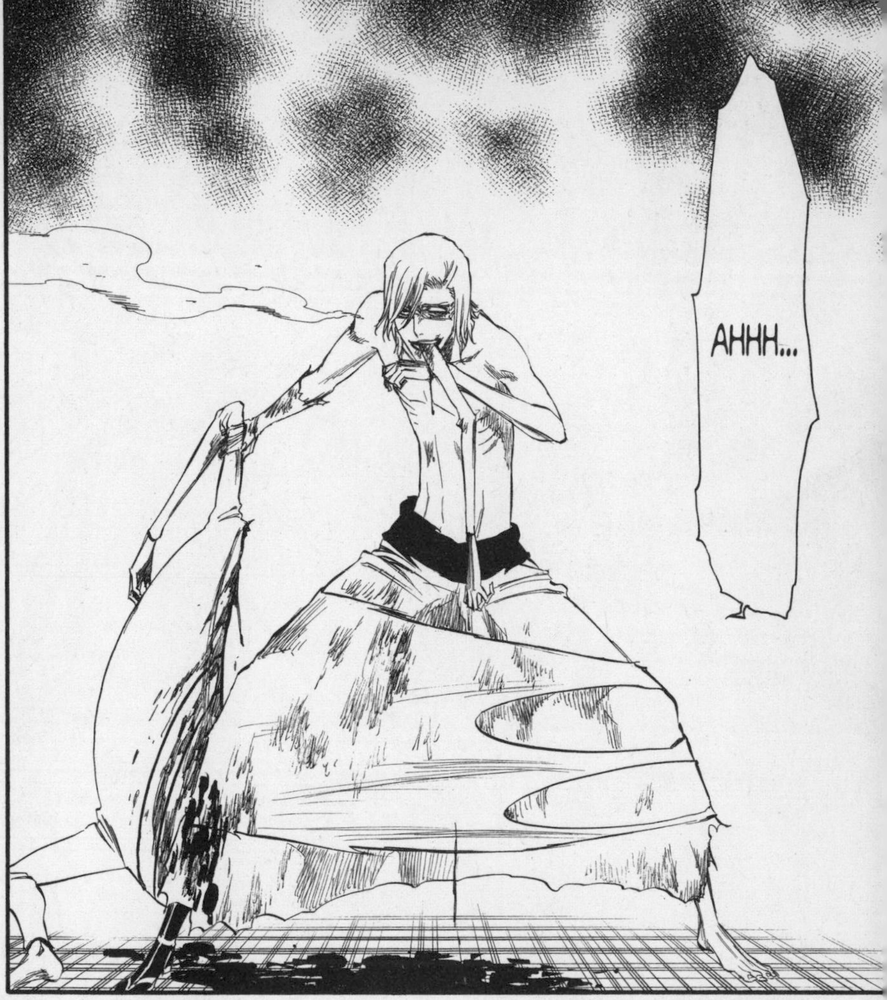
AHHH...
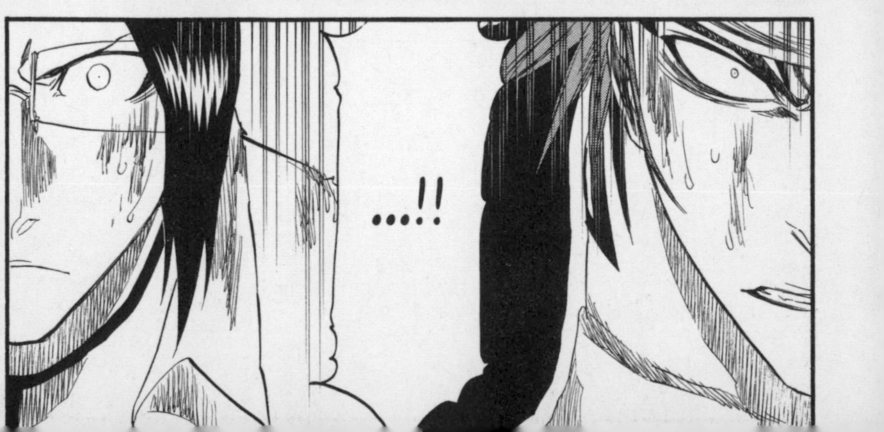
...!!

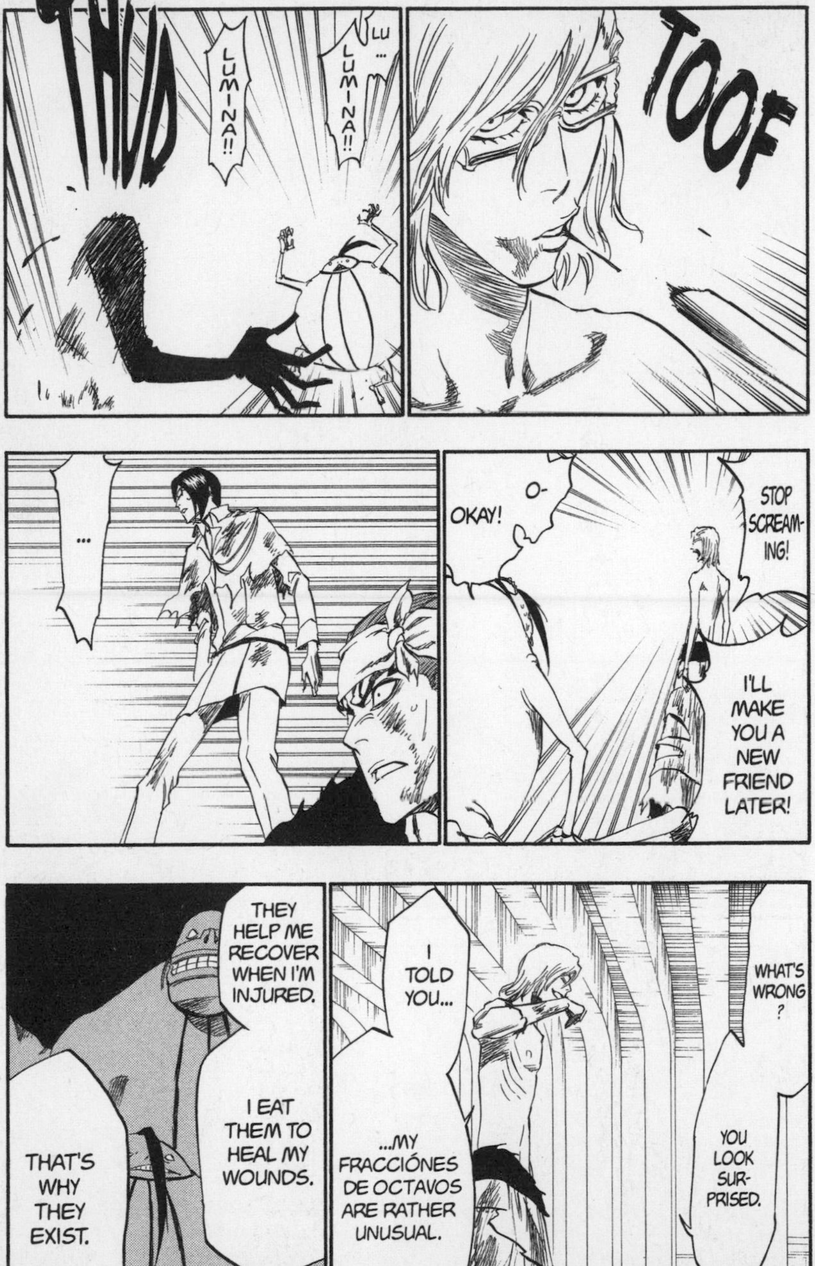
TOOF
LU... LUMINA!!
LUMINA!!
THUD
STOP SCREAMING!
I'LL MAKE YOU A NEW FRIEND LATER!
O- OKAY!
...
WHAT'S WRONG?
YOU LOOK SURPRISED.
I TOLD YOU...
...MY FRACCIÓNES DE OCTAVOS ARE RATHER UNUSUAL.
THEY HELP ME RECOVER WHEN I'M INJURED.
I EAT THEM TO HEAL MY WOUNDS.
THAT'S WHY THEY EXIST.

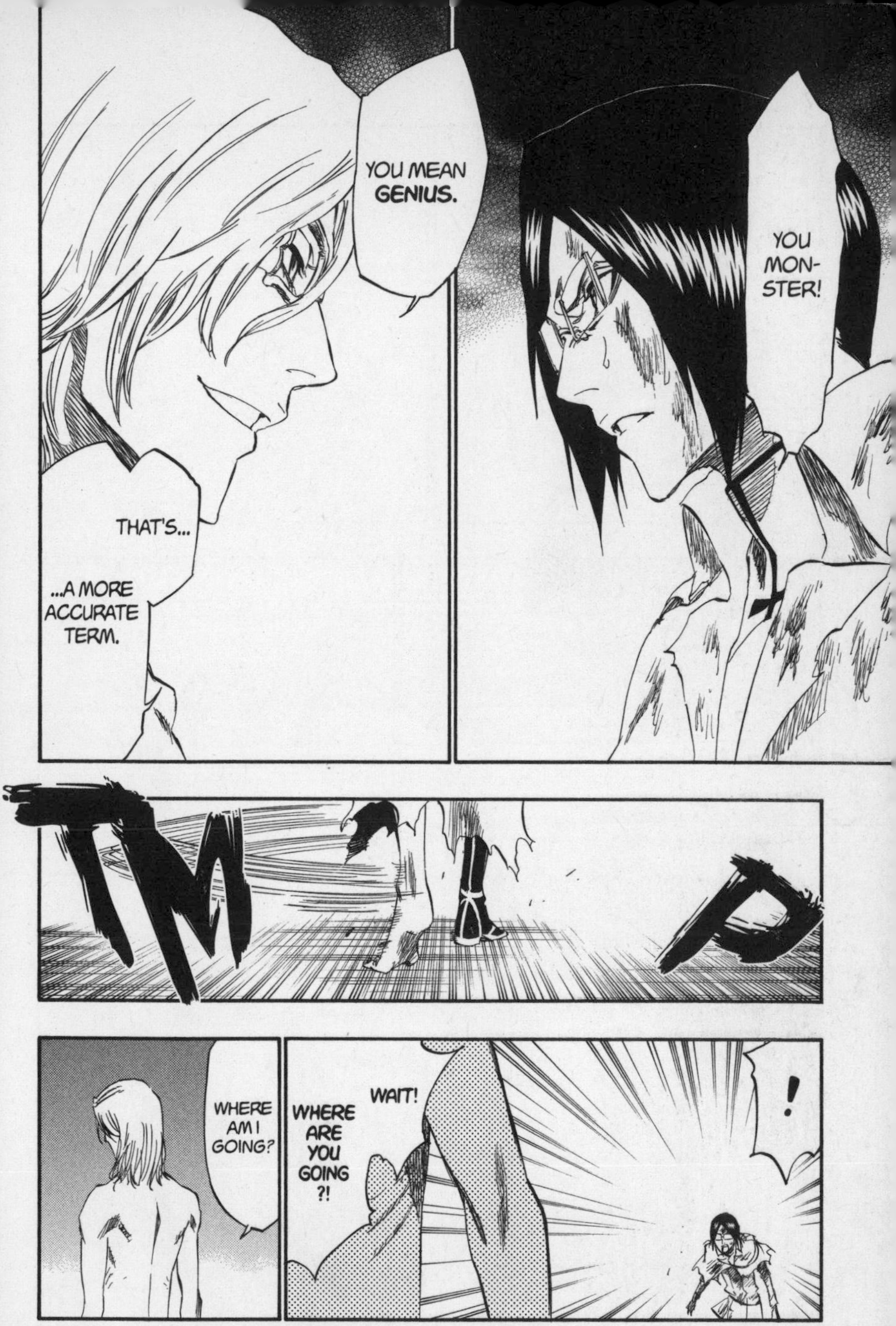
YOU MON-STER!
YOU MEAN GENIUS.
THAT'S...
...A MORE ACCURATE TERM.
TMP
!
WAIT!
WHERE ARE YOU GOING ?!
WHERE AM I GOING?

READ THIS WAY

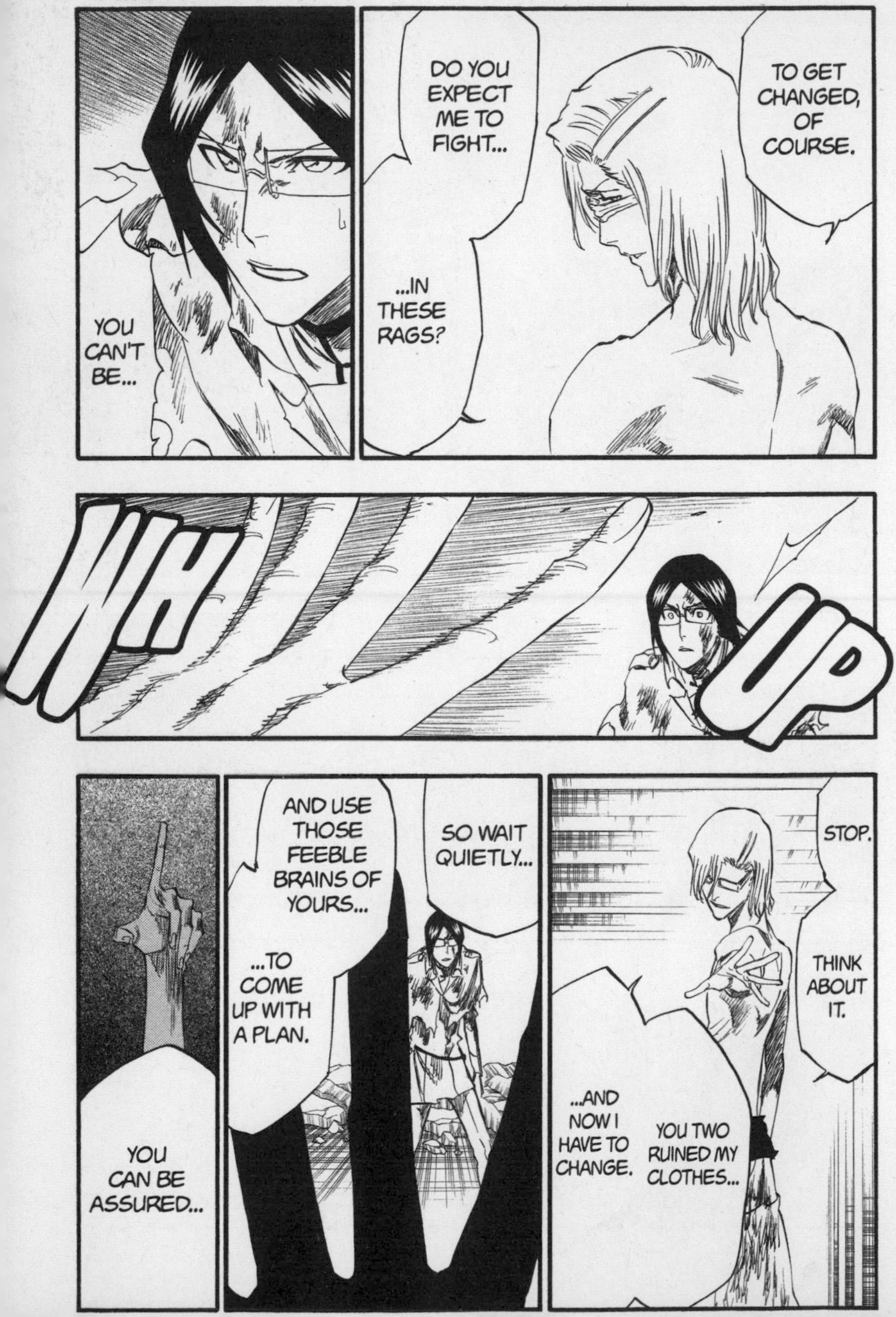
TO GET CHANGED, OF COURSE.
DO YOU EXPECT ME TO FIGHT...
...IN THESE RAGS?
YOU CAN'T BE...
WHUP
STOP.
THINK ABOUT IT.
YOU TWO RUINED MY CLOTHES...
...AND NOW I HAVE TO CHANGE.
SO WAIT QUIETLY...
AND USE THOSE FEEBLE BRAINS OF YOURS...
...TO COME UP WITH A PLAN.
YOU CAN BE ASSURED...

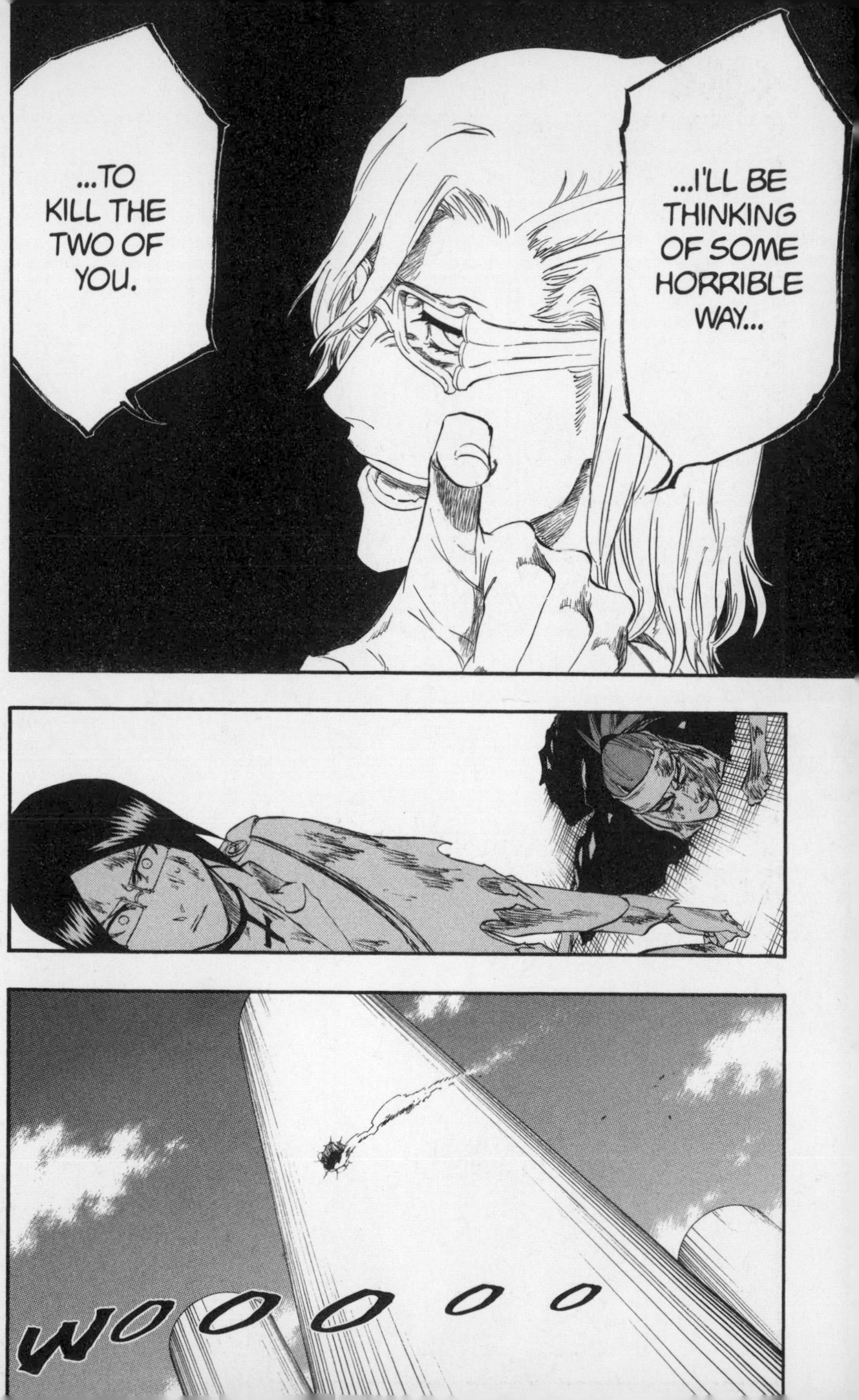
...I'LL BE THINKING OF SOME HORRIBLE WAY...
...TO KILL THE TWO OF YOU.
WOOOOOO

READ THIS WAY

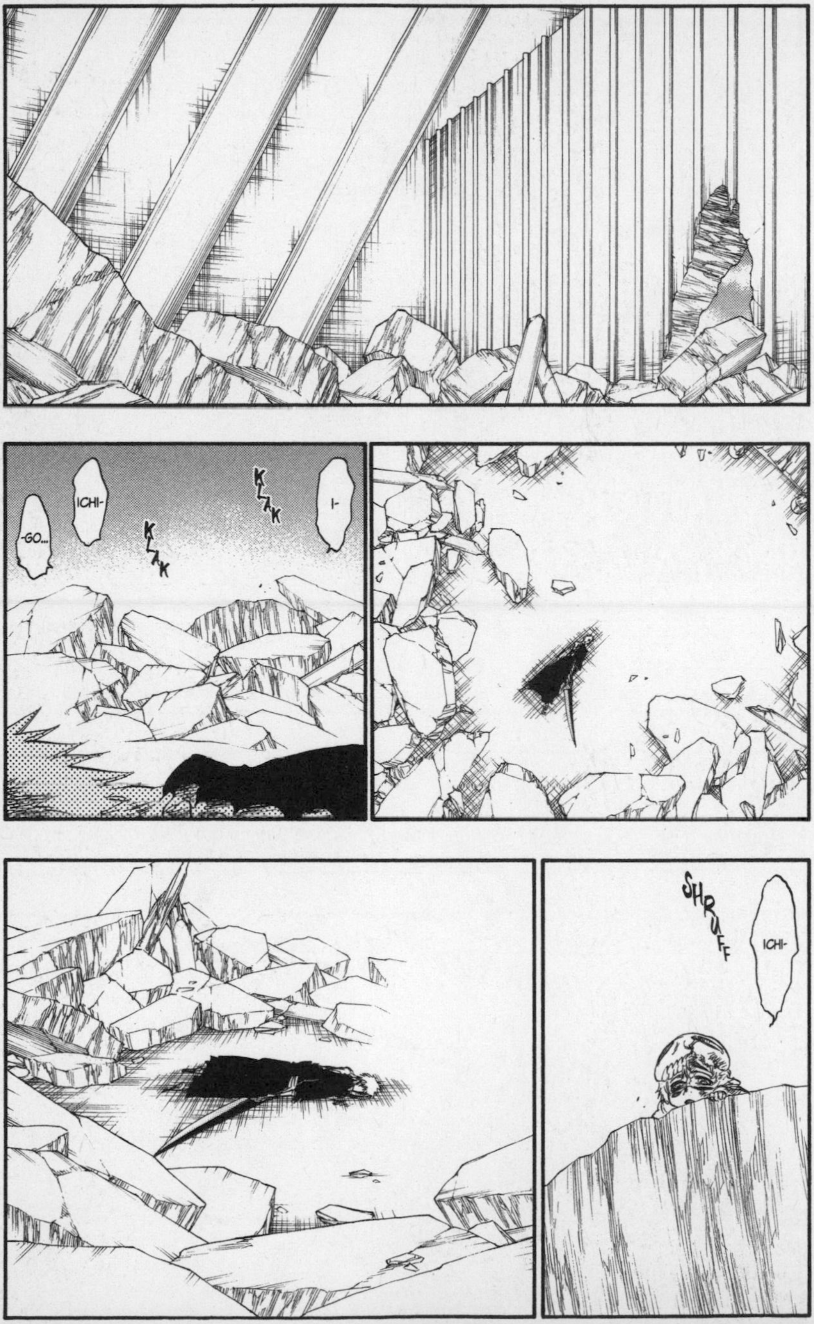
I-
KLAK
KLAK
ICHI-
-GO...
SHRUFF
ICHI-

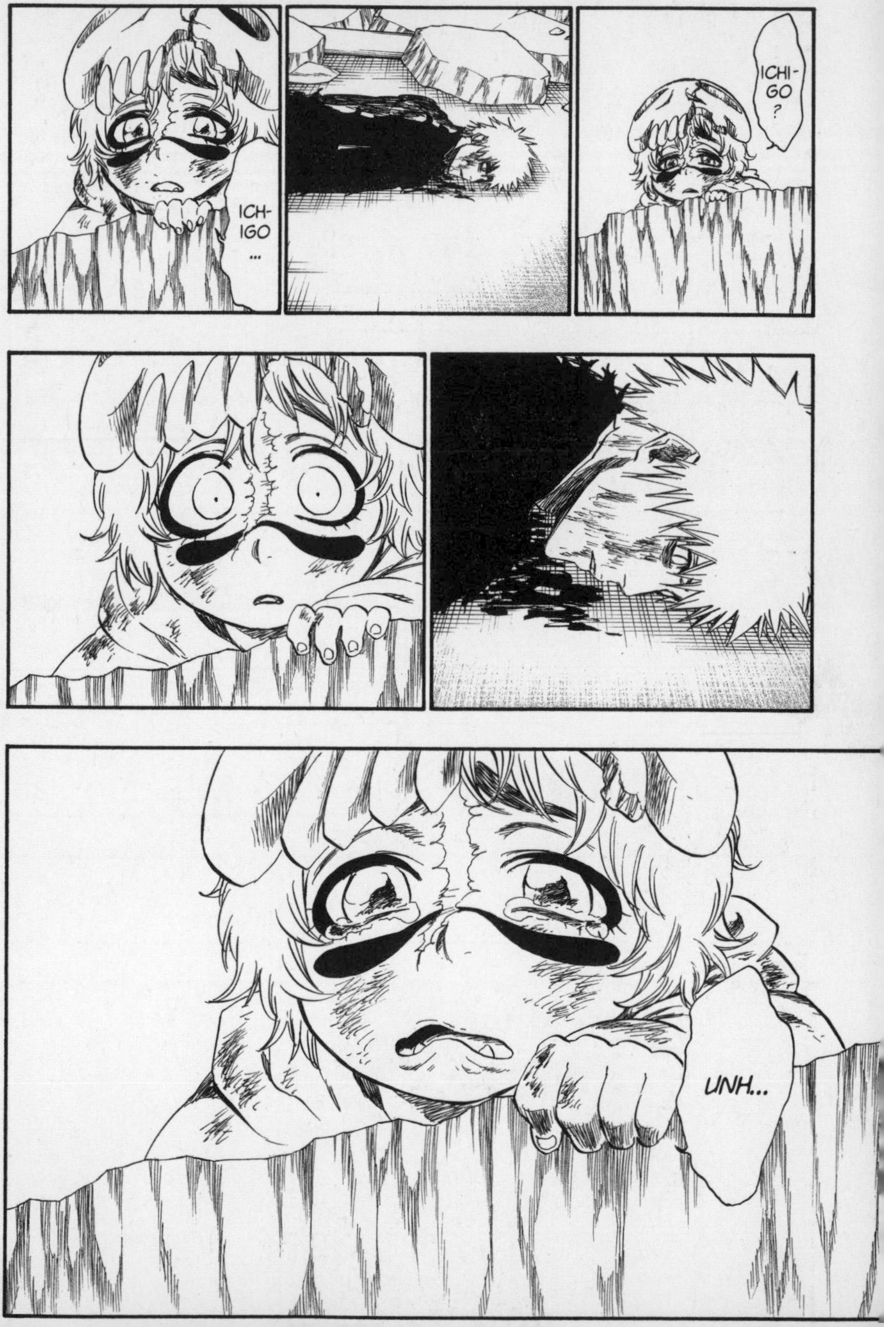
ICHI-GO?
ICH-IGO...
UNH...

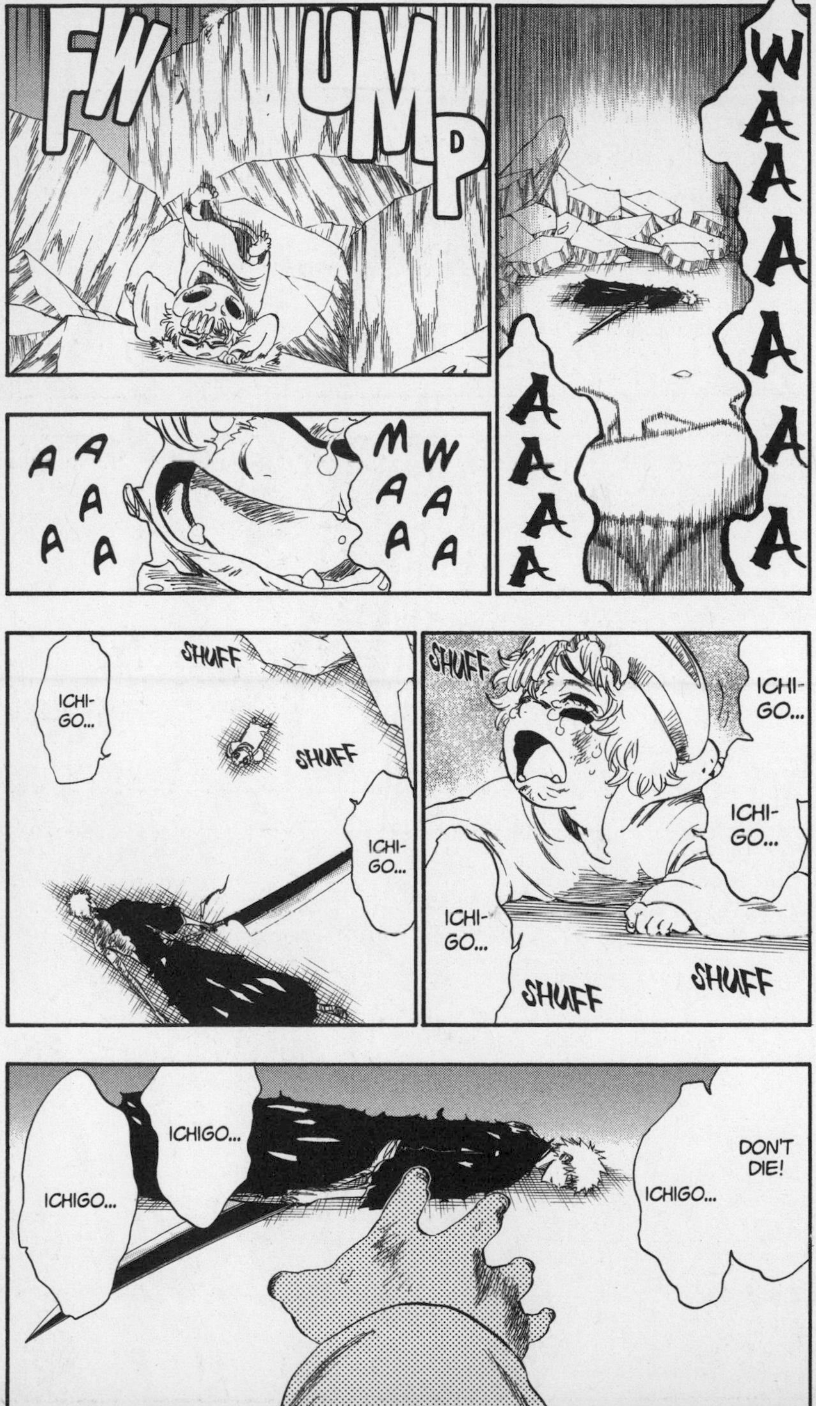

WAAAAAA
AAAA
FWUMP
MWAAAA
AAAAAA
SHUFF
ICHI-GO...
ICHI-GO...
ICHI-GO...
SHUFF
SHUFF
SHUFF
SHUFF
ICHI-GO...
ICHI-GO...
DON'T DIE!
ICHIGO...
ICHIGO...
ICHIGO...

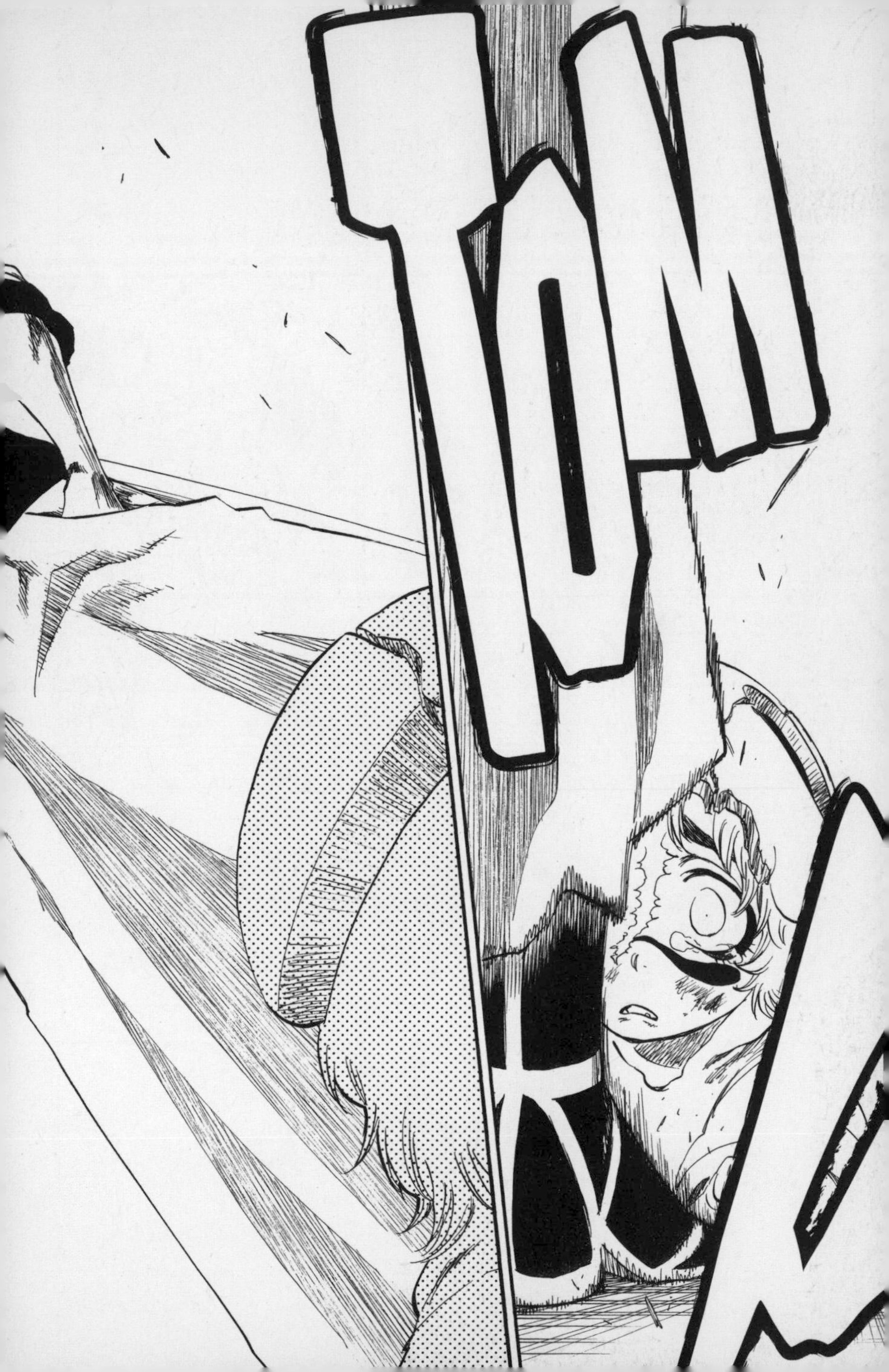
TOM

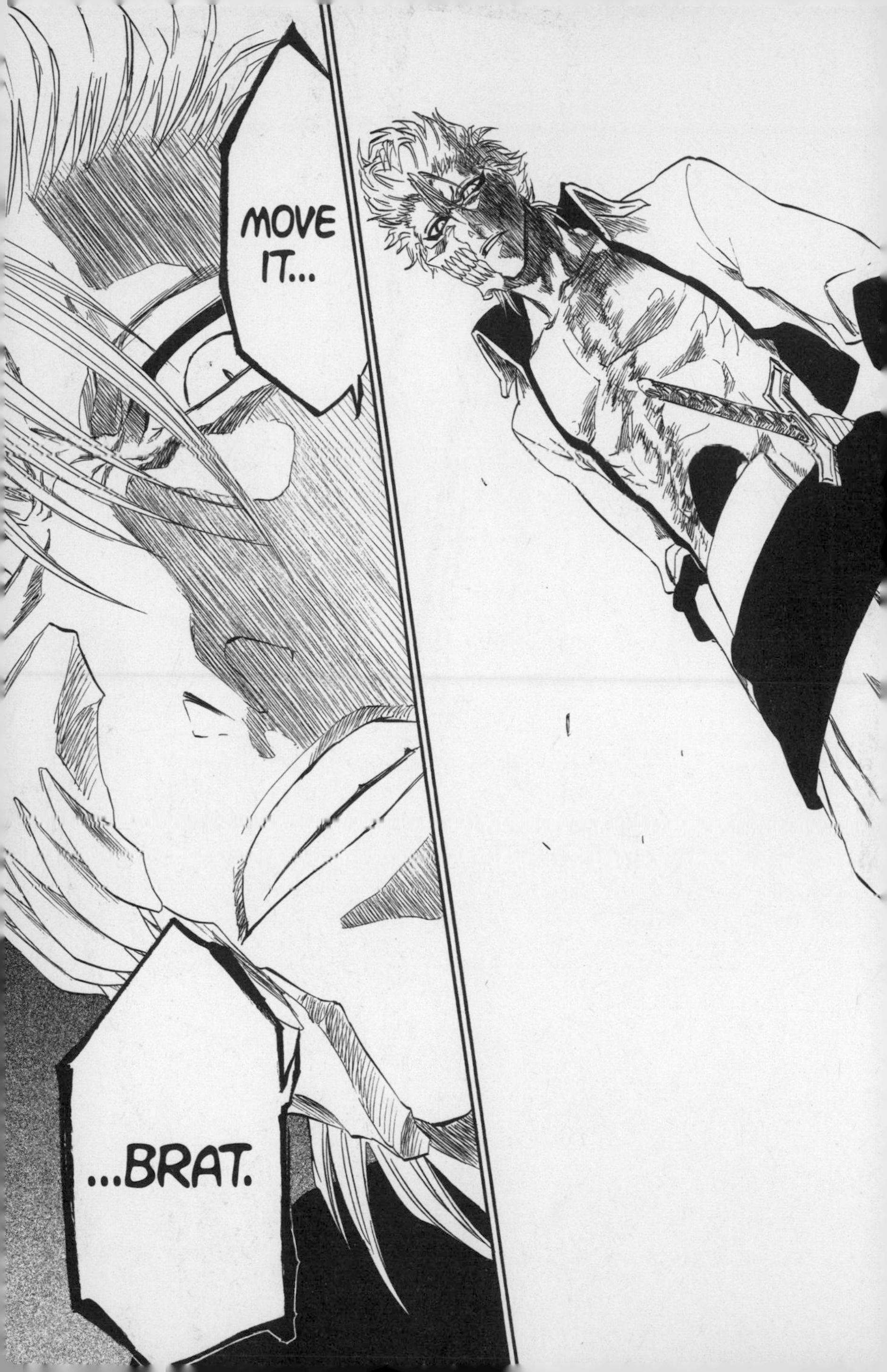
MOVE IT...
...BRAT.

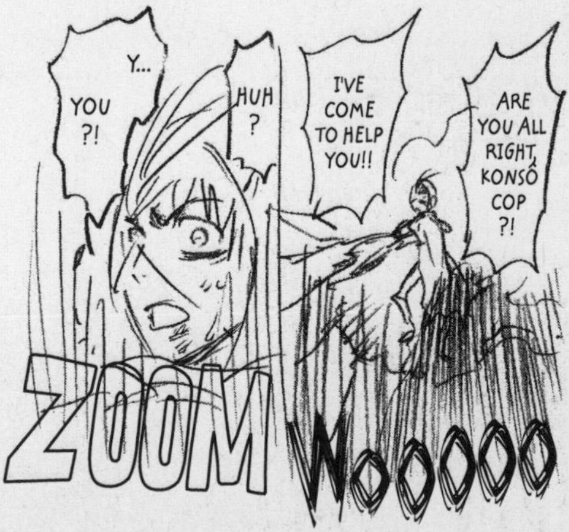
ARE YOU ALL RIGHT, KONSŌ COP ?!
I'VE COME TO HELP YOU!!
HUH ?
Y...
YOU ?!
WOOOOO
ZOOM

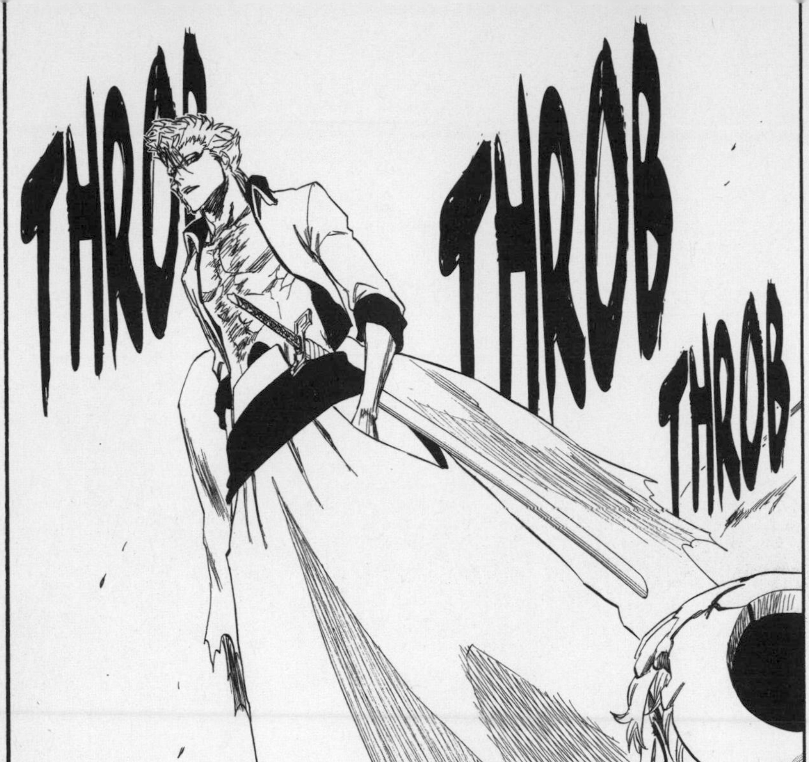
THROB
THROB
THROB
THROB

277. Corrosion of Conformity

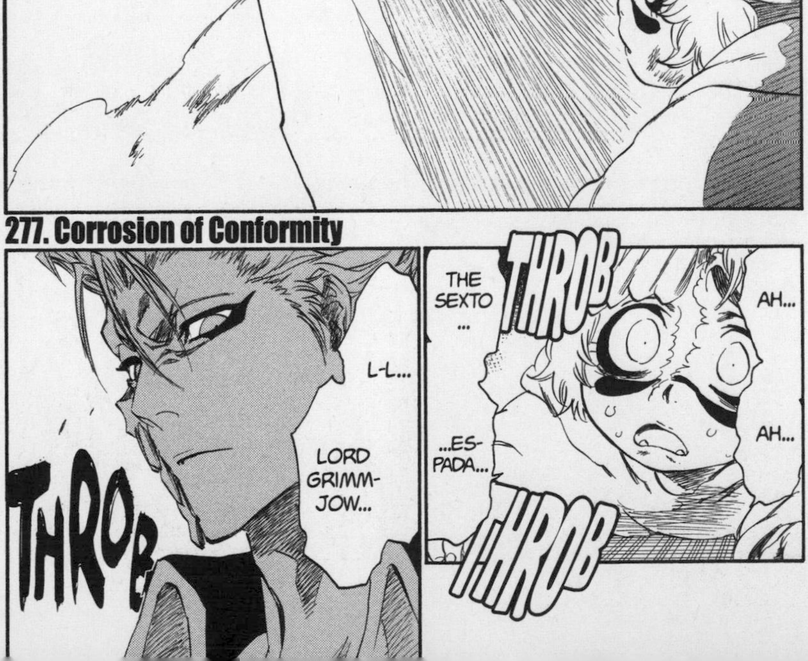
AH...
THE SEXTO
...
THROB
AH...
...ES-
PADA...
THROB
L-L...
LORD
GRIMM-
JOW...
THROB

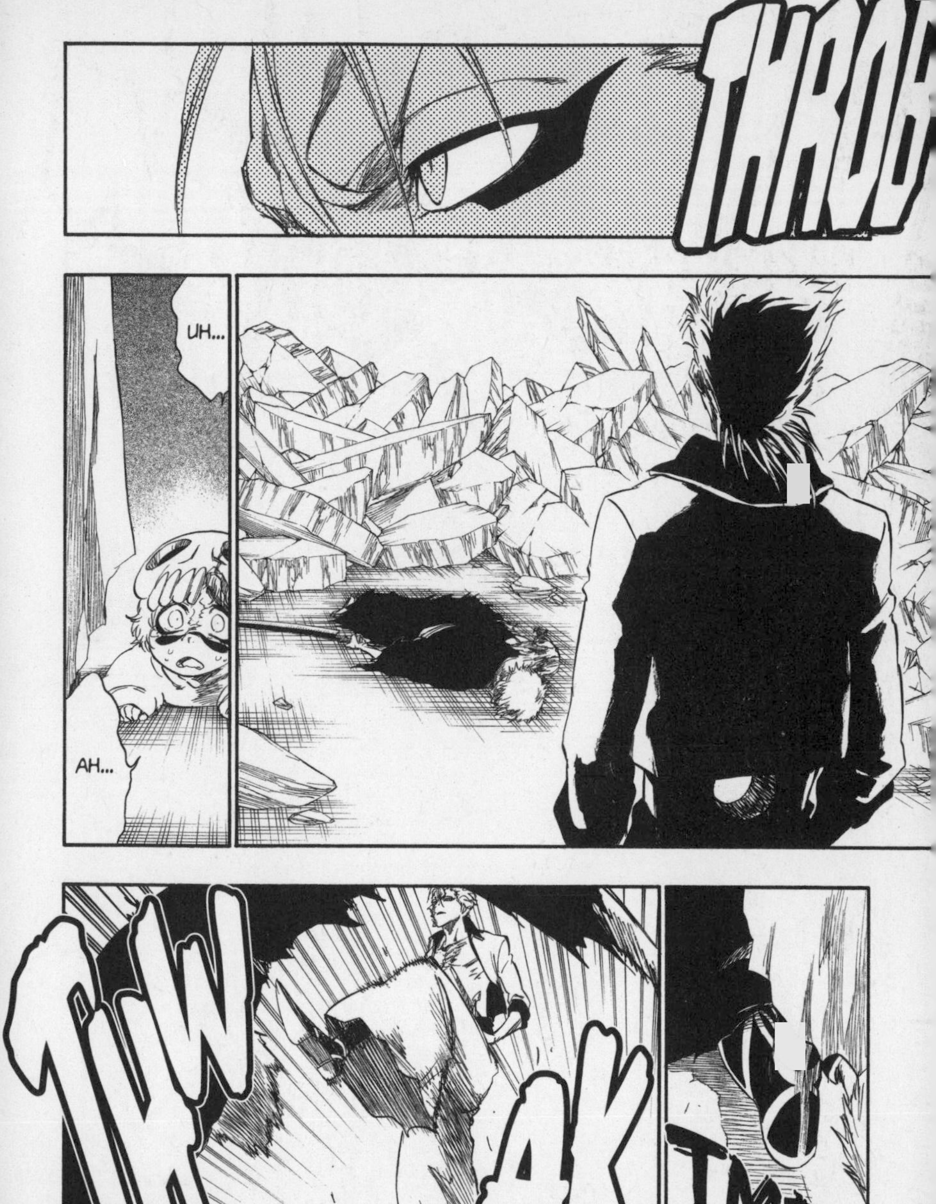
THROB
UH...
AH...
TMP
TWAK

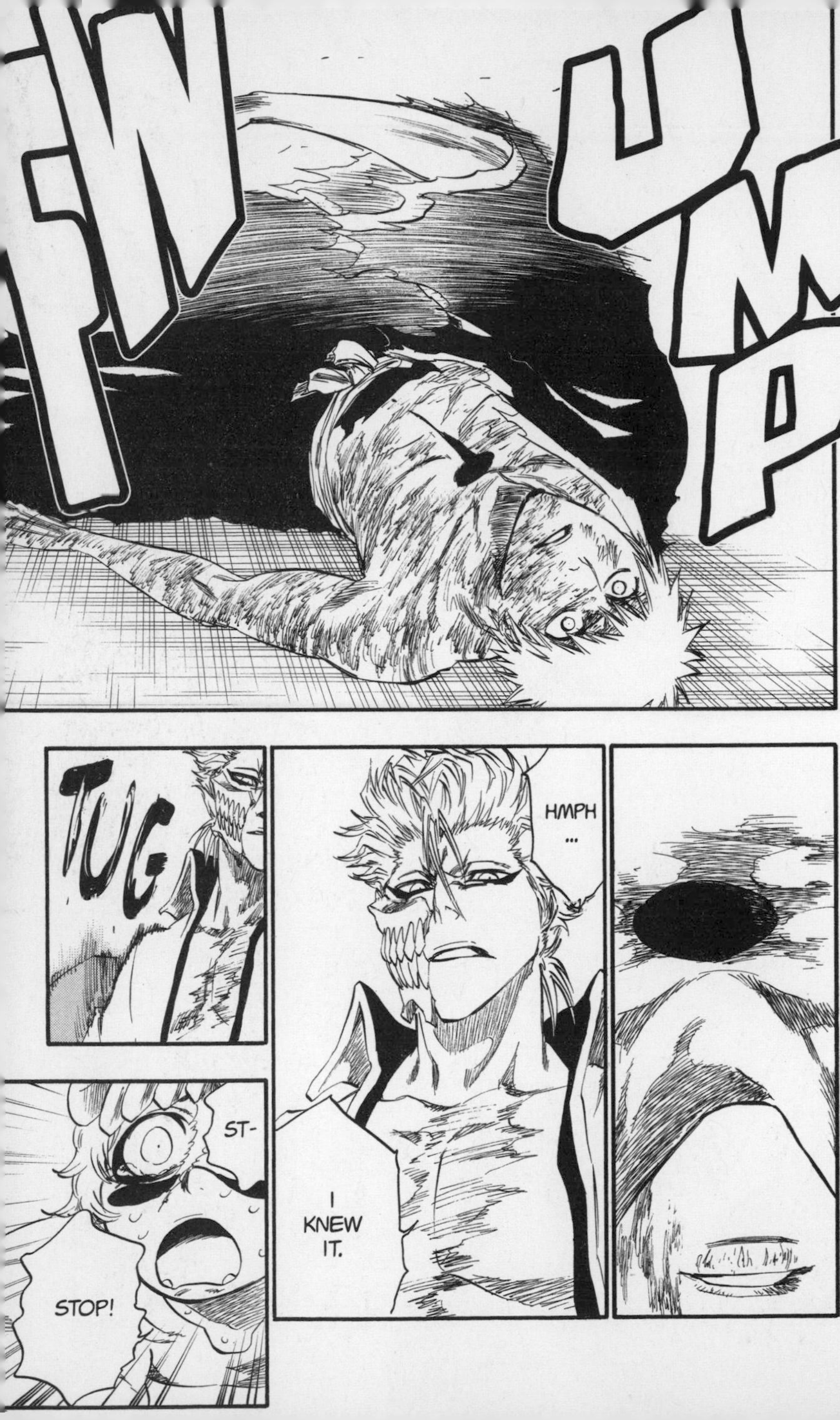
UMP
HMPH
...
I KNEW IT.
TUG
ST-
STOP!

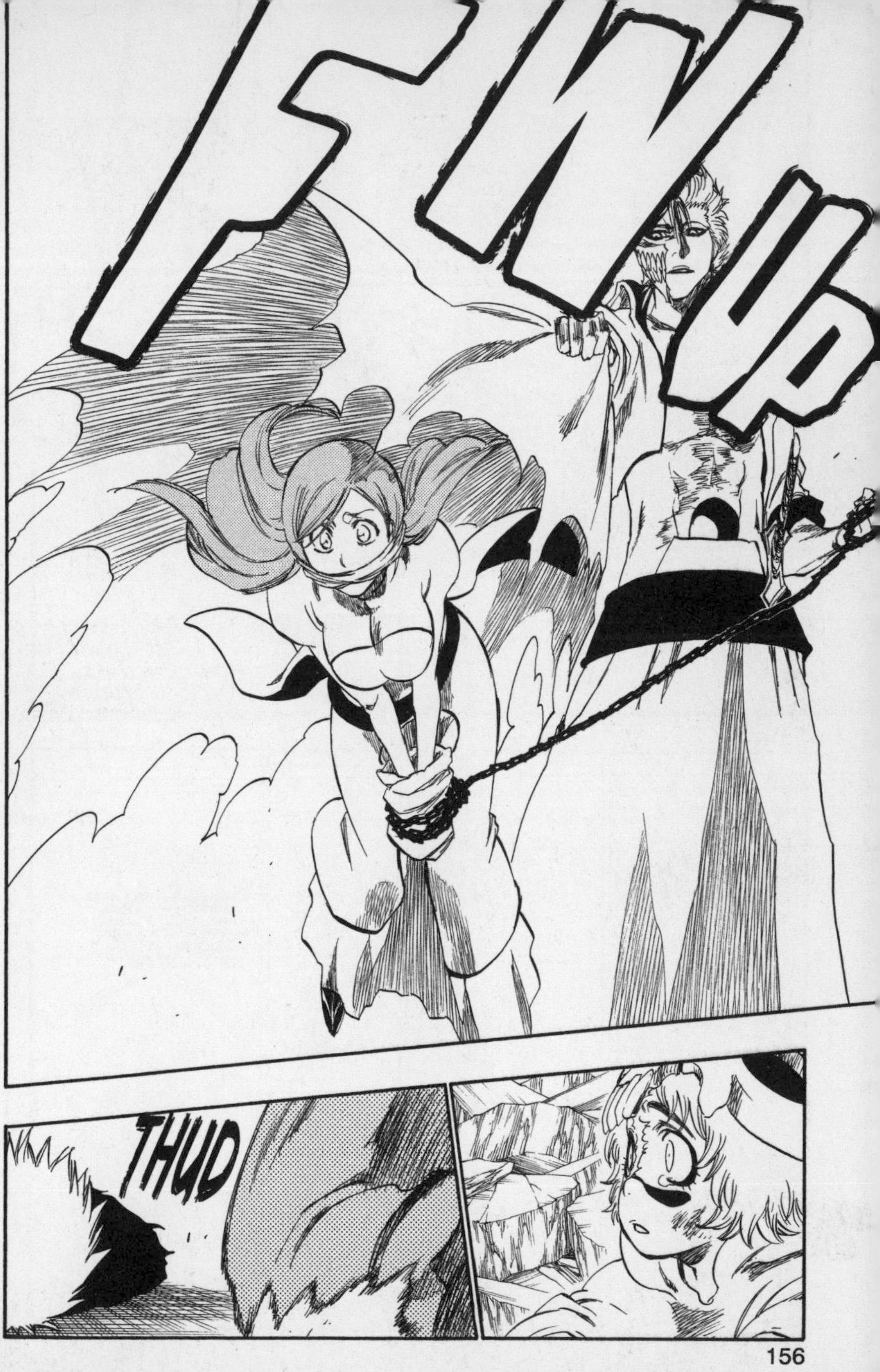
FWIP
THUD

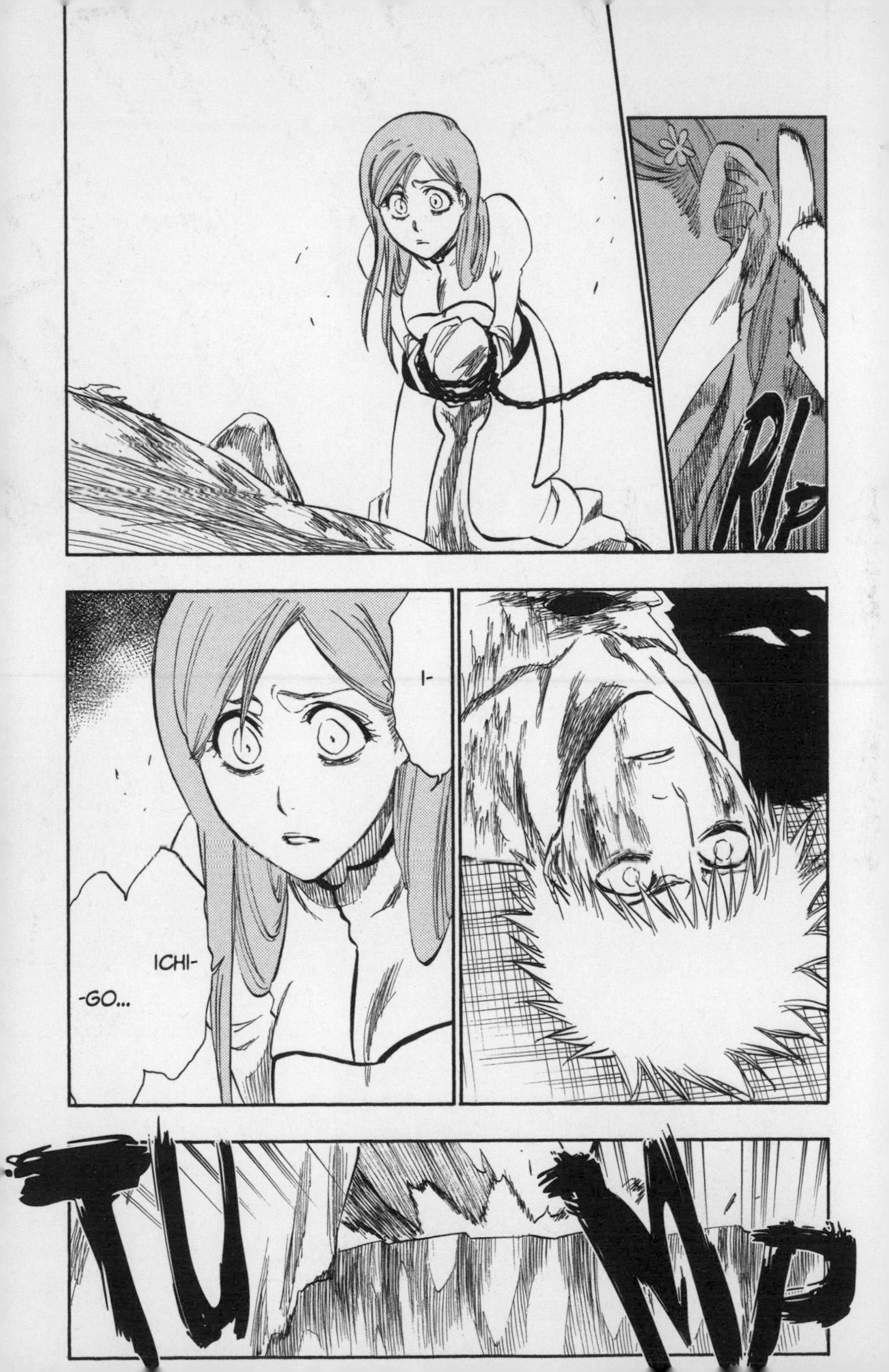
RIP
I-
ICHI-
-GO...
TUMP

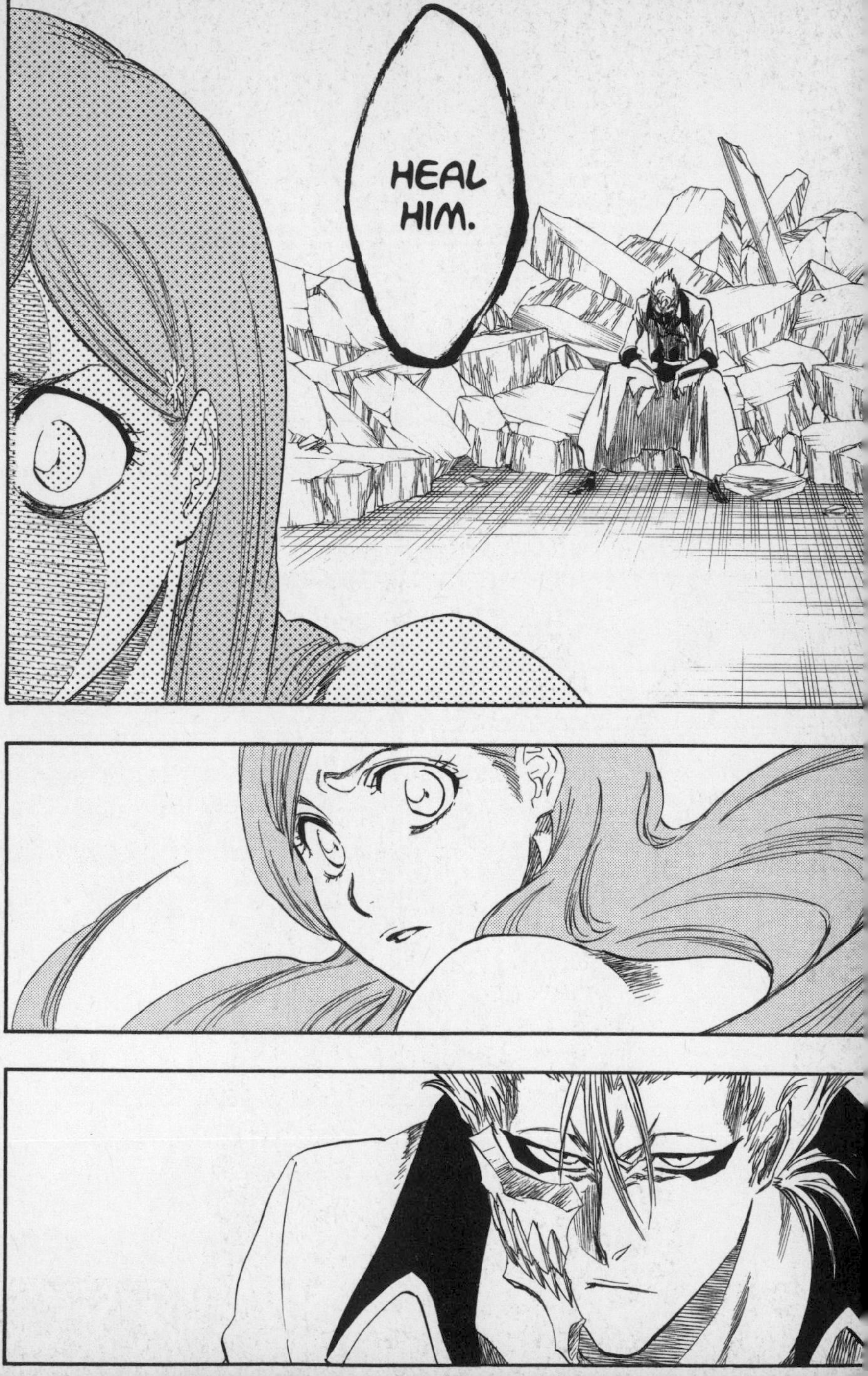
HEAL HIM.

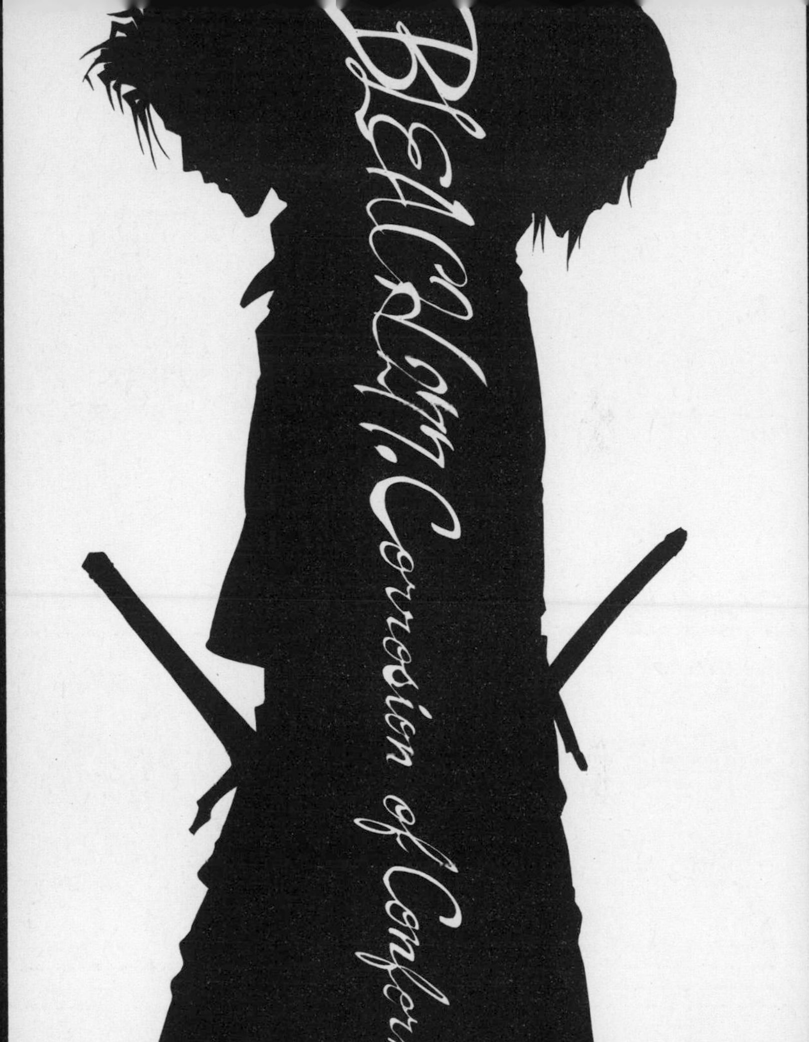
BLEACH 277. Corrosion of Conformity

BLEACH 277. Corrosion of Conformity

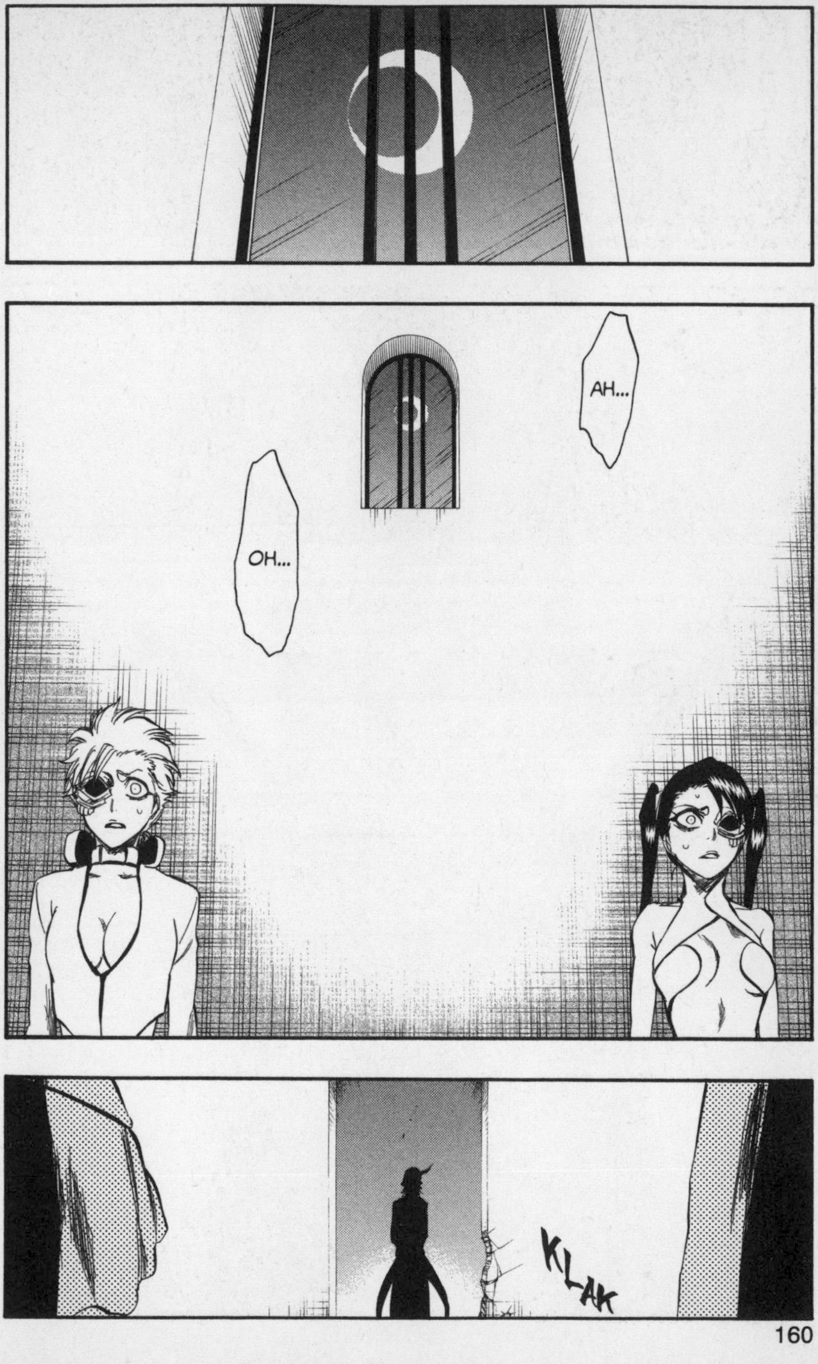
AH...
OH...
KLAK

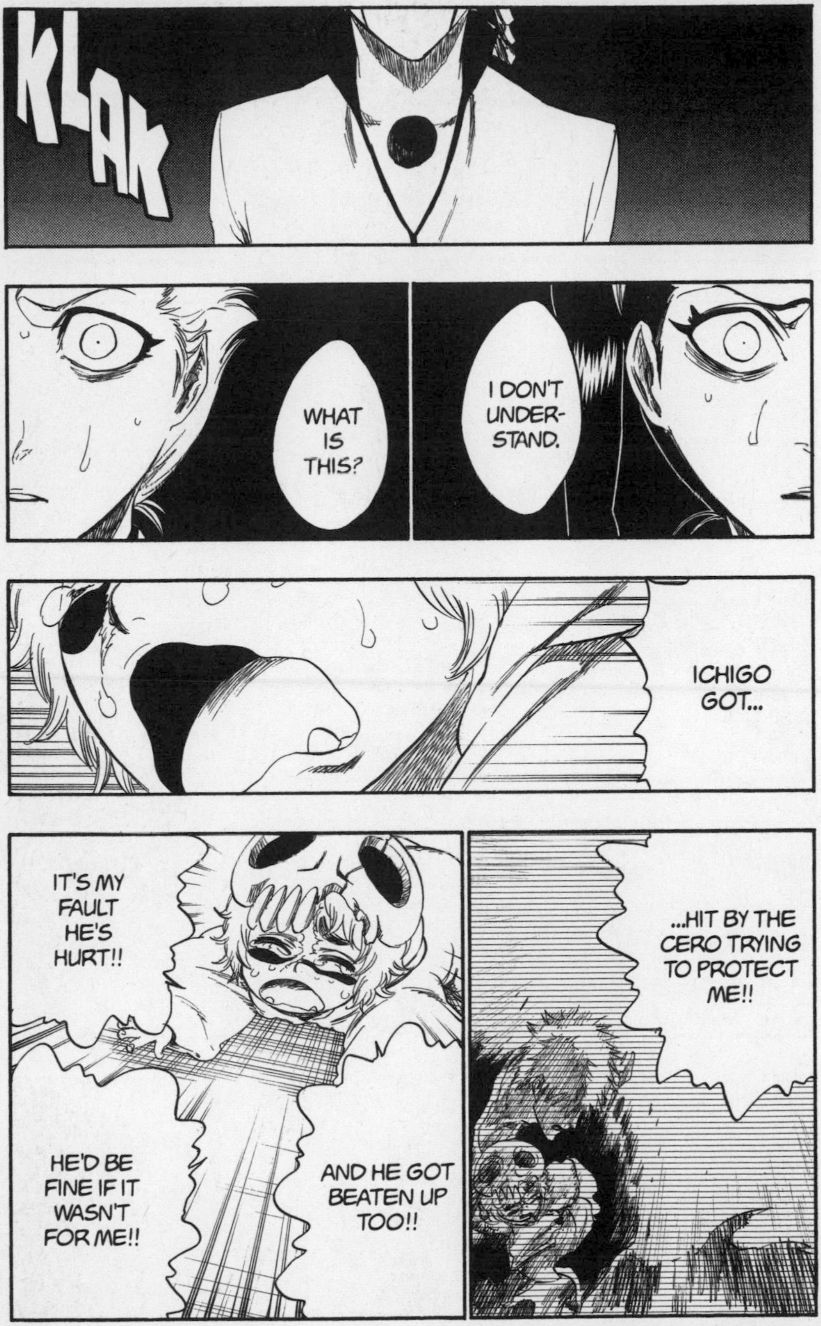
KLAK
I DON'T UNDER-STAND.
WHAT IS THIS?
ICHIGO GOT...
...HIT BY THE CERO TRYING TO PROTECT ME!!
IT'S MY FAULT HE'S HURT!!
AND HE GOT BEATEN UP TOO!!
HE'D BE FINE IF IT WASN'T FOR ME!!

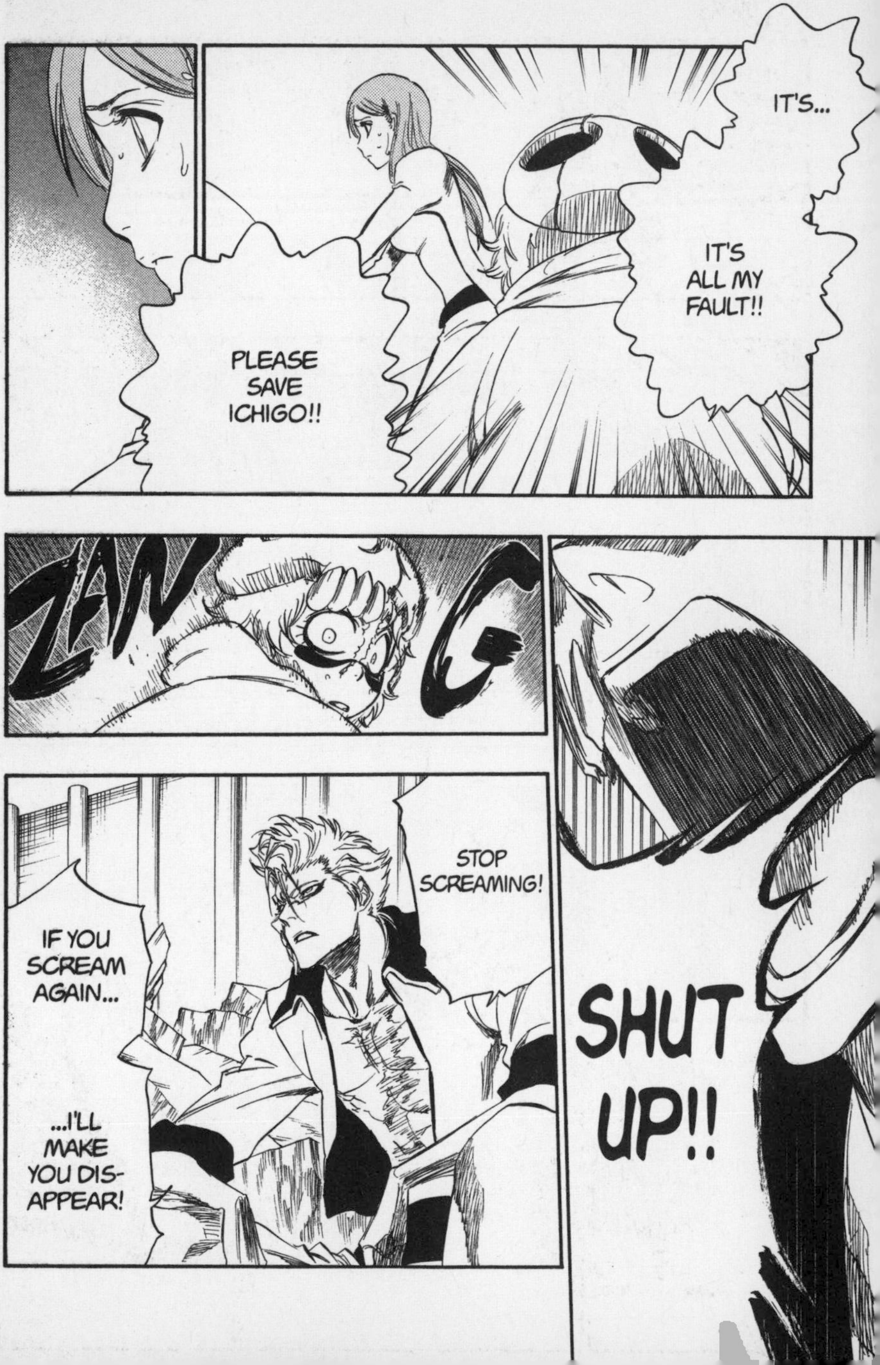
IT'S...
IT'S ALL MY FAULT!!
PLEASE SAVE ICHIGO!!
SHUT UP!!
ZANG
STOP SCREAMING!
IF YOU SCREAM AGAIN...
...I'LL MAKE YOU DIS-APPEAR!

NOW SHUT UP AND WATCH.

HE DOESN'T NEED YOUR HELP.

...

YES SIR.

...REJECT IT.

I CAN'T ...

WHO...

...IS SWIRLING AROUND ICHIGO'S WOUNDS.

TRE-MENDOUS SPIRITUAL PRESSURE ...

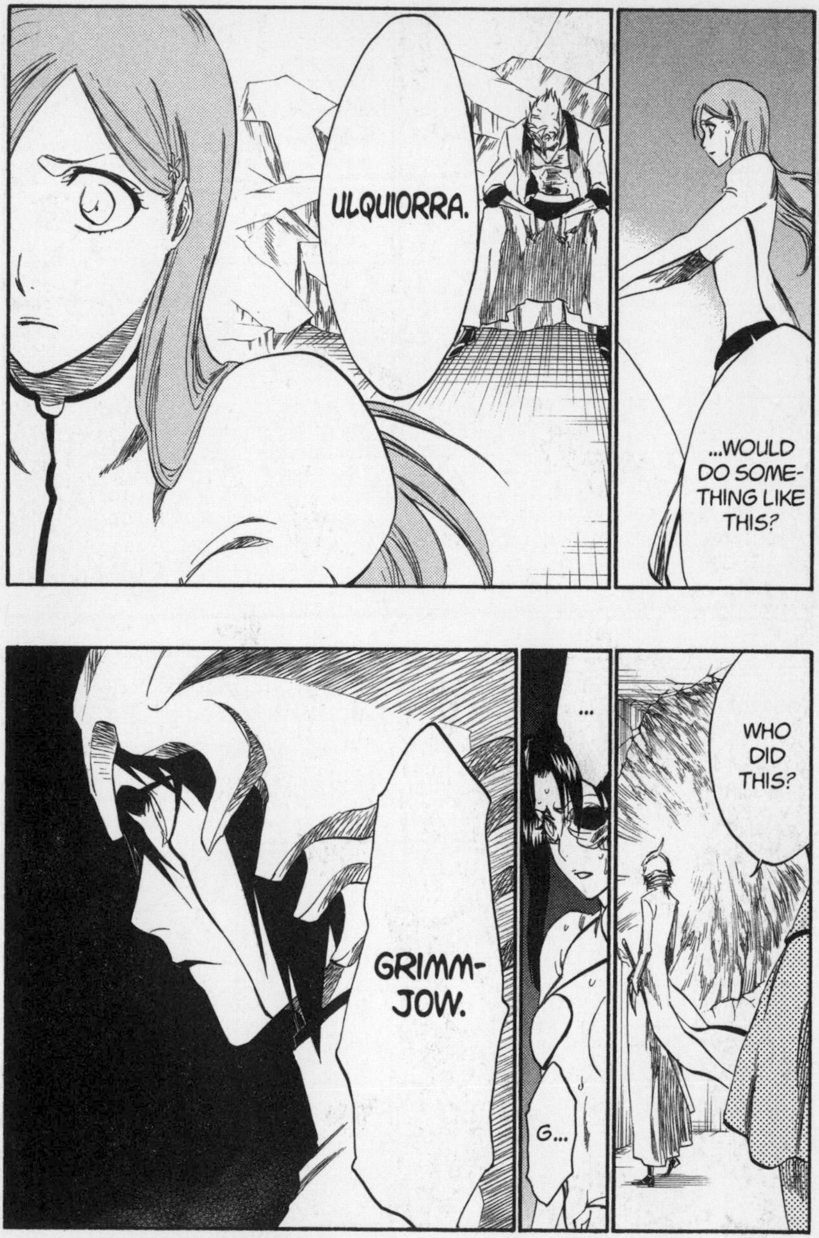
...WOULD DO SOMETHING LIKE THIS?
ULQUIORRA.
WHO DID THIS?
...
G...
GRIMMJOW.

READ THIS WAY

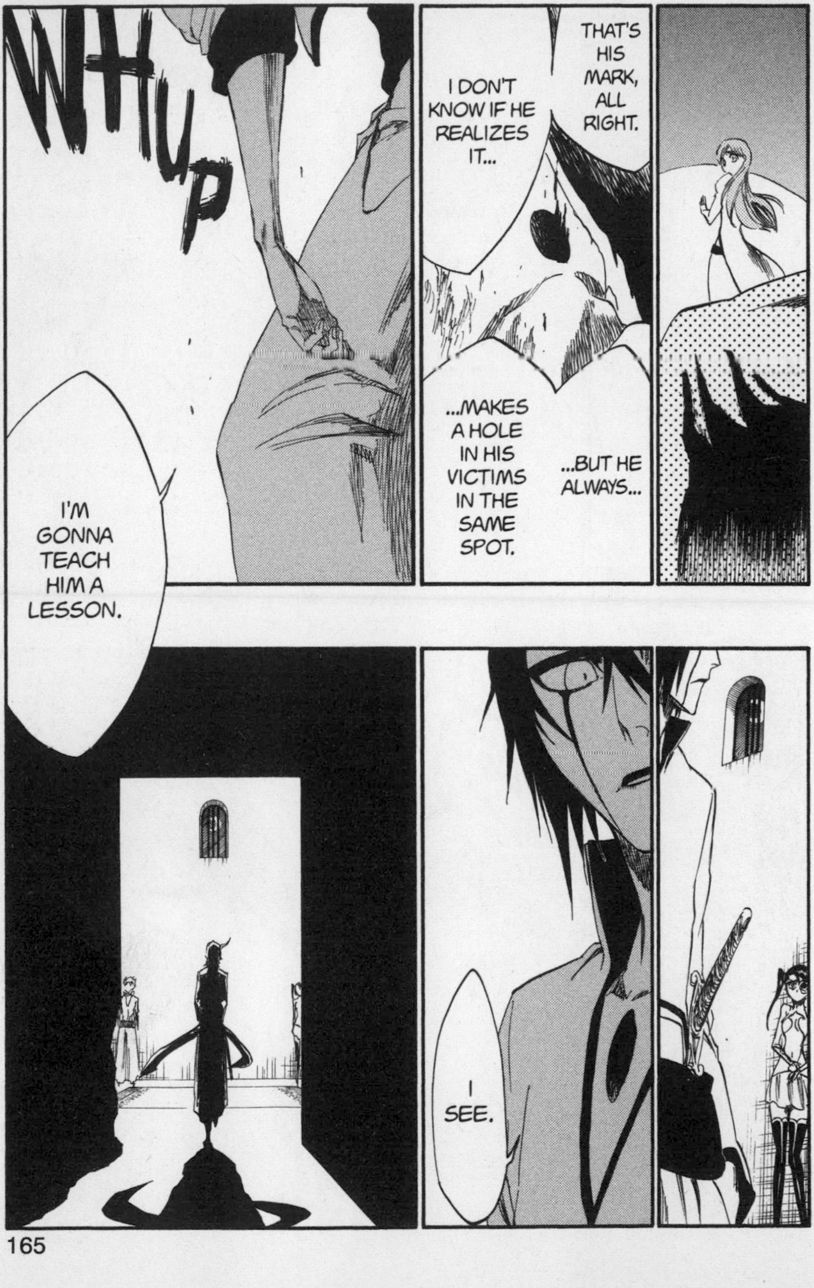
THAT'S HIS MARK, ALL RIGHT.
I DON'T KNOW IF HE REALIZES IT...
...BUT HE ALWAYS...
...MAKES A HOLE IN HIS VICTIMS IN THE SAME SPOT.
WHUP
I'M GONNA TEACH HIM A LESSON.
I SEE.

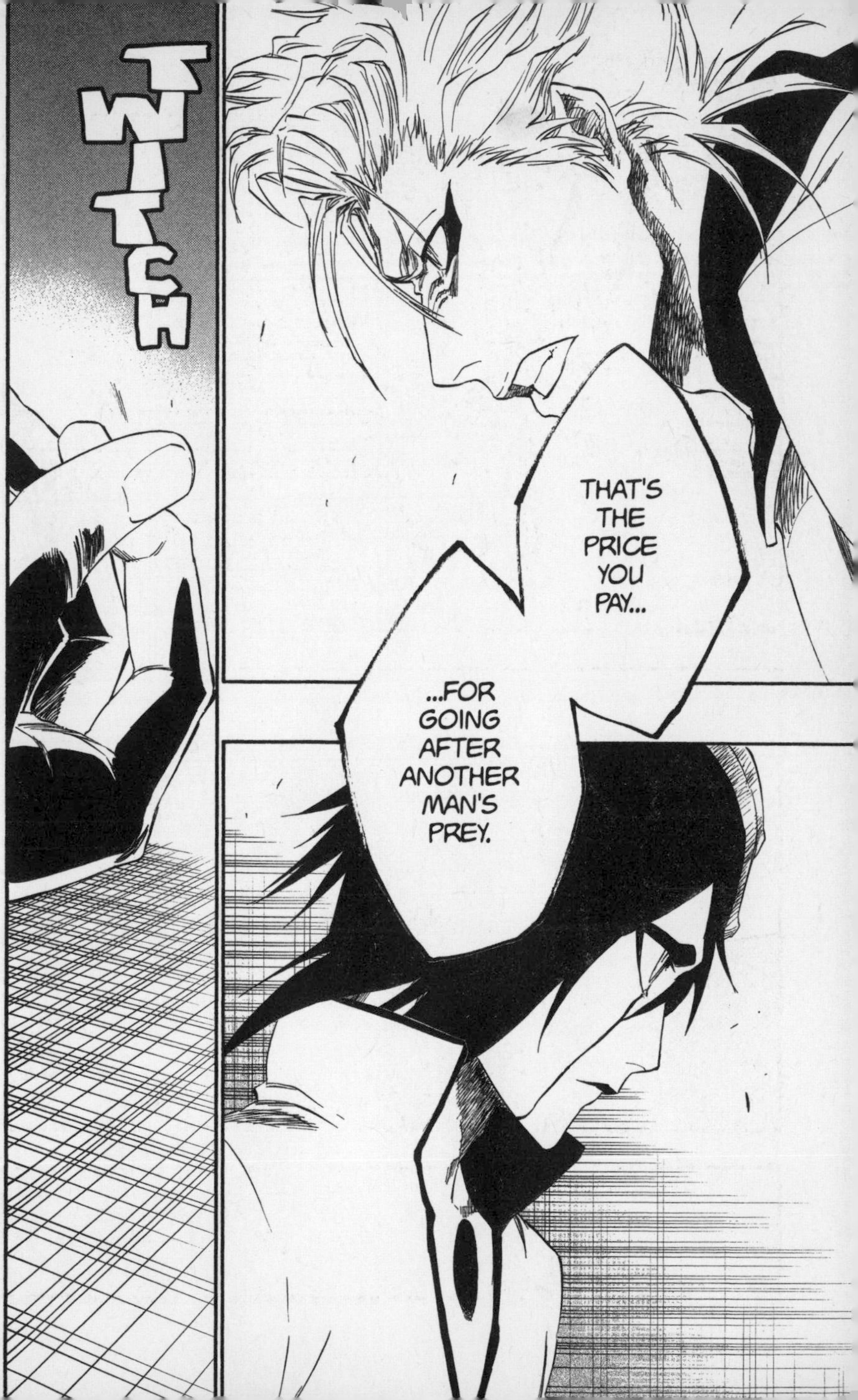
THAT'S THE PRICE YOU PAY...
...FOR GOING AFTER ANOTHER MAN'S PREY.
TWITCH

READ THIS WAY

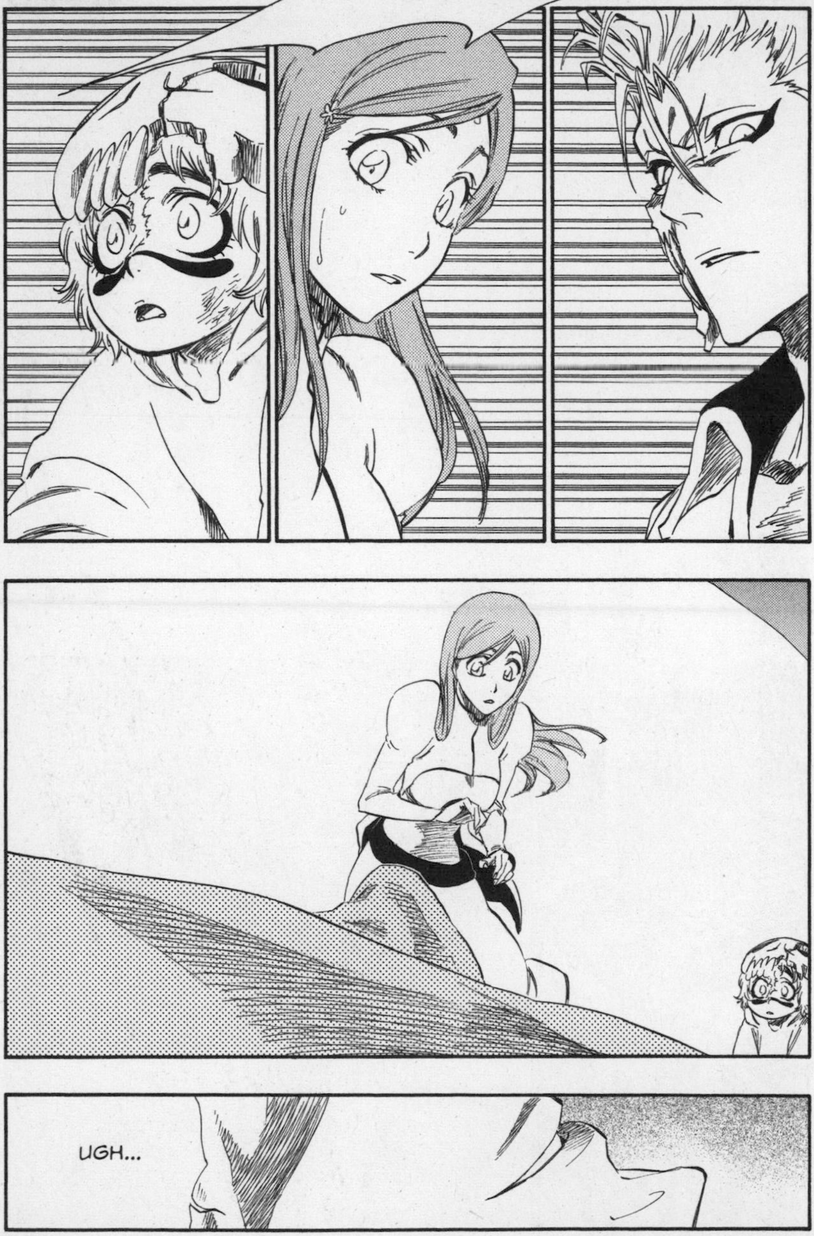
UGH...

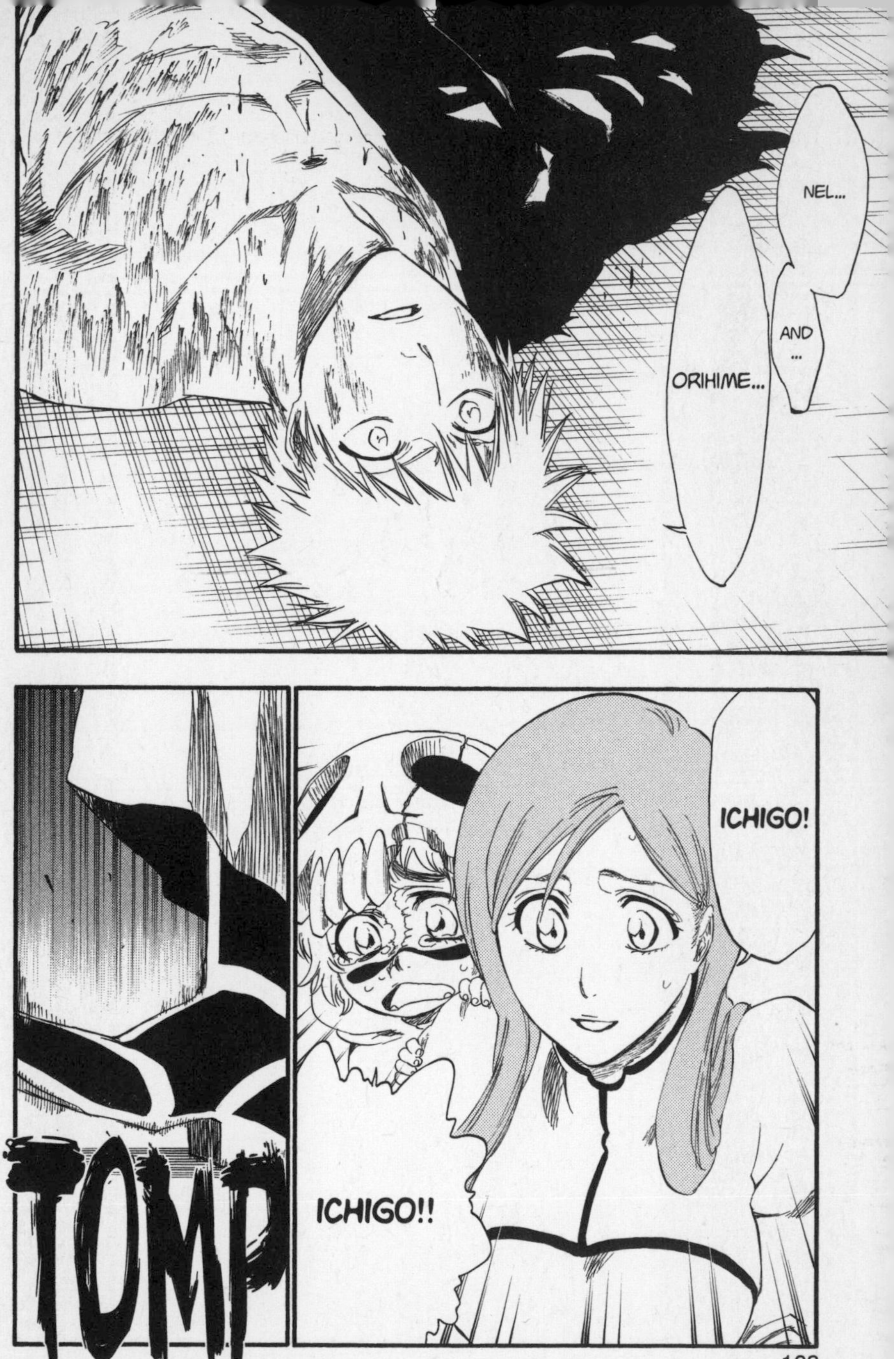
NEL... AND ...
ORIHIME...
ICHIGO!
ICHIGO!!
TOMP

READ THIS WAY

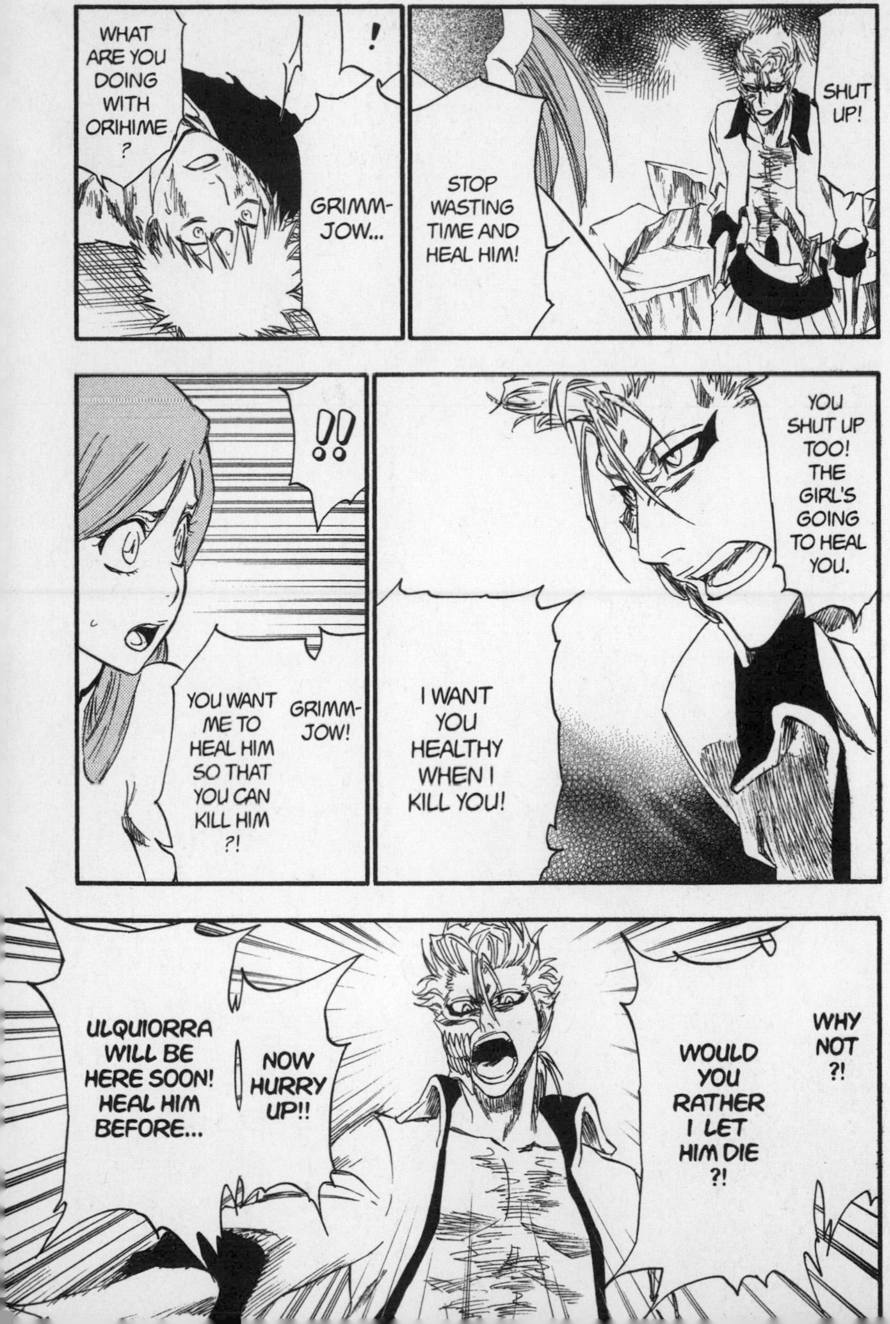
SHUT UP!
STOP WASTING TIME AND HEAL HIM!
!
GRIMM-JOW...
WHAT ARE YOU DOING WITH ORIHIME?
YOU SHUT UP TOO! THE GIRL'S GOING TO HEAL YOU.
I WANT YOU HEALTHY WHEN I KILL YOU!
!!
GRIMM-JOW!
YOU WANT ME TO HEAL HIM SO THAT YOU CAN KILL HIM?!
WHY NOT?!
WOULD YOU RATHER I LET HIM DIE?!
NOW HURRY UP!!
ULQUIORRA WILL BE HERE SOON! HEAL HIM BEFORE...

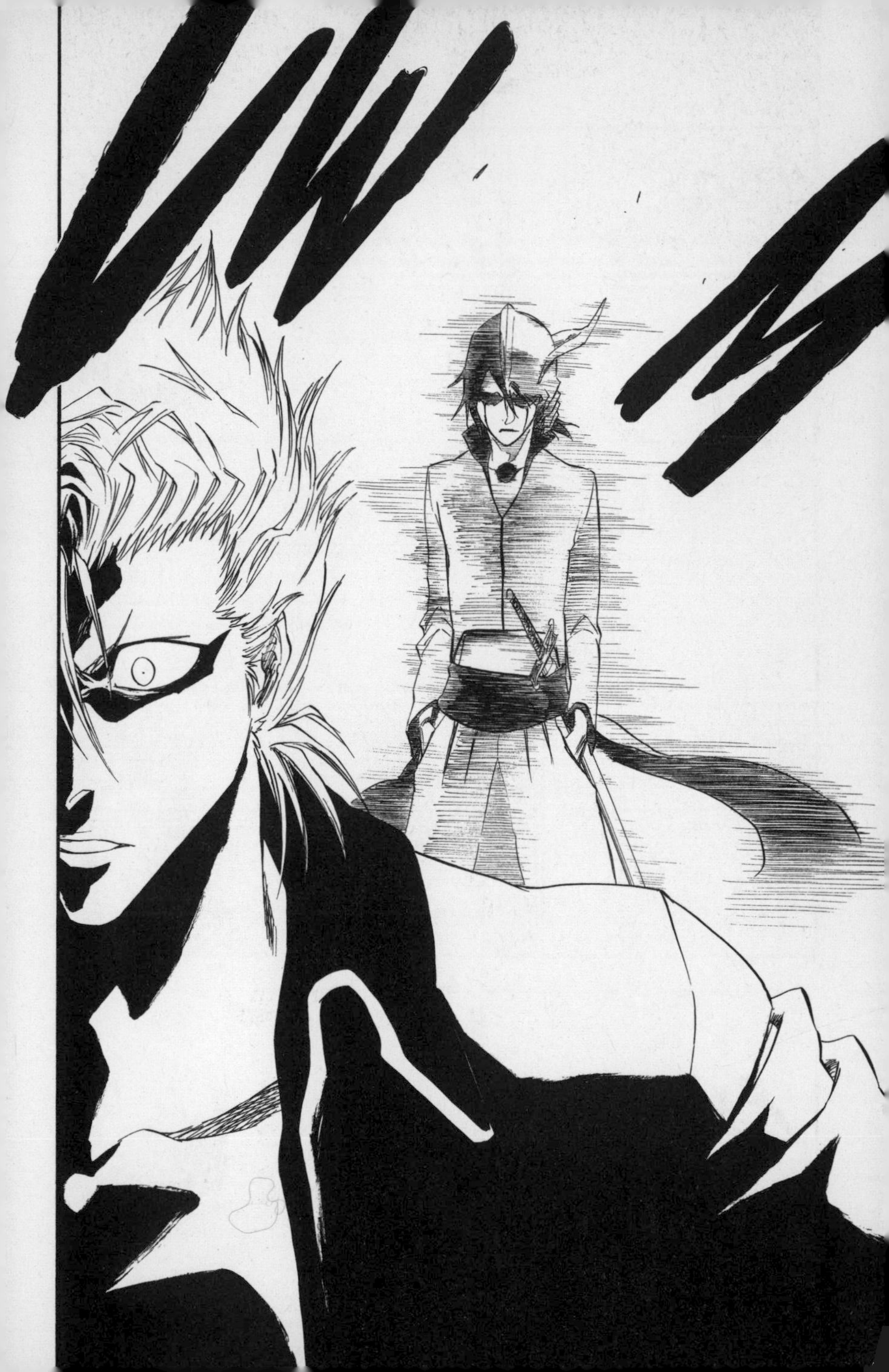

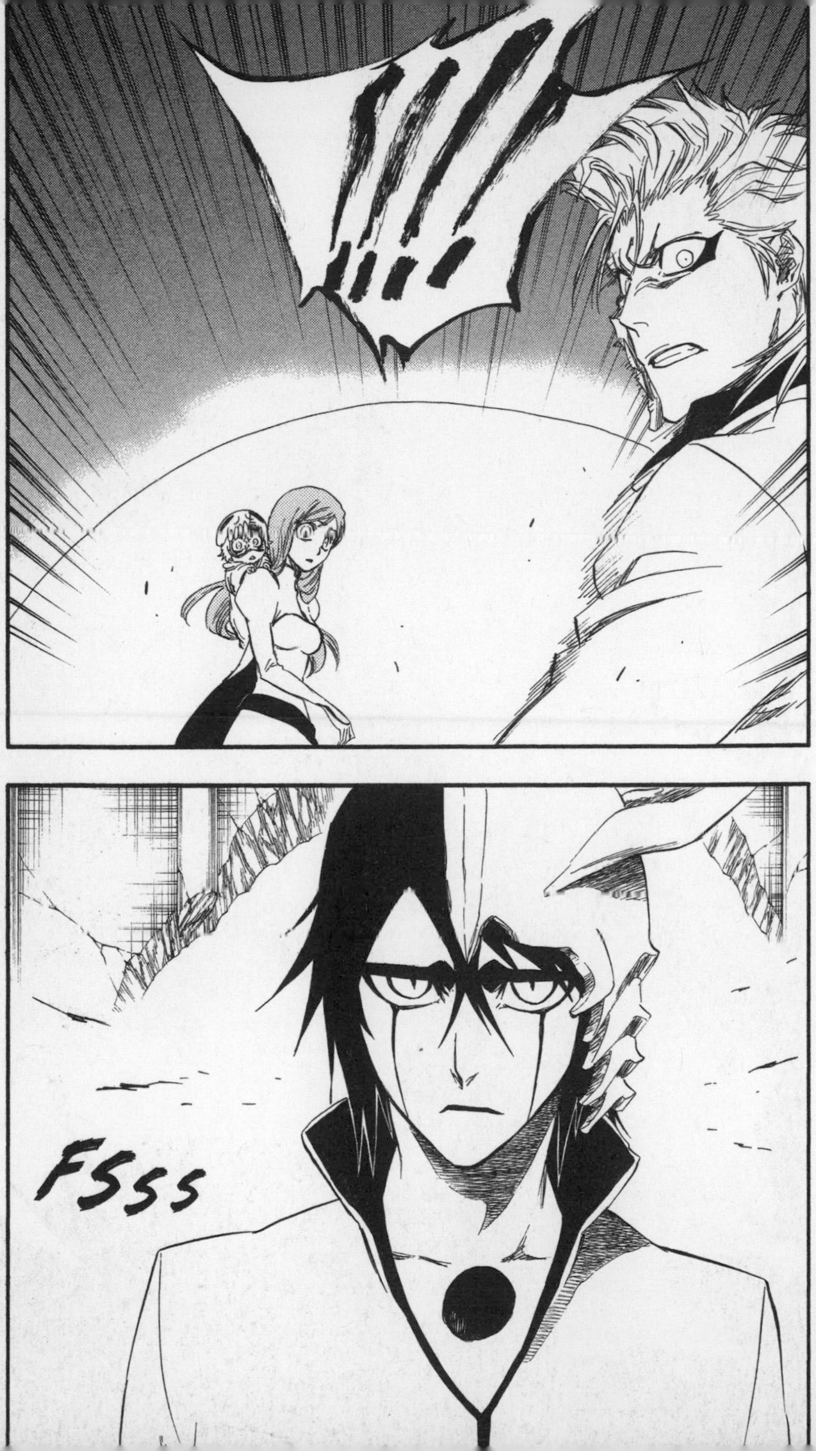
FSSS

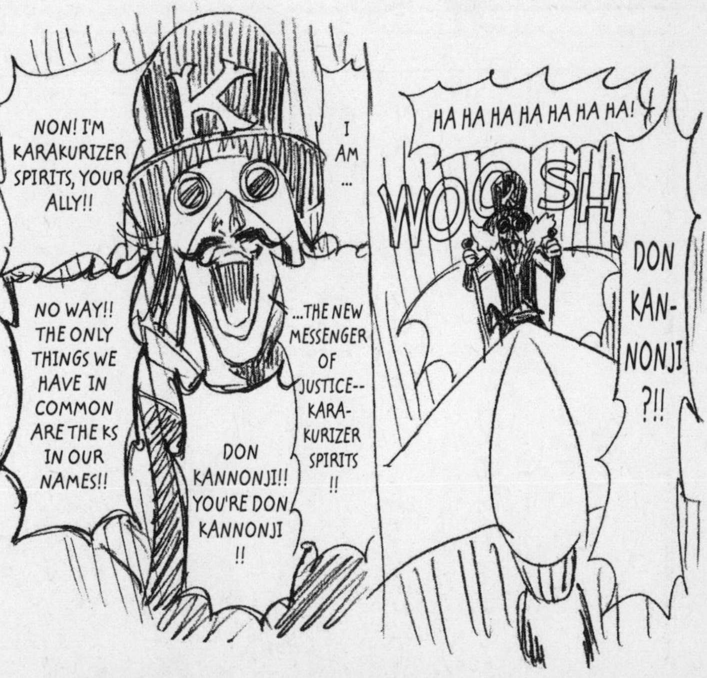
HA HA HA HA HA HA HA!
WOOSH
DON KAN-NONJI?!!
I AM...
...THE NEW MESSENGER OF JUSTICE--KARA-KURIZER SPIRITS!!
NON! I'M KARAKURIZER SPIRITS, YOUR ALLY!!
DON KANNONJI!! YOU'RE DON KANNONJI!!
NO WAY!! THE ONLY THINGS WE HAVE IN COMMON ARE THE KS IN OUR NAMES!!

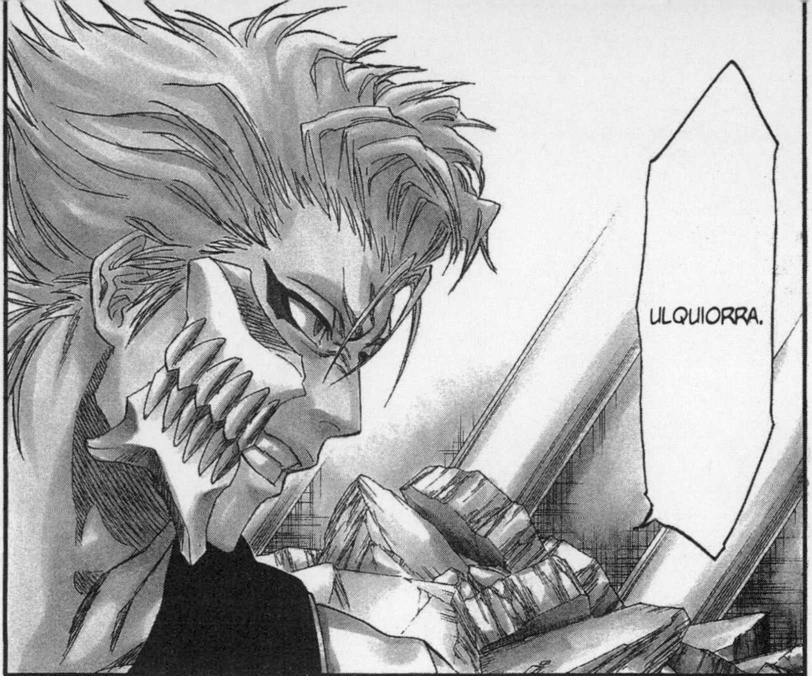
ULQUIORRA.

278. Heal for The Crash

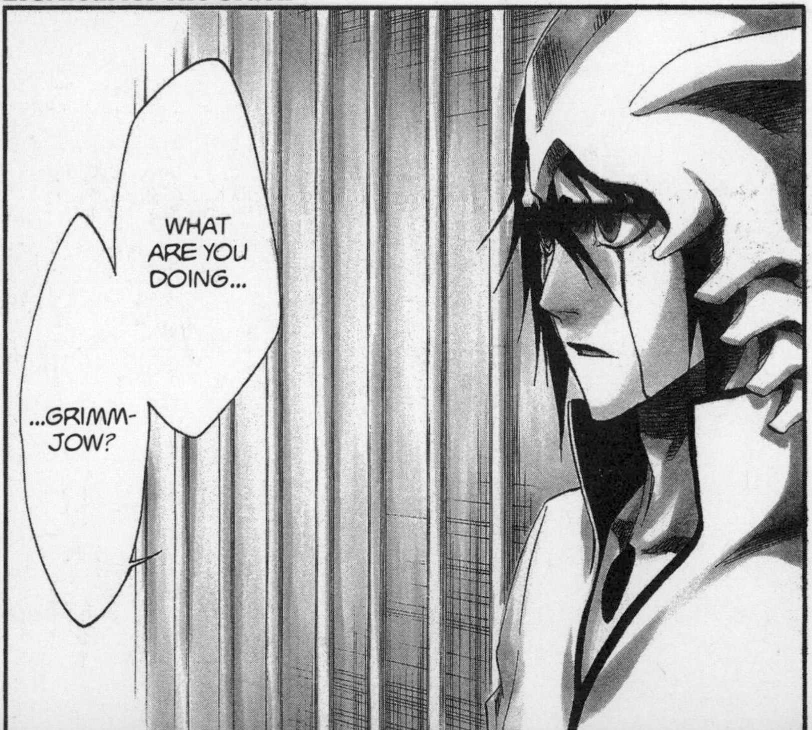
WHAT ARE YOU DOING...
...GRIMM-JOW?

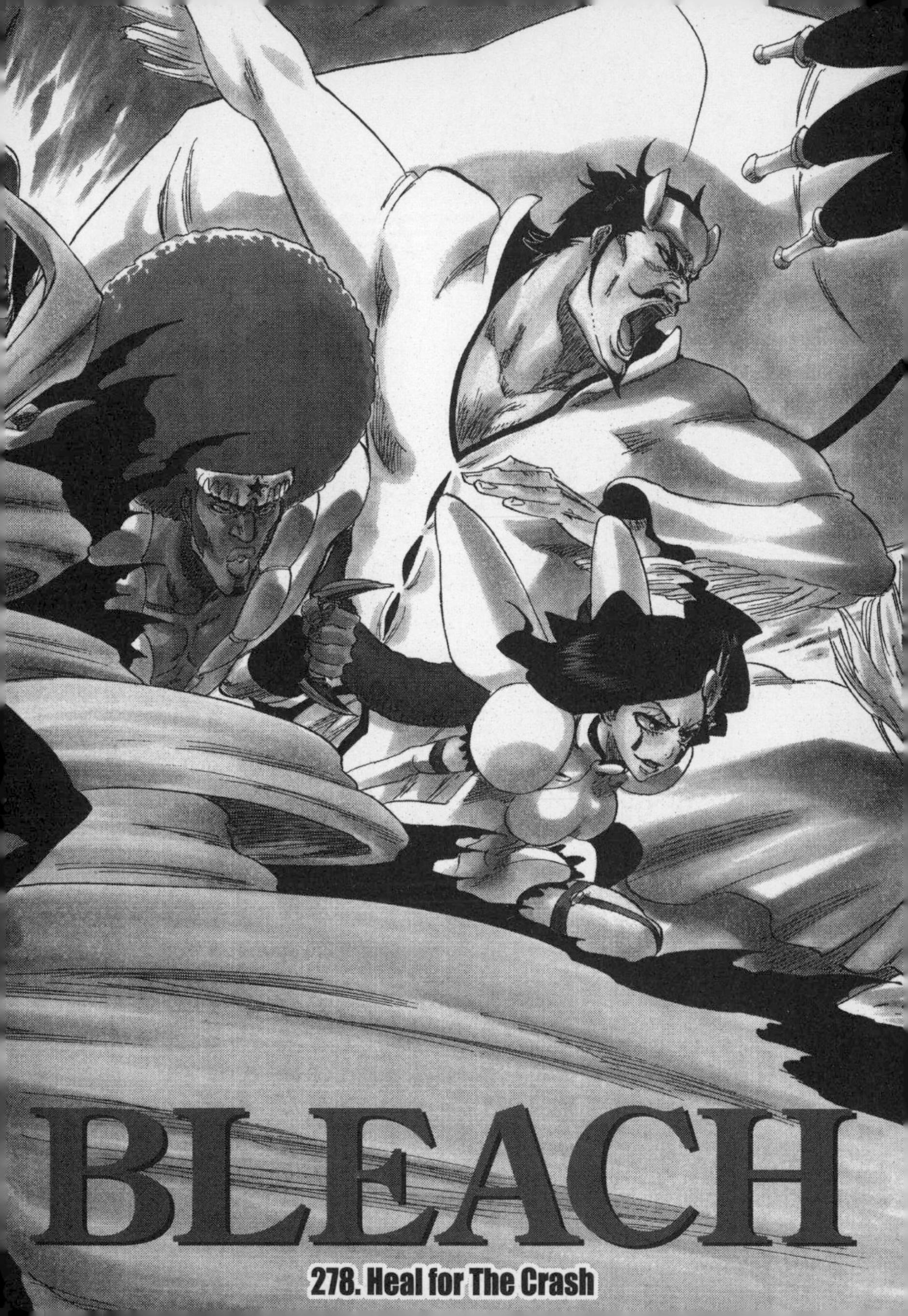
BLEACH
278. Heal for The Crash

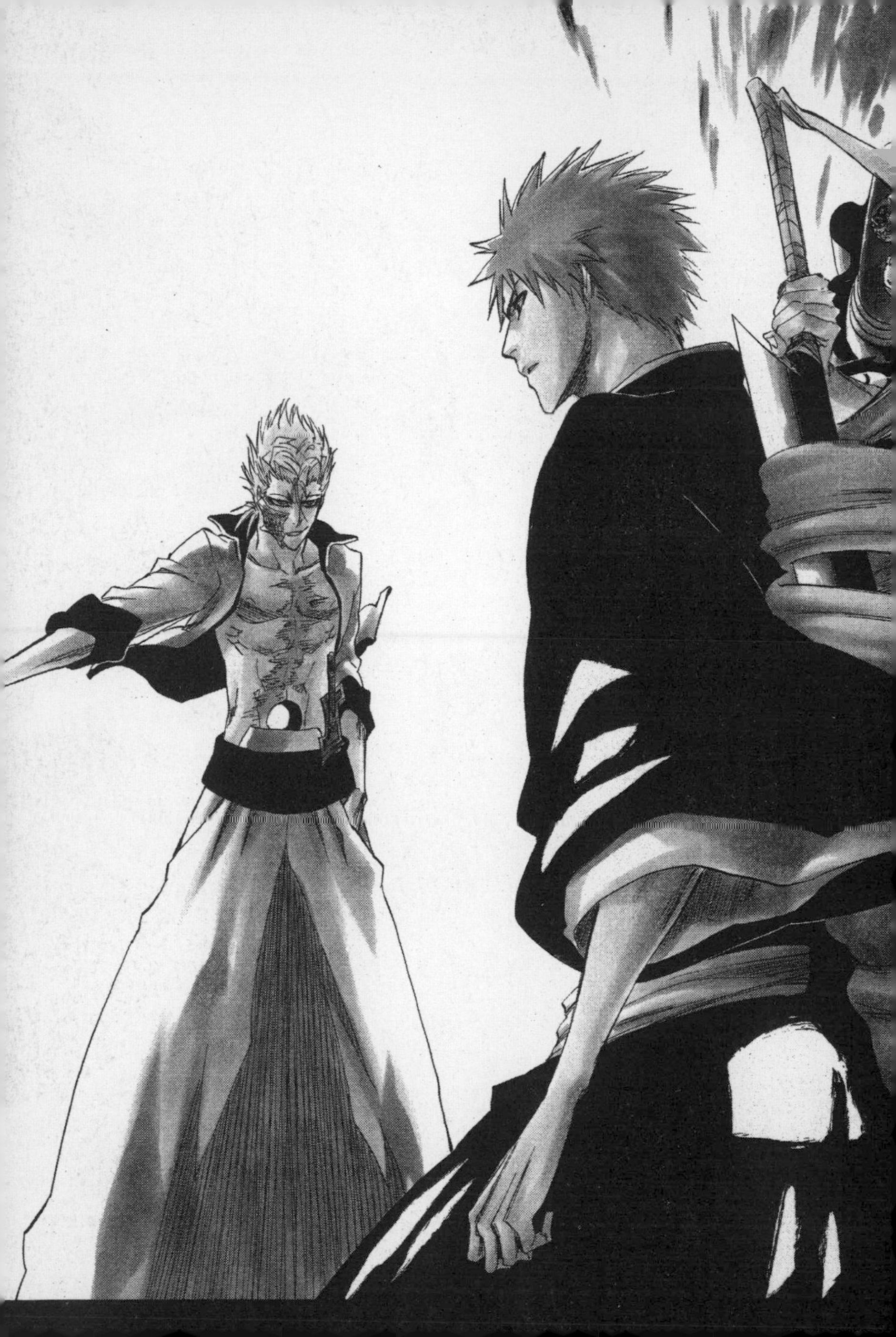

BLEACH
ブリーチ

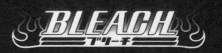

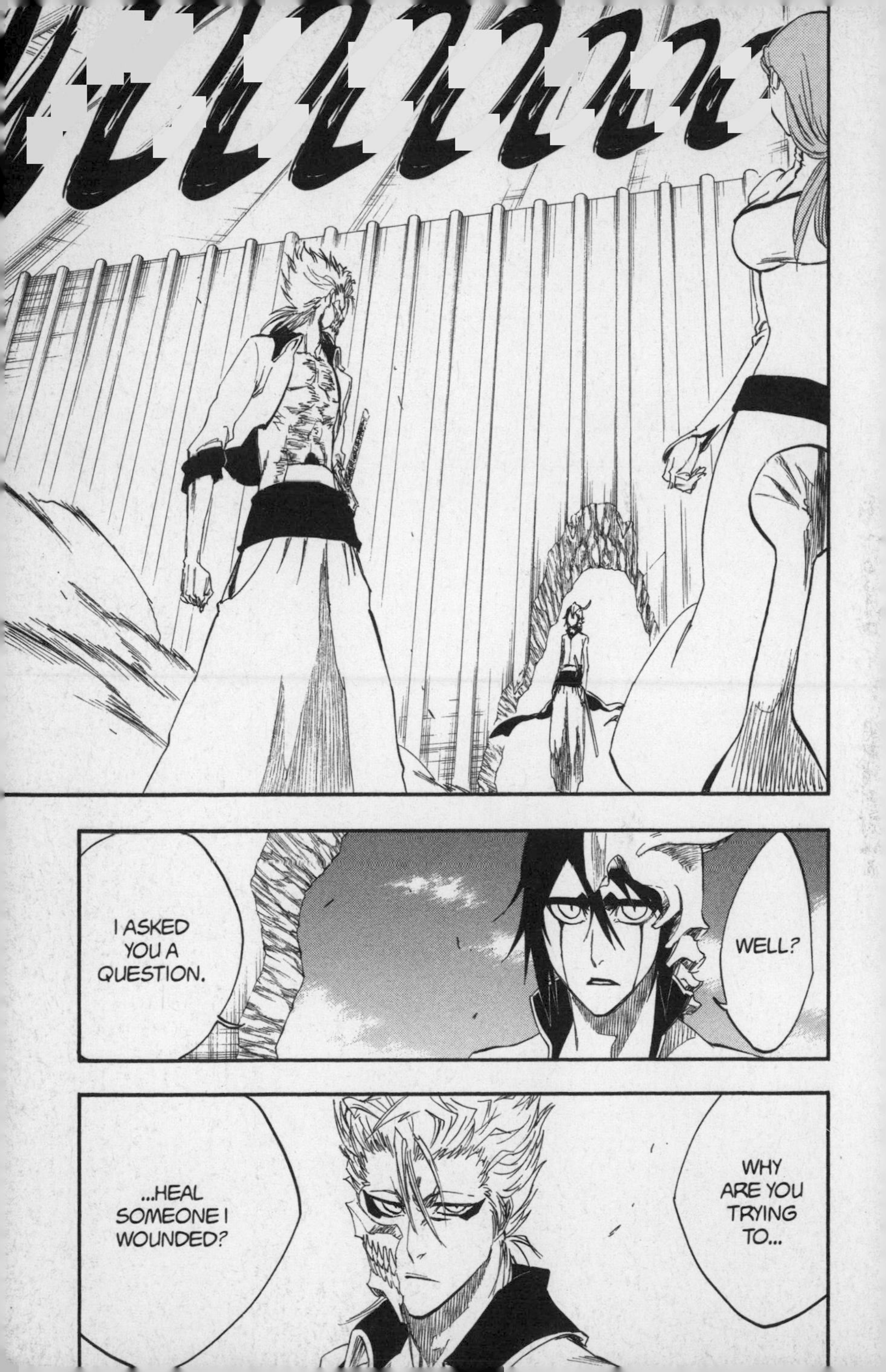
WELL?
I ASKED YOU A QUESTION.
WHY ARE YOU TRYING TO...
...HEAL SOMEONE I WOUNDED?

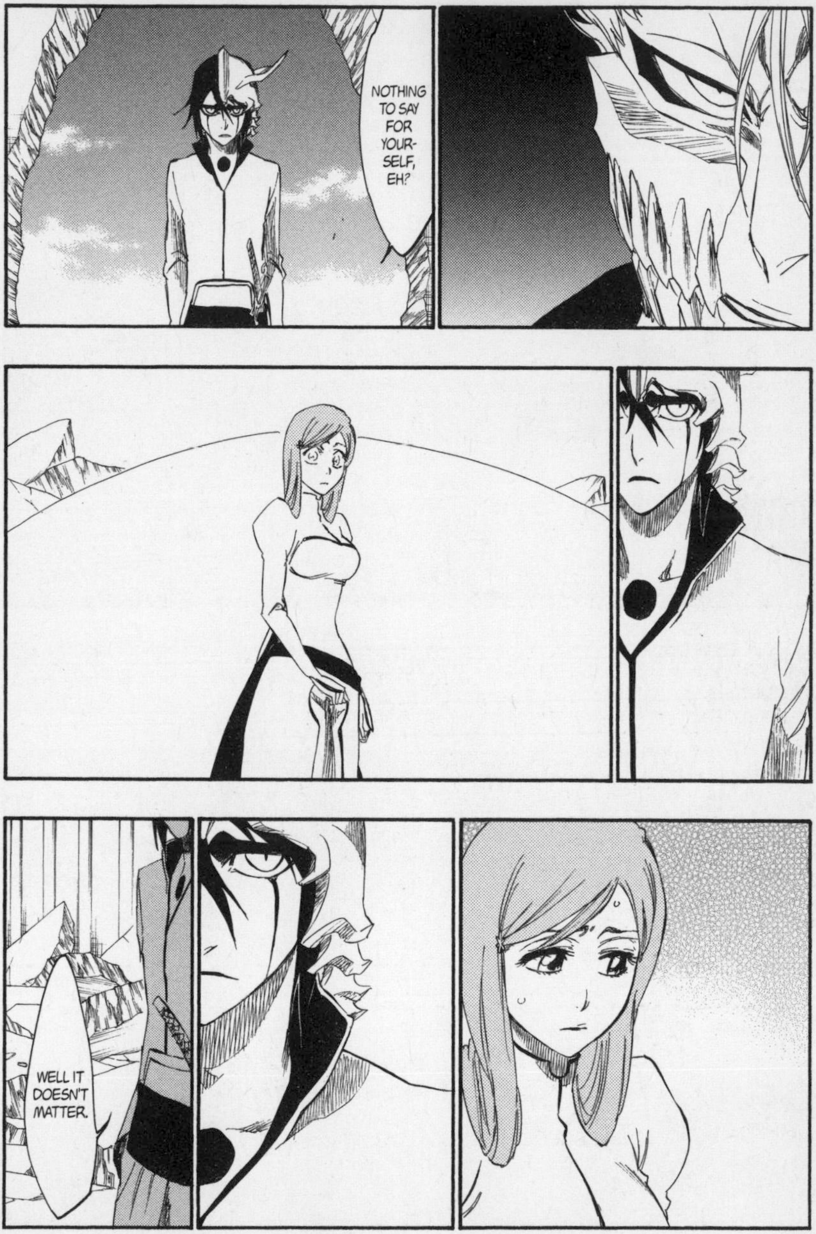
NOTHING TO SAY FOR YOUR-SELF, EH?
WELL IT DOESN'T MATTER.

READ THIS WAY

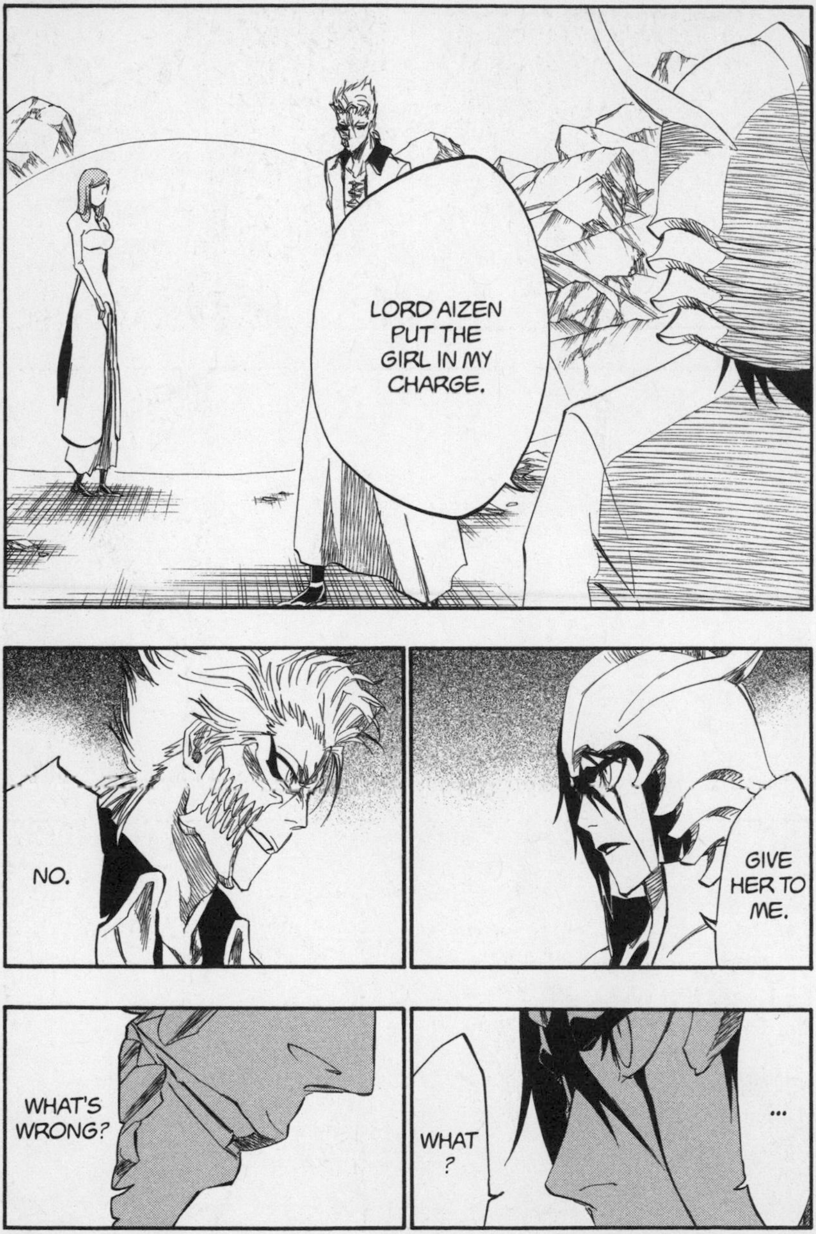
LORD AIZEN PUT THE GIRL IN MY CHARGE.
GIVE HER TO ME.
NO.
...
WHAT ?
WHAT'S WRONG?

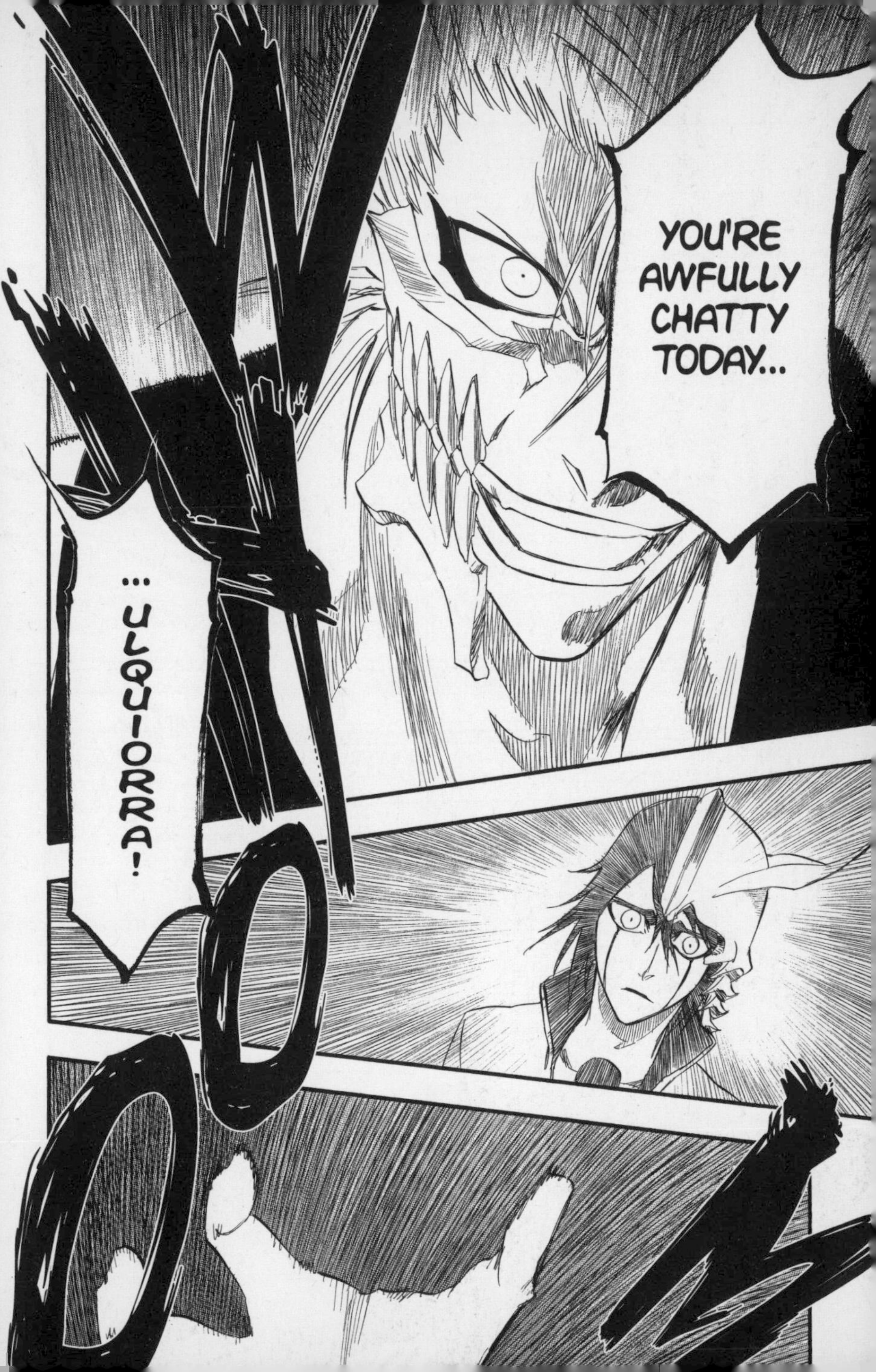
YOU'RE AWFULLY CHATTY TODAY...
...ULQUIORRA!

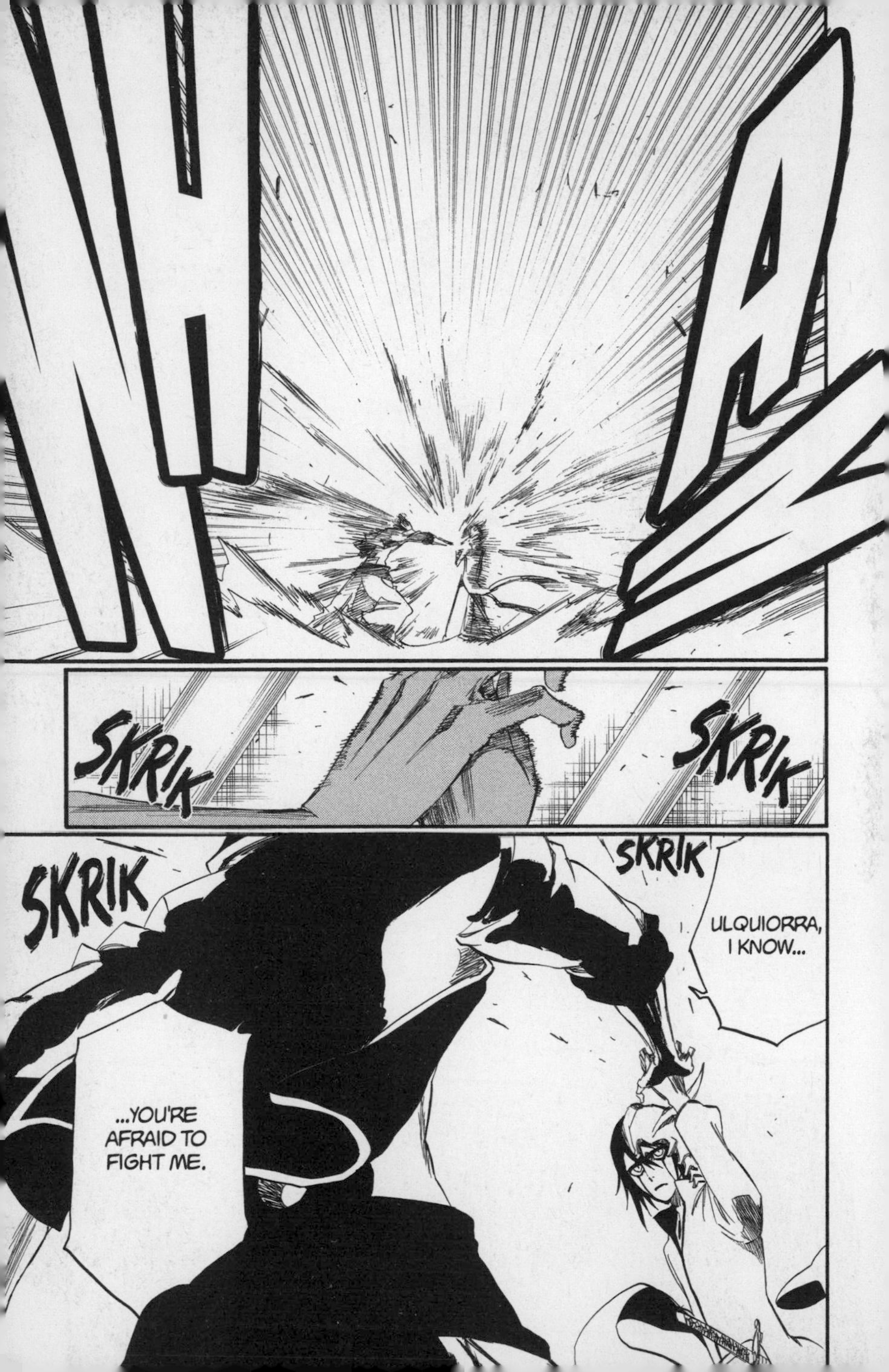
SKRIK
SKRIK
SKRIK
ULQUIORRA, I KNOW...
SKRIK
...YOU'RE AFRAID TO FIGHT ME.

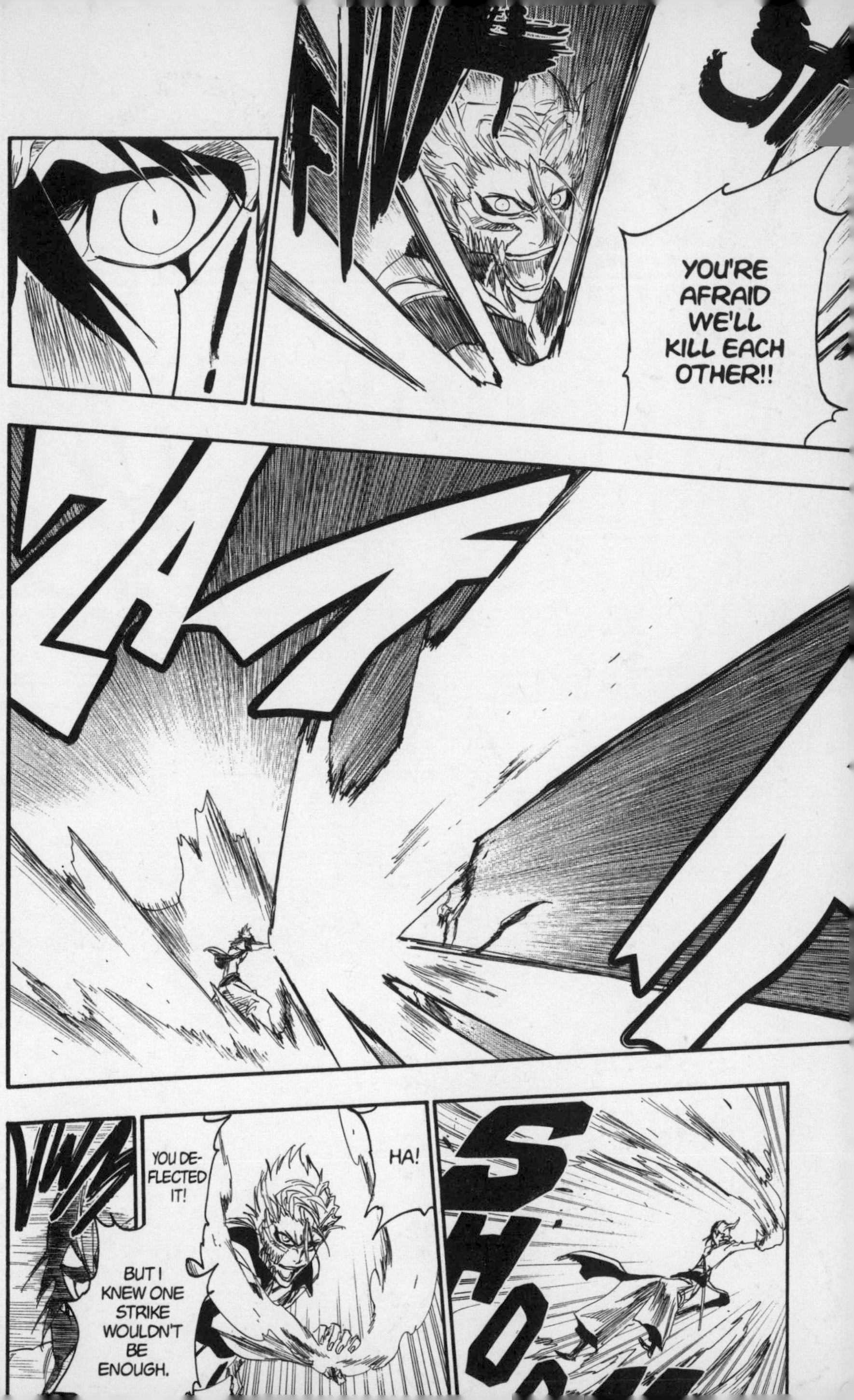
YOU'RE AFRAID WE'LL KILL EACH OTHER!!
HA!
YOU DE-FLECTED IT!
BUT I KNEW ONE STRIKE WOULDN'T BE ENOUGH.

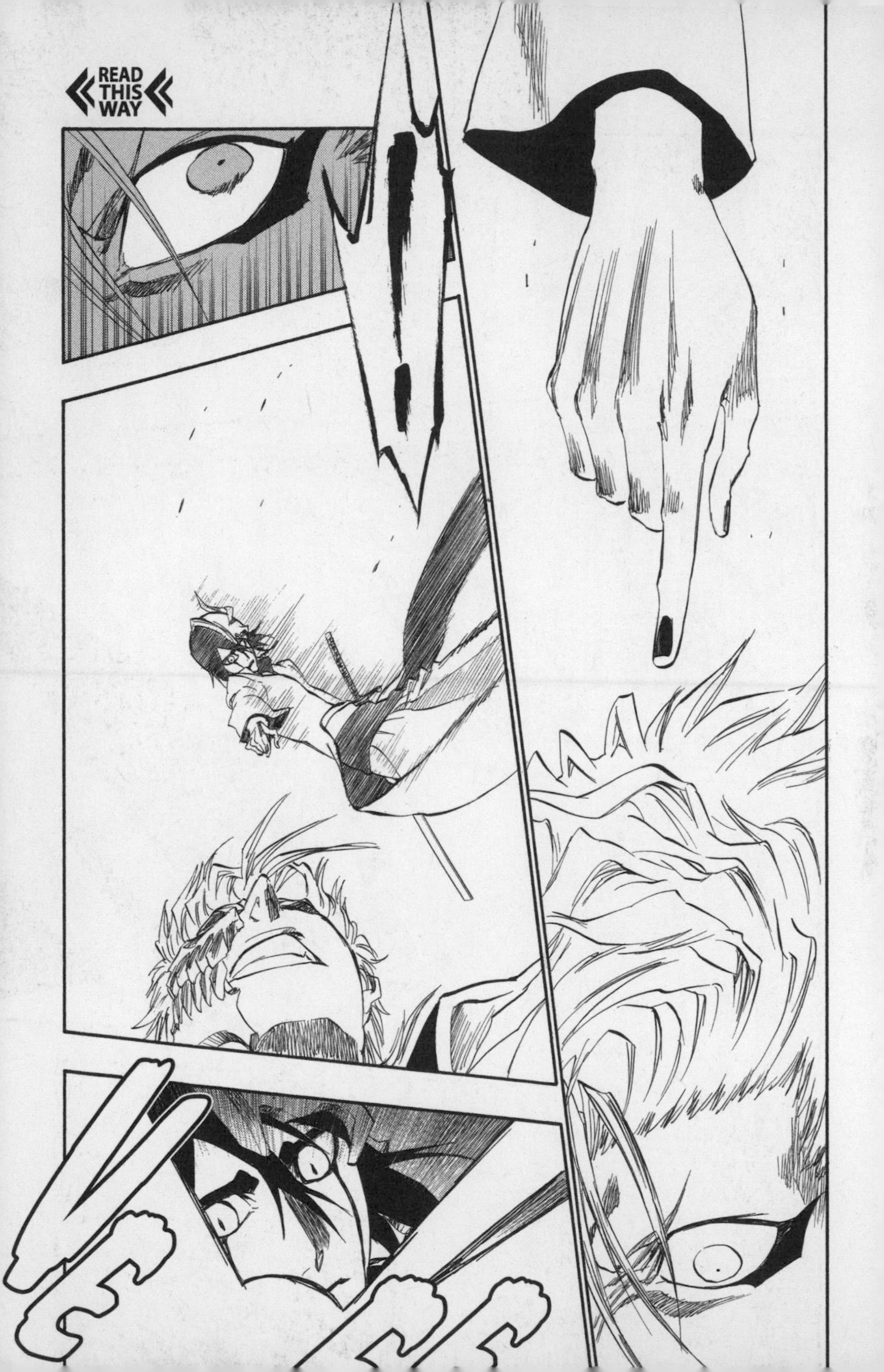
READ THIS WAY

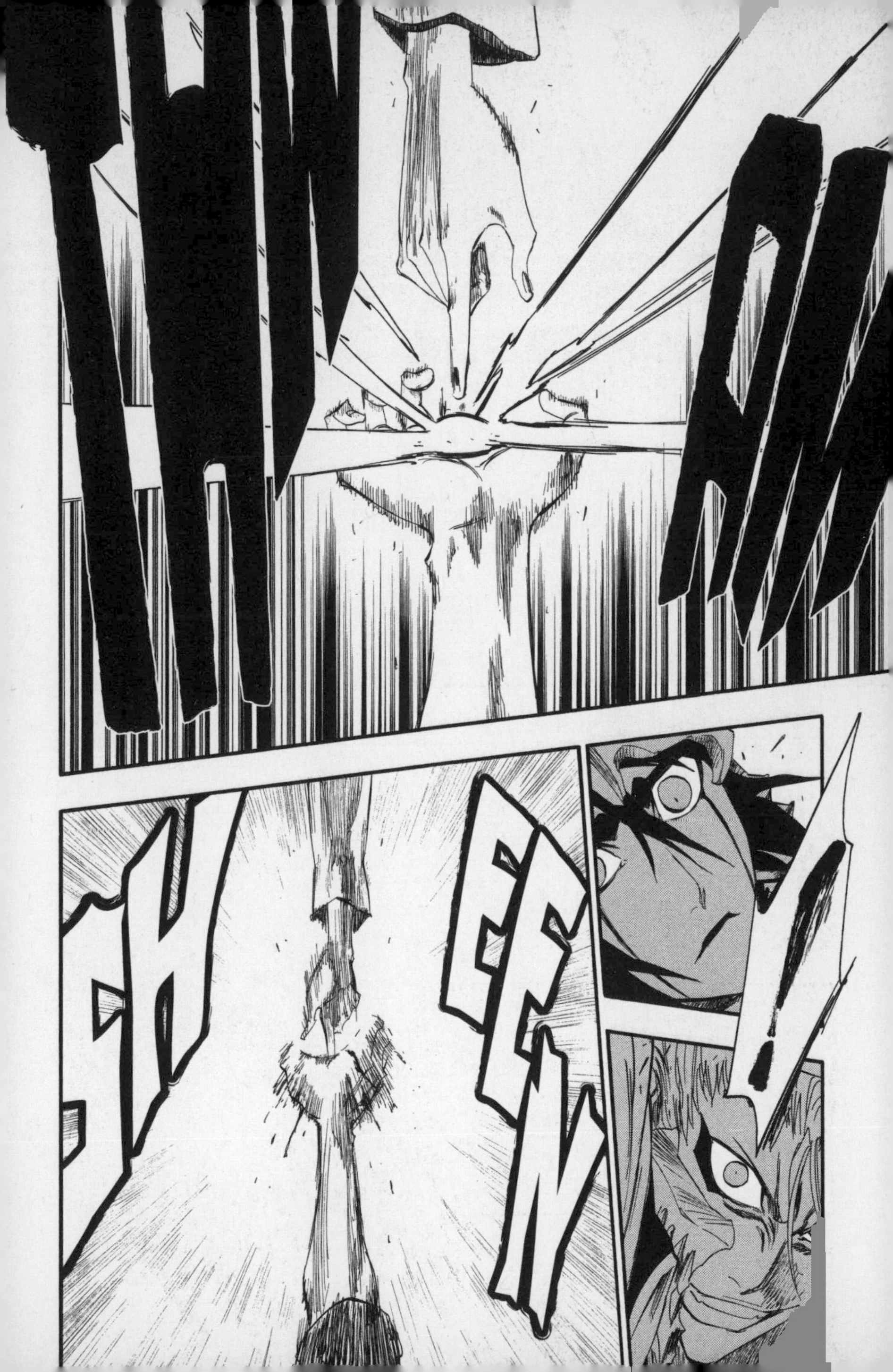
THWAM
SHEEN
!

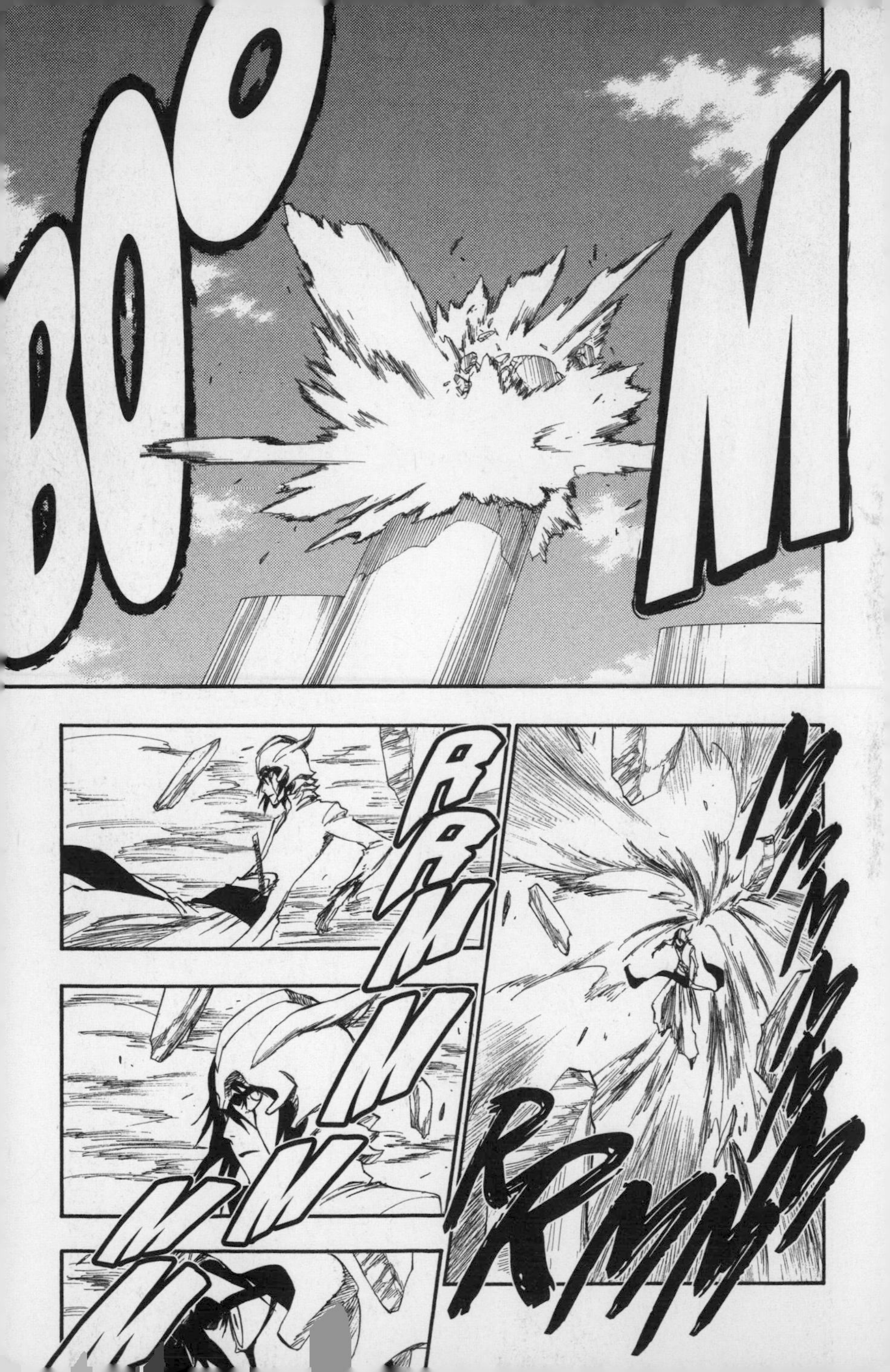
BOOOM
RMMMMMMMM
RRMMMMMM

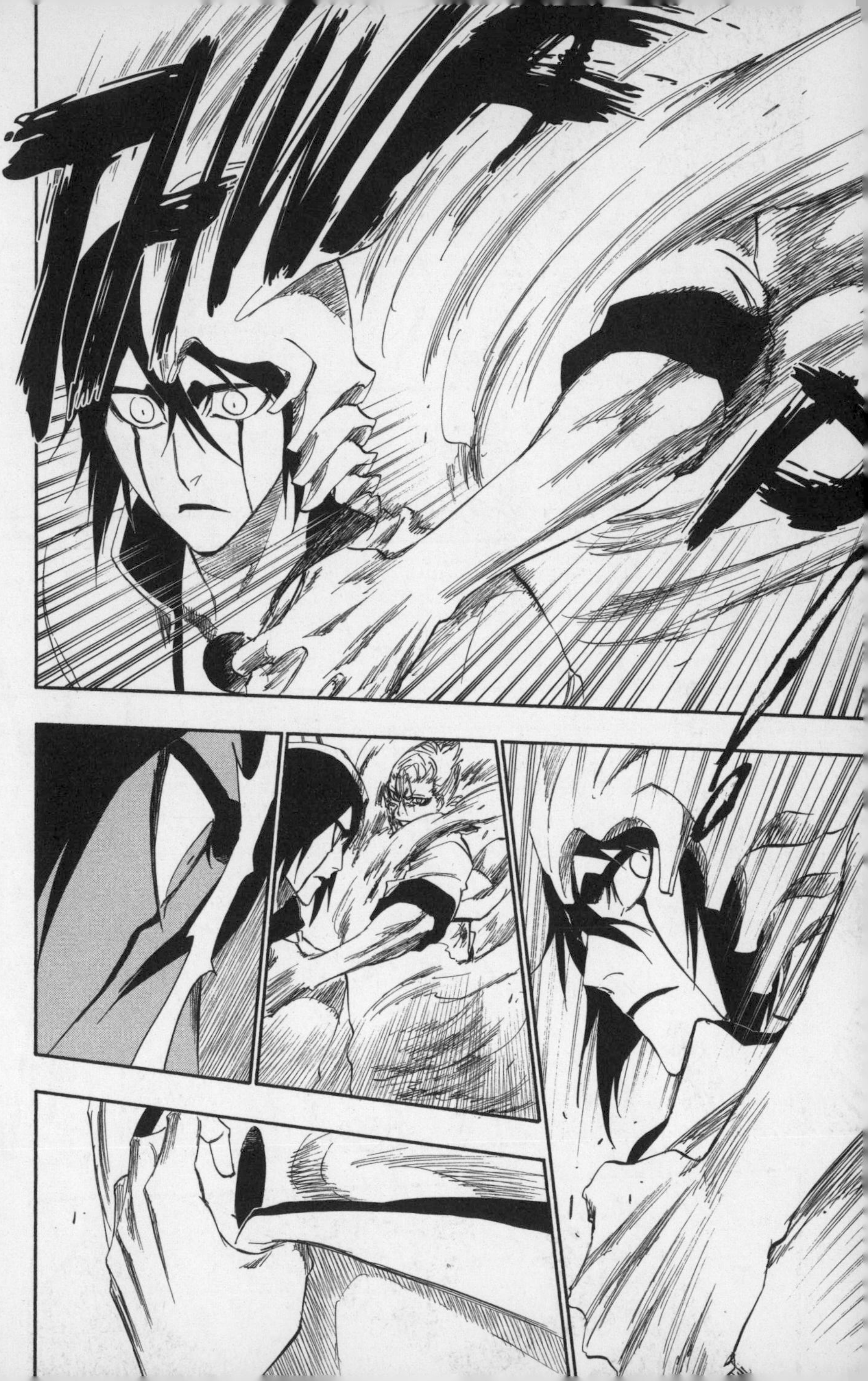
THWACK

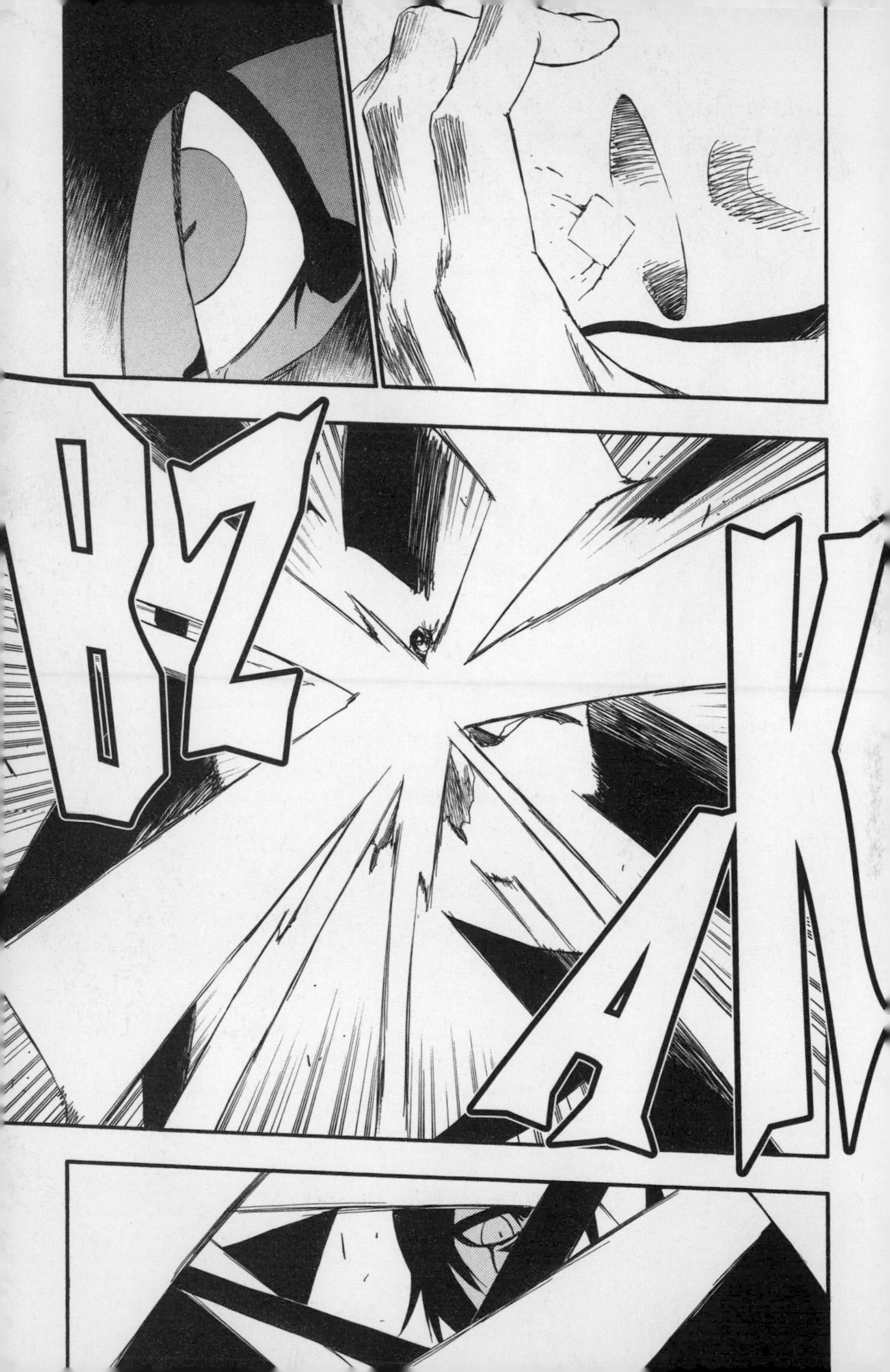
BZAK

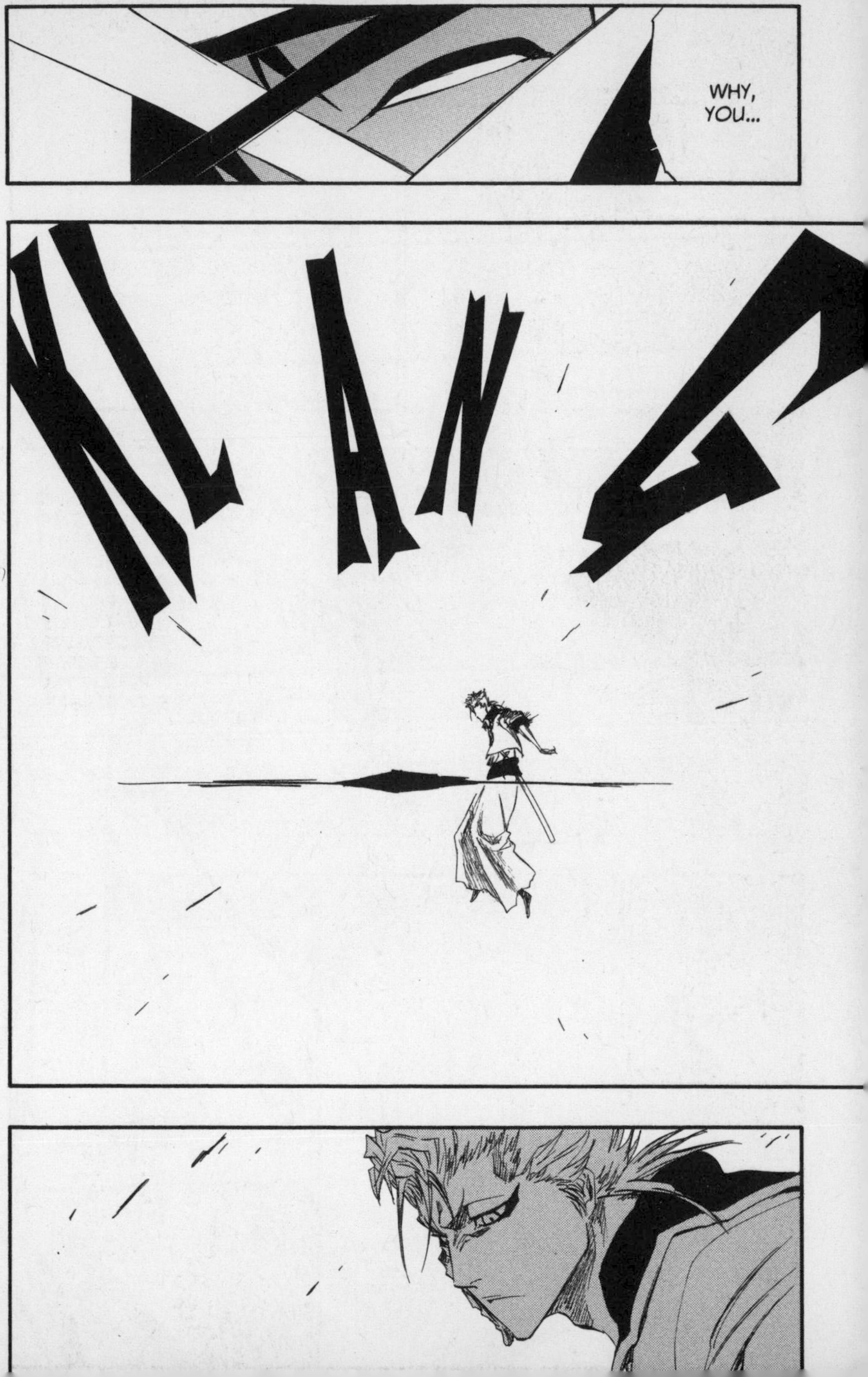
WHY, YOU...
KLANG

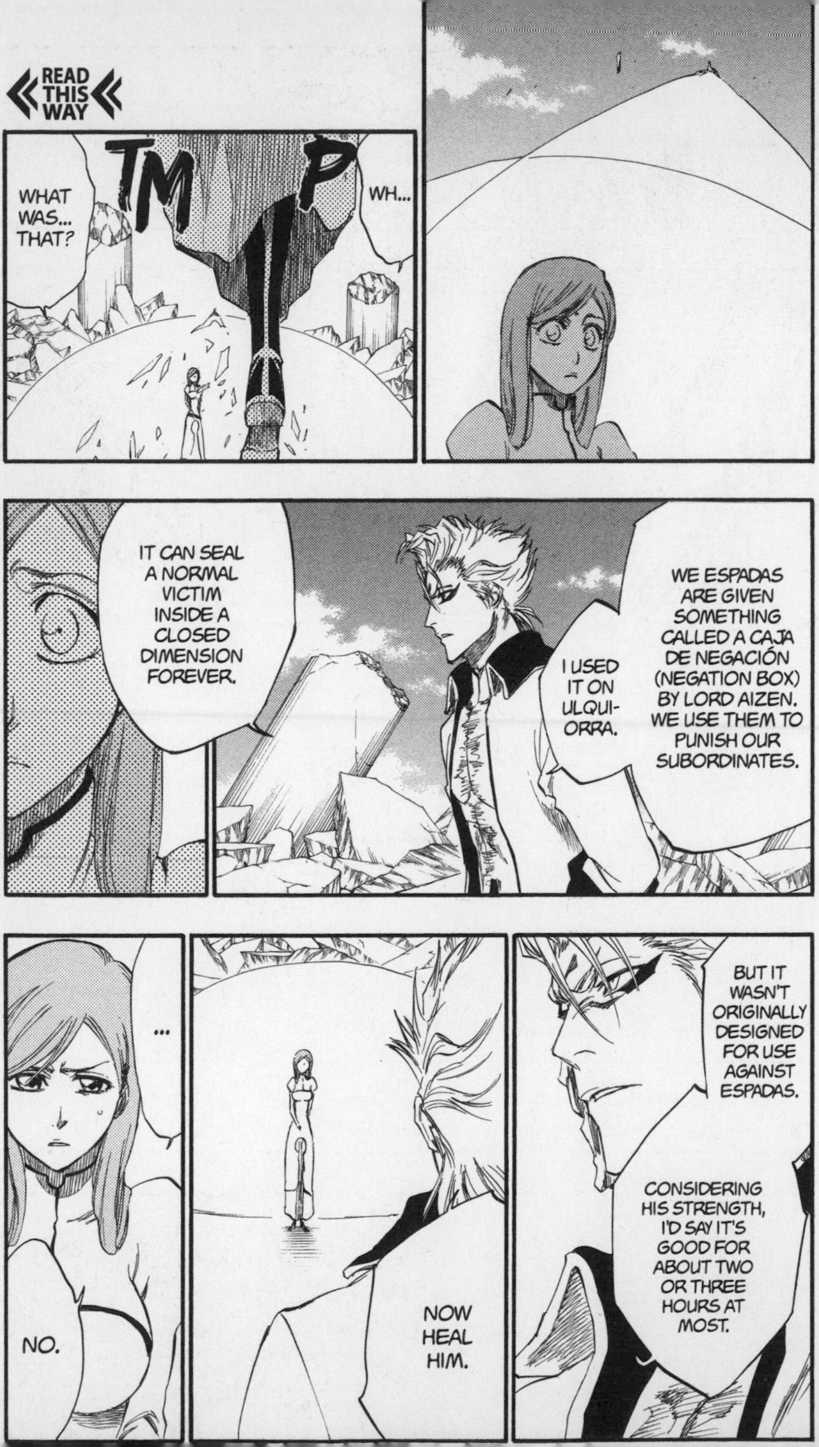
READ THIS WAY
WH...
TMP
WHAT WAS... THAT?
WE ESPADAS ARE GIVEN SOMETHING CALLED A CAJA DE NEGACIÓN (NEGATION BOX) BY LORD AIZEN. WE USE THEM TO PUNISH OUR SUBORDINATES.
I USED IT ON ULQUIORRA.
IT CAN SEAL A NORMAL VICTIM INSIDE A CLOSED DIMENSION FOREVER.
BUT IT WASN'T ORIGINALLY DESIGNED FOR USE AGAINST ESPADAS.
CONSIDERING HIS STRENGTH, I'D SAY IT'S GOOD FOR ABOUT TWO OR THREE HOURS AT MOST.
NOW HEAL HIM.
...
NO.

NO! I WON'T HELP YOU KILL HIM!

I WON'T DO IT!

HEAL HIM!

I'M NOT ASKING YOU, I'M TELLING YOU!

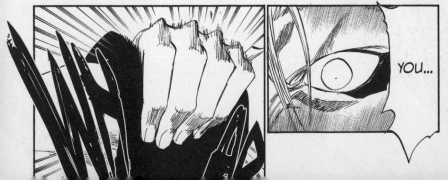

YOU...

LET
HER
GO.

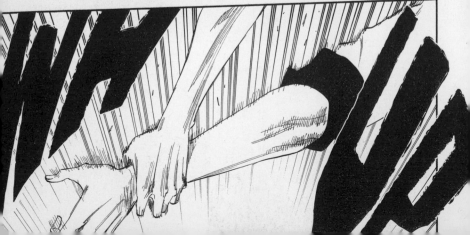

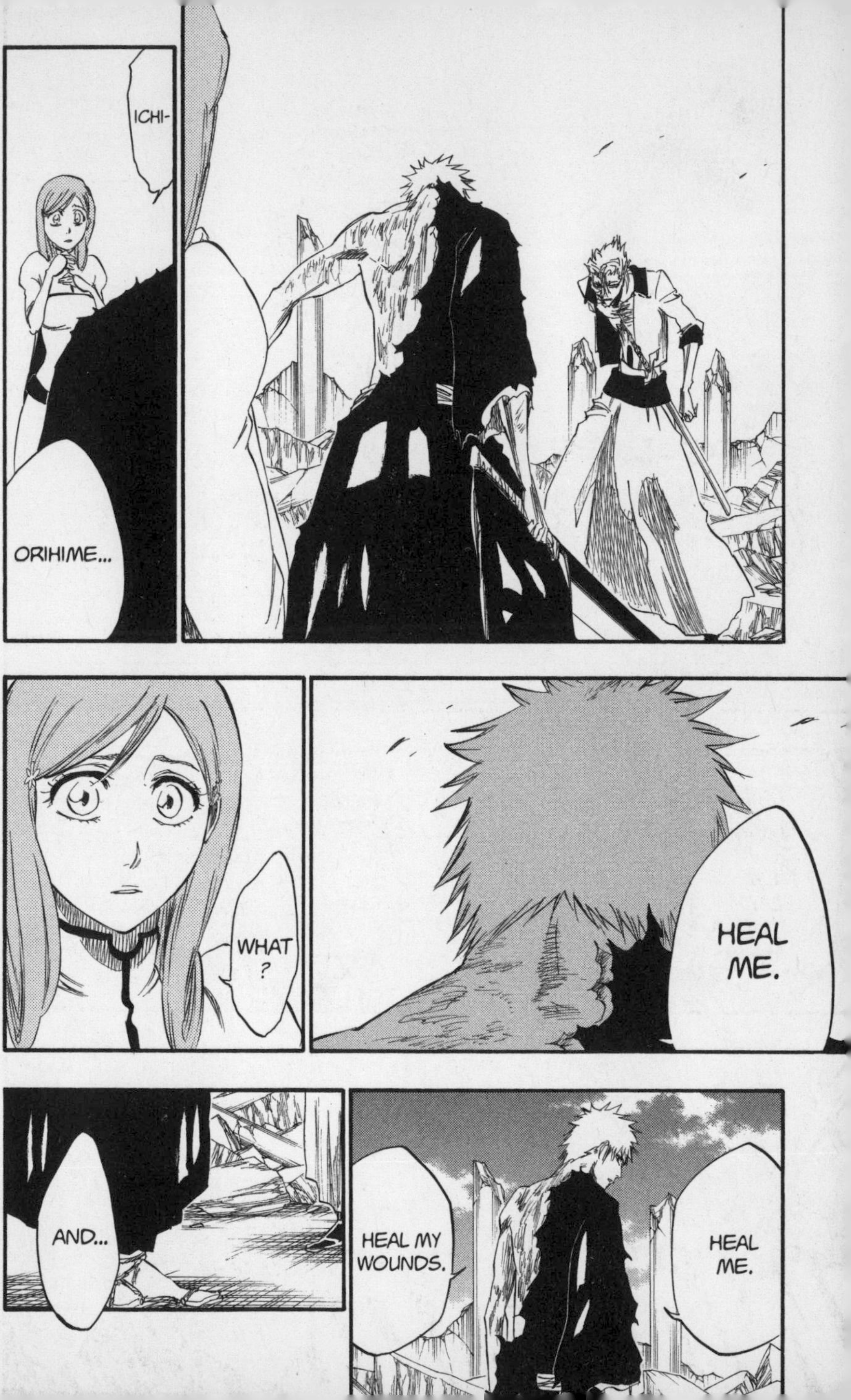
ICHI-
ORIHIME...
HEAL ME.
WHAT?
HEAL ME.
HEAL MY WOUNDS.
AND...

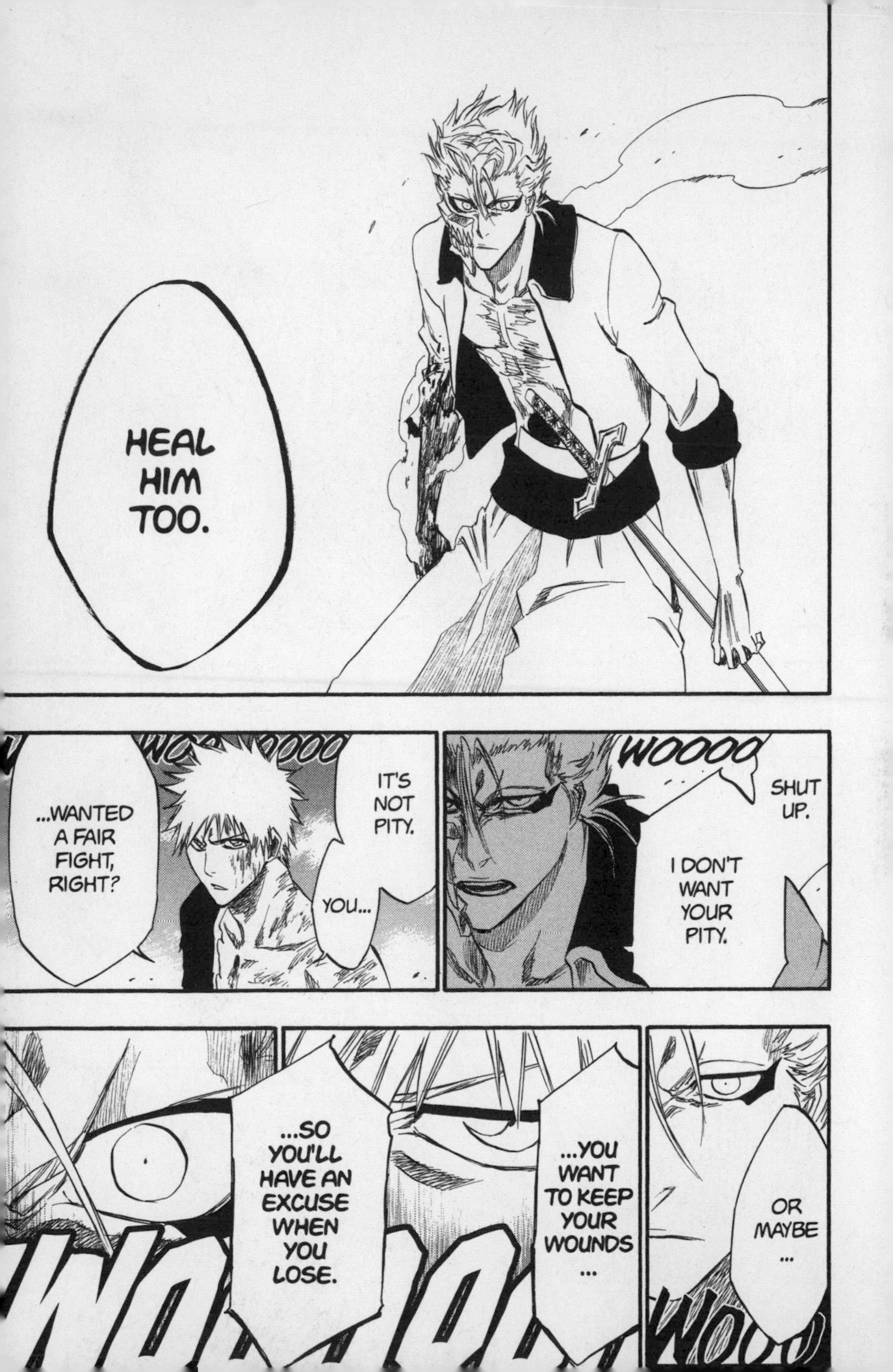
HEAL HIM TOO.
WOOOO
SHUT UP.
I DON'T WANT YOUR PITY.
IT'S NOT PITY.
YOU...
...WANTED A FAIR FIGHT, RIGHT?
OR MAYBE ...
...YOU WANT TO KEEP YOUR WOUNDS ...
...SO YOU'LL HAVE AN EXCUSE WHEN YOU LOSE.

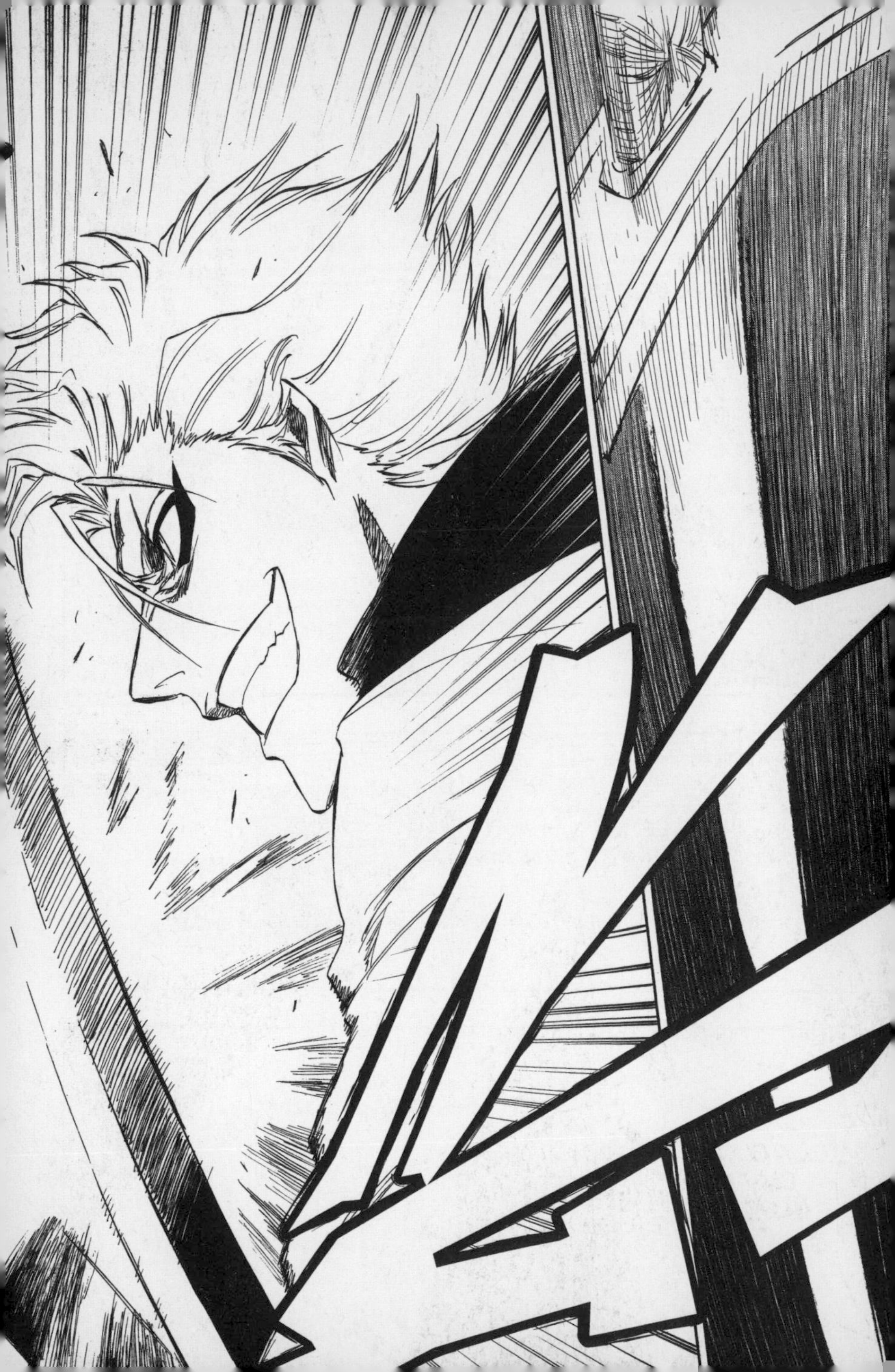

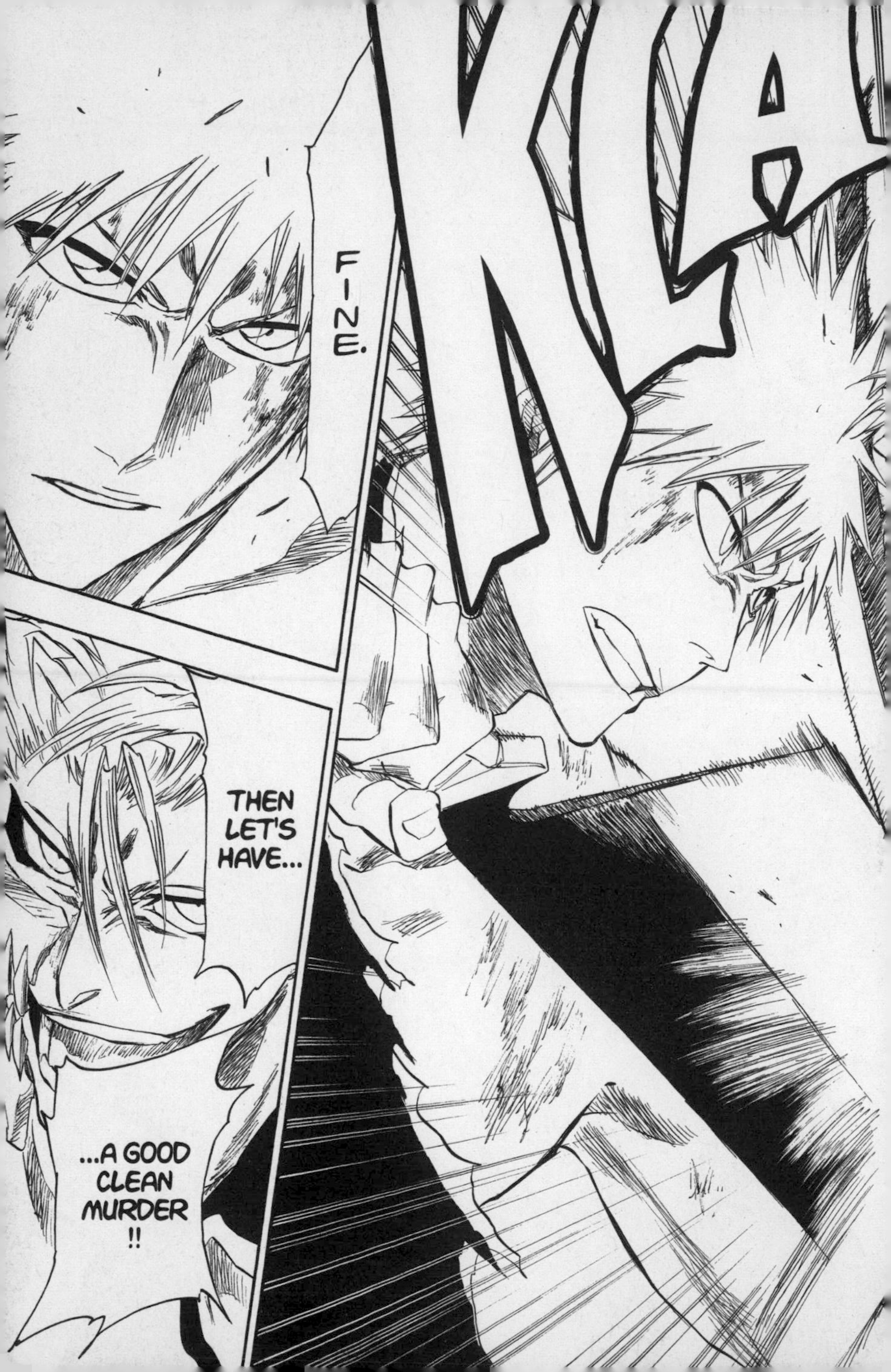
FINE.
THEN LET'S HAVE...
...A GOOD CLEAN MURDER!!

CONTI
NUED
IN
BLEACH
32

KONSÔ COP (K):	"WHAT THE HECK?! WHERE ARE THE PICTURES?! IS THAT IT?! DID THE STORY JUST END?!"
KARAKURIZER SPIRITS (S):	"THIS IS THE POWER OF THE SPIRITS."
K:	"HUH?! WHAT'RE YOU TALKING ABOUT?!"
S:	"NOW LET'S GO! THERE'S NO TIME TO WASTE! OUR JOURNEY HAS JUST BEGUN!"
K:	"HEY, THAT SOUNDS LIKE A LAST LINE! IS IT REALLY OVER?! ARE YOU SERIOUS?!"
EVERYONE:	HA HA HA
K:	"WHO JUST LAUGHED?! COME OUT HERE!! AND WHO THE HECK IS 'EVERYONE'?! IS THAT YOU URAHARA?! IS IT YOU GUYS?!"

AND THAT IS HOW...
...THE KONSÔ COP AND HIS NEW ALLY, KARAKURIZER SPIRITS, DEFEATED THE POWERFUL HOLLOW ZONZINE.

★ THANK YOU FOR READING!!

KARAKURIZER KONSÔ COP AND HIS FRIENDS
Complete Profiles!!

KARAKURIZER TINY DEVIL

THE ULTIMATE RIZER. A CHAMPION OF JUSTICE WHO WANTS TO RULE THE WORLD.

SPECIAL TECHNIQUE: RIZER RAISING HELL

KARAKURIZER SPIRITS

A MYSTERIOUS RIZER WHO APPEARED OUT OF NOWHERE. HIS IDENTITY REMAINS UNKNOWN.

SPECIAL TECHNIQUE: RIZER CANNONBALL

KONSÔ COP

THE MAIN CHARACTER, AS YOU KNOW. HIS HEART IS AS STRONG AS STEEL AND HE CAN MELT FROZEN HEARTS WITH HIS FIERY FISTS.

SPECIAL TECHNIQUE: RIZER BEAM

KARAKURIZER DELICATE

THE WEAKEST OF THE RIZERS. SOMEHOW HE MADE IT INTO THE ANIME AND SOMEHOW HE'S MANAGED TO SURVIVE. SOMEBODY PLEASE SAVE THIS MISERABLE WRETCH.

SPECIAL TECHNIQUE: RIZER CRY

KARAKURIZER EROTIC

HER APPEARANCES ARE FEWER AND FEWER THANKS TO HER DIRTY MOUTH. THIS TRAGIC RIZER, WHOSE PART IN THE *BLEACH* ANIME IS SHRINKING, IS ALMOST INVINCIBLE WHEN FACING BEAUTIFUL FEMALE ENEMIES.

SPECIAL TECHNIQUE: RIZER DIRTY DOGGY

KARAKURIZER BEAST

THIS SECOND ULTIMATE RIZER IS LOCKED IN A STRUGGLE FOR SUPREMACY WITH TINY DEVIL. SHE'S A CHAMPION OF JUSTICE WHO WILL TURN ANYONE, FRIEND OR FOE, INTO ASHES IF THEY GET IN HER WAY.

SPECIAL TECHNIQUE: RIZER DEADLY MAGNUM

Next Volume Preview

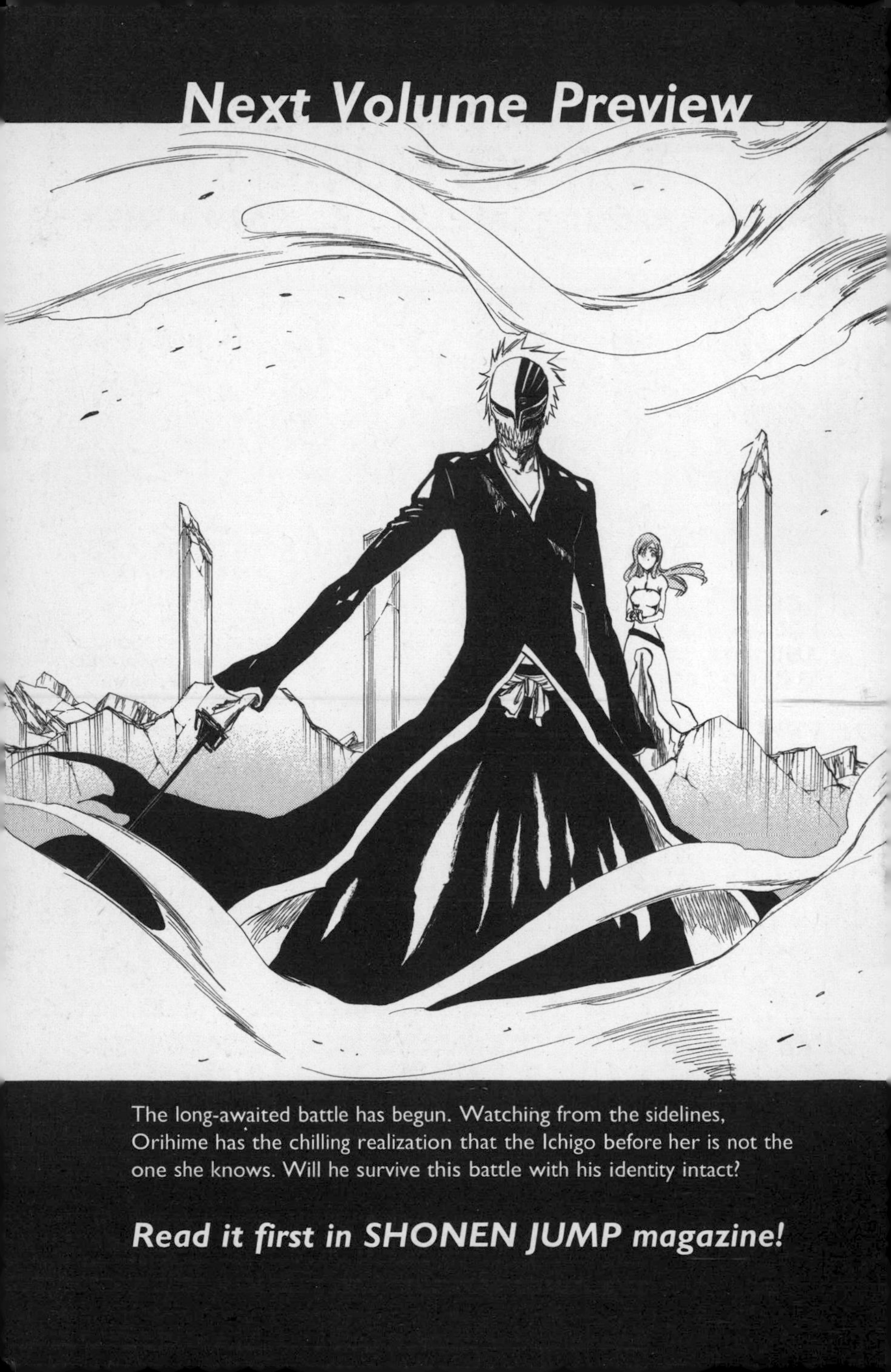

The long-awaited battle has begun. Watching from the sidelines, Orihime has the chilling realization that the Ichigo before her is not the one she knows. Will he survive this battle with his identity intact?

Read it first in SHONEN JUMP magazine!

BLEACH
Vol. 31: DON'T KILL MY VOLUPTURE
SHONEN JUMP Manga Edition
This volume contains material that was originally published in English
in SHONEN JUMP #87–89. Artwork in the magazine may have been
altered slightly from what is presented in this volume.

STORY AND ART BY
TITE KUBO

English Adaptation/Lance Caselman
Translation/Joe Yamazaki
Touch-Up Art & Lettering/Mark McMurray
Design/Sean Lee
Editors/Pancha Diaz and Yuki Takagaki

VP, Production/Alvin Lu
VP, Sales & Product Marketing/Gonzalo Ferreyra
VP, Creative/Linda Espinosa
Publisher/Hyoe Narita

Printed in the U.S.A.

Published by VIZ Media, LLC
P.O. Box 77010
San Francisco, CA 94107

10 9 8 7 6 5 4 3 2 1
First printing, June 2010

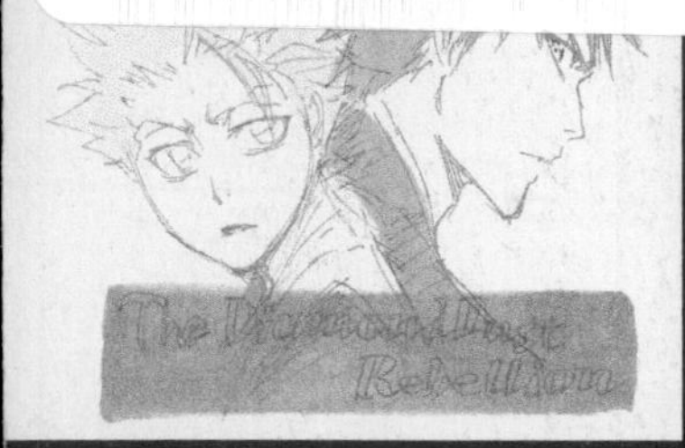

I got a fan letter the other day that said, "Congratulations on passing the 30-volume mark! Thirty is an excellent number! It's not too many or too few. But now you've entered dangerous waters."

I thought to myself, I need to work harder.
Oh, by the way, a second *Bleach* movie is coming out!

-Tite Kubo, 2007

BLEACH is author Tite Kubo's second title. Kubo made his debut with *ZOMBIEPOWDER.*, a four-volume series for *WEEKLY SHONEN JUMP*. To date, *BLEACH* has been translated into numerous languages and has also inspired an animated TV series that began airing in the U.S. in 2006. Beginning its serialization in 2001, *BLEACH* is still a mainstay in the pages of *WEEKLY SHONEN JUMP*. In 2005, *BLEACH* was awarded the prestigious Shogakukan Manga Award in the *shonen* (boys) category.

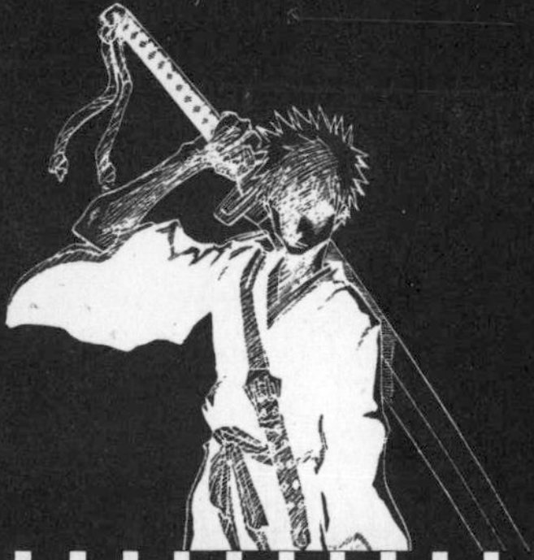